SECOND EDITION

BEHAVIOR THEORY
in Public Health Practice *and* Research

Bruce Simons-Morton, EdD, MPH
Scientist Emeritus
Eunice Kennedy Shriver National Institute of Child
Health and Human Development (NICHD)
National Institutes of Health (retired)

Marc G. Lodyga, PhD, CHES
Assistant Chair & Assistant Professor
Department of Behavioral Health & Nutrition
College of Health Sciences
University of Delaware

JONES & BARTLETT
LEARNING

World Headquarters
Jones & Bartlett Learning
25 Mall Road, 6th Floor
Burlington, MA 01803
978-443-5000
info@jblearning.com
www.jblearning.com

Jones & Bartlett Learning books and products are available through most bookstores and online booksellers. To contact Jones & Bartlett Learning directly, call 800-832-0034, fax 978-443-8000, or visit our website, www.jblearning.com.

23174-8

Production Credits

VP, Product Development: Christine Emerton
Director of Product Management: Matt Kane
Product Manager: Sophie Teague
Content Strategist: Sara Bempkins
Project Manager: Jessica deMartin
Senior Project Specialist: Jennifer Risden
Digital Project Specialist: Angela Dooley
Senior Marketing Manager: Susanne Walker
VP, Manufacturing and Inventory Control: Therese Connell

Composition: Straive
Project Management: Straive
Cover Design: Briana Yates
Media Development Editor: Faith Brosnan
Rights Specialist: Benjamin Roy
Cover Image (Title Page, Part Opener, Chapter Opener):
   © Chanchai howharn/Shutterstock
Printing and Binding: McNaughton & Gunn

Library of Congress Cataloging-in-Publication Data

Names: Simons-Morton, Bruce G., author. | Lodyga, Marc G., author.
Title: Behavior theory in public health practice and research / Bruce Simons-Morton, Marc G.Lodyga.
Other titles: Behavior theory in health promotion practice and research.
Description: Second edition. | Burlington, MA : Jones & Bartlett Learning,
    [2022] | Preceded by: Behavior theory in health promotion practice and
    research / Bruce G. Simons-Morton, Kenneth R. McLeroy, Monica L. Wendel.
    c2012. | Includes bibliographical references and index.
Identifiers: LCCN 2021003223 | ISBN 9781284231717 (paperback)
Subjects: MESH: Health Behavior | Health Communication | Social Marketing |
    Public Health | Behavioral Sciences
Classification: LCC RA776.9 | NLM W 85 | DDC 613—dc23
LC record available at https://lccn.loc.gov/2021003223

6048

Printed in the United States of America
25 24 23 22 21   10 9 8 7 6 5 4 3 2 1

We dedicate this book to Dr. Kenneth McLeroy who passed away in 2020, shortly after retiring as Professor Emeritus at the Texas A&M School of Rural Public Health after an illustrious career. Few people have been so committed to public health or so thoughtful about its importance in modern society. The authors owe Ken a great debt for his intellectual rigor, commitment to public health, and long-standing friendship.

Marc would like to thank his wife, Emily, for her encouragement, compassion, and endearment. You are an inspiration to our beautiful and intelligent daughter, Harper, and me. Thank you doesn't even begin to express my sincere gratitude. Marc would also like to thank Dr. Bruce Simons-Morton for his support, guidance, and mentorship. It has been an honor working with you.

Bruce is pleased to thank his wife, Denise, for her support, and Dr. Marc Lodyga for his essential contributions to the book. Bruce also wishes to recognize his many research and professional collaborators at the NIH, across the country, and abroad.

Contents

Preface ix

Acknowledgments xiii

SECTION 1 Theory in Context 1

CHAPTER 1 Health Behavior in the Context of Public Health . . 3

Health and Disease 4

    Disease Causation 5

    Dimensions of Health and Well-Being 6

Public Health 9

    Prevention 11

    Health Objectives for the Nation 13

    Health and Behavior 14

    Health Behaviors 14

    Prevention and the COVID-19 Pandemic . 17

Health Promotion 18

    Who Does Health Promotion? 18

    Certification as a Health Education
        Specialist (CHES) 19

    Health-Promotion Processes 19

Ecological Perspectives and
    Multilevel Programs 23

Theory and Practice 25

    What Is Theory? 25

    Theory and Health Promotion 26

    Why Are There Numerous Behavior
        Theories? 26

    Theory in Ecological Context 27

Caveats 28

Lessons for Public Health Practice . . . 29

Discussion Questions 30

References 30

CHAPTER 2 A Social Ecological Perspective 33

Introduction 34

    Social Ecology Conceptualizations 34

    Social Ecology and Public Health 35

Theory and Social Levels 36

    Intrapersonal (Individual) Level 38

    Interpersonal (Social) Level 39

    Organizational/Institutional Level 40

    Community Level 41

    Policy Level 42

    Physical Environment Level 43

    Cultural Level 44

    Economic Level 45

    Interactions Between Societal Levels 46

Intervening at Multiple Societal Levels . . 47

    Program Objectives 47

    Environments Matter 48

    Targets of Intervention 48

    Intervention Approaches 49

    Multilevel Intervention Considerations . . . 49

Lessons for Public Health Practice . . . 50

Discussion Questions 51

References 51

CHAPTER 3 Theories of Motivation and Behavior: A Public Health Primer 53

Introduction 54

    Motivation and Behavior 55

    Individual Variability 58

Behavior Theories 58

    Reinforcement Theory 58

    Psychoanalytic Theory 60

    Cognitive Psychology 64

Social Psychology 66
Sociology 67
Theory Commonalities 68
Lessons for Public Health Practice . . . 70
Discussion Questions 71
References 72

SECTION 2 Behavior Change Theories   73

CHAPTER 4 Self-Regulation and Social Cognitive Theory. . . . 75

Reinforcement 76
Self-Regulation 77
Social Cognitive Theory 79
Reciprocal Determinism 79
Self-Regulatory Processes 82
Social Influence 84
Other SCT Constructs 85
Applications of SCT 85
Diet and Physical Activity Self-Regulation
Change Among Obese Women 85
Checkpoints Program to Prevent Motor
Vehicle Crashes Among Young Drivers . . 86
Lessons for Public Health Practice . . . 88
Discussion Questions 89
References 89

CHAPTER 5 Self-Determination Theory and Motivational Interviewing. 91

Introduction 92
Self-Determination Theory Elements . 93
Psychological Needs 94
External and Internal Motivation 96
Motivational Interviewing (MI) 99
MI Assumptions 99
MI Methods 99
MI Spirit. 101
MI Process 102
MI Example: The Personal Trainer Study 104

The Marriage of SDT and MI 105
Lessons for Public Health Practice . . 106
Application Exercise 107
Discussion Questions 107
References 108

CHAPTER 6 Social Influence Theory: The Effects of Social Factors on Health Behavior . . . 109

Introduction 110
Psychosocial Theories That Emphasize
Social Influence 111
Elements of Social Influence 111
Social Norms 112
Social Influence Processes. 114
Context, Culture, Capital 117
Example: Electronic Cigarette Use . . . 122
Lessons for Public Health Practice . . 123
Discussion Questions 124
References 124

CHAPTER 7 Value Expectancy Theories. 127

Introduction 128
Four Expectancy Value Theories. 131
Theory of Reasoned Action. 132
Theory of Planned Behavior 137
The Health Belief Model 139
The Information–Motivation–Behavioral
Skills Model 143
Lessons for Public Health Practice . . 145
Discussion Questions 147
References 147

CHAPTER 8 Stages of Change: The Transtheoretical Model . . . 149

Introduction 149
Assumptions. 151
Stages 151
Change Dynamics. 153
Stage Tailoring 154
Cognitions 154

Change Processes 155

Matching Change Processes
and Methods to Stage 156

Examples 157

Lessons for Public Health Practice . . 157

Discussion Question 159

References 159

SECTION 3 Communi-cation and Messaging   161

CHAPTER 9 Health Communication and Social Marketing 163

Introduction 164

Information Revisited. 165

Cognitive Dissonance 165

Cognitive Resistance 166

Models of Communication Processes . . 167

Action Model 168

Interactive/Transactional Model 169

Intermediary Model 170

Ecological Model 171

Persuasion 171

Elaboration Likelihood Model 174

Inoculation Theory 175

Social Marketing 176

Processes 176

Ethics 177

Theory-Based Message Framing 178

Theory of Reasoned Action and Theory
of Planned Behavior 180

Health Belief Model 180

Social Cognitive Theory 180

Social Influence Theory 180

Diffusion Theory. 181

Theory-Based Social Marketing
Applications 181

Smoking Prevention 182

Preventing Excessive Drinking 182

Reducing Consumption of Sugared
Beverages 183

Increasing Face Mask Wearing to Prevent
COVID-19 183

Lessons for Public Health Practice . . 186

Discussion Questions 187

References 187

CHAPTER 10 Diffusion of Innovations Theory 189

Introduction 190

Key Concepts 190

Communication Channels 192

Social Systems 193

Time and the S-Shaped Diffusion
Curve 194

Innovation-Decision Process 194

Adopter Categories 196

Characteristics of the Innovation 199

Example: Diffusion of an Innovation
at the System Level 202

Innovation Characteristics of
Graduated Driver Licensing (GDL) 203

Communication and Relative Advantage. . 203

Lessons for Public Health Practice . . . 204

Discussion Questions 206

References 206

SECTION 4 Nothing So Practical as Theory   209

CHAPTER 11 Applications of Theory to Public Health Practice 211

Introduction 211

Theory in Practice 212

Program Planning Phases and Steps 212

Example: Theory-Based Planning to
Reduce College Drinking Problems. . . 212

Choosing a Theory 220

Theory Selection Principles 221

Common Errors in Selecting Theory 222

Lessons for Public Health Practice . . 223

Discussion Questions 223

References 223

CHAPTER 12 **Why So Many Theories?. 225**

Introduction 225

Behavior Theory and Public Health . . 226

   Personal-Health Behavior 227

   Health-Protective Behavior 227

   Health-Related Behavior 227

   Program Planning 227

   Multilevel Thinking 228

Many Useful Theories 229

   External Influences on Motivation and
      Behavior 229

   Internal Influences on Motivation
      and Behavior. 230

The Value of Each Theory 231

   Grand Theories of Behavior 231

   Somewhat Grand Theories of
      Behavior 231

   Possible Integration of Cognitions Across
      Theories 232

Theory as a Way of Thinking 233

Lessons For Public Health Practice . . 234

Discussion Questions 235

References 235

Glossary. 237

Index 245

Preface

Behavior is fascinating and complicated. Behavior theory can make sense of complicated behavior, helping us understand how people process information, make decisions, and cope with environmental conditions. A firm understanding of health behavior theory is a public health training requirement and an essential tool for use in public health practice. Hence, the goals for the book are to provide health educators, health-promotion specialists, and other public health professionals with a solid understanding of behavior theory and how it can be applied in practice and research.

Students will find this information about behavior theory immediately useful in many courses, particularly those involving research and program planning. Moreover, the book will be a useful reference for many years to come. Current public health professionals should be able to apply the substance of the book to the public health problems on which they work. Researchers will find the book of use as they explore how to frame research questions and design study methods. In the following pages, we address these issues: (1) What are the key features of this book? (2) How is this book different and better than other theory books? (3) Why did we write this book? (4) How could this book help you in your job? (5) How is the book organized?

1. What are the key features of the book?

The following features are designed to make the book as informative and useful as possible. Theory is presented in the context of multilevel program planning. The contents are logically organized, each section containing chapters on related topics. The chapters provide detailed descriptions of theory with practical examples of how it can be applied. The numerous evidence-based examples include many contemporary, popular, interesting, and important public health topics.

Examples include emerging and timely topics such as the COVID-19 pandemic, college drinking, vaping, compliance with medical recommendations, and physical activity, with special consideration to environmental, cultural, and economic impacts.

2. How is this book different and better than other theory books?

There are a number of books on behavior theory from which public health professionals can select, and each provides useful information. The existence of many books on behavior theory is a reflection of the recognized importance of behavior theory to public health. Because behavior is a fundamental element of nearly all health concerns, training for public health specialists includes behavior theory. Health promotion specialists, in particular, must develop a sophisticated grasp of theory because it is one of the essential tools for changing behavior. Thus, the book provides the information that public health professionals need to apply behavior theory for effective program development.

Some books are designed to provide only rudimentary descriptions of theory, with limited examples. Other books include detailed descriptions, each written by different authors. Each of these books can serve a useful role in public health and health-promotion curricula and merit a place on the bookshelves of practitioners, professors, and researchers.

We believe that our book's particular niche in this market derives from our efforts to provide an ecological conceptualization and a comprehensive overview of popularly employed theories, written in a manner that is accessible to a wide range of readers (including those outside public health with interest in behavioral science), with contemporary examples that illustrate how theory can be applied in the real world.

3. Why did we write this book?

Collectively, the authors of this book have been in the field for many years. We have conducted theory-based studies that have addressed a wide range of topics, including diet and physical activity promotion, substance use prevention, adolescent pregnancy protection, injury prevention, and compliance with medical regimens, to mention only a few. Our research has focused on children, adolescents, and adults. We have worked with at-risk populations such as children with diabetes, adults with hypertension, sexually active youth, low-income youth, and HIV-infected persons and their partners.

The authors have extensive experience with multilevel, theory-based program planning, development, and evaluation. We have conducted qualitative and quantitative need assessments and evaluations. We have conducted observational studies and randomized trials, including group randomized trials and community studies. As applied researchers, we have learned that theory is essential to both research and practice. The better one understands theory, the better able one is to practice. Theory informs research, and research findings determine the utility of theory.

We have written or edited books that were largely or partly devoted to behavior theory. As college professors, we have taught theory and methods courses. In particular, Dr. Lodyga's ongoing experience teaching both upper undergraduate and graduate-level courses using the first edition of *Health Behavior Theory in Health Promotion*

Practice and Research has firmly grounded the second edition. Mainly, it is the devotion to theory-based programming that explains our irrepressible urge to write a book about behavior theory. However, actually committing to the enterprise of writing this book, however rewarding, can only be explained by our poor judgment about just how challenging and time-consuming the task would prove to be.

4. How could this book help you in your job?

Our intended audience for this book includes public health students, as well as practicing public health professionals whose responsibilities include health promotion. Behavior theory is an essential tool that should be part of the arsenal of every public health professional, most of whom are responsible at some level for promoting healthful behavior. These responsibilities are likely to include personal-health behavior, health-protective behavior, and health-related behavior. These behaviors can be understood theoretically and addressed through theory-based programming. Theory provides a conceptual understanding about behavior that is fundamental to effective programming and necessary for effective needs assessment, program development, and evaluation. Moreover, behavior theory encourages logic-based and science-oriented approaches that ground public health professionals and public health practice. At a time when magical thinking is prevalent and disinformation common, public health, grounded in science, theory, and logic, is needed as an important counterbalance.

5. How is the book organized?

The book has four sections. Section 1 describes the important role of behavior theory in public health practice, provides an ecological framework, and includes brief reviews of the foundations of psychosocial theory. Section 2 encompasses five chapters, each describing a theory or cluster of related theories. Separate chapters are devoted to comprehensive theories of behavior, Social Cognitive Theory and Self-Determination Theory. Other chapters are devoted to theories that are popularly employed in public health, including social influence, expectancy values, and stage theories. Section 3 provides one chapter on communication theories and one on Diffusion of Innovation Theory. These chapters described the importance to behavior of information processing and how communication can promote shared understanding. Section 4 builds on the many examples provided in earlier chapters, addressing issues of how to apply theory to public health practice. The first of these chapters provides suggestions for how to select theory and why theory provides a useful way for public health professionals to think. The second chapter in this section, and the last in the book, addresses in some detail why there are so many behavior theories.

We hope you like and enjoy the book at least as much as we enjoyed writing it!

Acknowledgments

A book is a lonely undertaking, requiring hours of hard work, researching, reading, thinking, writing, revising, and rewriting. Ultimately, bringing a book to print takes more than committed authors, who after all seek merely to report the contributions of many others. Notably, we are in debt to theorists upon whose work the book is based, as well as the many researchers who have tested the utility of the theories. The authors are also grateful to our colleagues and students with whom we have interacted and collaborated over the years. In particular, we wish to acknowledge those who so graciously reacted to our ideas and commented on our work in progress. Notable among these, are coauthors of the first edition, Monica Wendel and Ken McLeroy.

The authors also wish to recognize the Jones & Bartlett Learning editors, Sophie Teague and Sara Bempkins, and their staff for their thoughtful and expeditious efforts rendering our manuscript into book form.

Theory in Context

The chapters in Section 1 provide a conceptual overview and background for the discussion of specific theories in later chapters. Chapter 1 deals with the importance of behavior to health and the importance of theory to health behavior. Chapter 2 describes ecological thinking and the role of theory in multilevel program planning. Chapter 3 provides an overview of foundational behavioral theory, which lays the groundwork for the many specific theories described in subsequent chapters.

CHAPTER 1	Health Behavior in the Context of Public Health......3
CHAPTER 2	A Social Ecological Perspective 33
CHAPTER 3	Theories of Motivation and Behavior: A Public Health Primer 53

CHAPTER 1

Health Behavior in the Context of Public Health

An ounce of prevention is worth a pound of cure.

Henry de Bracton

OUTLINE

1. Preview
2. Objectives
3. Health and Disease
   3.1. Disease Causation
   3.2. Dimensions of Health and Well-Being
      3.2.1. Physical Well-Being
      3.2.2. Mental Health
      3.2.3. Social Health
      3.2.4. Economic Health and Well-Being
      3.2.5. Interactive Dimensions of Health
4. Public Health
   4.1. Prevention
      4.1.1. Primary Prevention
      4.1.2. Secondary Prevention
      4.1.3. Tertiary Prevention
   4.2. Health Objectives for the Nation
   4.3. Health and Behavior
   4.4. Health Behaviors
      4.4.1. Personal-Health Behavior
      4.4.2. Health-Protective Behavior
      4.4.3. Health-Related Behavior
   4.5. Prevention and the COVID-19 Pandemic

5. Health Promotion
   5.1. Who Does Health Promotion?
   5.2. Certification as a Health Education Specialist (CHES)
   5.3. Health-Promotion Processes
      5.3.1. Program Planning, Implementation/Management, and Evaluation
      5.3.2. Change Processes
      5.3.3. Assessment, Evaluation, and Research
         5.3.3.1. Assessment Research
         5.3.3.2. Research on Determinants of Health Outcomes
         5.3.3.3. Research on Determinants of Health Behavior
         5.3.3.4. Efficacy and Effectiveness Research
6. Ecological Perspectives and Multilevel Programs
7. Theory and Practice
   7.1. What Is Theory?
   7.2. Theory and Health Promotion
   7.3. Why Are There Numerous Behavior Theories?
   7.4. Theory in Ecological Context
8. Caveats
9. Lessons for Public Health Practice
10. Discussion Questions
11. References

PREVIEW

Public health is generally more concerned with the health of populations than of individuals and with prevention rather than with treatment. Behavior theory is a central tool in the service of public health practice and research, and the selection and application of appropriate theoretical frameworks is a key competence of public health professionals.

OBJECTIVES

The discerning reader of this chapter will be able to:

1. Describe the dimensions of health and ways of measuring them on a population basis.
2. Describe the functions of public health, and explain how these functions serve the goals of prevention.
3. Describe the three ways the environment affects health behavior.
4. Describe the interactive relationship between health behavior and the environment.
5. Define and provide examples of personal-health behavior, health-protective behavior, and health-related behavior.
6. Describe the role of health promotion in public health.
7. Identify three distinct health-promotion processes.
8. Explain why health-promotion programs often include multiple components.
9. Identify three important ways theory is useful in health-promotion research and practice.

Health and Disease

Health is a highly valued quality, particularly when it has been compromised. Just recall how miserable you were the last time you had the flu or ask someone suffering from a major health problem about the importance of good health. In the absence of good health, the great wonder of life and its many rewards and challenges pales. Health is so central to our existence and so valued that we routinely greet our family, friends, and colleagues with a question about their health, "How are you?" and genuinely hope that the honest answer is "fine." While each of us knows when we are feeling well and when we are not well, health, itself, is a rather complicated **concept** with multiple dimensions.

According to the constitution of the World Health Organization (WHO, 2021), health is not merely the absence of disease or infirmity, but rather a state of complete physical, mental and social well-being. This lofty definition sets a high standard because few of us have actually experienced a complete state of well-being. Nevertheless, the definition introduces the idea that health includes physical, mental, and social dimensions, as shown in **Figure 1.1**. Because they are interactive, problems with one dimension of health can lead to problems in another dimension. For example, obesity and depression, chronic pain and drug abuse, and mental illness and homelessness are commonly associated. Conversely, problems in one area can be better overcome when the other dimensions are strong. Ultimately, health can be considered a resource for everyday life: ". . . the extent to which an individual or group is able, on the one hand, to realize aspirations and satisfy needs; and, on the other hand, to change or cope with the environment" (WHO, 2021).

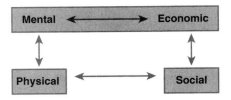

Figure 1.1 The interrelationship of physical, mental, and social dimensions of health

Disease Causation

Before we discuss the dimensions of health, it may be useful to recall that until relatively recently, there was only a limited understanding about the causes of ill health. Two centuries ago, it was thought that the then-rampant contagious diseases were caused by divine punishment, imprudent behavior, or bad-smelling environments (Goldstein, Dwelle, & Goldstein, 2015). However, by the end of the nineteenth century, it was understood that **germs** were responsible for the spread of contagious disease, and this new understanding eventually led to advances in bacteriology and medicine and ultimately to reductions in contagious diseases. Germ theory, of course, is the idea that disease is caused by microorganisms invisible to the naked eye. With the understanding that exposure to germs could occur through the water, air, or personal contact, it became clear that such exposures could be reduced through sanitation and personal hygiene and eventually through antibacterial treatments and vaccinations.

As important as germ theory has been to improvements in health, enabling the development of antibiotics and the promotion of sanitation, germs alone do not fully explain many modern health problems. Germs do not explain injury, cancer, stroke, diabetes, chronic obstructive pulmonary disease (COPD), or heart disease, which are the leading causes of death in the United States and most of the developed world. Moreover, not everyone exposed to pathogenic agents gets sick, so by itself, germ theory is not a complete explanation of disease. While germ theory remains an important explanation of disease, it may be more generally useful to think about disease in terms of the interactions among host, agent, and environment.

In the host–agent–environment model of disease, the host is the population at risk for becoming ill, the agent is a **pathogen** such as a germ or stressor, and the environment brings the agent and host into contact. The common cold serves as a classic example. People tend to get sick when they are exposed to the cold virus, a germ that is typically transferred from person to person. The environment contains the agent and provides conditions for acute or chronic exposure. Those not exposed to the virus cannot become infected. Among those exposed, the likelihood of infection depends on the **susceptibility** of the host and the extent and duration of exposure. A host may be more or less susceptible due to a variety of causes, including genetics, past experience, health status, environmental conditions, and health behavior. Hence, illness is probabilistic, depending on the complex relationships between host, agent, and environment.

This conceptualization works reasonably well to explain the spread of most infectious diseases, and it also provides a partial explanation for injury and chronic disease. Indeed, a version of the theory has been adapted specifically to explain injury causality (Haddon, 1968). The Haddon matrix, as it is called, conceptualizes injuries due to motor vehicle crashes as follows: (1) the agent would be another vehicle or roadside barrier (or after a crash, the secondary impact of the unrestrained passenger tossed against objects within the vehicle or, in the worst case, thrown from the vehicle); (2) the host is the vehicle occupant, who is susceptible to injury in a crash, particularly when not protected by a seat belt and airbag; and (3) the environment, including vehicle speed and position, traffic, and road conditions, which provides the opportunity and context for the host to come into contact with the agent. While drivers can sometimes speed, follow closely (tailgating), and text while driving without crashing, the more frequently and excessively they do so, the greater the likelihood or probability of a crash.

The host–agent–environment conceptualization also works well for chronic diseases, particularly if we appreciate that there are often many causal agents, each of which may be only partially responsible. These partial causes are known as **risk factors**, which are "...partial—i.e., not sufficient, not always necessary, but nevertheless contributing—component causes" (Krieger, 2008, p. 223; WHO, n.d.). Even genetic causes of disease are often best understood as risk factors. While certain maladies are caused by a single gene or allele, such as sickle cell anemia, mostly genes contribute to one's susceptibility, but do not by themselves cause disease. For example, a particular gene marker (CYP2A6) has been identified that increases susceptibility to lung cancer. Smokers with this gene are much more likely than smokers without this gene to get lung cancer, but of course smokers without the gene are more likely to get lung cancer than nonsmokers with or without the gene (Styn et al., 2013). In this case, genotype can be a risk or protective factor that interacts with the environment and the smoking behavior.

The considerable population variability due to socioeconomic status, sex, and race in the social and physical environment helps explain inequities in patterns of disease (Grossman, 2017). That is to say, the less privileged tend to suffer greater cumulative environmental exposure, including to pollution, violence, economic hardship, and other sources of stress, leading to greater

susceptibility to disease. Modern ecosocial perspectives link proximal and distal, biological, and social influences in a comprehensive explanation of inequities in health and disease. These important concepts are addressed in further detail in Chapter 2.

Dimensions of Health and Well-Being

At the individual level, one may think of being well or sick or relatively better or worse than usual. However, population health is generally measured by statistics describing the prevalence rate of health problems, expressed as the number of cases per 100,000 people or similar denominator (Office of Disease Prevention and Health Promotion [ODPHP], 2020a). Prevalence rates are useful for assessing health status and **enabling** comparisons over time and between various population groups. One of the more reliable and prominent measures of national health status is the rate and causes of specific disease **(morbidity)** and death (mortality) according to age, sex, region, and race. See **Table 1.1** for

Table 1.1 Measures of Health Status

Index	Definition
Mortality	Number of deaths in a population within a prescribed time period
Crude mortality	# deaths/year/1000 population
Cause-specific mortality	# deaths/specific cause/100,000 population
Life expectancy	Average # years life remaining
Infant mortality	# infant (0–1 years)/year/1000 live births
Longevity	Average length of life
Morbidity	Measure of disease incidence or prevalence in a given population
Disease incidence rate	# new cases/specific disease/year/1000 population at risk
Disease prevalence rate	# existing cases/specific disease/years/1000 population

Data from the Centers for Disease Control (https://www.healthypeople.gov/2020/about/foundation-health-measures/General-Health-Status).

Table 1.2 Ten Leading Causes of Death as a Percentage of All Deaths—United States, 1900 and 2018

Number	Year	
	1900	2018
1	Pneumonia	Heart disease
2	Tuberculosis	Cancer
3	Diarrhea and enteritis	Unintentional injury
4	Heart disease	Chronic respiratory disease
5	Stoke	Cerebrovascular
6	Liver disease	Alzheimer's disease
7	Injuries	Diabetes
8	Cancer	Influenza and pneumonia
9	Senility	Nephritis
10	Diphtheria	Suicide

Data from National Vital Statistics System, National Center for Health Statistics, CDC, 2018 (https://www.cdc.gov/nchs/nvss/leading-causes-of-death.htm, accessed 4-16-2020).

definitions of important population measures of health and disease: life expectancy, longevity, mortality, morbidity, and potential years of life lost.

Physical Well-Being

At the population level, physical health is usually measured by the prevalence of illness, disease, injury, and disability. The major threats to physical health have changed over the years. The leading causes of death are shown in **Table 1.2** for 1900 and 2018 (Centers for Disease Control and Prevention [CDC], 2020b). Notably, there has been a dramatic shift in the causes of death in the United States over the past century. In the early twentieth century, Americans were likely to die of infectious diseases such as tuberculosis and diarrhea, while today Americans mainly die due to injury and chronic diseases such as heart disease, cancer, and stroke.

This major shift in causes of death from infectious to chronic diseases has been referred to as the **epidemiological transition** (Omran, 2005; Wikipedia, n.d.). Accordingly, there have been dramatic decreases in mortality among infants and children. These changes can be attributed to improvements in nutrition, birth control, economic growth, access to medical care, but above all else to improvements in the physical environment, particularly sanitation and clean water. Meanwhile, the modern lifestyle typified by high-fat diets, low levels of physical activity, tobacco, and other drug use, among other factors, has increased the prevalence of chronic diseases, which are responsible for 70% or more of deaths in the United States (CDC, 2020b).

Mental Health

Mental health problems are among the most prevalent and costly of all health problems globally. While genetics contribute to mental health, many mental health problems are the product of physiological and environmental processes, much like physical health problems (National Institute of Mental Health [NIMH], 2020). Notably, the homeless, the disenfranchised, the impoverished, victims of violence, substance abusers, and other unfortunates are at particularly high risk for mental health problems, illustrating the importance of environmental factors in mental health and illness.

Mental illnesses are diagnosed by mental health professionals using various measurement methods, including self-reports, interviews, and observations, to determine an individual's inner feelings and ability to function within conventional society. The most common mental health problems are anxiety, depression, and other mood-, eating-, and stress-related disorders. Many of these mental health problems are transient and resolve over time, particularly when treated, but can sometimes be sustained and progressive. More serious psychological problems, including major anxiety, major depression, bipolar disorders, and dementia, are less prevalent but more debilitating (Patel, Minas, Cohen, & Prince, 2014).

Mental health problems are not only unpleasant and incapacitating, but also when untreated they are risk factors for other problems, such as job loss, relationship issues, suicide, drug dependency, and other self-destructive behaviors (Kessler, Alonso, Chatterji. & Yanling, 2014; Patel et al., 2014). During a typical year, about 25% of Americans are estimated to experience a mental health problem severe enough to cause functional impairment, making mental disorders the leading cause of disability in North America and Canada for those ages 15–44 (NIMH, n.d.; U.S. Surgeon General's Report, 1999). Fortunately, many mental health problems can now be identified and treated with success.

Social Health

A certain level of social interaction may be important for sustained mental health. Clearly, having good social relationships with family and friends and getting along with others at work, school, and in the community are indicators of social health and associated with a range of health outcomes (Bonner, 2018; Grossman, 2017). Social health is often measured by statistics on crime, poverty and joblessness, marriage and family dissolution, child abandonment, homelessness, and access to health. Where we live contributes to social health. Communities that are well organized, provide ample social services, include abundant open spaces, and offer good transportation are desirable places to live and are healthier in some ways than other communities. The Healthy Cities movement (Bloomberg.org, 2020; CDC, 2020a) seeks to improve the social, economic, and environmental qualities of cities by engaging local governments in a process of political commitment, institutional change, capacity building, partnership-based planning, and innovative projects. These programs promote comprehensive and systematic policy and planning focused on health inequalities, poverty, vulnerable groups, and participatory governance. The health of the cities and towns in which we live is a public health goal as well as a measure of health.

Economic Health and Well-Being

Health and well-being are not independent of economic status. While being rich does not necessarily bring good health and happiness, being poor emphatically contributes to health problems. Inequities in economic status are surprisingly high in the United States, much greater than any other highly developed country (Grossman, 2017). Inequities in the United States and elsewhere in the world in educational and employment opportunities and the availability of adequate housing contribute to poor health (WHO, 2009). Education level, income, and housing quality are highly associated with each other and with elevated exposure to water and air pollution. The best thing for public health is a fair economy that provides everyone with the essentials for healthful living, including a sound education, employment opportunity, and adequate housing (Grossman, 2017).

Interactive Dimensions of Health

Health is a complicated phenomenon, and health status can vary across physical, mental, and social dimensions, such that a person may be relatively well physically, but not so well mentally or socially. Also, these dimensions can be interactive, with problems in one dimension carrying over into the other dimensions. Being sick physically is stressful mentally, and both mental and physical health problems can be moderated by social factors. Mental health problems often contribute to physical and social health problems. Economic status interacts with each of the other health dimensions. For example, those who live in poorer neighborhoods have dramatically worse physical and mental health outcomes (WHO, 2020b). So, while it is useful to understand that there are several dimensions of health, it is just as important to appreciate that they are interrelated.

Public Health

At the outset of the chapter, it was noted that **public health** is primarily concerned with health at the population level. This is distinct from **medicine**, which is primarily concerned with the health of individual patients. Of course, public health and medicine intersect around issues of access, coverage, and quality. Historically, a major function of public health has been to provide medical services to those who are not insured and to provide certain special health services deemed vital to population health, such as immunizations and birth control. Accordingly, to the extent that public health is the provider of last resort, it can be thought of as the practice of medicine on a population basis.

Nonetheless, the primary function of public health is **prevention**. The American Public Health Association (2021) lists its overarching priorities as (1) building infrastructure and capacity, (2) ensuring the right to health and health care, and (3) creating health equity. A report from the Institute of Medicine (IOM, 1988) characterized the mission of public health as ensuring conditions in which people can be healthy by providing the following core services: (1) assessment of health status, (2) policy development, and (3) assurance of healthful living conditions. This broad mandate is reflected in the wide range of public health activities. For example, public health is largely credited with monitoring health status and behavior and identifying causes of disease (Goldstein et al., 2015). Also, public health efforts have improved water and food sanitation, increased vaccination rates, eradicated some diseases (e.g., smallpox) and fostered the control of others (e.g., HIV), and mitigated the effects of injuries and other problems. A more detailed list of essential public health services is provided in **Table 1.3**, including those devoted to measuring and monitoring health status and fostering access to care (Goldstein et al., 2015).

These public health functions have remained important even as contagious diseases have declined. Meanwhile, the increasing prevalence of chronic disease has challenged public health to increase its focus on lifestyle factors such as inactivity, poor diet, substance abuse, mental health, injury, and pollution (Goldstein et al., 2015). While public health remains concerned about outbreaks of infectious diseases such as flu epidemics and

Table 1.3 **Essential Public Health Services**

Assessment
1. Monitor health status to identify community health problems.
2. Diagnose and investigate health problems and health hazards in the community.

Health Education and Promotion
3. Inform, educate, and promote the health of the population (health education and health promotion).
4. Mobilize community partnerships to identify and solve health problems.

Policy
5. Develop policies and plans that support individual and community health efforts.
6. Enforce laws and regulations that protect health and ensure safety.

Services
7. Link people with needed personal-health services, and ensure the provision of health care when otherwise unavailable.

Infrastructure
8. Ensure a competent public health and personal healthcare workforce.

Evaluation and Research
9. Evaluate effectiveness, accessibility, and quality of personal and population-based health services.
10. Conduct research for new insights and innovative solutions to health problems.

U.S. Department of Health and Human Services. Public Health in America, Essential Public Health Services.

relatively new threats such as HIV, exotic biological agents, and environmental disasters, it must also increase its efforts to prevent and control chronic diseases.

Public health has long struggled to obtain and maintain resources needed for essential functions. Funding air and water pollution activities seems less urgent when these problems are reasonably under control, leading to funding reductions until problems worsen and become evident and problematic. Unfortunately, fixing environmental problems after they occur can be more difficult and expensive than preventing them. Similarly, the United States was woefully ill prepared for the COVID-19 pandemic because the prevention plans and materials developed during the Obama administration were eliminated by the Trump administration, which meant there was inadequate personal protective gear for healthcare workers,

among other glaring deficiencies. While the threat of contagious exotic diseases like COVID-19, caused by the novel (not previously experienced by humans) coronavirus, SARS CoV-2, is difficult (but not impossible) to prepare for in advance, just such preparations were undertaken by a public-health-minded administration, but eliminated by the subsequent administration.

Similarly, the impending climate change crisis is well understood, extensively measured, highly predictable, and certain to be devastating. Early steps to mitigate climate change were taken during the Obama administration, but the following administration systematically eliminated climate protection policies and practices. Unquestionably, climate change is an existential threat to human existence and a crucial public health challenge (Yale Climate Connections, 2019). Countless studies have documented the human causes of climate change, estimated the extent of damage, and determined the number of years remaining to reduce greenhouse gases and restore land and sea to prevent irreversible and catastrophic global warming and climate catastrophe (Romm, 2018). In addition to dangerous temperature increases and sea level rise, climate change increases the frequency and severity of weather events such as storms that cause flooding, pollution, dislocation, wildfires, crop destruction, and injuries (CDC, 2021). Sadly, the needed societal reforms to reduce the use of fossil fuels have not yet become sustained national priorities, and the longer the danger is ignored, the more difficult it will be to mitigate the extreme public health consequences.

Prevention

While public health has always emphasized prevention, the focus of prevention efforts has changed over time. The impending climate change crisis emphasizes public health concerns about the impact of dramatic changes in the physical environment on human health. At the same time, the recent novel COVID-19 pandemic underscores the continued importance of contagious disease prevention, even while chronic diseases account for the greatest burden. While investment in prevention has the potential to greatly reduce the costs associated with major health problems, consistent funding has been problematic. The United States spends more on health care, both as a proportion of gross domestic product and on a per capita basis, than any other nation in the world (Organization for Economic Co-Operation and Development, 2019), but ranks thirty-fifth among countries in terms of life expectancy (Central Intelligence Agency, 2020). Annually, the United States spends an estimated $3.6 trillion on health care, about $11,000 per person and 17.7% of GDP (Centers for Medicare and Medicaid Services, 2019). Sadly, the nation devoted only 2.65%

of total health expenditures to prevention in 2014, which is projected to fall to 2.4% by 2023 (Himmelstein & Woodhandler, 2016).

Prevention includes **risk reduction** and health protection, including the environment and healthcare access. Risk reduction includes things like decreasing the prevalence of uncontrolled hypertension, smoking and other substance use, injuries, unsafe sex, and violence. Increases in risk reduction efforts could reduce chronic disease prevalence by 40%–50% (Milstein et al., 2007). A sincere commitment to prevention has been recognized for decades as an essential part of national health planning (ODPHP, 2020b).

Prevention efforts are often described as primary, secondary, or tertiary (Goldstein et al., 2015). Next we describe for each level goals, target population, and examples. **Table 1.4** provides examples related to cardiovascular disease.

Primary Prevention

Primary prevention is concerned with the prevention of the onset of health problems among the general population. Primary prevention can focus on those at risk or even to prevent the development of risk factors (termed *primordial prevention*). Primary prevention activities include sanitation of water, food, and air; immunization; and health promotion to foster improvements in **personal-health behavior** and healthful environmental conditions. Screening for risk in some cases is considered primary prevention, for example, sedentary behavior, unsafe sex, substance use, lack of immunization, and mental health issues, some of which are both risk factors for other health problems and independent health outcomes. Examples of primary prevention objectives during the 2020 COVID-19 pandemic included social distancing, handwashing, and face mask wearing. With respect to cardiovascular disease, primary prevention activities include improving diet, increasing physical

Table 1.4 Categories of Prevention Related to Cardiovascular Disease

Prevention Level	Goal	Population Targets	Examples
Primordial	Prevent the development of risk factors	General population	Promote healthful diet, physical activity, no substance use, and safety behavior Develop healthful policies Create safe and healthful environments
Primary	Reduce risk, prevent onset	General population	Programs, policies, environments that improve diet, weight, physical activity, and prevent obesity; moderate substance use; and facilitate safe behaviors
Secondary	Early detection and treatment to reduce impact of existing disease	High-risk and confirmed cases (e.g., overweight, sedentary; smokers; elevated blood pressure, elevated cholesterol)	Screening for elevated cardiovascular disease (CVD) risk (e.g., elevated blood pressure, cholesterol; smoking) Promote risk reduction Enhance adherence to medical recommendations (e.g., low-dose aspirin, cholesterol medication, low-fat diet, exercise)
Tertiary	Reduce consequences, prevent recurrence, moderate severity, rehabilitate	CVD patients	Provide and promote aggressive medical treatment; medical follow-up, long-term medical management; enhanced adherence to medical regimens; rehabilitation services

activity, and maintaining healthful environmental conditions.

Secondary Prevention

Secondary prevention is concerned with detecting health problems and reducing their **consequences** through early detection and treatment among those who are at high risk or already afflicted. Secondary prevention is concerned with minimizing consequences, for example, reducing the severity of symptoms and the number of sick days, medical care visits, and emergency room visits associated with a particular health problem. Screening programs for detection of sexually transmitted diseases (STDs), cancer, diabetes, and breast cancer that allow early treatment, while fostering improved adherence to medical advice, are examples of secondary prevention. Examples of secondary prevention objectives during the COVID-19 pandemic included screening for detection and early treatment. Examples of secondary prevention of cardiovascular disease include screening for risk factors and fostering adherence to a medical regimen.

Tertiary Prevention

Tertiary prevention is designed to mitigate the severity and consequences of existing disease or injury. While secondary prevention is concerned with early detection, tertiary prevention occurs after the problem has fully manifested. The goal is to provide treatment and rehabilitation to reduce the negative impact and restore functioning. Examples of tertiary prevention include mental health counseling for rape victims, tracing those exposed to sexually transmitted infections, and rehabilitation for victims of stroke and other serious health problems. In addition to rehabilitation, tertiary prevention includes the prevention of recurrence, for example, of addictive behavior or repeated unintended pregnancy. Examples of tertiary prevention objectives during the COVID-19 pandemic included quarantining of victims, supplying hospitals with ventilators and related medical equipment, and developing rehabilitation of those successfully treated. Examples of tertiary prevention for cardiovascular disease include continuity of medical care and postevent and posttreatment rehabilitation.

Health Objectives for the Nation

To combat the most prevalent health problems, the United States has developed a national prevention agenda known as *Healthy People* (ODPHP, 2020b), which provides 10-year

goals and objectives. The agenda is renewed each decade through an elaborate process that involves input from a wide range of public health professionals. The leading health indicators for 2020, shown in **Table 1.5**, include goals related to health care, environmental quality, injury and violence, mental health, diet/

Table 1.5 *Healthy People 2020 Health Objectives*

1. Access to health services
2. Adolescent health
3. Arthritis, osteoporosis, and chronic back conditions
4. Blood disorders and blood safety
5. Cancer
6. Chronic kidney disease
7. Diabetes
8. Disability and secondary conditions
9. Early and middle childhood
10. Education and community-based programs
11. Family planning
12. Food safety
13. Genomics
14. Global health
15. Health communication and health IT
16. Healthcare-associated infections
17. Hearing and other sensory or communication disorders
18. Heart disease and stroke
19. HIV
20. Immunization and infectious diseases
21. Injury and violence prevention
22. Maternal, infant, and child health
23. Mental health and mental disorders
24. Nutrition and weight status
25. Occupational safety and health
26. Older adults
27. Oral health
28. Physical activity and fitness
29. Public health infrastructure
30. Quality of life and well-being
31. Respiratory diseases
32. Sexually transmitted diseases
33. Social determinants of health
34. Substance use
35. Tobacco use
36. Vision

U.S. Department of Health and Human Services, Topics & Objectives. Retrieved from https://www.healthypeople.gov/2020/topics-objectives

physical activity/obesity, reproductive health, and substance abuse. The leading indicators framework recognizes the biologic, social, economic, and environmental factors linked to health disparities. In addition to the leading indicators, *Healthy People 2020* includes 42 topics and 1200 objectives for reducing mortality and morbidity organized across life stages. Ultimately, the objectives can be and are used to establish resource priorities, plan prevention programs, and evaluate national progress. The 2030 leading indicators and objectives are currently in development. Since it was established in 1979, the *Healthy People* process of gathering data, convening experts, and developing leading indicators has become perhaps the most important national prevention initiative. The leading indicators and objectives provide guidance and direct resource allocation to state and local agencies for prevention.

Health and Behavior

Note that behavior figures prominently in the list of topics listed in Table 1.5. It is tempting to categorize some of the indicators as strictly behavioral, for example, physical activity, substance use, and sex, while immunization, environmental quality, and access to health care could be categorized as environmental. However, this would not be an accurate categorization because behavior and environment are not strictly independent.

Healthy People documents recognize the importance to health of both environmental factors and personal-health behavior. Because the success of public health efforts to control contagious diseases through improved air, water, and food quality, and because environmental factors are still hugely important in both contagious and chronic health problems, there had been a long-standing emphasis in public health on environmental approaches to prevention. Indeed, there is a long-standing debate among public health professionals about the relative importance of intervening to change the environment or intervening to change personal behavior. There remain strong advocates for both positions. This debate is complicated because the environment can be defined broadly to include not just water, air, and food, but also policies, practices, and conditions that greatly influence health behavior. For example, policies that would increase the availability of immunizations are important, but the act of getting immunized is a behavior. Probably all types and aspects of behavior are influenced by both physical and social environments. While pollution is an environmental problem, environmental laws and regulations to control pollution come about through the behavior of legislators and policy makers. While access to health care is largely a social condition, appropriately accessing health care is behavioral. Notably, changes in the environment often result in changes in behavior, and changing behavior generally requires alteration in related environmental conditions.

The early versions of *Healthy People* created confusion by categorizing certain health behaviors under the term *health promotion*. Hence, many people began to think that **health promotion** was synonymous with health behavior, rather than a process that seeks to foster improvements in environment and behavior. This was problematic to the extent it suggested that health behaviors were strictly under the control of the person and a matter of personal choice, which they are only to a certain extent. In general, both environment and personal choice are important, and environment and behavior are not separable. The continuing arguments about the relative importance of creating healthful environments or promoting personal-health behavior are understandable, but unproductive.

Health Behaviors

It is instructive at this point to clarify the common terms relating to health behavior. The first of these, personal-health behavior, refers to behaviors that relate to one's health. **Health-protective behavior** is undertaken specifically, if not exclusively, out of a concern for the health of others. The term **health-related behavior**, as used here, includes behaviors that affect the health (for better or worse) of others (for example, parenting, and regulatory behavior), regardless of their intent.

Personal-Health Behavior

Personal-health behaviors are defined here as behaviors performed by an individual that affect their health, even if the behaviors occur for reasons other than health. Health behaviors generally considered personal include some of those listed in *Healthy People*, shown in Table 1.5, including physical activity, diet, and substance use. Personal-health behavior is also implicated in the cause and prevention of many other topics listed in Table 1.5, for example, injury and violence.

Personal behaviors include elements of choice, but they are not necessarily always or fully under individual control. For example, there is substantial research indicating physical and social environment influences on personal-health behaviors such as diet, physical activity, and substance use. Notably, neighborhood characteristics are associated with the prevalence and amount of physical activity (Cerin et al., 2014). Because many personal-health behaviors are largely habitual, they do not require much conscious effort and for the most part are not always or fully motivated by a concern for health. For example, some people are highly concerned about the health properties and effects of the foods they eat, but most people most of the time are mainly concerned about the taste, convenience, cost, and familiarity of food. People drive fast because they are in a hurry or otherwise prefer to do so without much concern for health, despite the potential crash and injury consequences. The point here is that while personal-health behaviors may include aspects of personal choice, they are not fully volitional because they are influenced by other **motivation**, as well as current and past environmental factors. While it is theoretically possible for people to

behave in any way they wish (e.g., free will), in practice there are a lot of physical and social influences on any particular behavior at any particular time, not to mention the effect of lifelong environmental influences that precede and condition behavior.

While people are sometimes purposeful about their health-damaging behavior (driving fast, drinking too much, smoking, overeating, and the like), the idea should be resisted that personal-health behaviors are generally intentional and fully under the control of the individual. Substance abuse, for example, is maintained by the addictive properties of the substances, plus the substantial social and commercial factors that encourage use. Also, many people exercise for reasons other than health, for example, because they enjoy the process, the competition, the outdoors, social aspects, or possibly because they live or work near a lovely park where it is convenient to walk and spend time. Similarly, some people wear safety belts because they are required to by law, to satisfy other family members, to avoid the vehicle warning signs and sounds, or merely out of habit, and not necessarily or fully because safety belts protect their health. Personal-health behaviors contribute to their health but not always intentionally.

Examples of personal-health behavior with respect to preventing COVID-19 contagion include behaviors that protect a person from the virus such as proper handwashing and social distancing.

Health-Protective Behavior

Health-protective behavior is distinguished by its specific concern for the health of others. At the individual level, requiring that your child wear a safety belt or bicycle helmet, encouraging your partner to stop after two drinks, cooking low-fat meals for the family, and driving carefully are health-protective behaviors to the extent they are undertaken purposefully, if not exclusively, to protect or improve the health of others. Socially oriented, health-protective behavior is undertaken to improve the social conditions that contributed so importantly to health (Koh et al., 2020). Health-protective behavior is also practiced by health professionals, environmentalists, social workers, child advocates, and concerned citizens working together for changes that would improve health conditions. In almost every area of health, private and public groups with overlapping concerns undertake independent and concerted change efforts. For public health to be successful, substantial commitment to health-protective behavior by local institutions, policy makers, and concerned citizens is needed.

Adolescent substance abuse is one of many examples where public health, media advocates, criminal justice professionals, child advocates, and concerned citizens all are interested in prevention. Examples of health-protective behaviors related to the COVID-19 pandemic include individuals wearing face masks in public to prevent possible contagion to others, public testing for the virus or antibodies to determine who was infected and who were possibly immune to further infection, contact tracing of those who had been exposed so they could be quarantined, and providing health-care workers with appropriate personal protective equipment and medical equipment and supplies.

Health-Related Behavior

The term *health-related behavior* is often used interchangeably with the term *personal-health behavior*. However, at least when used in this text, the term *health-related behavior* refers exclusively to behavior that affects the health and health behavior of other people and not that of the person who engages in the behavior. As with personal-health behavior, health-related behavior is not always purposefully undertaken for health reasons, but affects others' health, nonetheless. The behavior of friends, family members, administrators, policy makers, regulators, and others affect the health

and behavior of others. The person who drives in a risky manner engages in behavior that endangers other vehicle occupants and road users, although health and safety considerations may have had little to do with the way the person drives. The parent who shops for groceries and prepares family meals is engaging in health-related behavior. The agents responsible for licensing commercial outlets for cigarettes, alcohol, or fast food may be primarily concerned with zoning and tax issues and not health, but nonetheless engage in health-related behavior. Legislators who passed laws subsidizing oil exploration and refining were motivated by economic and not health concerns, but their policies reflect health-related behavior. Similarly, land use decisions are often made mainly on the basis of concerns about transportation and commerce, with little concern for air quality or nonvehicular transportation routes, which are important to health.

It is useful conceptually and for programmatic purposes to distinguish health-related behavior from other forms of health behavior. One of the goals of public health is to create healthful environments and living conditions. Accordingly, it must seek to target not only those whose health and health behavior is of interest, but also the behavior of those whose actions contribute to or create environmental influences on personal health and behavior. It can be argued that the contribution to health of health-related behavior may be at least as great or greater than personal-health behavior. Motor vehicle crashes resulting in injury and death are only partly due to driver performance, as problematic as it sometimes is, and largely due to environmental factors. Although the crash rate declines as miles driven increase, actual crash risk increases the more one drives due to increased exposure in terms of the overall amount of time on the road. Therefore, policies that encourage people to drive are health related. Examples include the development of residential communities apart from business and commerce requiring daily commuting (vs. high-density urban development) and the development or failure to develop convenient public transportation and safe walking and cycling routes. The point here is that motor vehicle crashes are due not only to the personal-health behaviors of inattentive or reckless driving but also to the health-related behavior of community planners, roadway engineers, and government officials responsible for transportation policy. During the COVID-19 pandemic of 2020, policy makers made decisions requiring aspects of social distancing and then about relaxing these requirements and reopening commerce. While these decisions included elements of health-protective behavior, they were also based on economic considerations that were health related.

The concept of health-related behavior is essential to **multilevel thinking**, taking into account both the population of interest and the environmental influences on health and behavior. Indeed, it has been well argued that targeting only personal-health behavior without appreciation for the environmental

influences on behavior can be a form of victim blaming. Keep in mind health-related behavior affects the health and health behavior of others, although not necessarily intentionally and sometimes only as a side effect. Accordingly, it is essential to understand that substantial contributions to health occur from decisions and policies made at every level of society that often fail to take health into account appropriately or adequately. Hopefully, over the course of this text, as we come back to these concepts many times, you will appreciate why these distinctions are important and the advantages of thinking about health behavior in these ways.

Prevention and the COVID-19 Pandemic

Examples of the three categories of health behavior as they relate to the COVID-19 (first detected in 2019) pandemic (popularly termed *Covid*) are shown in **Table 1.6**. Accordingly,

Table 1.6 Examples of Each Category of Health Behavior from the COVID-19 Pandemic

Health Behavior	Whose Behavior?	Example
Personal health: Behaviors that affect one's own health, intentional or not	Everyone	Handwashing; social distancing
Health protective: Behaviors undertaken to affect the health of others	Everyone Public health professionals Policy makers	Wearing face masks; testing for disease and antibodies; developing and administering vaccines; providing personal protective and medical equipment; adopting policies to encourage social distancing and other safe behaviors
Health related: Behaviors that affect others' health, often unintended	Everyone Managers Public officials	Engaging in behaviors that could expose others to possible infection: not wearing masks; not social distancing; congregating in large groups Enabling congregation of groups opening businesses, workplaces Enabling congregation in public spaces

personal-health behaviors include handwashing and social distancing (mask wearing can provide minor personal protection), things under the control of individuals and largely engaged in for personal protection from contracting the disease. Health-protective behaviors of individuals include wearing face masks, honoring social distancing, and getting tested for the virus. Health-protective behaviors of public health officials include providing testing and establishing social standards for social distancing and mask wearing and the size of public gatherings. At the political level health-protective behaviors included the provision (or failure to provide) of testing equipment and materials, personal protective equipment for healthcare workers, and medical equipment and supplies for hospitals. Health-related behaviors would include those activities that could affect the spread of the virus, although they may have been undertaken for other reasons. Examples include individuals going unmasked in public and congregating in large groups. Examples of health-related behaviors by policy makers and businesspersons concern policies and practices regarding the congregation of large groups and reopening of businesses, worksites, and public areas for economic considerations while the epidemic was ongoing.

Health Promotion

Health promotion is a relatively recent concept, and there is a range of perspectives on what it entails. Over time it has been defined variously as a process concerned with changing personal behavior, empowering people to change, changing lifestyle, and changing environmental influences on behavior (Simons-Morton, Greene, & Gottlieb, 1995). Indeed, it is all of these things. We define health promotion as processes employed to foster healthful behavior and environmental conditions. There is modern agreement that health promotion is a process and not a particular set of health behaviors. The World Health Organization

(WHO, 2009, 2020a) defined health promotion as follows: "...the process of enabling people to increase control over, and to improve, their health. It moves beyond a focus on individual behaviour towards a wide range of social and environmental interventions." This is consistent with accepted definitions in the United States, Canada, and other countries.

Health promotion has become an integral part of public health and an essential element of public health training (Riegelman & Albertine, 2011). Most schools of public health have academic units that emphasize and train students in health promotion (Association of Schools and Programs of Public Health, n.d.), and many state and local health departments have health-promotion programs. Here we consider two questions of particular importance for this text and its focus on theory. Who is responsible for health promotion, and what are health-promotion processes?

Who Does Health Promotion?

Many public health and education professionals undertake health-promotion activities. The profession of **health education** is devoted to health promotion, and the public health subspecialty, health promotion, is primarily concerned with these processes, but other public health and other professionals (e.g., social workers, nutritionists, nurses, physicians, health psychologists, health communication specialists) engage in work consistent with health promotion, whether they consider this work health promotion or not. Moreover, every public health professional has some responsibility for health promotion because health behaviors and conditions are important in nearly every area of public health. Indeed, many people outside public health should be involved in health promotion, including teachers, youth workers, social workers, and others. The better the training in health promotion for health professionals, the better it is for the health of the nation. However, health promotion is not a simple process and cannot be practiced capably without substantial formal training.

Certification as a Health Education Specialist (CHES)

It is possible and desirable to become certified as a health education specialist (CHES). Eligibility requirements include at least a bachelor's degree in a relevant field and appropriate coursework. The National Commission for Health Education Credentialing (NCHEC) administers the CHES competency-based exam and manages the CHES certification process (NCHEC, n.d.). The following eight competency areas, each with multiple subcompetencies, define the role of the health education specialist: (1) assessment, (2) planning, (3) implementation, (4) evaluation and research, (5) advocacy, (6) communication, (7) leadership and management, and (8) ethics and professionalism. Those with advanced training and experience can qualify to take the Master Certified Health Education Specialist (MCHES) exam. The MCHES exam focuses on advanced aspects of the eight CHES competencies and subcompetencies.

It is also possible to become certified in public health (CPH) (National Board of Public Health Examiners, n.d.). The CPH exam covers 10 areas, many overlapping with the CHES, including the following: (1) evidence-based approaches, (2) communication, (3) leadership, (4) law and ethics, (5) health equity and social justice, (6) policy, (7) biology and risk, (8) program planning and evaluation, (9) program management, and (10) collaboration and partnerships.

Health-Promotion Processes

Most health-promotion programs have the main goals of providing services and activities

that: (1) improve behavior and health, and (2) strengthen the environmental healthfulness. However, under usual conditions health promotion cannot directly alter the environment—policy, regulations, or physical environments. Maybe some high-level government officials have the capability to establish a policy or regulation, but for most health-promotion professionals, policies, regulations, and environments are goals, not processes. Can you think of anyone in public health who could actually adopt a policy or pass legislation or directly change the physical environment? These things are mostly not under the control of public health professionals. They are complicated and political and involve many individuals and agencies with diverse goals and constituents. However, public health professionals should and do influence these outcomes. A key health-promotion process is fostering changes in the health-protective and health-related behavior of those who control or exert environmental, policy, and practice influences on health and health behavior. Hence, health promotion seeks to facilitate change at multiple social levels.

Health-promotion practice functions are not limited to any one specific health problem or behavior and can be applied to a range of settings, population groups, health problems, and risk factors. Practice processes include needs assessment and planning, implementation/anagement, and evaluation of health-promotion programs. Program implementation includes the application of change processes such as **communication** (Hickson, 2015). Research may be involved in each of these areas, but particularly in assessment and evaluation.

Program Planning, Implementation/Management, and Evaluation

A key health-promotion process is program development, which includes the establishment, implementation, evaluation, replication, and dissemination of programs. Health promotion should be conducted within the context of planned programs that have carefully identified goals and objectives, activities, and measures of success. The obvious advantages of careful planning include the increased likelihood of efficient, economic, and effective programs.

Program planning entails multiple functions, including determining and documenting a need for the program, developing components and plans, implementing interventions, and conducting evaluation. There are many important problems, and typically only those that are established as top priority receive proper programmatic resources. Therefore, considerable effort is required to establish the need for programs. Assessments are needed to determine prevalence, populations at risk, and goals and objectives. Once a health problem and population(s) at risk is established as a priority, a program, sometimes with multiple components, must be developed, conducted, and evaluated. Each program component would include goals, objectives, and **intervention** activities.

Planning and management responsibilities include competing for resources, including staff salaries, meeting and office space, equipment and materials, methods of recruiting participants, personnel to carry out and manage the programs, program guidelines and instructions, and money for travel costs, to name just a few. To secure resources, funding agencies or organizations must be convinced to support the program. This process includes submitting funding requests, applying for grants, and otherwise securing necessary program resources. Additional program management activities would include recruiting, training, supervising, and monitoring staff; procuring resources; developing intervention materials; and conducting interventions.

After a program is finally developed and implemented, it is necessary to secure the resources and support necessary for program maintenance and continuation. This has led to the idea of focusing on factors associated with program continuation in the planning, implementation, and evaluation of our programs and activities. One set of factors associated with program continuation refers to the extent to which a program is "institutionalized" or embedded in the host organization. That is, the extent to which the program has survived important organizational passages, such as budget cycles; the extent to which the program becomes established within the organization (having their own staff, space, management, etc.); and the extent to which the program is recognized to fulfill an important institutional niche.

Change Processes

An essential function of health promotion is the selection, adaptation, and implementation of change processes. A change process is the strategy and methods used to change behavior, usually addressing cognitions, skills, and environmental factors. With respect to reducing the prevalence of smoking in a particular population, it is necessary to identify the factors that encourage and factors that discourage smoking, including cognitions, quit skills, and environmental conditions. Change processes should be specific to the needs of the target population based on needs assessments. If the key predictors of smoking cessation (or not starting) are **attitudes** and skills, these should be a focus of the program and the methods employed. If social and physical environment factors are important (they usually are), somewhat different change processes might best be employed. Ultimately, change process considerations include the following: (1) the specific target population(s), (2) the key **determinants** of the target outcomes, and (3) change processes appropriate to program goals.

The general categories of change processes include **counseling, teaching**, training, communicating, social marketing, community development, organizational change, and advocacy, as described in **Table 1.7**. Probably most other change processes (e.g., peer education, community mobilization, advocacy, and

Table 1.7 Health-Promotion Change Processes

Process	Description
Teaching	Processes of facilitating change in knowledge, beliefs, attitudes, and behaviors through information and learning activities in a group setting
Counseling	Processes of facilitating change in knowledge, beliefs, attitudes, and behaviors through information and learning activities with one individual or in a small group
Communication, social marketing	Process of developing and delivering messages that are informative and persuasive
Organizational/Institutional change	Develop and promote healthful and safe worksite and school policies and practices through policy advocacy, worker organizations
Community development and social capital development	Political and social actions to improve health-related community involvement, resource allocations, program development, policies, and functioning; promote social capital and social support
Advocacy	Actions designed to gain political commitment, policy support, and social acceptance for healthful goals, policies, programs, and practices, including lobbying, organizing, protesting, and related activism

lobbying) are subsumed under these broad change process categories. Also, while each of these processes is discrete, with unique approaches to change, they overlap, can be combined, and employ similar methods. For example, information is a common element of all change processes, but how information is developed, transmitted, and communicated is unique to each process.

These general change processes are typified by conceptual and logistic considerations. For example, teaching is used when the target population is more or less captive and a structured curriculum can be developed, training usually focuses on preparing health professionals for work with individuals (but sometimes refers to instructing the target population in specific skills), counseling is used in settings where the target population can be seen in a one-to-one or small-group context, and social marketing is used when the population is "at large" and can only be reached through media. Communication strategies

are included in almost every health promotion program and are often adapted for use in each program component. Change processes employ a range of methods that tend to be theory based. Notably, specific activities based on methods can be developed to address specific objectives.

Change processes can be employed to address personal-health behavior, health-protective behavior, and health-related behavior. One of the functions of program development is to identify the targets of each component, one of which usually includes the **at-risk population**, the group about whose health and health behavior the program is concerned, and one or more other components that are concerned about environmental influences on the health and behavior of the at-risk population. These components identify those who control the environmental objectives and their health-related behavior. For example, in a program developed to improve the diet of preadolescent children, one component might target the children of interest, another component might target their parents, and a third component might target those who manage and prepare school meals. Each program component may employ one or several change processes.

Assessment, Evaluation, and Research

Numerous activities are required to determine the prevalence of health problems and health behaviors and identify at-risk populations; identify health problems and elucidate the personal and environmental determinants of health and behavior; and assess program **efficacy** and **effectiveness** and translation of effective programs from one setting or population to another. "In order for health promotion and disease prevention programs and interventions to be effective, they should be based on a body of relevant theory and research" (Columbia University, n.d.).

Assessment Research Most health-promotion research is designed to determine the prevalence of health problems and the populations most at risk. This information is essential for determining programmatic priorities, as well as determining program foci. Using surveys and applied behavioral epidemiology methods, this work is concerned with identifying rates of a health problem and how these rates vary according to the characteristics of the population of interest, such as by age, sex, race, or neighborhood. For example, we may be interested to know the prevalence of smoking by age and region so that programs can be developed for particular age groups or regions. Alternatively, we might be interested in determining the rates of childhood immunizations among different population subgroups.

Research on Determinants of Health Outcomes Health-promotion researchers are concerned about the factors associated with

health and behavior. For example, this research might seek to determine the environmental and behavioral factors associated with a flu outbreak. Environmental factors would include things like the virulence of the flu strain, population concentration, general health of the population, vaccine availability and distribution systems, healthcare access, other availability and access issues, and policies regarding minimizing contamination in public places and worksites. On the personal behavior side, this research would seek to determine what behaviors are important, including hygiene, safety, and healthcare-seeking behavior. This research would identify the factors that are linked to flu contagion and would help identify possible prevention objectives and program components.

Research on Determinants of Health Behavior Most health-promotion research is concerned about identifying factors associated with health behavior. Determinants of these behaviors can be cognitive, environmental, and interactional. This research would be concerned with identifying the relevant knowledge, beliefs, attitudes, and behavior of the population groups of interest with respect to the health behaviors of interest. It might also be concerned with the environmental influences on these behaviors. Some of these cognitions may not be inconsistent with logic and reality, in which case objectives can be created to alter incorrect perceptions. In cases where cognitions are inconsistent with healthful behavior but accurately reflect environmental conditions, it may be necessary to identify environmental objectives. Similarly, in addition to research on the influences on the behavior of a population at particular risk, this research might be interested in the influences on the behavior of medical care professionals, social workers, teachers, and others with respect to the behavior. This research would seek to understand the knowledge, attitudes, and behavior of these professionals and the environmental factors that influence their cognitions and behavior.

Efficacy and Effectiveness Research

A good deal of health-promotion research is designed to determine how well programs worked; what they accomplished; how they can be improved; how they can be modified for other contexts, populations, or problems; and how they can be translated to other settings and populations and disseminated. This research employs systematic methods to assess **process**, **impact**, and **outcome evaluation** to determine efficacy and effectiveness within experimental or quasi-experimental program designs. Much of this research seeks to determine program efficacy, which is how well it worked under relatively ideal conditions, or its effectiveness, which is usually tested under typical rather than ideal conditions, or sometimes under well-controlled conditions but in comparison with another program or approach of equal or near equal magnitude. Efficacy and effectiveness research preferably are conducted using experimental or quasi-experimental designs in which participants or groups (e.g., schools or communities) are randomized to treatment conditions. The replication of efficacy and effectiveness research in various contexts provides the evidence base for health-promotion practice.

Ecological Perspectives and Multilevel Programs

One of the primary themes of this text that should now be apparent is that behavior and health can best be understood as the product of a web of related factors. Chapter 2 is devoted to this topic and here we provide a brief introduction. Notably, the environment influences behavior and behavior influences the environment. Bandura (1986) conceptualizes this as the interrelationships between the **person**, **behavior**, and **environment**.

Person factors include personality attributes and cognitive processes of the individual. The environment includes both physical and social factors that influence or affect opportunity or provide **reinforcement**, including **norms**, structures, policies, programs, practices, economic factors, and social influences. Behavior is not only a result but also an effect, as it responds to and interprets the environment and modifies it to some extent. Ultimately, these experiences are interpreted by each person according to their unique character, past experience, and cognitions. The environment reinforces future behavior, for better or worse. Over the course of a lifetime a person learns from their experience how to judge environment cues and the likelihood of reinforcement. Thus, person, environment, and behavior interact constantly.

While this simple model is useful for understanding these relationships in general ways, just how person, behavior, and environment interact is quite complex. One of the main ways people learn is through the response of the environment to behavior. Getting tested for coronavirus exposure or symptoms provides a useful example of the complexity of behavior–environment interactions. Let's say you and I both seek to be tested. Given the lack of national policy with dedicated resources, testing varies dramatically across the nation. Accordingly, each of us could experience somewhat unique experiences, shorter or long wait times, more or less courteous and efficient treatment, or shorter or longer periods before getting test results. Depending on our personalities and situational context (e.g., how concerned we are that we might be positive for the virus or susceptible to its effects), past experience, and cognitions, our behaviors will be variably reinforced, leading to increased or decreased likelihood of engaging in similar behavior in the future. Each of us may engage in more or less the same behavior, but experience different responses from the environment, with variable effects on future behavior.

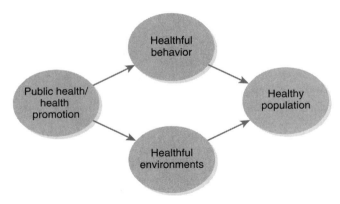

Figure 1.2 The goals of public health and health promotion are to foster healthful behavior and healthful environments

Adding to the complexity, *person* is a dynamic concept. People have competing motivations and priorities influenced by their environment and their behavior that they develop and change over the course of a lifetime. Schedules and responsibilities change, and motivation wanes. Keep the following points in mind as we move forward: (1) behavior is influenced by its interaction with the environmental and personal factors; (2) each person develops uniquely due to the interaction of genetic, as well as immediate and lifelong environmental, factors; and (3) the environment not only influences behavior but is also influenced by behavior and understood uniquely by the person.

Health promotion is concerned not only about understanding the nature of these multilevel influences, but also about what we can do to make them health enhancing. If health and behavior are influenced at many levels, most of which are beyond the control of the person whose health is of concern, our efforts to facilitate changes in personal-health behavior will be limited by the extent to which these behaviors are supported at other societal levels.

Accordingly, a fundamental health-promotion task is to develop effective interventions at multiple levels. Remember, health promotion is concerned about and seeks to understand and influence the behavior of individuals with respect not only to their personal-health behavior, but also the behavior of others, the health-protective and health-related behaviors exercised by family members, friends, neighbors, health and education professionals, regulators, policy makers, and others, representing various societal levels. Therefore, many health-promotion programs address behavior at multiple levels. Fortunately, many of the theories and principles of behavior change discussed in this text have relevance to personal-health behavior and health-related behavior.

As illustrated in **Figure 1.2**, the goals of public health and health promotion are to foster improvements in personal-health behavior and healthful environments. This simple **ecological** model makes sense in the context of personal-health behaviors being influenced by other environmental factors. Of course, if we want to facilitate change in peoples' behavior and health, we can work with them directly, and we can seek to alter the environmental influences on their behavior. Health promotion is always concerned about behavior, but this can be personal-health behavior, health-protective, and health-related behavior. As shown in Table 1.6, if we want to alter environmental influences on personal-health behavior, we need to identify and intervene with those individuals whose behavior affects the health and behavior of the population of concern.

Take, for example, the diet of preadolescent children. Children have some responsibility for what they eat, exercising personal preferences at every meal. However, they are also influenced by what foods are available, how they are served, and by what their parents and friends want them to do, possibly by what their friends prefer. Accordingly, a health-promotion program designed to improve children's diet might address children's personal behavior with respect to their food choices, parents' health-related behavior with respect to food purchase and preparation, and school food service directors' health-protective behavior with respect to the healthfulness of school meals.

Theory and Practice

Here we provide a brief introduction to the role of theory in public health programming. A more extensive discussion is provided in a subsequent chapter.

What Is Theory?

A **theory** can be described as the possible relationships between **constructs** or sometimes as a **hypothesis** supported by data. We tend to think about hypotheses as being very specific, testable statements that are a standard part of every research proposal, but they are really just statements about expected relationships. We often attempt to understand the data from daily life by developing a personal hypothesis and then evaluate the hypothesis as we collect additional information through experience. For example, the last time you got a cold you might have thought to yourself, I got cold germs from someone at work who was sick and left germs in the kitchen or on a doorknob. Maybe you decide that you could avoid getting sick in the future if you washed your hands more consistently and thoroughly, particularly after touching doorknobs and objects

in public spaces. You do this conscientiously for some time without getting sick again. Your behavior becomes habitual and is reinforced when a good friend encourages this behavior, or you come across an article that reports that handwashing is one of the best ways to avoid picking up germs. Assuming you avoid for a time picking up a new cold, you might conclude from the evidence that your hypothesis is correct. Now that you have some evidence, it is possible to develop your hypothesis further, maybe even develop a theory.

A theory is not necessarily the truth, but it describes relationships, defines terms, and is stated in such a way as to be testable. Indeed, one of the great strengths of a theory is that it facilitates research that tests the utility of the theory and the extent of its application. In the case of the theory that germs cause disease and handwashing can prevent contagion, there is a lot of evidence supporting it. Indeed, handwashing to prevent contagion is consistent with what is known about germs and the spread of contagious disease.

Unlike our simple example of handwashing to prevent contagious disease, general theories of behavior such as **operant** conditioning, values expectancy, social cognition, and persuasion apply to a wide range of behaviors. However, they may have started out as simple hypotheses. Indeed, operant conditioning prides itself on being the scientific observation of how people respond to the environment (i.e., how reinforcement influences the frequency of a response). Similarly, the premise of the transtheoretical model is that the methods people use in their independent efforts to change their behavior can be identified (according to stage) and employed programmatically. Most theories started out as ideas or hypotheses and eventually became more elaborate theories of behavior through research. Generally, as an applied field, health promotion is less interested in testing a theory than in applying it; however, a lot can be learned about theory from the careful evaluation of programs, particularly well-controlled evaluations. Therefore, theory is one of the essential tools for effective health-promotion practice and research. Even if we could somehow conduct successful health-promotion programs without using theory, we would not be able to interpret the results and generalize them to other contexts and health problems. Theory can assist not only in the development of the program, but also in the interpretation of how it did or did not work, allowing improvements in future iterations of the program. The trail-blazing social psychologist Kurt Lewin noted, "If you want to truly understand something, try to change it."

Theory and Health Promotion

Theory is useful in health promotion in several ways. First, it provides conceptual context for understanding behavior. For example, operant conditioning provides the perspective that behavior is a matter of reinforcement, and this helps us understand how environments influence behavior and how alterations in the environment can change behavior. Second, theory guides research that seeks to identify the determinants of health-related behavior, and it guides program planning with respect to objectives and change processes. For example, effective health-promotion programs typically address cognitions, but it can be unclear which cognitions are associated with particular health behaviors. Theory provides us with logical candidate variables that can be assessed, objectified, and targeted for intervention. Third, theory suggests intervention methods that can be incorporated into health-promotion practice. Another quote by Kurt Lewin applies: "There is nothing as practical as a good theory." Fourth, theory enables interpretation of program results.

The better **health-promotion specialists** and other public health professionals understand theory, the more effective they will be. In this text we describe many of the most relevant and popular theories used in health

promotion. We believe that most of these theories are relevant to a wide range of behaviors, and each of these theories is particularly useful for certain behaviors under certain situations. Some of these theories are specific to certain kinds of behavior, while other theories are broadly applicable to almost any behavior.

At first it can be confusing that there are many different theories, and some of them seem to overlap, each using somewhat unique terms for similar concepts, and sometimes employ a term for a meaning somewhat different from the meaning for that term in another theory. There are many behavior theories because there are many kinds of behavior, many facets of behavior, many contexts for behavior, many influences on behavior, and many different ways of understanding behavior. Consequently, new theories or variations on existing theories are constantly being developed. However, all behavior theories derive from a focus on how behavior is influenced by (1) the environment (broadly defined to include social context, policy, and community); (2) cognitive information processing; and (3) individual differences within the context of personality. The last two chapters discuss these core foundations of theory in more detail. The text's middle chapters focus on theories that have been widely used in health-promotion research and practice.

Why Are There Numerous Behavior Theories?

Because there are a lot of theories, the tendency has been to teach each one separately to maintain its integrity. This is sometimes referred to as the "theory of the week" approach. While this approach can be frustrating for students because it is difficult to digest so many different theories in a short period of time, to their credit, professors want to make sure that students develop familiarity with many different theories. What can suffer in a theory-of-the-week approach is a broader understanding of how theories are related, which may be most relevant for any particular problem, and how theory can be used to guide and evaluate practice. There is no easy solution to this problem, but the approach taken in this text is to first orient the reader to ecological models of behavior and then to conceptually organize related theories within each chapter, sometimes only one theory and sometimes several closely related theories to a chapter.

The student then must do the real work of figuring out how to apply each theory to relevant problems. (We discuss the process of selecting theory in a later chapter.) This work involves reviewing the literature to see how theory has been applied previously, learning everything possible about the problem of interest, and then creatively applying theory to the development of a program. Admittedly, this is not easy. Indeed, those of us who have worked in this area for decades are still learning about theories and their use. Most of us become particularly familiar with one or two theories and tend to think about health behaviors from those perspectives. Fortunately, researchers have left a thoughtful trail of publications describing the application of theory to various health problems and behaviors. It is up to us to review and interpret the literature carefully and build on the findings from past research and when possible to apply theory in interesting ways and extend research on that theory.

Theory in Ecological Context

As discussed earlier, many health-promotion programs have multiple components, each addressing a different population. Most programs have at least one component directed at personal-health behavior, but many programs also have components directed at the health-protective or health-related behavior of those whose behavior affects health or environmental influences on health and behavior. For example, if we were interested in improving the diets of preadolescent children, as previously discussed, it would make sense to have one component that addressed the children's knowledge, attitudes, and skills. This component might be based on a particular theory of behavior, for example, social cognitive theory, reasoned action, or **attribution** theory. However, children have only so much control over their diets, so another program component might address school lunch. Those with control over what is served in the school lunch (or breakfast) program would include school administrators, cafeteria managers, and cooks. A multidimensional program might include separate components for each of these. A goal of each component would be to modify the composition of foods offered in school lunch, but the target population for that component would be unique. These program components would undoubtedly address the knowledge, perceptions, attitudes, and behavior of these target populations and the environmental influences on these cognitions and behaviors. The theory employed for each component might be unique. Another component might address the knowledge, attitudes, and behavior of family members in a manner that would lead to changes in the family environment with respect to food and eating. This component might employ the same or a different theory than the one employed to address the children directly. Another program component, or a separate program altogether, might be directed at increasing the availability of healthful foods at local grocery outlets. Such a program component would benefit from theories relating to organizational change, community development, and social change. While all of these components would have the goal of improving child nutrition, each would target a unique population with control over the specific objectives of that component. Accordingly, different theories might be employed in each component because of the nature of the behavioral goals, target of the intervention, social context, and programmatic considerations.

Caveats

Let's be clear about some issues that may be lingering about theory and the orientation of this text.

1. **Prevention.** Prevention is a primary concern of public health. Prevention is concerned with healthful behavior and environments. Behavior and environment are not independent.

2. **Health Promotion Facilitates Change.** Health promotion has sometimes been accused of blaming the victim, encouraging people to change when they are not able. This accusation has come about, we believe, because of two unfortunate misconceptions. The first is the idea that health promotion seeks to make people responsible for behavior over which they have little control. Our discussion of the terms *personal-health behavior*, *health-protective behavior*, and *health-related behavior* is meant to help dismiss this misconception. Health promotion is concerned about both the cognitive and environmental influences on behavior. Indeed, health promotion is, or should be, just as concerned with health-protective and health-related as with personal-health behavior.

   Another misconception is that health promotion is somehow manipulative. Nothing could be further from the truth. There are many change processes and methods available for use in health promotion, but education is central to all of them, and education is empowering, not manipulative. Education is an essential function of public health and a fundamental element of personal freedom and democracy, not a matter of manipulation. To be clear, health promotion, broadly speaking, is an educational enterprise that has as its goal improvements in the ability of individuals to manage their behavior and changes in the environment that are conducive to healthful living.

3. **Imperfection in the Cognition–Theory–Change Continuum.** We do not suggest that health behavior is simply a matter of personal cognitions and environmental influences. Nor do we contend that behavior is always logical and predictable. We recognize that behavior is complicated. Often, even the person engaging in the behavior is unsure why. Behavior is not simply a matter of the sum of cognitive factors that support the behavior minus the factors that discourage it, although this is largely true. A thorough if incomplete understanding of these factors is invariably informative and useful. Information about key cognitions is generally predictive of behavior, and theory and good measurement help us better explain behavior, not completely, but within the bounds of probability and with a level of accuracy that can guide and enable program development. That is, we can develop an understanding of particular behaviors well enough to develop programs that target important variables and lead to behavior change. However, there will always be a lot of uncertainty and variability because people and environments are complex and unique. The more narrowly we can focus on a particular population group, the better we can assess the factors related to their health and behavior, and the better we can develop programs that are consistent with their needs. However, health promotion programs invariably and appropriately address a wide range of individuals, with unique dispositions and environments, requiring creative and adaptable program planning.

4. **Whose Behavior Anyway?** Hopefully, the chapter has made it clear that theories about individual behavior are relevant not only to personal-health behavior, but also to health-protective and health-related behavior. While the target of the intervention may be unique, the determinants of behavior change are the same. Health

promotion has moved beyond a limited focus on personal-health behavior to a concern with the multilevel influences. We now frame individuals' behaviors as part of a broader system in which behavior affects and is affected by other people, settings, and broader social and environmental influences. Finally, we try to balance the focus on the behavior of the at-risk population with a complementary emphasis on the behavior of individuals and groups who contribute to environmental influences on individual behavior through health-protective or health-related behavior.

5. **The Value of Theory.** Theory is a tool for use in public health program development, implementation, and evaluation. Sadly, lots of programs are enacted without an ounce of theory. Programs can be better when theory is applied to their conceptualization, identification of objectives, implementation methods, and evaluation.

6. **Ecological Perspectives and Multilevel Programing.** While most theories of behavior were developed with personal behavior in mind, many of these theories can be extended to health-related and health-protective behavior, and other theories have been developed to explain community and other collective behavior. We argue that health-promotion professionals should take an ecological perspective with respect to health behaviors of interest. Even if the program focuses only on the individual level, an ecological perspective appreciates the environmental influences on behavior and suggests other levels and other types of behavior that could be addressed. Not every program can develop and implement program components at multiple levels, but ecological thinking enables appropriate program planning for the components that are developed.

Lessons for Public Health Practice

1. Public health is mainly concerned with prevention.
2. Prevention invariably involves behavioral and environmental change.
3. Health promotion is a process that seeks to facilitate healthful behavior and environments.
4. Health promotion is an essential public health activity, many public health professionals have health-promotion responsibilities, and health promotion is also a public health specialty.
5. Health educators and other public health professionals with training in health promotion can become certified health education specialists (CHES).
6. Personal-health behavior includes elements of choice and environmental influence.
7. Health-protective behavior is purposefully undertaken with a concern for others' health.
8. Health-related behavior affects others' health, often as a side effect rather than a purposeful concern for health.
9. Theory can guide the development and evaluation of health-promotion programs.
10. Recognizing that there are influences on health at many societal levels, health-promotion programs tend to have multiple components addressing personal-health behavior and health-related behavior.

Discussion Questions

1. How have the 10 leading causes of death changed since 1900, and why?
2. Why are health objectives in *Healthy People* important to public health practice?
3. What public health professionals are responsible for health promotion? What public health specialties are primarily responsible for health promotion?
4. How is health promotion different from public health?
5. Describe two health-protective behaviors for preventing the spread of the coronavirus.
6. Describe how theory can contribute to health-promotion program development.

References

American Public Health Association. (2021). Our mission. Retrieved from https://www.apha.org/about-apha/our-mission

Association of Schools and Programs of Public Health. (n.d.). Retrieved from https://www.aspph.org

Bandura, A. (1986). *Foundations of thought and action: A social cognitive theory*. Englewood Cliffs, NJ: Prentice Hall.

Bloomberg.org. (2020). Partnership for healthy cities. Retrieved from https://partnershipforhealthycities.bloomberg.org

Bonner, A. (2018). *Social determinants of health: An interdisciplinary approach to social inequality and wellbeing*. Bristol: Bristol University Press. DOI:10.2307/j.ctt22p7kj8

Centers for Disease Control and Prevention. (2018). Learn about mental health. Retrieved from http://www.cdc.gov/mentalhealth/learn/index.htm

Centers for Disease Control and Prevention. (2020a). 500 cities project. Retrieved from https://www.cdc.gov/places/about/500-cities-2016-2019/index.html

Centers for Disease Control and Prevention. (2020b). Leading causes of death and injury. Retrieved from https://www.cdc.gov/injury/wisqars/LeadingCauses.html

Centers for Disease Control and Prevention. (2021). Climate effects on health. Retrieved from https://www.cdc.gov/climateandhealth/effects/default.htm

Centers for Medicare and Medicaid Services. (2019). National health expenditure data. Retrieved from https://www.cms.gov/Research-Statistics-Data-and-Systems/Statistics-Trends-and-Reports/NationalHealthExpendData

Central Intelligence Agency. (2020). The world factbook. Retrieved from https://www.cia.gov/the-world-factbook

Cerin, E., Cain, K. L., Conway, T. L., van Dyck, D., Hinckson, E., Schipperijn, J., . . . Sallis, J. F. (2014). Neighborhood environments and objectively measured physical activity in 11 countries. *Medicine and Science in Sports and Exercise*, 46(12), 2253–2264. DOI:10.1249/MSS.0000000000000367

Columbia University. (n.d.). Health promotion research and practice. Retrieved from https://www.publichealth.columbia.edu/academics/degrees/master-public-health/certificates/health-promotion-research-and-practice

Goldstein, R. L., Dwelle, T., & Goldstein, K. (2015). *Introduction to public health: Promises and practices* (2nd ed.). New York: Springer Publishing Co.

Grossman, M. (2017). *Determinants of health: An economic perspective*. New York: Columbia University Press.

Haddon, W., Jr. (1968). The changing approach to the epidemiology, prevention, and amelioration of trauma: The transition to approaches etiologically rather than descriptively based. *American Journal of Public Health and the Nation's Health*, 58(8), 1431–1438. DOI:10.2105/ajph.58.8.1431

Hickson, F. (2015). Concepts in health promotion. In W. Nutland & L. Cragg (Eds.), *Health promotion practice* (2nd ed.). New York: Oxford University Press.

Himmelstein, D. U., & Woodhandler, S. (2016). Public health's falling share of US health spending. *American Journal of Public Health*, 106(1), 56–57. DOI:10.2105/AJPH.2015.302908

Institute of Medicine. (1988). *The future of public health*. Washington, DC: Academy Press.

Kessler, R. C., Alonso, J., Chatterji, S., & Yanling, H. (2014). The epidemiology and impact of mental disorders. In V. Patel, H. Minas, A. Cohen, & M. J. Prince (Eds.), *Global mental health* (pp. 82–101). New York: Oxford University Press.

Koh, H. K., Bantham, A., Geller, A. C., Rukavina, M. A., Emmons, K. M., Yatsko, P., & Restuccia, R. (2020). Anchor institutions: Best practices to address social needs and social determinants of health. *American Journal of Public Health*, 110(3), 309–316. DOI:10.2105/AJPH.2019.305472

Krieger, N. (2008). Proximal, distal, and the politics of causation: What's level got to do with it? *American Journal of Public Health*, 98(2), 221–230. DOI: 10.2105/AJPH.2007.111278

Milstein, B., Jones, A., Homer, J. B., Murphy, D., Essien, J., & Seville, D. (2007). Charting plausible futures for diabetes prevalence in the United States: A role for system dynamics simulation modeling. *Preventing Chronic Disease*. Retrieved from http://www.cdc.gov/pcd/issues/2007/jul/06_0070.htm

National Board of Public Health Examiners. (n.d.). Credentialing public health leaders. Retrieved from https://www.nbphe.org

National Commission for Health Education Credentialing. (n.d.). Retrieved from https://www.nchec.org/ches

National Institute of Mental Health. (n.d.). Statistics. Retrieved from https://www.nimh.nih.gov/health/statistics/index.shtml

National Institute of Mental Health. (2020). Mental illness. Retrieved from http://www.NIMH.nih.gov/health/statistics/mental-illness.shtml

Office of Disease Prevention and Health Promotion. (2020a). General health status. HealthyPeople.gov. Retrieved from https://www.healthypeople.gov/2020/about/foundation-health-measures/General-Health-Status

Office of Disease Prevention and Health Promotion. (2020b). *Healthy people 2030*. Retrieved from https://www.healthypeople.gov/2020

Omran, A. R. (2005). The epidemiologic transition: A theory of the epidemiology of population change. *The Milbank Quarterly, 83*(4), 731–757.

Organization for Economic Co-Operation and Development. (2019). General government spending. Retrieved from https://data.oecd.org/gga/general-government-spending.htm

Patel, V., Minas, H., Cohen, A, & Prince, M. J. (Eds). (2014). *Global mental health*. New York: Oxford University Press.

Riegelman, R., & Albertine, S. (2011). Undergraduate public health at 4-year institutions. It's here to stay. *American Journal of Preventive Medicine, 40*(2), 226–231. DOI:10.1016/j.amepre.2010.10.013

Romm, J. J. (2018). *Climate change: What everyone needs to know*. New York: Oxford University Press.

Simons-Morton, B. G., Greene, W. A., & Gottlieb, N. (1995). *Introduction to health education and health promotion* (2nd ed.). Prospect Heights, IL: Waveland Press.

Styn, M. A., Nukui, T., Romkes, M., Perkins, K. A., Land S. R., & Weissfeld, J. L. (2013). CYP2A6 genotype and smoking behavior in current smokers screened for lung cancer. *Substance Use & Misuse, 48*, 490–494. DOI:10.3109/10826084.2013.778280

U.S. Surgeon General. (1999). *Mental health: A report of the Surgeon General – executive summary*. Rockville, MD: U.S. Department of Health and Human Services, Substance Abuse, and Mental Health Services Administration, Center for Mental Health Services. National Institutes of Health, National Institute of Mental Health.

Wikipedia. (n.d.). Epidemiological transition. Retrieved from https://en.wikipedia.org/wiki/Epidemiological_transition

World Health Organization (WHO). (n.d.). Environment, climate change and health. Retrieved from http://www.who.int/phe/en/

World Health Organization. (2009). Milestones in health promotion: Statements from global conferences. Retrieved from https://www.who.int/healthpromotion/Milestones_Health_Promotion_05022010.pdf

World Health Organization. (2020a). Health promotion. Retrieved from https://www.who.int/topics/health_promotion

World Health Organization. (2020b). Mental health. Retrieved from https://www.who.int/health-topics/mental-health#tab=tab_1

World Health Organization. (2021). Constitution. Retrieved from https://www.who.int/about/who-we-are/constitution

Yale Climate Connections. (2019). How climate change threatens public health. Retrieved from https://yaleclimateconnections.org/2019/08/how-climate-change-threatens-public-health/

CHAPTER 2

A Social Ecological Perspective

Health behavior is influenced not only by individuals' own cognitions but also by their relationships with others, affiliations with organizations, location within communities, physical environment, connections with culture, and the politics and economics of the time.

OUTLINE

1. Preview
2. Objectives
3. Introduction
   3.1. Social Ecology Conceptualizations
   3.2. Social Ecology and Public Health
4. Theory and Social Levels
   4.1. Intrapersonal (Individual) Level
   4.2. Interpersonal (Social) Level
   4.3. Organizational/Institutional Level
   4.4. Community Level
   4.5. Policy Level
       4.5.1. Examples of Policies That Affect Health
       4.5.2. Policy Analysis
       4.5.3. Policy Intervention
   4.6. Physical Environment Level
   4.7. Cultural Level
   4.8. Economic Level
   4.9. Interactions Between Societal Levels
5. Intervening at Multiple Societal Levels
   5.1. Program Objectives
   5.2. Environments Matter
   5.3. Targets of Intervention
   5.4. Intervention Approaches
   5.5. Multilevel Intervention Considerations
       5.5.1. Multiple Causes
       5.5.2. Interrelated Levels
       5.5.3. Adjacent Societal Levels
       5.5.4. Environment and Behavior
       5.5.5. Altering Cognitions of the Targets of Intervention
6. Lessons for Public Health Practice
7. Discussion Questions
8. References

PREVIEW

Health behavior is influenced not only by individuals' cognitions but also by their relationships with others, their affiliation with organizations, their location within communities, their physical environment, the politics and economics of their time, and connections with their culture.

OBJECTIVES

At the end of this chapter, the reader should be able to:

1. Describe why social ecological thinking is important to public health.
2. Identify societal levels that make up the social ecology of behavior and health.
3. Explain how a particular personal-health behavior may be affected by each societal level.
4. Describe how societal levels interact.

5. Describe how socioeconomic disparities affect behavior and health.
6. Explain the concept of target of intervention.
7. Explain how health-promotion intervention can be directed to each societal level.

Introduction

Social ecology considers the interrelationships of social levels with behavior and health. Health behavior is influenced not only by individuals' own **cognitions** but also by their relationships with others, affiliations with organizations, location within communities, physical environment, connections with **culture**, and the politics and economics of the time. The effects of each societal level vary considerably, with substantial disparities in income, education, housing, and healthcare access contributing to disparities in health and behavior. The principles of social ecology and the behavior and health effects of social levels are central concerns of public health. We can best understand and foster improvements in health behavior through analyses of the influences of each societal level and their interactive effects. Understanding these influences is an important element of cultural competency and a requirement for effective public health practice.

In Chapter 1 we introduced a number of important concepts that will be emphasized throughout this book, including (1) the conceptualization of disease as the relationships between the host, the agent, and the environment; (2) the role of various types of behavior, including personal-health behavior, health-related behavior, and health-protective behaviors, in the causes and prevention of diseases and promotion of health; (3) the idea that behavior shapes and is shaped by the physical, social, and economic environments (Venkataramani, Chatterjee, Kawachi, & Tsae, 2016); (4) the concern that behavior should be viewed within the context of individuals' developmental history and their social context (Bronfenbrenner, 1979); and (5) appreciation that the effects of each social level on behavior

and health vary dramatically according to economic status (Grossman, 2017). This chapter further develops these themes of behavior affecting and being affected by the social and physical environment and how social disparities contribute to these relationships.

Social Ecology Conceptualizations

The prominent idea that health behavior is a matter of personal choice has long been challenged by the modern contention that individual behaviors should be understood within broader social contexts. Behavior is the product of individual choice to the extent that it has been influenced by previous experience; social relations, norms, and values; and social contexts of family, neighborhood, community, culture, public policy and economics.

As described by the developmental psychologist Urie Bronfenbrenner (1979), human behavior may be viewed as occurring within multiple systems or levels. These systems include individuals with unique and varied cognitions and life experiences, families and other social relationships, organizations such as schools and work, communities, and cultures. According to Bronfenbrenner, characteristics of the combined influences at each of these societal levels affect what individuals believe and how they behave. Bronfenbrenner referred to the study of these various **social systems** as "levels of analysis" (see **Figure 2.1**), referring to the characteristics of each societal level and their interactions. Bronfenbrenner was primarily interested in influences on human development during the lifespan, but his concepts form the bases of modern social ecological thinking about society, health, and behavior. Just to take a simple example, smoking behavior is affected by our individual **beliefs**, attitudes, and values (individual level), which are the product of immediate and distant social influences (interpersonal level). Our cognitions and behavior with respect to smoking

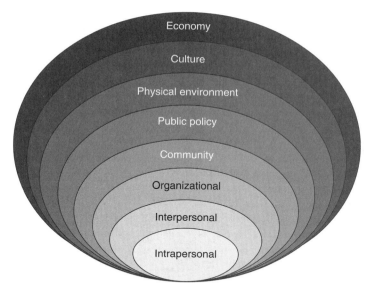

Figure 2.1 The social ecological model

are influenced by the norms of groups to which we belong (group level). Smoking behavior is also conditioned by the norms of the communities within which we reside (community level) and those of our general culture (cultural level). Policies affect the availability, cost, and locations where tobacco can be used. These levels are highly interactive. Thus, to understand behavior and behavior change, it is useful to examine each societal level and their interactions.

Social Ecology and Public Health

Application of Bronfenbrenner's social ecological model to health and behavior has made multilevel thinking standard in modern public health training and practice. At a practical level multilevel approaches have been employed to increase vaccinations by reducing barriers to vaccinations (Nyambe, Van Hal, & Kampen, 2016) and improving access to health care for adolescents and young adults (Harper, Steiner, & Brookmeyer, 2018).

Social ecological concepts are integral to public health training and practice, including

as follows: (1) core competencies for public health on the national public health certification examination; (2) multidimensional bases for several of the leading volumes on theory and practice in the field (Glanz, Rimer, & Viswanath, 2015; Green & Kreuter, 2005; Simons-Morton, Green & Gottlieb, 1995; Simons-Morton, McLeroy, & Wendel, 2011); (3) framework for curricula for numerous public health schools and programs; and (4) as a model for interventions to reduce health disparities (Paskett et al., 2016). Public health theorists have renamed and defined Bronfenbrenner's levels to better accommodate the concerns of the field. McLeroy, Bibeau, Steckler, and Glanz (1988) proposed five societal levels that closely correspond to Bronfenbrenner's levels and include the following: (1) individual, (2) social relations, (3) organizations, (4) community, and (5) public policy. To these five levels, we add (6) physical environment, (7) culture, and (8) economics. It is this eight-level framework that we use for discussion of ecological perspectives.

Ecological frameworks are based on evidence that no single factor or level fully explains why some people or groups are at a higher risk for certain health and behavior problems. In practice, a social ecological approach to health-promotion planning requires analyses of each societal level and their interactions across levels. Such analyses enable us to understand and address the factors at each level that influence behavior and health and the interrelationships between levels. Notably, the levels in some ways are overlapping and interactive. Social ecology considers each level and their interactions to be of importance. Therefore, public health practitioners can best understand health behaviors and create appropriate interventions by addressing multiple levels as relevant and feasible.

Figure 2.2 provides a representation of the ecological model of development and behavior. The figure illustrates that health and behavior are the product of the influences of the various social levels. Essentially, our relationships with other people, including family, friends, neighbors, coworkers, teachers, clergy, and even casual acquaintances, and the broader social and physical environment affect our knowledge, attitudes, values, and behavior. If many of our close friends or family members use tobacco, we may develop relatively positive or accepting attitudes toward smoking. Our attitudes toward smoking, however, may also be affected by our friends and peer group. We often make friends of those with whom

we have frequent contact, such as neighbors, school or work mates, club or religious organization members, or those with whom we exercise, play sport, game, or otherwise spend time. Thus, friendship patterns are affected by organizational memberships and processes within neighborhoods, work, and schools. Organizations are affected by characteristics of the people who are members and its culture. Public policies regarding taxes, employment, education, business, housing, and transportation greatly influence both health and behavior. Culture and economics provide powerful and complicated effects on each of the other levels as well as on health and behavior directly.

Theory and Social Levels

The conceptualization and analysis of behavior and health from a social ecological perspective is guided by a range of theories and concepts. Indeed, social ecology perspectives are imbedded within many theories. Think of social ecology as processes similar to the many lines of code that make your computer function. You might be using a certain program, and that is what allows the program to work, and it reflects what you see on your screen, but there are many processes working behind the scenes to enable the operation of the program and your

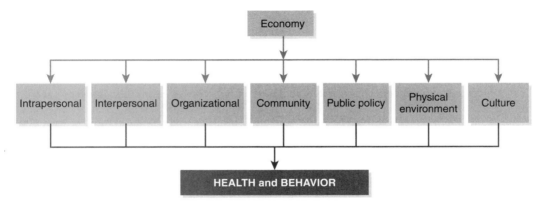

Figure 2.2 Relationship of levels of analysis to behavior

computer. Likewise, social levels of influence are continually operating in the background, providing context for behavior and health. Indeed, an appreciation of social ecology facilitates understanding behaviors and theories presented in this book. Public health is concerned with multiple social levels because health behaviors are influenced by factors at each level.

Each societal level derives mainly from one or a few disciplines, each with particular concerns, a body of knowledge, intervention approaches, and theoretical concepts of human behavior. Indeed, the term *level* may not provide adequate description, because each level actually represents complex systems. Nonetheless, analyses of the role that each level plays with respect to particular behaviors and health outcomes provide practical information for program planners and

intervention development. The theoretical concepts at each level are elaborated by theories discussed in later chapters. The theoretical concepts are generally applied to particular levels. However, many of these concepts are relevant at every level as they are applied to health-related and health-protective behaviors. Most health-promotion programs target individuals whose behavior and health are of concern (let's call this the at-risk group). However, many programs also target individuals who control or influence the behavior and health of the at-risk group. These may be friends, family, teachers, healthcare providers, community representatives, politicians, and policy makers.

In the following sections, and shown in **Table 2.1**, we describe how analyses of each societal level can guide health-promotion intervention.

Table 2.1 Social Ecology: Theories at Eight Levels of Analysis

Ecological Level	Disciplines	Concerns	Approaches	Theoretical Concepts
Intrapersonal	Psychology	Human development Cognitions Self-variables (concept, efficacy, esteem, motivation) Behavior	Education and training Counseling Persuasion Reinforcement	Personality Operant conditioning Cognitive consistency Knowledge, beliefs, perceptions, attitudes, values
Interpersonal	Social psychology	Social relationships and support Norms Social roles Family environment	Casework Training Social assistance Social media Network analyses	Social learning Family development Social influences, networks
Organization	Sociology Anthropology Business	Purpose and structure Performance Cultural norms Regulations	Management, leadership, and development Innovation Consultation Access	Diffusion and adoption of innovations Leadership and management

(continues)

Table 2.1 Social Ecology: Theories at Eight Levels of Analysis *(continued)*

Ecological Level	Disciplines	Concerns	Approaches	Theoretical Concepts
Community	Political science Sociology Social work Community development Community psychology	Local policies, practices, leadership Social interactions Political engagement Empowerment Discrimination Poverty Mobilization	Political and social engagement Community development Conflict resolution Partnerships Coalitions	Complex systems Communities Resources Power/conflict Engagement
Public Policy	Political science Public administration	Legislation Policy Regulations Taxes Gender equality	Political action Policy analysis Advocacy	Policy Political action
Physical Environment	Urban planning Environmental psychology Public health Physical education	Land use Pollution Contagious disease Built environment Transportation Housing	Surveillance, risk assessment Policy development Policy advocacy	City planning Political action
Culture	Sociology Cultural anthropology	Cultural literacy Conflict resolution Social engagement Discrimination Stigma	Mass media Qualitative methods	Functionalism Conflict and power Social interaction Discrimination
Economy	Economics Political science Sociology	Economic growth Wealth distribution Education, training, employment disparities	Taxation Policy (labor/ employment, finance, health, welfare)	Macroeconomics Microeconomics

Intrapersonal (Individual) Level

Individual factors or theories, largely from psychology, help us understand how within-person characteristics affect behaviors. The intrapersonal level is concerned with personal-health behaviors and their unique cognitions, including knowledge, beliefs, attitudes, values, and skills. Influences from other levels aside, cognitions are associated with personal behavior, at least within the context of the prevailing social and physical environment. Therefore, behavior change is largely the result of changes in cognitions.

Many studies have demonstrated the strong relationship between cognitions and health behaviors. Without question, knowledge, beliefs, perceptions, attitudes, skills, and values are related to behavior. All of the individual-level theoretical concepts assume **cognitive consistency**, which posits that information is related to knowledge, beliefs, and attitudes, and these cognitions influence behavior. Therefore, new information is the primary driver of change, whether it is acquired passively or through targeted intervention. However, it has long been understood that the relationship between cognitions and behavior is complex and variable. Accordingly, knowledge, what is actually true and known to be true and correct, is associated with beliefs, which are what a person thinks to be correct but are not necessarily correct, and attitudes, which include affective considerations (how strongly beliefs are held). Some cognitions have more powerful influences on values and behavior than others. Consequently, most cognitive theories are concerned with nuanced explanations of the relationships between these variables. Cognitions are thought to vary according to particular behaviors, particular conditions, and interactions with other societal levels. This is why need assessments and research on cognitive determinants of behavior are so important for effective intervention. For example, attitudes about smoking are associated with smoking behavior (Cheney, Gowin, & Clawson, 2018), but there are many specific attitudes about smoking, with variable strength of **association** with smoking behavior. If information is to be effective at reducing smoking prevalence, it would need to address the salient attitudes of the specific population of interest.

Notably, it is possible to develop effective interventions only to the extent that we understand which cognitions are important. The **logic model** is that cognitions underlie behaviors, and changing them produces behavior change. Therefore, analysis at the individual level is concerned with identifying important cognitions of the target population. Then intervention approaches and strategies can be developed to facilitate changes in target cognitions.

Interpersonal (Social) Level

The interpersonal level of the social ecological model, based mainly on social psychology and sociology, focuses primarily on social roles and interpersonal influences on behavior, including **social norms** and support. Of concern are the health-related behaviors of those who affect personal-health behavior. Family, friends, peers, acquaintances, neighbors, and coworkers exert social influence directly through persuasion or shared social norms. According to social influence theories and research, being accepted by others or part of a group or social network has many advantages, providing friendship, sense of belonging, social identity, and opportunity. Therefore, these relationships exert powerful influences on cognitions and behavior. Some social influence is direct and purposeful, such as parents and teachers trying to influence the values and behaviors of children and adolescents. Social influences can also be unintentional, occurring indirectly from **expectations** or **perceptions** of expectations about how one should behave. Whether direct or indirect, social influences encourage conformity of belief and behavior. People most proximal to us will have the most influence on behavior.

Social Cognitive Theory (Bandura, 1986) is the most prominent and complete social **learning theory**, but the Theory of Reasoned Action and other cognitive theories are concerned with social, along with other social-cognitive variables. Accordingly, individual cognitions and behavior are not independent of the cognitions and behaviors of others. For example, adolescent vaping is often influenced by the attitudes and behavior of peers toward smoking. An adolescent is more likely to vape if their friends vape because peers affect normative expectations and demonstrate how to use the device. Notably, students attending schools with high rates of e-cigarette use are more likely than others to smoke (Lippert, Corsi, & Venechuk, 2019). Research with college students indicates that the high rates of vaping can be explained, at least in part, by interpersonal factors (Cheney et al., 2018).

Social influence theory and research helps us understand the mechanisms through which interpersonal relationships affect behavior. Thus, family members, friends, peer groups, and neighbors may be important **targets of intervention**. Approaches to change at this level focus on the social influences of key others. Interventions can be directed toward increasing functional and emotional support among family members and to alter peer norms (Das, Salam, Arshad, Finkelstein, & Bhutta, 2016). Social network analysis is a useful approach for determining social contacts and sources of influence. Social network theory is concerned with our social interactions, how many people we interact with, and with whom they interact. Our social networks determine what information we obtain and how we interpret and value that information.

Organizational/ Institutional Level

For better or worse, most of us spend a good deal of time within specific organizations, including school, work, clubs, and other social groups. Organizations or institutions also set standards for their members, such as banning smoking at the worksite, not hiring smokers, or providing **incentives**, such as life or health insurance discounts for those who quit smoking or lose weight. Some community organizations participate in broader communitywide efforts to provide health-promotion services and to improve the health of the broader community. Organizations may provide direct services to their members, such as smoking cessation and weight-loss programs, or they may provide insurance or other coverage for health-promotion services. The stated and actual culture of organizations exerts powerful influences on the beliefs and behaviors of their members.

Partly as a result of the amount of time we spend in these settings, organizations can be important foci for health-promotion and disease-prevention activities. Organizations also provide access to important populations in health promotion, including employees at the worksite, children and adolescents in schools, and religious organizations, which are frequently engaged in health-promotion efforts. At the organizational level, health promotion seeks to affect the health-protective and health-related behaviors of key individuals who manage organizations. For example, many worksites offer health and life insurance discounts to nonsmokers, potentially strengthening employee interest in smoking cessation; other employers and worksites provide physical activity, screening and follow-up programs, and other health-promotion services on-site, which may serve to reduce barriers to program participation. Many large companies and organizations promote health by offering on-site healthcare services, fitness centers, and bike share programs. Some employers offer health-promotion programs to their employees at reduced or no cost because such programs may reduce lost time at work due to illness and reduced healthcare costs. Policies, such as no smoking on campus, at the worksite, and in restaurants, have been useful in thwarting smoking in communal areas, which has decreased smoking rates and improved quality of life for nonsmokers. In K–12 schools, institutions often implement after-school programs to increase physical activities and social relations. Many schools offer free preventative testing such as eye and hearing tests and per-participation physical examinations. At the university level, schools reduce sexually-transmitted infections (STIs) by offering free condoms, provide counseling services to improve mental health, and offer free or low-cost immunization services.

Because of important differences in populations, regulations, policies, organizational missions, goals, and other factors, specific models for health-promotion practice have been developed. For example, the area of school health has developed a variety of models for school health promotion that includes not only educational curriculum directed at students but also changes in food service, student physical activity, health-promotion programs for faculty and staff, community and family involvement, a healthful and secure physical and social environment, counseling services, and school health services, and these models have been applied successfully in practice (Clift & Jensen, 2005).

Worksite health-promotion programs generally focus on employees, but sometimes include family members. These programs emphasize their potential to improve morale, reduce absenteeism, improve recruitment and retention, enhance productivity, and reduce healthcare costs by changing behavior and reducing risk. Comprehensive worksite programs frequently include components that focus on smoking cessation; weight loss; hypertension, cholesterol, diabetes, and other screening programs; physical activity; stress management and reduction; changes in food service; and components that focus on the social environment at work and may include programs to control healthcare costs more directly. One study reported significant effects for up to 2 years of a comprehensive worksite health-promotion program on smoking prevalence, physical activity, diet, sleep, and seat belt use (LeCheminant & Merrill, 2012). Many civic organizations serve health functions or support health through their programs. These are discussed in the next section on community.

A key health-promotion goal at the organizational level is to foster the adoption of healthful programs, policies, and practices. Organizations are instrumental in adopting and diffusing **innovations**, many of which have health implications, for example, policies and programs regarding smoking, discrimination, and diet. As with all health promotion, the key at the organizational level is to address the cognitions of those individuals whose behavior determines how operations affect personal-health behavior directly and indirectly through effects on the environment.

Community Level

Many public health programs are applied at the community level. Communities are studied within the disciplines of political science, sociology, community psychology, and social work, as well as public health. Generally, we think of a community as people who share common geography, culture, conditions, and/or interests. Cyber communities are now ubiquitous and there are many communities of individuals with collective professional, political, intellectual, social, or recreational interests that may have amorphous boundaries. Here we focus on local communities with specific geographic boundaries. Such communities are composed of the residents and the community groups to which they belong.

Primary community concerns are local policies, practices, and leadership, as well as citizen involvement, engagement, and empowerment. These factors determine the personality of the community. Community organizations exert important influences on government policies, provide direct health-related services, and foster civic involvement. Public health practice commonly works with community organizations on specific programs, for example, adolescent substance abuse prevention, flu vaccinations, vision health, and local nonvehicle transportation safety. Many of these organizations have strong commitments to their communities and ties with government organizations and structures, making them excellent public health partners.

Actions to affect these community outcomes include political and social engagement, community development, advocacy, and conflict resolution. Theoretical concepts at this level include community development, resource allocation, power and conflict, and citizen participation. Community health promotion seeks to employ evidence-based programs to support healthful behaviors and environments with substantial community participation (The Community Guide, n.d.).

Behavior change at the community level is important because the community is responsible for resources available. This includes access to public parks to improve physical activity, implementing neighborhood farmers' markets to provide healthy food to those in low access areas, and providing affordable transportation for individuals to reach access to care. Communities are also responsible for monitoring risk factors that affect health such as violence, population density, social isolation, and local gun or drug trading.

Policy Level

Public policy can support or undermine health and healthful behavior. Public policy is of academic concern mainly to the disciplines of political science and public administration. We use the term *public policy* to include local, state, and federal policies, statutes, procedures, and laws, and their regulation, interpretation, and enforcement of these policies. Policies of concern to public health can include those that focus on the physical environment, health care, crime (e.g., when and what drug use is a crime?), housing, transportation, safety, and so on. Examples of policies that are health protective include mandatory seat belts and child restraints, speed limit laws, restrictions on tobacco and alcohol sales, subsidized vaccinations, and medical marijuana. However, most policies are health related in that they affect health and behavior, despite that not being the main intent.

Examples of Policies That Affect Health

Housing policies are strongly associated with health (Desmond, 2017). Unfortunately, policies in many communities are unfavorable to low-income residents. Some communities allow only single-family homes in certain areas, thereby reducing available

housing and increasing costs. Renters generally experience severe consequences for temporary lapses in payment, regardless of cause. Ultimately, low-income renters face many obstacles obtaining suitable housing, particularly housing with convenient transit. The lack of stable housing undermines health and frustrates public health program effectiveness.

Likewise, transportation policies in many communities discourage healthful behavior and impose severe injury risks. Public transportation and related land use policies often encourage growth in outer suburbs rather than dense housing in metropolitan area, which is burdensome for the many workers who must travel great distances, with greater than necessary risk for injury. Land use policies tend to favor motor vehicles at the cost of pedestrians and bicyclists, which can negatively affect safety and physical fitness. Housing and transportation policies are not designed to affect health, but they often do.

Policy Analysis

Policy analysis focuses on the process of policy development from policy formulation (defining the problem, setting policy objectives, and drafting action plans) and its potential health impact. Sometimes, policy implementation, including how the policy is employed, and regulations regarding the policy are essential, for example, in determining eligibility for government-supported health care. While advocacy can include working directly with decision makers, at its core it is a process of providing relevant information to potentially affected constituents and decision makers.

Policy Intervention

Approaches to influencing policy, derived mainly from policy development and political action theories, include political action, policy analysis, and advocacy. Policy objectives are important in public health, but policy is not an intervention in the sense of something than can be imposed. Instead, policy objectives can be supported through advocacy by public health and community group efforts to influence policy makers to adopt healthful policies. For example, a variety of groups and organizations in many communities are interested in encouraging transportation that is not totally dependent on automobiles and seek to improve policies and practices related to safe pedestrians and bicyclists, high-density housing development near metro and transportation hubs, and services for HIV, substance abuse, and mental health. The hard work at this level is to identify or develop model policies, enlist sponsors within the power structure, convince and obtain the support of key individuals and organizations, organize within and across interest groups, attend and comment at public hearings, and otherwise participate in the political processes that result in policies. Advocacy focuses on public support for the policy.

We generally think that public policies emerge from a broad recognition that something, tobacco use, for example, is a problem. Once the problem is identified and appropriately framed as a priority, legislation, laws, or policies are developed and considered by legislative and policy bodies, such as state and federal congress and regulatory agencies. In the case of tobacco, tax increases on cigarettes by municipalities, states, and the federal government reduce smoking prevalence, even if a central purpose of the tax is to raise revenue and not necessarily to discourage smoking. Similar tax increase examples, benefiting health behavior, include sugar-sweetened beverages, alcohol, and fossil fuels. Once particular laws are passed, they are assigned to a specific government agency to implement or carry out the policy. Sometimes this is based on evidence related to health. For example, the Institute of Medicine found that raising the smoking age to 21 could prevent approximately 223,000 premature deaths, 50,000 fewer deaths from lung cancer, and 4.2 million years of life lost for those born between 2000

and 2019 (Public Health Law Center, 2016). Eventually, the minimum age to buy tobacco products like cigarettes, electronic cigarettes, and vaping products that contain nicotine could be raised from 18 to 21 years. These policies have contributed to the reduction in tobacco use in the U.S. from 20.9% in 2005 to 13.7% in 2018 (Centers for Disease Control and Prevention [CDC], 2020).

The great success of efforts to alter policies regarding smoking have prompted the development of similar policy approaches to address obesity, physical activity, injuries, motor vehicle safety, and other major public health problems. For example, recent attention has focused on characteristics of the physical and built environment that may affect levels of physical activity and how characteristics such as the availability of neighborhood sidewalks and safe places to walk can be modified in ways that would increase physical activity. However, policy is rarely this orderly, involving messy competition from interest groups with different objectives, often resulting in compromised or even fully unhealthful policies. Follow the forces at work on any particular policy or budget consideration regarding land use, for example, zoning, road construction, housing density, public transportation, health and social programs, and you will find developers, business leaders, and citizen groups competing for political influence.

Physical Environment Level

There is a growing recognition of the powerful effect of the physical environment on health, including in the following ways: (1) disease transmission through water and air; (2) stress from noise, population density, or physical threats; (3) unsafe or contaminated areas; and (4) infection transmission. The physical environment is a primary concern for the disciplines of environmental psychology, public health, urban planning, human ecology, and physical education. Traditional concerns about air and water pollution remain central in public health, but land use has become of particular concern, due perhaps to increasing population density. Land use involves the fair allocation and safe use of air, water, transportation, housing, and public space. It has become abundantly clear that the "built" or man-made environment may affect risk factors for injury, including transportation and playgrounds, chronic diseases due to physical inactivity and obesity, and quality of life. Characteristics of the physical environment that have been linked to these risk factors include land use (land use density, diversity, open spaces); accessibility (distances between destinations); design (neighborhood aesthetics and enjoyable scenery); and transportation infrastructure (sidewalks, street design). The presence of sidewalks, neighborhood layout and design, and access to local shopping and parks are associated with physical activity and quality of life (Sallis, Floyd, Rodreguez, & Saelens, 2012).

Housing and transportation are important concerns at the physical environment level. Where one lives matters to health. Low-income housing tends to reside in areas that are more polluted and violent, with fewer parks, options for fresh food, access to health care, and employment opportunities (Desmond, 2017). The lack of transportation options, particularly inexpensive public options, reduces employment opportunities and increases transportation-related injury risks.

The effects of the physical environment on health and behavior can vary over time. The COVID-19 pandemic required a new imagining of how people could safely engage with each other and with grocery stores, worksites, schools, and playgrounds. Communities developed new protocols to distance people, created contactless delivery systems, installed Plexiglas between people, and closed playgrounds.

Cultural Level

Culture, a primary interest in sociology and cultural anthropology, is a complex concept with many direct and indirect effects on health and behavior (Triandis, 2004). Basically, culture reflects shared conventional norms in the form of beliefs, values, and norms and group practices defined by habit, customs, language, geography, race/ethnicity, and religion (Hruschka & Hadley, 2008, p. 947). Culture affects how people think and talk about health problems, habits, and practices. Culture can be either positive or negative. For example, culture contributes to norms for appropriate civil behavior. However, cultural biases can also contribute to bias and inequality. Cultural norms, for better or worse, are often institutionalized by policies and practices, resulting in inequalities in access to and delivery of health care (Napier et al., 2014). Cultural bias also influences individual and institutional practices regarding immigration and immigrants, race relations, sexual orientation, housing, science and evidence, employment, social services, and health care, resulting in health-damaging disparities (Napier et al., 2014). The civil rights movement, including, recently, Black Lives Matter, has been a reaction to the long-standing **discrimination** resulting in poor health and safety outcomes of Blacks and Hispanics in the United States (Colen, Ramey, Cooksey, & Williams, 2018). Police brutality is the product of a culture of repression, bias, and power dynamics. Aspects of racial discrimination are institutionalized in health care, housing, and policing, to mention only a few obvious examples. Accordingly, cultural competency, defined as an appreciation of cultures other than one's own, is an essential competency of public health (Napier et al., 2014). Given long-standing cultural biases in the United States, it is imperative that public health and health promotion develop and adopt models of practice that strengthen our ability to work within multicultural contexts. This is more difficult than it might seem, in part because of the tendency to assume one's cultural perspective to be universal when often they are particular to one's group (e.g., religion, profession, race, socioeconomic status, sexual orientation), and not necessarily shared by everyone.

Cultural bias has been ascribed to tribalism, the strong attachment to racial, ethnic, cultural, religious, and political groups (Chua, 2018). In a popular book describing the entire human history Harari (2011) argues that *Homo sapiens* have come to dominate the world through our unique collective propensity to embrace abstract concepts such as nationality, religion, geography, and race. These collective abstractions are often shared and valued within groups (e.g., families, races, tribes, nationalities) to the extreme exclusion and repulsion of other groups. Chua (2018) documents how tribal affiliations not only bind, but also exclude. Thus, there is a long human history of racial and cultural extremism and war. Culture is so powerful and insidious that entire lives are devoted and sometimes lost to defend particular cultural perspectives. Discrimination against African Americans is rooted in slavery, the Civil War, reconstruction, and the long, sad history of systematic bias. Currently in the United States there is a culture war against immigrants, who, like ethnic citizens, are easy targets because they have little power. In the inherent culture battles fought in every country and community, the health of the residents is at stake. Of course, great cultural advances have occurred in modern society, for example, in the areas of sexual identity, racial justice, abortion rights, special needs individuals, and smoke-free environments. However, these have generally not advanced to fair and satisfactory levels.

It is difficult to think about culture change as a specific public health goal, but establishing a high level of cultural competence among public health professionals is essential if programs are to function optimally. A lack of cultural competence contributes to inequalities in health care and prevention programs. Therefore, it is a public health goal to foster cultural competence among public health professionals and to counter cultural biases within health care and public health practice that impede the public's health.

Important theoretical concepts about culture include functionalism, conflict and power, and social interaction. Functionalism emphasizes the advantages of belonging to a cultural group or holding a particular cultural identity. Conflict and power are concerned with how cultural groups attempt to overcome or dodge social disadvantages and avoid or create conflict. Social interaction theories seek to understand how people's social interactions are related to cultural identity. Qualitative methods are commonly employed to study culture, while social media is now a common way for culture to promote or discourage certain cultural identities.

Economic Level

Macroeconomics (how countries and governments deal with economic growth, price stability/inflation, employment, and distribution of income and wealth) is profoundly associated with all other levels and directly to health and behavior. Microeconomics, which involves the financial actions of individuals and businesses, is also important to health, but mainly as it is influenced by macroeconomics. Notably, over the past 6 to 8 decades at least, world economic growth has been responsible for profound improvements in sanitation, nutrition, and habitat (Roser, 2013). It is generally fair to say that on the whole, the human population alive today has it better economically than any previous population. However, it is also the case that economic disparities are also great and increasing in many countries, including the United States (Congressional Budget Office, 2019), with substantial implications for health and behavior (World Health Organization, 2013).

Disparities in education, income, and housing are negatively associated with longevity, health status, and healthful behavior in the United States (Grossman, 2017). Grossman (2017) details the extent to which lower-income populations are at greater risk to negative health outcomes relative to higher-income populations and are more susceptible to environmental threats such as lead poisoning from outdated household paint, infectious diseases such as COVID-19, obesity, and chronic diseases. Sadly, disparities in income growth have persisted for decades, with the slowest growth and greatest disparities for Black workers relative to White and Hispanic workers (Gould, 2019). Wage disparities also persist among women compared to men. The greatest disparities in wage growth are between the lowest and highest income brackets. Perhaps the single most important way to improve health in the country would be to improve the economic status of the poorest populations. This can only be done by creating an economy that provides everyone with the essentials for healthful living, including a sound education, employment opportunity, and adequate housing (Grossman, 2017; Committee on Health, Education, Labor, and Pensions, 2013).

The principal economic approaches at federal, state, and local levels include policies related to the economy, taxation, labor rights, corporate responsibility, welfare, health care, and public health. While public health generally does not intervene at this level, understanding the underpinning economics of health, health care, and health behavior is essential. Moreover, the amount of funding for public health is determined by macroeconomic policy.

Interactions Between Societal Levels

It should be evident that societal levels are interactive rather than independent. These interactions develop and magnify over the life course, the longer and greater the exposure to each level the greater their effect on behavior and health. While each level deserves particular analyses, interactions among levels make it difficult to determine which level is most important with respect to any particular health concern. As shown in Figure 2.2, economics are particularly powerful influences on each of the other societal levels, the economy itself

being a reflection of the aggregated values of the other societal levels. Notably, economic disparities are at the core of many health problems because low income is directly associated with poor education, housing, employment, and environment, and indirectly with public policy, culture, and interpersonal relations. Notably, many public policies exacerbate health problems of lower-income persons (Grossman, 2017). Thus, many health-damaging personal-health behaviors are the result of broader societal influences.

Substance abuse is a case in point. Viewed from the cultural perspective that has dominated the problem, addiction is a personal failing, and the solution is for interdiction to reduce availability of drugs, legal sanctions on individuals for illegal use, and medical treatment for individual addiction. Viewed from an alternative cultural perspective, addiction is a systemic problem, often exacerbated by income disparities, and the solution is to treat it from a harm-reduction perspective. Harm reduction includes reducing predatory drug dealing by decriminalizing drugs, working with the individuals and communities to minimize the harmful effects of drug use, making available drug alternatives and safe places to use, providing job training, and subsidizing mental health services for those who need it (Marlatt & Witkiewitz, 2010). This is not to say there is no need for legal approaches to addiction prevention. It is to say that treating addiction as a strictly personal weakness rather than a social problem exacerbates the problem and prevents the development and funding of meaningful social solutions. Substance abuse is a concern at multiple societal levels. For example, families, organizations, communities, and public policy are in constant interaction about the best ways to think about it and provide prevention and treatment services. Culturally competent public health professionals recognize the interactive effects of multiple levels on health and behavior and seek to foster the most healthful approaches.

Intervening at Multiple Societal Levels

Multilevel intervention programming seeks to account for independent and interactive influences on health and behavior at each societal level. If health and behavior are dependent on environmental factors, then it is important to identify those factors and intervene to alter them. In many cases, interventions targeting multiple levels, rather than just individual cognitions, may be more effective in achieving sustainable behavior change. But what does it mean to intervene at multiple levels?

Program Objectives

Programs typically focus only on objectives directly related to the at-risk population, consisting of those whose health and behavior are of programmatic concern (the at-risk population). Typically, this involves informational interventions designed to alter cognitions to be consistent with healthful behavior. At the same time, to the extent we recognize that environmental factors are important to the health and behavior of the at-risk population, we should also address these factors. We do this by identifying the key people at those levels who can alter or influence those objectives through health-protective or health-related behaviors. These individuals are the targets of the intervention at these levels. The target outcomes are the behaviors, practices, policies, and environmental, cultural, and economic conditions related to the health and health behavior of the at-risk population. To achieve change in these outcomes, it is necessary to intervene with the key influencers at each societal level. The objectives would be to change the cognitions of these influential people to be consistent with the targeted outcomes. Changing cognitions requires that information be delivered in a manner that challenges existing cognitions. Information can be delivered in a wide range of forms, including persuasion, advocacy, and political action. Information can focus on the link between the target outcome (e.g., policy) and the desired health and health behavior of the at-risk population. As shown in **Table 2.2**, at the intrapersonal (individual) level, we seek to alter

Table 2.2 Multilevel Intervention: Targets and Outcomes of Intervention at Multiple Levels

Health-Promotion Intervention	Societal Level	Target of Intervention	Target Outcomes
Information to alter cognitions: • Knowledge • Skills • Beliefs • Attitudes • Values • Behavior Delivered via: • Education • Training • Persuasion • Advocacy • Policy analyses • Political action	Intrapersonal	At-risk population	Personal-health behavior
	Interpersonal	Social network	Health-protective; health-related
	Organizational	Leaders	Health-protective; health-related (policies and practices)

cognitions related to motivation for improving particular personal-health behaviors, while at other levels, we seek to alter cognitions of those in a position to create healthful environments to do so, or at least to not engage in behaviors that are damaging to others' health.

Environments Matter

Individual cognitions are critical motivators of behavior, but **agency**, the ability to act volitionally, depends greatly on environmental factors. The purpose of intervening at societal levels beyond the intrapersonal and interpersonal levels is to alter key environmental factors such that they support healthful behavior. Desirable outcomes of intervention would be changes in the environment, including policies and practices, consistent with healthful personal-health behavior. If our primary interest is increasing physical activity, we would seek to create healthful physical environments, such as increasing open space and safe transportation routes for pedestrian and bicycle mobility, and opportunities for physical activity, such as physical education and active recreational programs. Creating environments that support physical activity requires interventions that focus upstream from the individual to community and regional decision makers. Thus, we would identify objectives and possible intervention targets at organizational, policy, community, and neighborhood levels (overlapping levels, of course). Intervention at these levels would be directed at the cognitions and behaviors of those who can influence these environmental changes (who become the targets of interventions at these levels). Once we know the desired outcomes, we need to intervene with those who control those outcomes. We do that by providing information.

Public policy is a prominent public health concern given its potential for widespread impact on the population. As noted, public health can be substantially impacted, for better or worse, through public policies related to housing, transportation, criminal codes, environment, and health care, to mention only the most obvious. Therefore, policy advocacy is a cornerstone of intervention to improve policy so that it contributes maximally and positively to public health. Policy advocacy provides methods for fostering adoption of particular policies by decision makers (Collins, 2005). Advocacy generally involves the following: (1) research and verification of proposed policies and development of new policies; (2) working with decision makers; (3) mobilizing the relevant community; and (4) communicating the advantages and support for particular policies (O'Connell, 2020). While advocacy is a political process, at its core it is a communication process. Those potentially affected by policy have a right to be informed and involved in its determination. Frequently, policies are developed by special interests with no particular concern for public health, and it is a responsibility of public health professionals to advocate for appropriate, fair, and healthful policy.

Targets of Intervention

Recall that many of the theories described in this book are about information processing, the process by which people receive and interpret information and form cognitions that contribute to their behavior. Our psychological and interpersonal theories help us to conduct analyses at various levels, identify the individuals and groups who exert control at each level, and identify objectives for appropriate health-protective and health-related behaviors. Of course, information about public health must compete with the vast deluge of information on a wide range of topics people, including decision makers, get from friends, colleagues, commercial enterprises, political groups, the media, and other sources.

If we are interested in improving healthful dietary behavior in a particular population, there are numerous possible targets of intervention. Let's use childhood obesity, for example. Objectives for the at-risk population might be to alter their dietary behaviors through education providing information directed at the cognitions and skills related to healthful dietary behavior. However, we might also target the cognitions of household members who purchase and prepare the family meals. We might also want to influence the local grocery store to carry and display healthier foods. If we are interested in putting in place local policies requiring restaurant menus to display food content and calories, we may need to influence local decision makers, such as the mayor or city council members. If we want to change the content and types of foods served at school cafeterias, we may need to target not only principals and superintendents but also food service personnel.

Intervention Approaches

As illustrated in Table 2.2, intervention can include many forms, but each is designed to provide information to those with some control over the target outcomes. While the effects of societal levels on health and behavior are generally well understood, fostering change at these levels is complicated. It is important to clearly distinguish the target outcomes, including policies, practices, environmental and economic conditions, and cultural preferences, from the cognitive changes of those with influence over these outcomes. It can be argued that we should intervene as much as possible at all levels of the ecological model or justify why certain levels were omitted. However, given limited resources of money, time, and staff, the foci of our programs on the possible social levels must be selective, identifying the most critical and likely to change environmental factors, target populations, and the cognitions required for behavior change.

There is a key difference in how theory can be applied with respect to the personal-health behavior of an at-risk population, and how it can be applied to decision makers regarding health-related policies and practices. In typical public health programs, need assessments based on theory are conducted to guide program development. Intervention at the policy level, for example, would have in common some features of standard program development, including problem analyses and the development of target outcomes. However, it is not generally possible to conduct formal need assessments with policy makers. Instead, policy advocacy must rely on general theoretic tenets. For example, let's suppose you, as a public health professional, were interested in hiker/biker routes in your local community because the availability of this form of mobility increases physical activity and reduces driving, among the many public health benefits. Such routes are established (or not) by land use and transportation policies. If you wanted to foster or alter the adoption of a policy under consideration, you would engage in policy advocacy. Possibly, after doing the preliminary work of analyzing policy and talking with decision makers and constituents, and remembering the chapter you studied in grad school about diffusion of innovations (see Chapter 10), you would develop a communication campaign that emphasized the relative advantages, examples of its success and popularity elsewhere, data regarding public sentiment, the potential for local variation, and so on. Thus, theory would guide the development of the information campaign to foster healthful policy.

Multilevel Intervention Considerations

While multilevel intervention is desirable, it can be complicated due to a range of considerations, including the following.

Multiple Causes

The level and approach to intervention should depend on an understanding of the environmental conditions and social factors that contribute to the problem of interest. Using tobacco as our example again, we should ask how individual characteristics, family, social networks, organizations, public policy, the physical environment, and culture may contribute to the problem of tobacco use.

Interrelated Levels

Knowing how each level affects the other can inform decisions about the levels on which to intervene and what the objectives of those interventions might be. Accordingly, in addition to intervening to affect individual smoking behavior, we might intervene with the smoker's family or friends to alter social support for quitting, or with the community to alter environmental or policy conditions with respect to smoke-free environments. These environmental factors become the objectives for intervention at that level, and those who control those environmental factors become the targets of intervention at that level. Educational interventions would then be directed at the cognitions of these target populations to facilitate environmental changes.

Adjacent Societal Levels

It can be useful to think about each level of the ecological model as the context for adjacent levels. For example, in addition to addressing individual cognitions, we might also address the cognitions and behaviors of peers, family, neighbors, and other social contacts. Communities and organizations, such as schools, churches, and workplaces, may also have powerful influences on our behavior and serve as important access points for populations and subgroups. Similarly, if our concern is with policy, for example, tobacco policy, it may also be useful to focus on the cognitions of policy developers consistent with prevention.

Environment and Behavior

Even if intervention is at the individual level, it is useful to know what and how environmental factors are associated with the behavior of interest and who controls those factors. An ecological perspective on health promotion requires that for every issue we consider both behavioral and environment factors. Even when it is not

possible to intervene at multiple levels, cultural competence requires that we understand the multilevel influences on health and behavior.

Altering Cognitions of the Targets of Intervention

While it may be necessary to intervene at multiple societal levels to change the policies and practices contributing to the personal-health behavior of the at-risk population, all change strategies are essentially informational. Information can be provided in many different ways, not necessarily only in the form of documents, lectures, and curricula. We may provide information to individuals at the intrapersonal and interpersonal levels through education, **training**, and **persuasive communication**, or to policy makers through advocacy or policy analyses, but in all cases we provide information designed to change the cognitions of the target population. Therefore, cognitive theories, such as those detailed in later chapters, are relevant at each level. The determinants of behavior are the same for smokers as for the purveyors of smoking, for those at risk for HIV, and for those responsible for HIV policy. They are based on individual cognitions of the target population. It might require unique methods for reaching different targets, but the objective is always to alter cognitions leading to change in behavior. These are topics for discussion in the following chapters. For now, it is mainly important to recognize that behavior theory is relevant theory for use in developing programmatic activities at each societal level.

Lessons for Public Health Practice

1. The social ecological perspective is that health and behavior are influenced by multiple social levels.
2. Social ecology concepts are employed to develop and conduct analyses at multiple levels.

3. There are eight levels for potential analyses: (1) intrapersonal; (2) interpersonal; (3) organizational; (4) community; (5) policy; (6) culture; (7) environment; and (8) economy.
4. Cognitions affect goal-oriented behavior, for which people have agency or control to the extent the environment allows and supports such behavior.
5. It is common to think of most health and behavior issues involving individual and environmental levels, where the environment involves all of the levels other than the individual level. Sometimes intrapersonal/individual and interpersonal factors are combined and considered as the psychosocial level.
6. Societal levels are interrelated, each level exerting influence on the other levels.
7. Even theories concerned with distal social levels such as public policy and economics, rely on information as the means of changing cognitions related to behavior. If we wish to change behavior, we must determine and address the cognitions related to the intervention objectives for each societal level.
8. Intervention at multiple levels may be more effective than intervention at a single level.
9. Behavior theory can provide guidance at each level.

Discussion Questions

1. What are the 8 levels of potential analyses?
2. Why is analysis at the interpersonal level important?
3. How might socioeconomic disparities affect substance use behavior?
4. How might the unsafe alcohol behavior of a particular population be influenced by interpersonal, cultural, community, and policy factors?
5. Why is it useful to conduct analyses at multiple levels, even if the intervention is only at the individual, personal-health behavior level?

References

Bandura, A. (1986). *Social foundations of thought and action: A social cognitive theory.* Upper Saddle River, NJ: Prentice Hall.

Bronfenbrenner, U. (1979). *The ecology of human development: Experiments by nature and design.* Cambridge, MA: Harvard University Press. Retrieved from https://ebookcentralproquest.com/lib/detail.action?docID=3300702

Centers for Disease Control and Prevention (CDC). (2020). *Current cigarette smoking among adults in the United States.* Retrieved from https://www.cdc.gov/tobacco/data_statistics/fact_sheets/adult_data/cig_smoking/index.htm

Cheney, M. K., Gowin, M., & Clawson, A. H. (2018). Using the ecological model to understand influences on college student vaping. *Journal of American College Health, 66*(7), 597–607. DOI: 10.1080/07448481.2018.1440578

Chua, A. (2018). *Political tribes: Group instinct and the fate of nations.* New York: Penguin Press.

Clift, S., & Jensen, B. B. (Eds.). (2005). *The health promoting school: International advances in theory, evaluation and practice.* Copenhagen: Danish University of Education Press.

Colen, G. C., Ramey, D. M., Cooksey, E. C., & Williams, D. R. (2018). Racial disparities in health among nonpoor African Americans and Hispanics: The role of acute and chronic discrimination. *Social Science and Medicine, 199,* 167–180.

Collins, T. (2005). Health policy analysis: A simple tool for policy makers. *Public Health, 119,* 192–196. DOI: 10.1016/j.puhe.2004.03.006

Committee on Health, Education, Labor, and Pensions. (2013). Dying young: Why your social and economic status may be a death sentence in America. United States Senate, 113th Congress, Senate Health 113-820. Washington DC: U.S. Government Publishing Office,

22–267. Retrieved from https://www.govinfo.gov/app/details/CHRG-113shrg22267

Congressional Budget Office. (2019). *The distribution of household income, 2016.* Retrieved from https://www.cbo.gov/publication/53597

Das, J. K., Salam, R. A., Arshad, A., Finkelstein, Y., & Bhutta, Z. A. (2016). Interventions for adolescent substance abuse: An overview of systematic reviews. *Journal of Adolescent Health, 59*(4 Suppl), S61–S75. DOI: 10.1016/j.jadohealth.2016.06.021

Desmond, M. (2017). *Evicted: Poverty and profit in the American city.* New York: Crown Publishing Group.

Glanz, K., Rimer, B. K., & Viswanath, K. (Eds.). (2015). *Health: Theory, research, and practice* (5th ed.). San Francisco, CA: Jossey-Bass.

Gould, E. (2019). *State of working American wages over the last 40 years.* (2019). Retrieved from https://www.epi.org/publication/swa-wages-2019/?referringSource=articleShare

Green, L., & Kreuter, M. (2005). *Health program planning: An educational and ecological approach* (4th ed.). New York: McGraw-Hill.

Grossman, M. (2017). *Determinants of health: An economic perspective.* New York: Columbia University Press.

Harari, Y. N. (2011). *Sapiens: A brief history of humankind.* New York: Harper.

Harper, C. R., Steiner, R. J., & Brookmeyer, K. A. (2018). Using social-ecological model to improve access to care for adolescents and young adults. *Journal of Adolescent Health, 62,* 641–642. DOI: 10.1016/j.jadohealth.2018.03.010

Hruschka, D. J., & Hadley, C. (2008). A glossary of culture in epidemiology. *Journal of Epidemiology & Community Health, 62,* 947–951. DOI:10.1136/jech.2008.076729

LeCheminant, J. D., & Merrill, R. M. (2012). Improved health behaviors persist over two years for employees in a worksite wellness program. *Population Health Management, 15*(5), 261–266, DOI:10.1089/pop.2011.0083

Lippert, A. M., Corsi, D. J., & Venechuk, G. E. (2019). Schools influence adolescent e-cigarette use, but when? Examining the independent association between school context and teen vaping over time. *Journal of Youth and Adolescence, 48* 1988–1911. DOI: 10.1007/s10964-019-01106-y

Marlatt, G. A., & Witkiewitz, K. (2010). Update on harm-reduction policy and intervention research. *Annual Review of Clinical Psychology, 6,* 591–606. DOI: 10.1146/annurev.clinpsy.121208.131438

McLeroy, K. R., Bibeau, D., Steckler, A., & Glanz, K. (1988). An ecological perspective on health promotion programs. *Health Education Quarterly, 15*(4), 351–377.

Napier, A. D., Arcano, C., Butler, R., Calabrese, J., et al. (2014). Lancet and University College of London

Commission on Culture and Health. Retrieved from https://www.thelancet.com/action/showPdf?pii=S0140-6736%2815%2960226-4

Nyambe, A., Van Hal, G., & Kampen, J. K. (2016). Screening and vaccination as determined by the social ecological mode and the theory of triadic influence: A system in review. *BMC Public Health, 16,* 1166. DOI: 10.1186/s12889-016-3802-6

O'Connell, S. (2020). Policy developments and policy advocacy. National Democratic Institute. Retrieved from https://www.ndi.org/sites/default/files/Policy%20Development%20and%20Advocacy%20Workbook_EN.pdf

Paskett, E., Thompson, B., Ammerman, A. S., Ortega, A. N., Marsteller, J., & Richardson, D. (2016). Multi-level interventions to address health disparities show promise in improving population health. *Health Affairs, 35*(8), 1429–1434. DOI:10.1377/hlthaff.2015.1360

Public Health Law Center Tobacco Control Legal Consortium. (2016, October). *Tobacco21: Tips and tools.* Retrieved from https://www.publichealthlawcenter.org/sites/default/files/resources/phlc-Tobacco-21-Tips-Tools-2016.pdf

Roser, M. (2013). *Economic growth.* Retrieved from https://ourworldindata.org/economic-growth#citation

Sallis, J. F., Floyd, M. F., Rodreguez, D. A., & Saelens, B. E. (2012). Role of built environments in physical activity, obesity, and cardiovascular disease. *Circulation, 125*(5), 729–737. DOI:10.1161/CIRCULATIONAHA.110.969022

Simons-Morton, B. G., Green, W. H., & Gottleib, N. H. (1995). *Introduction to health education and health promotion.* Long Grove, IL: Waveland Press.

Simons-Morton, B. G., McLeroy, K., & Wendel, M. L. (2011). *Behavior theory in health promotion practice and research.* Burlington, MA: Jones & Bartlett Publishers.

The Community Guide. (n.d.). *About the community preventive services task force.* Retrieved from https://www.thecommunityguide.org/task-force/about-community-preventive-services-task-force

Triandis, H.C. (2004). The many dimensions of culture. *The Academy of Management Perspectives, 18,*1, 88–93.

Venkataramani, A. S., Chatterjee, P., Kawachi, I., & Tsae, A. C. (2016). Economic opportunity, health behaviors, and mortality in the United States. *American Journal of Public Health, 106,* 478–484. DOI:10.2105/AJPH.2015.302941.

World Health Association. (2013). *Economics of the social determinants of health and health inequalities: A resource book.* Retrieved from https://apps.who.int/iris/bitstream/handle/10665/84213/9789241548625_eng.pdf;jsessionid=64CC5A10CC0ACF3F5F2563D4AEB1561D?sequence=1

CHAPTER 3

Theories of Motivation and Behavior: A Public Health Primer

There is nothing so practical as a good theory.

—Kurt Lewin

OUTLINE

1. Preview
2. Objectives
3. Introduction
    3.1. Motivation and Behavior
    3.2. Individual Variability
4. Behavior Theories
    4.1. Reinforcement Theory
        4.1.1. Operant Conditioning
        4.1.2. Self-Management and Self-Regulation
    4.2. Psychoanalytic Theory
        4.2.1. Unconscious Drives
        4.2.2. Personality Traits
        4.2.3. Gestalt Theory
        4.2.4. Developmental Theory
        4.2.5. Summary of Psychoanalytic-Based Theory
    4.3. Cognitive Psychology
        4.3.1. Cognitive Consistency Theory/Dissonance
        4.3.2. Values Expectancy Theories
    4.4. Social Psychology
    4.5. Sociology
5. Theory Commonalities
6. Lessons for Public Health Practice
7. Discussion Questions
8. References

PREVIEW

A theory is a description of hypothesized relationships. Developing a firm understanding of behavior theory is a core competency for public health professionals. This chapter provides an overview of behavior theory and describes the purpose it serves in public health research and practice. Specifically, the chapter notes the common elements of cognitive theories, explains why there are numerous theories, and describes the unique contributions of major scientific theories of motivation and behavior to applied behavioral science.

OBJECTIVES

Upon completion of this chapter the reader will be prepared to:

1. Describe the major scientific perspectives that have shaped modern theories of motivation and behavior.
2. Describe the relationship between motivation and behavior according to operant theory.

3. Describe the relationship between motivation and behavior according to cognitive theories.
4. Explain why theory predicts behavior and behavior change.
5. Identify theory commonalities.
6. Note the functions of psychosocial theory in health-promotion practice.

Introduction

A *theory* is simply a description of hypothesized relationships. For example, a prominent climate change theory hypothesizes that the persistent and massive emissions of greenhouse gases due to human fossil fuel consumption contributes massively to global warming. A tremendous amount of research supports the theoretical relationship between fossil fuel consumption and global warming (Wallace-Wells, 2019). Research seeks to test aspects of the theory, and the findings provide evidence about the theory. Over time, as the many complex relationships are clarified, the theory is refined. Hence, theory-guided research about global warming has improved our understanding of the environment and provided ideas about what needs to be done if we are to prevent more serious environmental degradation. Of course, many theories turn out not to be valid. Examples of theories that did not stand the test of science include that the world is flat, gold could be created in a laboratory, and the Internet would usher in a golden age of reason.

In science, a theory typically starts out as conjecture by a researcher or theorist about the possible relationships between certain factors and an outcome. After reading, thinking, talking, and reading some more, the conjecture becomes a hypothesis or crude *conceptualization* of relationships among constructs. The conceptualization is discussed and debated among colleagues. Sometimes, conditions that limit the conceptualization to specific outcomes or conditions are specified. Preliminary research leads to refinement and elaboration,

until finally, a model of the possible relationships is fashioned. The constructs are defined in ways that make them measurable. Research determines the validity of the specified relationships, leading to further refinements and sometimes to a formal, defensible, and testable theory.

The essential elements of a theory are called constructs. Each construct represents a complex image or idea that eventually is defined specifically to become a measurable **variable**. Constructs are the building blocks of theory. In our examples of global warming, the primary constructs include the combustion of carbon-based fuel and atmospheric concentrations of carbon, but many other constructs must also be measured and accounted, including the historical record (for comparison), weather, and many chemical and physical variables.

Once a theory is developed, it is then possible to develop specific hypotheses and conduct research to determine the extent to which the hypotheses are valid and the implications of the findings for the theory. Researchers must develop valid measures of the key *constructs*. Constructs are formally defined as variables and measures are developed. It is not unusual for a construct to be defined such that several variables emerge and are defined. If constructs are the building blocks of theory, measured variables are the building blocks of research. Once a useful measure has been developed, cross-sectional and prospective observational (nonexperimental) studies can be conducted to test the strength of the hypothesized relationships. Eventually, experimental studies isolate the effects of one or a few particularly important variables and the conditions under which they operate (or not). Of course, a lot of research is needed to fully explore the utility of a theory. Often it is useful for the theory to be considered from the perspective of various disciplines, each with its own methods and orientations (Kuhn, 1996). In any case, research findings tend to suggest modifications of the theory, often for particular purposes, and these variations need to be verified by additional research. Once a theory has been validated, the measured variables allow researchers to evaluate how behavior has changed due to exposure to a program.

In the same fashion that theory has been developed to explain the complex human–environmental interactions leading to global warming, which stimulated research demonstrating the large contribution to global warming from the buildup of greenhouse gases from fossil fuel consumption, theories have also been developed to explain human behavior and its variability. Behavioral theories describe the hypothesized relationships of environmental and personal factors such as **personality** and cognitions with specific behaviors (e.g., smoking, wearing seat belts, appointment keeping) or types of behavior (e.g., substance use, safety, adherence), and how these relationships operate under varying conditions. Because human behavior is complex and multifactored, no single theory explains it fully. However, theories provide considered hypotheses about what and how certain factors influence behavior. In the social and behavioral sciences, we are generally interested in theories about the relationships between **psychosocial** factors and behavior and the situations and environmental conditions that affect these relationships.

Some behavioral theories are mainly concerned with relationships between the environment (physical and social) and behavior, while other theories are mainly concerned with the relationships between cognitive factors and behavior. Some theories are concerned with how the cognitive interpretations and perceptions of external, socioenvironmental factors affect behavior. Numerous observational (i.e., cross-sectional or prospective measurement) and experimental studies have been conducted using and evaluating behavioral theories. Experimental studies include randomization of willing participants to treatment conditions to determine if certain stimuli or interventions alter behavior, if certain beliefs or attitudes

are associated with a particular behavior, or if changing certain cognitive factors leads to a change in behavior. Research to determine the extent to which neighborhood, class, culture, race, income, and other socioenvironmental factors are associated with behavior does not lend itself to experimentation, so it is generally observational. Confidence about the relationships between broad environmental factors and behavior can eventually be established when a preponderance of research findings from observational (nonexperimental) studies accumulates.

In short, theories describe hypothesized relationships that can be evaluated by research. Theories seek to explain and predict behavior. Prominent behavior theories, such as those discussed in later chapters of this book, have been well studied, providing great confidence in their validity, at least for certain purposes and in certain contexts. In public health our task is to determine which theory is most relevant for a particular health problem, behavior, situation, and population, and how best to apply it in developing effective programs. Therefore, theory is an essential analytic tool for understanding behavior, as well as developing, conducting, and evaluating programs. Application and choosing the appropriate theory will be discussed later in the book.

Motivation and Behavior

Why do humans behave as they do? The nature of human behavior has been of general public interest since the beginning of civilization, as evidenced by the many rules guiding human behavior described in historical religious documents, philosophical writings, and ruler dictates. Early Greek philosophers pondered what behavior is most appropriate for a "considered life." However, until the last few centuries, human behavior was considered to be largely preordained at birth, due mainly to destiny, decree, tradition, or meddling gods. Surprisingly, self-awareness and rational thought were not major themes until the past century or so (and do not seem to be exercised as routinely as one would hope). However, in modern Western culture, there has been a dramatic evolution in thinking about human behavior and what governs it. The resulting behavioral and social sciences are concerned with advancing an empirical understanding of human behavior based on research.

Philosophy and religion are important human preoccupations that provide strong influences on moral values and behavior. Philosophy and ethics are concerned mainly with the purpose of life, while religion is concerned mainly with humans' relationships with god. Indeed, ethical considerations of right and wrong, the proper way to lead one's life, how to treat our fellow world travelers, and other core values are matters of religion and philosophy. Philosophy relies on principles of logic and reasoning, while religion relies on the teachings of religious leaders, prayer, ritual, and faith. Conversely, the behavioral and social sciences emphasize empirical approaches to understanding the nature of human behavior and the influences of individual and environmental factors on behavior. In this context, philosophy and religion, as important as they are to behavior, can be thought of as important cultural influences on health and health behavior.

The theoretical concerns in this book are those most relevant to public health, and particularly to health promotion, which we view as a public health subspecialty based on behavioral and social sciences. As noted in Chapter 1, health promotion is concerned with programmatic efforts to facilitate improvements in environmental conditions and behavior related to health. Theory is one essential tool for understanding the influences on human motivation and behavior and how to alter them to promote healthful behavior. Given the central concern to health promotion of **facilitating** healthful **behaviors** and environmental conditions, it is important to understand the motivation of the individuals about whose health and behavior we are concerned and

the motivation of those who influence or control environmental conditions.

For the purposes of this chapter, we discuss theory mainly as it relates to individual and proximal (close in time and space) social behavior, while recognizing the profound influences of more distal social environmental factors such as community, policy, culture, and economics. Understanding and altering motivation for change is one of the key issues at both the individual and societal levels.

Motivation and behavior are closely related, but they are not the same thing. Behavior is observable, and its frequency, amount, and intensity can be objectively measured. *Motivation*, on the other hand, is internal and personal, so it is not generally observable and can only be measured indirectly. Think about motivation being the likelihood of behaving in a certain way. Some individuals and groups are more likely than others to smoke marijuana, exercise, take their medicine, or drive fast, particularly in certain environmental (social and physical) contexts. To understand these behaviors, it is necessary to know what motivates them, more specifically what motives precede them. Not surprisingly, theories about behavior are really theories about what motivates behavior.

Motivation can be influenced by internal or external factors, as shown in **Figure 3.1**. Internal factors include basic **personality traits**, memory of past experience, and other cognitive and emotional processes. Of course, internal motivational factors are influenced by external factors and stored in memory, including those that occurred in the distant past, those that occurred recently, and those that are present and ongoing in the here and now.

External factors can be physical or social. The difference between internal and external factors has been described as push vs. pull forces. Internal factors push the person toward certain actions, while external factors pull the person toward certain actions. Internal factors **predispose** the person in certain ways, while external factors provide stimuli that

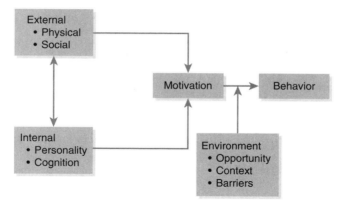

Figure 3.1 Influences on motivation and behavior

pull people toward actions that promise likely reinforcement. For example, people tend to eat when they are hungry (push) but eat more food when served a large portion than when they are served a small portion (pull) (Wansink & Kim, 2005). Similarly, while some people may be psychologically predisposed to exercise, people walk more when the near environment is safe and convenient (Sallis, Floyd, Rodriguez, & Saelens, 2012).

External influences on motivation can be social as well as physical. While some people are more conforming than others, humans tend to follow whatever rules are in place and are otherwise influenced by the behavior and attitudes of others. Hence, external and internal factors are interrelated. The external environment influences internal cognitions, and internal cognitions interpret the environment. One can seek a park in which to exercise or take a walk because a park is nearby, or some combination of each. As noted, motivation is the likelihood to behave in a certain way, but motivation is complex, and being motivated does not inevitably lead to an increase in the behavior, only an increased likelihood. As shown in Figure 3.1, opportunity and context (and cognitive evaluations of context) mediate the relationship between motivation and behavior.

Although there is little disagreement on the general elements of motivation, theories vary considerably with respect to emphases.

For behaviorists, motivation is mostly about the amount of reinforcement required to alter the frequency of a behavior. For psychoanalytic theorists, motivation is psychological, not always conscious, greatly influenced by early childhood relationships, and cognitions. For personality theorists, motivation is the tendency of a person for whom certain personality traits are particularly strong to behave in a certain way compared to someone for whom that trait or those traits are not as strong. For social-psychologists, motivation is largely about the effect of social relations on behavior. For sociologists, motivation is largely the product of group affiliation and culture. For most applied behavioral scientists, the most important aspect of motivation is cognition, the thought processes that include knowing, believing, perceiving, valuing, and feeling. This is because cognitions, like personality, are associated with behavior, but are vastly more amenable to change.

There are a range of cognitive theories of motivation and behavior, each providing important perspectives on particular aspects or types of behavior. Some theories seek to integrate these various influences on behavior. Social cognitive theory, for example, includes cognitive and environmental factors. Self-determination theory suggests that people are motivated by their sense of self and the extent to which they are able to satisfy needs for competence, relatedness, and autonomy and develop abilities to regulate their behavior. While behavioral theories are best understood with the individual in mind, they are also completely relevant when considering the behavior of policy makers and others who control health-related behavior and environmental conditions.

Individual Variability

Behavior theory is probabilistic. It seeks to understand how people behave generally, rather than how a particular person behaves at particular moments in time. Psychology is interested in the uniquely individual motivation and behavior of particular clients and employs theory as a way of understanding and treating behavior. From both a clinical and population perspective, individuals are unique in many important ways due to genetic and environmental factors. That is, a person is the product of unique genetic makeup, modified over time by environmental experiences, producing distinct cognitions. Even the contribution of personality to individual variability is somewhat malleable over a lifetime. Birth order, gender, sexual orientation, family, geography, culture, life experiences, and other factors contribute to a person's psychological makeup. Identical twins have the same genetic makeup and share many psychological and behavioral characteristics, but also vary in many ways, respond uniquely to the environment, interpret stimuli differently, and have particular proclivities and independent cognitions. Substantial individual variability from many sources exists more or less in any particular population. While there would be a lot of inherent commonality within populations of pregnant women, breast cancer patients, or marijuana users, there would also be considerable variability. Accordingly, behavior theories seek to predict variability beyond these basic individual characteristics. The utility of theory, then, is its ability to explain meaningful amounts of variability in behavior, but

given the vast individual variability and the substantial contribution of the unique social and physical environments each person experiences, no theory can be expected to account for behavior in its entirety.

Behavior Theories

Behavior theories share common themes concerning the interplay among environmental and experiential factors and unique individual and cognitive factors. All behavioral theories agree with the central tenet that humans learn from experience, and their behavior is influenced by their environment. Just how people learn from experience, both lifelong and immediate, is one of the principal considerations of behavior theory. In the following paragraphs, we provide brief reviews of major psychological and social science theories and their contributions to behavioral science and health promotion. The goal is to orient the reader to the rich array of disciplines interested in human behavior but is limited to cursory examination of the major disciplines and leaves out many other important disciplines.

Reinforcement Theory

The early reinforcement theorists, Pavlov, Watson, and Skinner, were termed "behaviorists" because they proposed that only observable measures of the prevalence, variability, or changes in behavior should be considered; psychological processes of personality and cognition should be ignored because they were not observable. These theorists emphasized the important influences on behavior of environmental factors that precede (antecedent stimuli) and follow (consequent) behavior. *Classical conditioning* theory is concerned with conditioned responses, which are automatic responses (such as salivation, hunger, and eating) to stimuli such as the sight or smell of food. Stimuli are **antecedent** (prior) events that trigger a **response**. The neurophysiology of conditioned responses to stimuli and the effect of various schedules of reinforcement remain active fields of research. However, the modern cousins of classical **conditioning** (automatic responses to stimuli), operant conditioning and **self-management**, are more informative and important to our discussion.

Operant Conditioning

Operant conditioning is concerned with how people "learn" to respond (behave) from the consequences of behavior. *Operants* are responses that are controlled by their consequences. There is no question that behavior tends to recur when rewarded. As shown in **Figure 3.2**, stimuli elicit responses (behaviors) that have the potential to be reinforced. Behaviors that are reinforced are likely to be repeated so they can again be reinforced. Positive consequences encourage recurrence of the behavior, while negative consequences, or the lack of positive consequences, discourage recurrence. Technically, the term *reinforcement* describes a consequence that increases the likelihood of a response.

It is also the case that behavior sometimes occurs when reinforcement is likely or possible but does not actually occur. The anticipation of possible reinforcement can influence behavior. Antecedent events known as stimuli indicate that reinforcement is likely, thereby prompting the behavior in anticipation of reinforcement. Among smokers, lighting up is stimulated by normal physiology as residual nicotine in the bloodstream diminishes and also by external stimuli that are associated (cognitively by the respondent) with the rewards of smoking, like a cup of coffee an advertisement, seeing someone else smoke, or taking a break from

work when smoking normally occurs. The relationships between stimuli, consequences, and responses are shown in Figure 3.2. Stimuli that are linked to reinforcing consequences prompt the response in anticipation of reinforcement. Essentially, the frequency of a behavioral response is the product of its likely consequences. Stimuli indicate the promise that reinforcement is likely, prompting the behavior. After a certain period of "learning" about consequences and stimuli, many behaviors become habits and need little actual reinforcement for their continuation.

Think about the effect of stimuli and reinforcement as they occur naturally over the course of a lifetime. People learn how to behave by storing in memory the past consequences of their behavior. For example, when the response of eating all the food served has been reinforced throughout one's life, it becomes a habit. When brushing and flossing teeth are reinforced by attentive parents, these behaviors become lifelong habits that need no further reinforcement. In short, the reinforcing consequences of life experiences create patterns of habitual behavior that do not need continual external reinforcement. Hence, past experience is profoundly influential.

From this we can appreciate that the environment, to the extent that it determines behavioral consequences, governs modern life. Driving is reinforced by virtue of the environmental design of modern municipalities, with many roads and lots of parking for suburban commuters. People who live in cities tend to walk because it is generally more convenient and a lot less expensive than driving and parking (Sallis et al., 2012). In areas with concentrations of fast-food restaurants, people frequently eat fast food, and where there are a plethora of alcohol outlets, people tend to drink frequently (Milam, Johnson, Furr-Holden, & Bradshaw, 2016). Bars increase drinking, parks increase physical activity, and roads increase driving. The ways communities are planned, organized, and managed provide environments that influence population behavior.

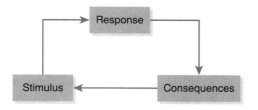

Figure 3.2 Stimulus—response model of behavior

The principles of operant conditioning apply to child raising, supervising staff, getting elected to office, and most health behaviors, including medication adherence, diet, physical activity, substance use, and safety behavior. Not surprisingly, the principles of operant conditioning are routinely employed to great effect in marketing (Grossman, 2017). In stores and on websites, marketers place their products strategically, packaged in colors and shapes likely to attract targeted customers, with advertisements designed to stimulate perceived need. Operant conditioning is also the basis for self-management training, one of the most powerful and widely employed change methods.

Self-Management and Self-Regulation

Modern programs for substance abuse, weight loss, and other behavior management programs (Kazdin, 2020) and health-promotion programs (Elder et al., 2007) employ self-management practices. Self-management skills facilitate **self-regulation** of the environment and responses to the environment. Self-regulation enables cognitive management of stimuli and responses to stimuli and consequences. An **applied behavioral analysis (ABA)** is a key self-management activity (see example in Chapter 5). An ABA assesses the frequency and timing of the behavior and associated antecedents and consequences. An ABA provides a behavioral baseline and specifies stimuli, contexts, and thoughts related to them and possible reinforcement. A key goal is to gain individual control over environmental stimuli. For example, diabetic patients learn from an ABA what antecedent events stimulate inappropriate eating, how to avoid exposure to those stimuli, and how to alter undesirable responses to them (Klein, Jackson, Street, Whitacre, & Klein, 2013). Rather than uncontrolled external stimuli and reinforcement controlling behavior, self-management provides the participants with cognitive skills that enable them to

manage their own behavior. Self-management skills include managing stimuli (for example, by avoiding, preventing, or interpreting them) and responses to them (for example, by setting goals, maintaining records, and self-talk). Thus, rather than thoughtlessly responding to stimuli, the respondent evaluates and manages stimuli. Rather than simply responding to possible reinforcement, one manages one's own responses. Thus, self-management embraces the principles of operant conditioning, while recognizing the importance of cognitive processing of stimuli, individual proclivities, attitudes, values, and stored memories of relevant past experiences.

In summary, Reinforcement Theory initially was concerned only with externally observable behavior, but eventually it was understood that cognitions were important in the process of interpreting stimuli and linking them to potential reinforcement. As these cognitive processes were revealed, they became the tools of self-management training programs. Cognition, of course, is important to behavior beyond stimuli and reinforcement.

Psychoanalytic Theory

For behaviorists, motivation is mainly a matter of reinforcement. If you provide enough of the right type of reinforcement, provide certain antecedent cues that reinforcement might occur (e.g., stimuli), and change the environment in certain ways, predictable response (change in the frequency of the behavior) is likely, if not certain. However, from other perspectives (and also for many contemporary behaviorists), a person is not an empty vessel responding automatically to possible consequences and manipulated by environmental cues. Instead, each person is a psychologically and cognitively active player with unique characteristics who considers, interprets, values, and reacts more or less purposefully, or at least consistently, to the environment. Basically, Psychoanalytic Theory is concerned with self-centered behavior, behaviors that satisfy personal drives related to needs and wants.

Unconscious Drives

Our discussion of psychological and social-psychological processes starts with Freud because his thinking was revolutionary and stimulated great advances in research and understanding (DK, 2017). To Freud, the innate desire for pleasure, the fear of pain, and the inevitability of death are the primary motivators of behavior. These innate drives are self-centered in the sense that they motivate behavior to satisfy them. Freudian psychologists, also known as psychoanalytic theorists, came to believe that people behave largely according to internal motivation stemming from basic, largely unconscious, drives related to pain and pleasure. Freud believed that basic drives are genetically programmed but modified by early childhood experience.

As children develop, they must resolve many psychological dilemmas that otherwise would keep them from maturing and developing normal social relationships and developing and achieving realistic aspirations. The job of parents and other caretakers is to socialize children so that as they mature, they are able to restrain their impulsive and self-centered behavior and direct their psychological **drive** toward socially acceptable ends. Unfortunately, children's relationships with their parents and the process of developing independence from parental dominance are generally challenging and imperfect, with lifelong influences on personality and motivation. Individuals may not even be aware of how childhood experiences have modified their management of basic drives.

Freud advanced the idea that many aspects of personality and motivation are not conscious to the individual, arguing that people often are unaware of why they behave as they do. Freud viewed the unconscious self as active and powerful, driving the person to fulfill selfish needs and desires that affect how they interact with the environment. Developing consciousness of self is a lifelong process to which some devote more energy than others. In the Freudian view, each person interacts with the environment in unique ways depending in part on personality. Each person may be born with certain tendencies in how they think and behave, and these tendencies are expressed in self-centered behavior. Unconscious drive is an important issue in psychological counseling and mental wellness activities, but in public health it is mainly something to keep in mind as a factor that explains some of the variance in behavior and intervention effectiveness.

Personality Traits

Psychoanalytic Theory led to a long and continuing fascination with personality and its role in motivation and behavior. *Personality* is a dynamic and organized set of characteristics possessed by a person that uniquely influences his or her cognitions, motivations, and behaviors in various situations (DK, 2017). Personality traits are relatively "… enduring patterns of perceiving, relating to, and thinking about the environment and oneself that are exhibited in a wide range of social and personal contexts" (American Psychological Association, https://dictionary.apa.org/personality-trait). Personality traits present early in life are likely to be retained throughout one's life, but personality can continue to evolve over the entire course of one's lifetime. Personality has been classified according to absolute type (e.g., introverted or extroverted), but is more often thought of in terms of traits that vary from person to person. Theorists generally assume that traits (1) are relatively stable over time; (2) differ among individuals (e.g., some people are outgoing while others are shy); and (3) influence behavior.

A variety of personality inventories of traits have been developed. Five basic characteristics are commonly emphasized: extraversion, openness, agreeableness, conscientiousness, and emotional stability. These traits, which can be measured by the NEO Personality Inventory (McCrae, Costa, & Martin, 2005), are defined as follows:

1. Extraversion—outgoing and stimulation-oriented vs. quiet and stimulation-avoiding
2. Neuroticism—emotionally reactive, prone to negative emotions vs. calm, imperturbable, optimistic
3. Agreeableness—affable, friendly, conciliatory vs. aggressive, dominant, disagreeable
4. Conscientiousness—dutiful, planful, and orderly vs. laidback, spontaneous, and unreliable
5. Openness to experience—open to new ideas and change vs. traditional and oriented toward routine

The Myers-Briggs Type Indicator, a popularly employed personality self-assessment tool, includes four dichotomous dimensions of personality: extroversion vs. introversion, sensing vs. intuition, thinking vs. feeling, and judgment vs. perception (Briggs & Myers, 1995). The inventory provides scores for each of these dimensions. Extroverts are relatively action oriented and seek breadth of knowledge and frequent social interaction, while introverts are more thought oriented, seek depth of knowledge, and prefer infrequent but substantial interactions. Sensing and intuition represent different ways of gathering information. Thinking and feeling reflect diverse methods of evaluating information. Theoretically, by understanding one's own pattern of thinking and valuing, one can better understand oneself and gain better control over decision making.

Theorists and researchers disagree about the extent to which personality is innate or environmental and the extent to which personality traits change over time and vary according to culture and socialization. Observational studies of twins separated at early ages suggest that both nature and nurture operate (Bronfenbrenner, 1986). The relative importance of genetics and environment in the development of personality is not known and may vary greatly from one individual to the next. The important point is that people exhibit unique personality traits that are not simply the product of genetics and fixed at birth. Genetics matters, of course, but personality is also a function of lifelong environmental influences. As shown in **Figure 3.3**, personality traits can be understood to develop as the product of inate drives, leading to self-centered behavior, moderated by socializing influences. Personality traits have unique genetic origins in the form of inherited drives, which leads to selfish behavior that would be unrestricted were it not for parental and societal influences. Thus personality traits are influenced over time by these socializing influences. Nonetheless, personality traits contribute to **individual differences** in how people interpret and respond to the environment.

The contention that personality traits affect motivation is compelling because the traits are measurable and associated with particular behaviors and also because we all know people who strongly exhibit certain traits, people who are particularly extroverted, aggressive, impulsive, rational, or emotional. Some traits are of particular interest in modern public health because programs can be developed that are tailored to fit or account for certain personality traits. However, for the most part, in public health it is useful to appreciate that there is

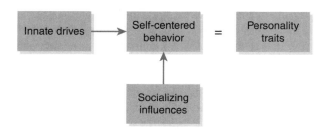

Figure 3.3 Conceptualization of personality development

variability in personality that can contribute to the relative effectiveness of programs. Also, in public health, as in all professions, an appreciation of the variability in personality traits of supervisors, colleagues, clients, and students can be invaluable.

Gestalt Theory

Psychoanalytic Theory influenced many great thinkers and stimulated new theories. Gestalt Theory, for example, was developed by Wertheimer (1938) and championed by Kurt Lewin (1951), both of whom were trained in Psychoanalytic Theory. Gestalt Theory suggests that people do not experience the environment in the same way because the mind alters the structure and meaning of experience based on impressions from past experience. Gestalt Theory has contributed greatly to an understanding of the role memory plays in behavior by suggesting that people do not record events in their memories the way they actually happened. Instead, they record factual and emotional impressions of what happened. Gestalt Theory helps explain why two observers of an event, for example, a car crash or robbery, often describe it quite differently. Gestalt Theory helps us understand why people view similar behavioral consequences differently, such that some people may be motivated by a seemingly trivial material incentive and others are not. It also helps us understand why people who have frequently experienced prejudice during their lives might interpret as prejudice events such as not being selected for a job or having to wait for a long time in the waiting room for a doctor's appointment (maybe it was prejudice, maybe not). Fundamental principles of public health practice derived from Gestalt Theory include the importance of assessing and developing an understanding of the target population's perceptions and conducing pilot tests of intervention messages and components with a sample of the actual target population to gain an understanding of how they interpret and react to the **message**, the source, and the intent.

Developmental Theory

Not surprisingly, the intellectual founders of developmental theory, Piaget and Inhelder (1962) and Erikson (1963), were trained in Psychoanalytic Theory. Developmental Theory is concerned with how aspects of personality and developmental challenges (such as independence and initiative) mature with age. Piaget determined that children develop in predictable ways, partly from inevitable physical and cognitive maturation, but also greatly from life experience (does this remind you of Freud?). Piaget's research documented the ages at which children are able to learn and understand certain concepts owing to their intellectual developmental. He also demonstrated that childhood experiences contribute to the variability in individual development, including many aspects of motivation. Accordingly, from a developmental perspective, motivation can be understood, at least partly, as the product of lifelong experience. For example, children who are appropriately challenged and socialized tend to develop self-confidence and the ability to get along with others.

Erikson built on Piaget's work and is best known for demonstrating that development is a lifelong process, not one that ends after childhood. He found that development advances in stages and that successful advance through a particular stage predicts success through future life stages, and the reverse. Moreover, the failure to fully develop certain fundamental capabilities impedes future development. Social competence and cooperation, for example, are essential capabilities in modern society, and the earlier and better these are learned, the greater the capacity for achievement and positive social relationships. Erickson believed that there are eight stages of development that are overlapping and ongoing throughout life. These include hope, will, purpose, competence, fidelity, love, caring, and wisdom. The research and thinking of Piaget, Erikson, and other developmental psychologists demonstrated the profound influence of life experience on adjustment, motivation, and behavior. Developmental psychology provides essential background for health-promotion specialists who work with children and adolescents and also provides a useful perspective for those who work with adult populations.

Maslow (1971) conceptualized human motivation as a pyramid of needs. At the base are physiological needs for sustenance and safety. Belonging and love are the next set of needs, followed by esteem, and finally **self-actualization**. To become self-actualized, meaning to reach one's full potential, the needs lower on the pyramid must first be substantially fulfilled. These need categories are generally thought of as overlapping, with greater fulfillment of lower-level needs contributing to greater fulfillment of higher-level needs. The conceptualization of a hierarchy of needs helps to explain why people whose basic needs have been poorly satisfied struggle to find fulfillment and independence. Maslow's thinking contributed immensely to the human potential movement that has promoted self-actualization therapy and related activities. Maslow and other humanist psychologists stimulated new thinking about human potential that evolved into the field of positive psychology. Positive psychology emphasizes happiness and well-being. Research has established that happiness is best realized with income security and through close and positive social ties to family and friends, exercise, and meditation (Seligman & Csikszentmihalyi, 2000).

Summary of Psychoanalytic-Based Theory

Psychoanalytic Theory stimulated a great deal of research and theory about the person, including motivation from basic drives, personality, unconscious drives, and cognitive processing of information. Both Behaviorism and Psychoanalytic Theory recognize the importance of environmental influences on behavior, but Psychoanalytic Theory, and the many theories that it stimulated, also emphasized the uniqueness of the individual, learning from socializing experiences, and cognitive processing of environmental stimuli.

Cognitive Psychology

This discussion of cognitive psychology will be brief because considerable space is devoted to these topics in later chapters. Cognitive psychology is concerned with how people process information. At a fundamental level, it is concerned with memory, attention, and cognition. The focus here is on information processing as it relates to decision making and related cognitive processes that affect behavior. That is, how do people make decisions, to the extent they do so intentionally? Briefly, we introduce Consistency Theory, the Health Belief Model, Theory of Reasoned Action, and Social Cognitive Theory.

Cognitive Consistency Theory/Dissonance

People constantly process information from all possible sources, including the physical and social environment, reading, TV, advertising, and conversations with family and friends. How information from these many sources is related to the core cognitions of knowledge, beliefs, attitudes, and behavior is central to most cognitive theories. Festinger's (1957) Consistency Theory suggested that new information sets up **cognitive dissonance**, or inconsistency, with current knowledge, beliefs, attitudes, and behavior. This dissonance creates tension that contributes to accepting, rejecting, or selectively interpreting the information. Accordingly, learning and change are motivated by cognitive dissonance. The premise is that people strive somehow to accommodate new information in relation to what they already know or believe, how they feel, and how they behave. New information creates "cognitive dissonance." Consistency Theory is intuitive because we have all experienced a change in understanding (knowledge), attitudes, and behavior from exposure to new information. Sometimes, we already know something about a subject, for example, that physical activity is good for health, but reading something new about particular benefits of physical activity or how to work out requires that we reconsider our original understanding. It encourages us to gain a new perspective on the subject, thereby changing our attitudes and behavior (or maybe just our intentions). Sometimes our behavior provides new information that changes cognitions. The informational feedback from a really good workout, for example, could change our attitudes and beliefs about exercise, at least for a time.

Consistency Theory suggests intervention possibilities. Theoretically, presenting information that creates cognitive dissonance should motivate change in cognitions and behavior. The key to successful informational interventions, of course, is delivering salient messages that reach the target population, engage their attention, and alter their understanding, creating dissonance between their current understanding, attitudes, and behavior.

The premise of cognitive dissonance is that it is uncomfortable when existing cognitions are challenged by new information (see **Figure 3.4**). Of course, to an extent people can and often do tolerate certain inconsistencies between knowledge, attitudes, and behavior. For example, many smokers recognize the health implications of their behavior and are reminded routinely but continue to smoke anyway. Sometimes people modify their attitudes and beliefs to fit their behavior, rather than the reverse. Indeed, a variety of coping strategies are employed to resolve or prevent such inconsistencies. **Confirmation bias**, attending only or mainly to information that is consistent with existing cognitions, is a common strategy. Similarly, there is a tendency for people to assume that the information you get is the totality of it (ease of reputation or availability heuristic), rather than a piece of a larger puzzle. If you mainly associate with others who hold the same attitudes and prefer the same behaviors, you might think these cognitions and behaviors are universal or at least superior to other possible cognitions and behavior. People commonly mistake a particular case or piece of information as the general case. For example, a smoker who learns about someone who died at the age of 90 or so and was a lifelong smoker may think this to be general rather than unusual. Apart from coping, environmental opportunity varies considerably, so regardless of the cognitive dissonance that one may suffer, behavior change may not always be possible. A smoker suffering from the dissonance between the knowledge that smoking is a health hazard may not quit when the environment is not supportive of this change in behavior. Nonetheless, the fundamental assumption is that information, when delivered effectively, increases knowledge, changes attitudes, and alters behavior.

Values Expectancy Theories

Consistency Theory, at least in part, gave rise to **values expectancy** theories, which are concerned with how people make decisions (process information) based on their beliefs and attitudes. An attitude is an emotional

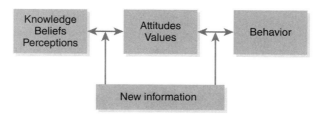

Figure 3.4 Consistency theory

disposition about an idea, person, thing, event, or behavior. Over time, attitudes are formed by a series of beliefs which result in **value** being placed on the outcome. Some attitudes are strongly held, others not so much. Attitudes can be general (I hate swimming) or specific (I like swimming in the ocean). Attitudes are related to values (exercising is more/less important than eating well or watching TV). Attitudes are made up of beliefs, which are what we think or perceive to be true but may or may not be factual. Many different beliefs can be involved in particular attitudes. The Health Belief Model posits that beliefs about one's susceptibility to a health problem and its severity affect motivation to take a specific action. Reasoned action argues that the likelihood of taking an action is based on beliefs and attitudes about the behavior and social norms. The Information Motivation Behavior model adds to these values expectancy theories the importance of cognitive skills. Having or not having particular cognitive skills influences behavior in profound ways. For example, many medical regimens are quite complicated, requiring substantial cognitive skill to master. Consider the many complex requirements of a person with diabetes who must carefully manage diet, frequently test blood sugar levels, dose with an appropriate amount of insulin, taking into account the time of day, exercise, sleep, and stress. In this case skills motivate compliance, and the lack of skills undermines the motivation to comply.

Values expectancy theories hold in common with Consistency Theory concerns about the relationship between cognitions and behavior and appreciation for the important role of information in behavior change. Ultimately, these theories envision the person as a sort of rational being weighing the available information as they form or reconsider their beliefs and attitudes and determine the advantages and disadvantages of engaging in a particular behavior now and in the future. This central conceptualization is the basis for most health-promotion interventions consisting of information designed to alter rational decision making.

Social Psychology

Social psychology is generally interested in social influences and contexts. Social-psychological research has demonstrated the importance of social context across a wide range of behaviors, including competitiveness, cheating, helping behavior, and conformity. People often behave differently in one social context than another. Your behavior is probably not always the same when you are with your parents as when you are with your friends or on your own or when you are at a party compared to when you are at school. Each social setting—home, work, school, the local pub, clubs, groups—exhibits and often reinforces unique and powerful normative expectations for behavior, with which most people in those settings tend to conform.

In addition to being influenced by context, behavior is influenced by other people. People tend to behave in ways that are similar to those with whom they associate. One well-studied example of social influences on health behavior is the effect of friends on adolescent substance use. Early adolescents with friends who smoke or drink are several times more likely to take up smoking or drinking than their contemporaries with no such friends (Simons-Morton, 2007). One explanation is that adolescents who smoke or drink exert pressure on their friends to take up these behaviors. It could also be, however, that adolescents take up these behaviors (or not) to conform and fit in with their friends. These are known as socializing effects or *socialization*. However, it is also likely, at least for some youth, that they make friends who smoke and drink because they are interested in these behaviors and form relationships at least in part on this basis. This is known as an effect of *selection*. Whether we are influenced by our friends or we select friends with common interests, our behavior tends to vary in the presence of others. For example, an adolescent might be more or less likely to accept the offer of a cigarette from an acquaintance depending on which of his other friends is also present, among other factors.

These concepts about social influences are important in health promotion because successful interventions often take them into account. With respect to social influences on smoking among adolescents, health-promotion programs commonly seek to alter exaggerated perceptions of social norms (everyone my age drinks alcohol). Social psychology is of particular relevance to public health because it has provided experimental research on a range of socially mediated health behavior such as adolescent substance use. For more on this, see Chapter 6.

Sociology

Members of the same family, school, church, neighborhood, profession, nationality, and race often share common beliefs, attitudes, and behaviors (Macionis, 2016). Some of this similarity is due to the tendency of people with similar interests and backgrounds to congregate, and some of it is the tendency of people to conform to social norms and other social influences. Although there is considerable overlap, social psychology is primarily interested in social influence and context, while sociology is interested in the broad influences of being part of a group including family, school, work, club, gang, as well as identifying as a patient, victim, or category (e.g., white, immigrant, gay). Consider how important it is to us to be a member of a group (and remember that Maslow's hierarchy of needs places belonging and love very highly, with esteem, achieved largely through group affiliation, at the next higher level). At a basic level, growing up in a family provides substantial socializing influence through intentional parenting and through **modeling** and other unwitting processes. School provides powerful influences as students are sorted out academically and sort themselves out into peer groups. Youth who go to parochial school are socialized differently than those who go to public school. Youth who are in the school band are socialized in certain ways by this experience, while youth who get involved in gangs are socialized in different ways. If you had gone to law school (like your dad wanted you to) or medical school (like your uncle expected you to), you would have been socialized very differently than you are now being socialized as a public health professional.

In addition to group behavior, sociology is concerned with issues of social class, deviance, power, status, justice, gender, race, culture, discrimination, and their effects on developmental processes, behavior, and health. Sociology seeks to understand individual behavior within the context of the groups to which the individual belongs and the normative influences of one's class, race, gender, and nationality. Growing up in the United States is a dramatically different cultural experience than growing up in Nigeria or Saudi Arabia, countries with very different national cultures, politics, religions, and economic policies. Of course, within one's country of origin, experience varies considerably among people from different social classes, races, and religions. We grow up not only as citizens of a particular country, but also as members of families, churches, schools, teams, religious organizations, communities, and the like. Later we join political parties, become members of one profession or another, and spend our day in certain workplaces. Each of these affiliations shapes our values and behavior in important ways. Sometimes group membership just happens to us, for example, when a person is diagnosed with cancer, he or she suddenly belongs to the group of cancer victims and their families. Sometimes group membership, being of a certain race, color, class, or gender, is the source of prejudice or privilege. In some cases, such as being a member of a gang, group membership is associated with crime and other social deviance (Fergusson, Swain-Campbell, & Horwood, 2002).

Ultimately, family, race, neighborhood, nationality, religion, gender, and class form a sort of web of culture that can be so dominant and all-encompassing that the individual within the web is not aware of its influence (Glass & McAfee, 2006). Our culture can be inseparable from identity (take the extreme example of a suicide bomber acting out of cultural commitment). Culture refers broadly to patterns of human activity and the symbolic structures that give such activities significance and importance. Our cultural experiences influence how we understand new information and interpret experience. For example, in most modern Western societies, science and empirical evidence are generally viewed as objective and valid, and people tend to be impressed with research findings and the opinions of scientists. Alternatively, in other societies and subgroups within Western societies, mysticism and religious dogma largely determine attitudes and values and the interpretation of events. One of the key sociology lessons about culture is that it is very difficult for people who do not share the same social background to understand and communicate with each other. This is a major challenge to public health professionals, who need to understand the populations with whom they work to be effective, but who often come from unfamiliar backgrounds and subcultures. Similarly, those of us who work with teenagers appreciate that they form unique and variable cultures and are not just younger versions of adults. Early, middle, and late adolescent boys and girls are quite different from each other both developmentally and socially. Within age groups, adolescents can belong to or identify with quite different subgroups typified by music preferences, social activities, dress, and other characteristics.

Discrimination and disparities related to group characteristics, particularly race, culture, and sexual orientation, are now recognized as important contributors to health and behavior. Racial disparities in economic opportunity and health remain in the United States as a sad legacy of slavery. Immigrants to the United States have long been discriminated against, but perhaps never as greatly as in the recent past. Indeed, persistent racial disparities in income are well documented (Grossman, 2017). More subtle but important aspects of discrimination include access to health care, school quality, and housing practices.

Sociological perspectives have figured prominently in the definition of health promotion. Considerable academic debate has attempted to emphasize health-promotion concerns with social and environmental objectives and not just with individual health behavior, as emphasized in *Healthy People* (U.S. Department of Health & Human Services, 2020) and elsewhere. Notably, Buchanan (2006) and others have argued that public health should be concerned with social justice, empowerment, and healthful environments and not only personal-health behavior. The argument is that environmental factors, including economic opportunity, fair policies, and access to decent housing, schooling, and health care are major determinants of health, so improving these social factors should be the focus of public health and health promotion. While there is no question about the importance of these considerations, there is always a question in health promotion about how much of our meager resources should be devoted to each societal level. Never has this been truer than now as the world confronts the dramatic challenges of climate change, overpopulation, and food and habitat insecurity.

Theory Commonalities

Each of the theoretical perspectives on motivation and behavior discussed in this chapter are concerned with the interrelationships among (1) environment, (2) person, and (3) behavioral experience. The differences in the theories are important mainly because of their relative emphases. For behaviorists, people learn from the consequences of their behavior, therefore, they are motivated by the environmental reinforcement of one's behavior. Psychoanalytic Theory suggests that people are motivated by basic drives that vary according to personality shaped by the interaction between their need-oriented behavior and the socializing effects of their formative relationship experiences. Social psychology emphasizes how perception and behavior are conditional on social context, while sociology emphasizes group membership and broad cultural influences on attitudes, values, and behavior.

In brief, while behavior is complicated, the major influence on behavior is the environment, understood and interpreted uniquely by the person based on their personality, past experiences, and cognitive processing. Clearly, particular behaviors are more or less likely depending on opportunity, social context, and social influence. Behavior, of course, once it occurs, provides information about the **reinforcing** properties of the behavior and about how reinforcement varies within particular social contexts. In general, environment and behavioral experience are processed somewhat uniquely by the individual and stored as impressionistic memories that anchor cognitions.

As noted, cognition is what we think, feel, and remember. Specifically, cognitions include knowledge, beliefs, attitudes, and values. Even modern proponents of operant conditioning emphasize the cognitive processes involved in recognizing stimuli and interpreting possible consequences of behavior. Humans are thinking creatures and can anticipate reinforcement and often respond to the possibility of reinforcement without being reinforced at all, or at least not every time. Although reinforcement and other influences on behavior can be direct, virtually all theoretical perspectives view cognitions as intermediate to behavior. For example, the way social influences work is through the cognitions of

beliefs, attitudes and values. Personality and lifelong socioenvironmental factors influence how new information and experience is cognitively processed. The argument here is that people learn from their experiences and store what they have learned in memory, so that new experiences are understood and interpreted cognitively.

One's culture, being a member of a certain family, attending a certain church, living in a certain neighborhood, being a certain race, determine what experiences people have and how they interpret these experiences. Cultural experience is stored in memory and shapes the cognitive lens through which new environmental exposures are interpreted. So basically, all behavioral theories are concerned with the interactions between the person, behavior, and environment, where the person includes personality, cognitive, and psychosocial factors; behavior includes current and past actions; and the environment includes both physical and social components.

The general proposition that motivation and behavior are the product of experience that is interpreted uniquely by the person has led to attempts to create a single theory that would make sense of it all. Self-Determination Theory (SDT) (Deci & Ryan, 2008; see Chapter 9) is one particularly grand theory that emphasizes both external and internal motivation. SDT emphasizes internal motivation from innate psychological needs. Social Cognitive Theory (SCT) is perhaps the best known and most elaborated theory linking reinforcement, cognition, and behavior (Bandura, 1986), as described more fully in a subsequent chapter. SCT is grounded in operant conditioning theory, while SDT is more oriented to personality and drive theory, but both theories recognize both unique individual characteristics and dynamic cognitive processes designed to foster self-regulation. The goal of these theories is to facilitate individuals' control of their behavior and their environments and employ many of the cognitive skills as self-management. Bandura recognized that people anticipate and interpret their experiences in ways that shape their behavior through reciprocal interactions between the person, the environment, and behavior. These three elements are interrelated and mutually influential—reciprocal. For Bandura, each person is uniquely shaped by his or her personality, childhood relationships, previous experience, and environmental influences. Experience provides **feedback** (reinforcement) from which people learn, and this learning is stored in memories that anchor cognitions. The social and physical environment, operating proximally in the here and now, and distal factors operating over the more distant and longer term, provides opportunity for experience, feedback, and context for interpreting these experiences. Thus, there is a constant and dynamic interaction between the person, representing both personal characteristics shaped by a lifetime of experience, and cognitive processing, and the environment, representing both lifetime exposure and immediate circumstances, and behavior.

Lessons for Public Health Practice

The contention that motivation and behavior are learned from experience is not a revolutionary idea and is not really a matter of debate. However, the nuances of how learning occurs and its variability in the population is enormously complex. Therefore, few theories fully explain behavior in specific ways that would hold for all populations and situations, and many theories tend to be somewhat narrowly focused. Some theories are concerned with specific types of behavior, for example, addiction or adherence. Some theories are primarily concerned with populations, such as theories about how race and gender influence behavior. Other theories are concerned with social context, family, and culture. Still

other theories are wholly concerned with information processes, such as how information of various types from various sources influence cognitions. These theories can best be understood as the elaboration of the basic behavior, person, and environment interactions described in this chapter. In this chapter we have emphasized the following main points.

1. Theories provide hypotheses about behavior that allow applied behavioral scientists to develop useful behavioral assessments and programs consistent with target behavior needs. Theories guide research and enable the interpretation of program results. Over time and with the accumulation of research, it becomes clear which theoretical perspectives can most usefully be employed in programs to address specific behaviors and populations.

2. A firm understanding of a range of theories is essential to the development, implementation, and evaluation of health-promotion programs. Theory-based programs are superior to theory-less programs in many ways, including that their evaluations can be interpreted.

3. Most behavioral theories are really theories about what motivates behavior. Motivation can best be thought of as the tendency to behave in certain ways. Factors that influence motivation tend to be external (environmental) or internal (cognitive).

4. Operant conditioning emphasizes the importance of external consequences and stimuli on the likelihood and frequency of behavioral responses. Essentially, behavior is learned based on experience with reinforcement. Behaviors that are reinforced tend to recur, and those that are not reinforced tend not to recur. All aspects of health-promotion practice should be informed by the simple and powerful principles of operant conditioning.

5. Ultimately, the goal of operant conditioning, at least modification, is self-regulation,

which can be accomplished by learning self-management skills enabling some level of control over stimuli and reinforcement.

6. People are not a blank slate. They come into the world with certain inherited traits that determine their predilections. Genetically inherited personality traits, while reasonably stable over time, are only one important aspect of character, and their influence is modified by socialization and other life experiences.

7. People are cognitive beings, capable of learning and developing unique beliefs, attitudes, and values.

8. Past experience is stored as memories that anchor cognitions, including their emotional valence, and guide the interpretation of new experiences. Beliefs and attitudes are based on the impressions from these memories. New experiences, including information, must compete with these existing cognitions.

9. Cognitive dissonance can occur when new information challenges current beliefs and attitudes. However, while people tend to be logical much of the time, they can also resort to rationalizations that serve to reduce tension caused by inconsistencies between cognitions and behavior.

10. Cognitive theories provide roadmaps for understanding behavior and how new information can lead to changes in cognitions and behavior.

11. People are socially influenced, not just as children, but throughout life. We are subject to the ways of thinking and behaving of our culture, our community, our family, and our friends. We sometimes behave differently in one social context than another.

12. Behavior theories apply not only to the at-risk population, but also to other targets of intervention, those with influence at particular societal levels. These include family and friends, policy makers, planners, politicians, bosses, and so on. While the goals of a program vary by level, the principles of behavior are the same for every person. Everyone's behavior is the product of external environmental and internal cognitive and personality factors.

13. There is no one theory of behavior because behavior is complicated. There is value in all of the major theories of behavior, but each may have particularly relevant applications.

14. Ultimately, behavior is influenced by information from a wide range of sources, including experience, and if we want to influence behavior, we need to provide new information that is useful and persuasive.

Discussion Questions

1. What is theory and why is it important?
2. What are the primary sources of motivation?
3. What is personality? Is personality fixed at birth?
4. Why is information so important to behavior?
5. How is behavior influenced by social context?

References

American Psychological Association Dictionary of Psychology. Retrieved from https://dictionary.apa.org/personality

Bandura, A. (1986). *Foundations of thought and action: A social cognitive theory.* Englewood Cliffs, NJ: Prentice Hall.

Briggs, I. M., & Myers, P. B. (1995). *Gifts differing: Understanding personality type.* Mountain View, CA: Davies-Black Publishing. Retrieved from https://www.mbtionline.com

Bronfenbrenner, U. (1986). Ecology of the family as a context for human development: Research perspectives. *Developmental Psychology, 22*(6), 723. DOI:10.1037/0012-1649.22.6.723

Buchanan, D. R. (2006). A new ethic for health promotion: Reflections on a philosophy of health education for the 21st century. *Health Education and Behavior, 33*(3), 290–304. DOI:10.1177/1090198105276221

DK. (2017). *The psychology book: Big ideas simply explained.* New York: DK Publishing.

Deci, E. L., & Ryan, R. M. (2008). Self-determination theory. A macrotheory of human motivation, development and health. *Canadian Psychology, 49,* 182–185. DOI: 10.1037/a0012801

Elder, J. P., Lytle, L., Sallis, J. F., Young, D. R., Steckler, A., Simons-Morton, D., . . . Ribisl, K. (2007). A description of the social–ecological framework used in the trial of activity for adolescent girls (TAAG). *Health Education Research, 22*(2), 155–165. DOI: 10.1093/her/cyl059

Erickson, E. H. (1963). *Childhood and society.* New York: W.W. Norton.

Ferguson, D. M., Swain-Campbell, N. R., & Horwood, L. J. (2002). Deviant peer affiliation, crime and substance use: A fixed-effects regression analysis. *Journal of Abnormal Child Psychology, 30*(4):419–30. DOI: 10.1023/a:1015774125952.

Festinger, L. (1957). *A theory of cognitive dissonance.* Evanston, IL: Row, Peterson & Company.

Glass, T. A., & McAfee, M. J. (2006). Behavioral science at the crossroads in public health: Extending horizons, envisioning the future. *Social Science and Medicine, 62*(7), 1650–1671. DOI:10.1016/j.socscimed.2005.08.044

Grossman, M. (2017). *Determinants of health: An economic perspective.* New York: Columbia University Press. DOI: 10.7312/gros17812

Kazdin, A. E. (2020). *Behavior modification in applied settings* (7th ed.). Long Grove, IL, Waveland Press.

Klein, H. A., Jackson, S. M., Street, K., Whitacre, J. C., & Klein, G. (2013). Diabetes self-management education: Miles to go. *Nursing Research and Practice, 2013,* Article 581012. DOI: 10.1155/2013/581012. ID 581012.

Kuhn, T. S. (1996). *The structure of scientific revolutions* (3rd ed.). Chicago: University of Chicago Press.

Lewin, K. (1951). *Field theory in social science; selected theoretical papers* (D. Cartwright, Ed.). New York: Harper & Row. DOI:10.1177/000271600135

Macionis, J. L. (2016). *Sociology* (16th ed.). New York: Pearson Publishing.

Maslow, A. (1971). *The further reaches of human nature.* New York: Viking Press.

McCrae, R. R., Costa, P. T., & Martin, T. A. (2005). The NEO P1-3: A more readable revised NEO personality inventory. *Journal of Personality Assessment, 84*(3), 261–270. DOI: 10.1207/s15327752jpa8403_05

Milam, A. J., Johnson, S. L., Furr-Holden, C. D. M., & Bradshaw, C. P. (2016). Alcohol outlets and substance use among high schoolers. *Journal of Community Psychology, 44*(7), 819–832. DOI: 10.1002/jcop.21802

Piaget, J., & Inhelder, B. (1962). *The psychology of the child.* New York: Basic Books.

Sallis, J. F., Floyd, M. F., Rodriguez, D. A., & Saelens, B. E. (2012). Role of built environments in physical activity, obesity, and cardiovascular disease. *Circulation, 125*(5), 729–737. DOI:10.1161/CIRCULATIONAHA.110.969022.

Seligman, M., & Csikszentmihalyi, M. (2000). Positive psychology: An introduction. *American Psychologist, 55*(1), 5–14. DOI: 10.1037//0003-066x.55.1.5.

Simons-Morton, B. G. (2007). Social influences on adolescent substance use. *American Journal of Health Behavior, 6,* 672–684. DOI: 10.5993/AJHB.31.6

Wallace-Wells, D. (2019). *The uninhabitable earth: Life after warming.* New York: Dugans Books.

Wansink, B., & Kim, J. (2005). Bad popcorn in big buckets: Portion size can influence intake as much as taste. *Journal of Nutrition Education and Behavior, 37*(5), 242–245.

Wertheimer, M. (1938). Laws of organization in perceptual forms. In W. Ellis (Ed.), *A source book of Gestalt psychology* (pp. 71–88). London: Routledge & Kegan Paul. Retrieved from Arizona State University, Classics in the History of Psychology Web site: http://psy.ed.asu.edu/~classics/Wertheimer/Forms/forms.htm (Original work published 1923)

U.S. Department of Health and Human Services. (2020). *Healthy People 2030.* Retrieved from www.healthypeople.gov/2020/

Behavior Change Theories

The first two chapters in Section 2 describe Social Cognitive Theory and Self-Determination Theory, which are comprehensive theories of behavior that describe the relationships with behavior of the person, the environment, and cognitions. Each of the other chapters in Section 2 deals with a specific theory or group of related theories such as value expectancy, stage, and social influence theories.

CHAPTER 4	Self-Regulation and Social Cognitive Theory........ 75
CHAPTER 5	Self-Determination Theory and Motivational Interviewing 91
CHAPTER 6	Social Influence Theory: The Effects of Social Factors on Health Behavior 109
CHAPTER 7	Value Expectancy Theories. 127
CHAPTER 8	Stages of Change: The Transtheoretical Model......149

Self-Regulation and Social Cognitive Theory

People self-regulate by processing information in advance of and as a result of their behavior.

OUTLINE

1. Preview
2. Objectives
3. Reinforcement
4. Self-Regulation
5. Social Cognitive Theory
    5.1. Reciprocal Determinism
        5.1.1. Environment
        5.1.2. Behavior
        5.1.3. Person
    5.2. Self-Regulatory Processes
        5.2.1. Observational Learning
        5.2.2. Cognitions
            5.2.2.1. Behavioral Capability
            5.2.2.2. Self-Efficacy
            5.2.2.3. Outcome Expectations
    5.3. Social Influence
    5.4. Other SCT Constructs
6. Applications of SCT
7. Diet and Physical Activity Self-Regulation Among Obese Woman
8. Checkpoints Program to Prevent Motor Vehicle Crashes Among Young Drivers
9. Lessons for Public Health Practice
10. Discussion Questions
11. References

PREVIEW

Social Cognitive Theory (SCT) provides a comprehensive explanation of the dynamic interactions between the environment and behavior that forms the basis for self-regulation processes involved in goal-directed behavior.

OBJECTIVES

The objectives of this chapter are for readers to be able to:

1. Describe self-regulatory processes.
2. Explain how Social Cognitive Theory provides a comprehensive theory of self-regulation.
3. Explain basic differences in cognition for goal-directed and impulsive behavior.
4. Define and describe the relationships between stimuli, response, and reinforcement.
5. Explain the reciprocal determinism concept of Social Cognitive Theory.
6. Describe how the environment influences behavior.
7. Explain how people learn from observation.

8. Describe the role of outcome expectations in behavior.
9. Apply the concepts of self-efficacy and behavioral capability to a health behavior program.
10. Identify intervention methods suggested by SCT constructs.

Reinforcement

We eat because we get hungry, and the thought of eating is a **stimulus** or cue that can be reinforced by eating. In addition to hunger, a variety of stimuli, such as seeing something good to eat, observing others eating, remembering how good something tastes, or exposure to an advertisement, can serve as stimuli that remind us to eat. Thus, stimuli draw our attention to the possibility of reinforcement.

Behavior that is reinforced tends to recur, and behavior that is not reinforced tends not to recur. Anything that increases the frequency of a behavior is considered to be reinforcing. Negative reinforcement is something unpleasant that leads to a change in behavior when it is removed (e.g., the craving for nicotine is reduced temporarily by smoking, hunger by eating, and fatigue by sleeping). A positive consequence that occurs after a response reinforces a recurrence of the response, for example, praise from a parent, teacher, or friend for a good behavior increases the likelihood of its recurrence. Reinforcement can result from a response to something internal, such as hunger or other craving, pain, or low blood sugar, or something external, such as money, tokens, or coupons that can be exchanged for desired objects or privileges. Feedback, praise, attention, **social approval**, and achievement are other examples of reinforcers. Reinforcement that is intermittent and not consistent can be as powerful as regular reinforcement. However, consistent lack of reinforcement serves to reduce the frequency of the behavior, sometimes to extinction. However, behaviors that have been reinforced over time tend to become habitual, even in the absence of further reinforcement. These are the basic principles of reinforcement theory, or operant conditioning, which is concerned with how behavior is guided by reinforcement (Kazdin, 2020).

Stimuli indicate that a response is likely to produce a certain consequence. This relationship between stimuli, responses, and consequences is shown in **Figure 4.1**. Over time, stimuli become linked in a person's mind to the likelihood of particular consequences. When these expected consequences are positive, the response is reinforced, even when no actual reinforcement is provided. This is a key principle of behavior, frequently employed as a marketing strategy to stimulate consumer anticipation of reinforcement from a purchase. It is also the key social marketing principle. A beer commercial with beautiful young people on a beach is a stimulus designed to link drinking beer to positive social consequences, designed to increase sales of that brand (or of beer in general). The more clicks and longer glances Facebook or Google can elicit for their sponsors, the more revenue they generate.

Of course, behavior is informed by other than direct reinforcement. One does not need to fall off a roof to know to be cautious up there because people learn from the experiences of others, as well as from their own. Also, there is considerable variability in susceptibility to particular stimuli according to individual preferences and goals. Moreover, people can manage their exposure and responses to stimuli through self-regulatory processes.

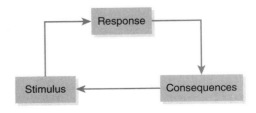

Figure 4.1 Stimulus–response model of behavior

Self-Regulation

Self-regulation is the process by which people manage their behavior to achieve personal goals. This process is often referred to as **self-directed** or **goal-directed behavior**. Self-direction requires agency whereby the individual has reasonable control. Behaviors over which the individual has little control include those that are automatic responses (like hunger), impulsive (lashing out in response to an insult), and dominated by the external environment (cold weather causes us to shiver or dress warmly). Within the context of personal agency, people typically pursue goals that are momentary and transient, such as the fleeting desire to own a special but expensive object, have sex, or eat a succulent meal. People also pursue goals that are longer-term and sustained, such as losing weight, getting fit, seeking approval, developing satisfying personal relationships, and achieving success. Sometimes goals conflict. A person may at the same time wish to lose weight and eat without reservation, become fit and laze about.

Self-regulation is the process by which people manage (self-direct) their behavior to achieve their goals (Vohs & Baumeister, 2016). Many prominent health problems are due largely to self-regulation failure, for example, overeating, substance abuse, and noncompliance with a medical regimen. A lack of self-regulatory skills renders individuals particularly susceptible to external environmental conditions as well as to self-destructive impulsiveness. Emotional problems, underachievement, and health-damaging behaviors can all be attributed in part to self-regulation deficiencies, along with environmental and biological factors (Carver & Schier, 2016). Those with poorly developed self-regulatory skills may be the most susceptible to societal forces that promote immediate gratification of impulses to overindulge, for example, by overeating, using drugs, and engaging in violent behavior.

Each of us struggles constantly to balance impulses to satisfy immediate wants with the need to control these same impulses for long-term benefits. To function well in modern society considerable impulse control is necessary; success in many endeavors demands substantial sacrifice of immediate for long-term goals. The development of self-regulation is an important and notable hallmark of psychological maturity, a goal of parents and teachers, a characteristic of individual personality, and a prerequisite for conventional acceptance and achievement. Ultimately, impulse control and the ability to sacrifice immediate satisfactions to achieve long-term goals are basic developmental standards for measuring maturity and are essential for most forms of conventional success. Our evolutionary past has programmed us with powerful impulses for sex, food, and other gratifications, and in modern society each individual must develop the means to control and balance these impulses to enable productive, goal-directed activity (Blair, 2016).

It is now generally assumed that people self-regulate by processing information in advance of and as a result of their behavior in a sort of constant, dynamic feedback loop influenced by cognitive, behavioral, and emotional processes. Both stimuli and reinforcement provide information that is processed in relation to past experience stored in memory. Thus, stimuli linked to reinforcement in memory is likely to elicit a response. The basic idea is that people estimate the likely effects of an anticipated action on goal satisfaction to guide action. Reconciling competing goals requires complex decision making that balances estimations of immediate and future consequences of behavior, including the reaction of others. Typically, programs designed to facilitate self-regulation begin with an applied behavioral analysis, as shown in **Table 4.1**. This exercise involves the learner in the process of identifying the pattern of their responses, including the stimuli and consequences. Thus, the participant can learn to control stimuli, evaluate the value of the consequence, and gain control of behavior.

Table 4.1 Applied Behavioral Analysis

Time/location	Antecedent Behavior	Consequence
8:00 A.M.	[indicate specific antecedents]	[indicate the strength of each consequence from low to high (1–5)]
9:00 A.M. School	[indicate specific antecedents]	[indicate the strength of each consequence from low to high (1–5)]
10:00 A.M.	[indicate specific antecedents]	[indicate the strength of each consequence from low to high (1–5)]
12 noon	[indicate specific antecedents]	[indicate the strength of each consequence from low to high (1–5)]
Etc.	[indicate specific antecedents]	[indicate the strength of each consequence from low to high (1–5)]

Instructions:
1. Record the time and location of every occurrence of the behavior over a period of time.
2. Identify the antecedents of each event, including any possible environmental or physiological cues, actions or comments of others, etc.
3. Record details about the behavior, such as its intensity or amount.
4. Record details about the consequences of the behavior, including physiological, psychological, and social consequences, and indicate strength on a scale from 1 to 5.

Self-regulatory processes apply more to deliberative (those consciously considered) than to immediate, impulsive actions. For example, self-regulatory processes apply reasonably well to deliberative actions such as what food to order or prepare or whether to go to the gym or watch TV after work, at least within the context of personal goals. However, behavior is not always fully reasoned. Often, rather than gathering and weighing all the facts, it is easier to rely on intuitive judgments, which may not be consistent with the best information (Kahneman, 2011). Intuition is largely based on general **heuristics** (a sort of general sense about particular things, ideas, or situations) developed with experience over time that allow us to act without serious consideration. Accordingly, we intuitively understand that particular food groups (milk, beef, potatoes) are good or not so good for our health, without reexamining the evidence each time we shop. Decisions that require immediate action, for example, reacting when another driver cuts you off dangerously or a peer invites you to smoke a joint, are particularly challenging because they require immediate action in the context of heightened emotions. Emotional situations tend to be dominated by intuition rather than reasoned action. One can be highly **deliberative** about many behaviors, but when confronted with an emergency, primitive fight-or-flight mechanisms dominate (Kahneman, 2011). Therefore, while self-regulation is an important process for deliberative decision making and goal-directed behavior, only very well-established self-regulatory processes are sufficient to manage immediate, emotion-provoking stimuli.

Social Cognitive Theory

Most theories of behavior employed in health-promotion activities are concerned principally with the initiation of behavior and less about the maintenance of behavior. Fostering the ability to maintain healthful behavior over long periods of time, namely self-regulation, is a primary health-promotion goal. To understand the long-term maintenance of health behavior, it is important to consider the role of self-regulation as described by Social Cognitive Theory (SCT). SCT provides a comprehensive conceptual framework that describes the dynamic interrelationships of self-regulatory processes involved in goal-directed behavior. Goal-directed behavior includes most purposeful behaviors that employ cognitive decision making.

The central concept of SCT, **reciprocal determinism**, posits that the person, behavior, and environment interact, and each influence the other in a reciprocal and dynamic fashion (Bandura, 1986). SCT represents a revolutionary way of thinking about how people learn from experience and regulate their own behavior. It has been known for many decades that the environment provides cues (stimuli) about possible consequences and opportunities for behavior and feedback from behavioral experience. SCT describes how individuals evaluate their environment, including the likelihood of reinforcement of particular behavioral responses to a stimulus. This evaluation, based on past experience and individual preferences, consists of a rapid processing of information that enables quick decisions. SCT argues that the process of decision making is simplified by the development of generalized **outcome expectations** and the values placed on them, termed **expectancies**, and the potential for reinforcement in a given situation (similar to Kahneman's heuristics). Hence, without recalling any particular past experience, and the individual can quickly, without conscious thought, based on this sort of heuristic, decide how the current situation fits into the general pattern or impressions of past experiences evaluate the potential for reinforcement in that situation.

Reciprocal Determinism

The grand concept of SCT is reciprocal determinism. Reciprocal determinism is a self-regulatory feedback loop in which person, environment, and behavior are dynamically interrelated. The term *person* refers to the individual, with a unique personality, experiences, and learned behavior. The *environment* represents the external social and physical milieu with various stimuli and potential reinforcements. *Behavior* includes responses to particular stimuli to achieve immediate and long-term goals. The constant and dynamic reciprocity of these three components makes them integral, such that a change in behavior interacts with the environment and the unique goals and expectations of the person. Each person responds to the environment somewhat uniquely, based on past experience and personal factors. The environment influences behavior by providing context, opportunity, and feedback, which are processed and acted upon uniquely by the person, based on past experience, personality, and goals.

The concept of reciprocal determinism is consistent with the tenets of multilevel programming in health promotion. In general, modern health-promotion practice assumes that each person is more or less unique, learns from experience, stores generalized impressions (outcome expectations) of the likelihood of reinforcement in various situations, makes decisions based on cognitive evaluations in relation to goals, and has reasonable control over personal behavior.

Environment

The broad physical and social environment sets the stage for behavior, providing cues and opportunities for experience and reinforcement. The environment includes both physical and social elements. Home, school, and work, for example, are physical places that provide certain social contexts. Family influences on behavior are profound owing to the amount of time family members spend together and the values they share. In similar fashion, people who go to a certain school are shaped somewhat in certain ways that are unique from how those who go to a different school are shaped, given the variability in values, expectations, and norms.

Opportunity is the aspect of the environment that allows us to try out certain behaviors and gain feedback from the experience. Opportunity varies considerably among individuals and groups. When cigarettes are available at home or from friends, the opportunity to smoke is great, increasing the likelihood of experimentation and reinforcement. Children who grow up being offered fresh fruits and vegetables gain experience and develop preferences for and generalized expectations about eating these foods that are different from youth who grow up without such opportunities. People who are exposed to other cultures and peoples may be more accepting of local diversity than those who did not have these kinds of opportunities. Opportunity enables behavioral responses, which provides feedback from which people learn.

A child is unlikely to wear a bicycle helmet if one is not available, but even when one is available, the child may not always wear it. When parents regularly reinforce a child's use of bicycle helmets by expressing approval, helmet use becomes more likely. Of course, reinforcement is complicated by the unique ways people experience consequences. Some children may wear their bicycle helmet to avoid their parents' nagging, while others may refrain from wearing a helmet because their parents' nagging provides a valued source of attention. Nagging in this case actually reinforces noncompliance. Also, the reinforcement that parents provide their children for wearing bicycle helmets may be less powerful than the perceived reinforcement from peers to not wear a helmet. Then again, it may be that parental admonishments about bicycle helmets are unheeded because they are not **contingent**, that is, parents impose no actual or valued consequence for nonuse.

The environment also provides feedback to behavioral responses in the form of consequences. The lack of consequences is also informative. Feedback about consequences is a form of information that is stored in memory and used to evaluate the likelihood of future consequences in similar contexts. Thus, a person learns over time that reinforcing consequences can be expected under certain conditions and not in others.

Some consequences are more reinforcing than others. Material **rewards**, for example, are powerful consequences of behavior, and therefore highly reinforcing. Material rewards are often used in the initial stages of a project or program to get people to try the behavior and gain experience. One simple example of the use of material rewards to increase healthful behavior was provided by The Safety Belt Connection Program (Simons-Morton, Brink, & Bates, 1987). To increase safety belt use among drivers at employee parking lots, inexpensive material incentives were provided, and group rates of weekly safety belt use were recorded on large thermometer-type signs located at the parking lot. These simple individual and group rewards led to significant and substantial increases in safety belt use rates compared with use in the comparison parking lots.

Social consequence is another very powerful class of reinforcement. In general, people tend to behave in ways that they think will bring them social reinforcement, which may include attention, praise, acceptance, and the like. To please mom or dad, children will button their coats, wear bicycle helmets, and eat vegetables. To please their friends (gain social reinforcement), people often behave in ways they otherwise would not. Therefore, social consequences are contextual. People adapt their behavior to the environmental setting and social context. A teen may be unlikely to start smoking (cigarettes or marijuana) on his or her own, but more likely when encouraged by peers.

The value of consequences is subjective and therefore does not have uniform effects on behavior (Kazdin, 2020). That is, people evaluate the consequences of their behavior according to their goals, values, and past experience. The tasks for health-promotion specialists interested in understanding and influencing behavior include the following: (1) identifying incentives that may encourage initiation of the target behavior; (2) appreciating the variability in reinforcement provided by consequences; (3) determining how the proximal social environment and the distal community and policy environment can be shaped to reinforce health-promoting behavior and discourage health-damaging behavior; and (4) facilitating self-regulation of behavior.

Behavior

In public health we usually think of behavior as an outcome of interest, but it is also an input. Notably, people learn from the consequences of behavioral responses. The environment provides opportunities for behavior, and these responses provide feedback. When people first smoke cigarettes or drink alcohol, for example, they get feedback about the intoxicating effects, the reactions of their peers, and sometimes the consequences of being found out by parents, school officials, or law officers. Some feedback may not be reinforcing, for example, smoking initially burns the lungs and alcohol tastes unpleasant, as least at first for many people. Other feedback may depend on the social context, personal goals, and **generalized expectations**. Sometimes a healthful behavior is not initially rewarding, for example, quitting smoking or starting to exercise. In these cases, behavioral maintenance may depend on copious amounts of positive reinforcement in the form of praise, records of achievement, and the like.

It is also the case that behavior can change the environment. A physiological example would be that eating a large meal results in a rapid increase in blood sugar levels, which stimulates the production of insulin, resulting in a rapid decline in blood sugar levels, which increases the sensation of hunger (moderate intake results in only moderation of blood sugar levels). Eating to excess often results in biological changes that increase the likelihood of more eating to satisfy the resulting hunger. In the same manner, a person tends to eat or drink more (alcohol) when servings are large than when they are small, probably because the size of the serving serves as a stimulus (Kersbergen et al., 2018). Preparing and serving smaller portions alters the environmental stimuli and reduces consumption. Similarly, dieters realize that they are more likely to eat if they see certain foods, so they modify the environment by not buying certain foods or put them out of sight. Runners create schedules and make commitments to running mates, thereby committing themselves to exercising and creating a reinforcement schedule. Conversely, when cigarettes and alcohol are handy, their likely use increases. For better or worse, these behaviors create stimuli that are linked to reinforcement and repetition of the behavior. The main point is that behavior provides feedback from which learning occurs.

Person

The third leg of triadic reciprocity is the person. The person interacts with the environment and behavior. If there were no such thing as "person," specific consequences would alter behavior the same with every person, but they do not. As discussed in Chapter 2, some of this variability is due to personality characteristics and some of it from the individual generalized expectations developed from previous experience. Each person evaluates the likelihood of reinforcement based on past experience and personal goals. Self-directed behavior results in decisions about behavior based on the evaluation of the likelihood of reinforcement in relation to personal values and goals. The person assesses opportunities for reinforcement by discriminating between similar stimuli and considering the value of the likely consequences. What is important is that the uniqueness of each individual creates variability in the population in terms of their environment and their behavioral responses to reinforcement. In public health this wide individual variability can be accommodated by creating a range of programs and appeals.

Self-Regulatory Processes

Self-directed behavior is the product of self-regulatory skill applied to achieve personal goals by interpreting stimuli, anticipating and evaluating possible consequences, controlling the environment, and taking action (Carver & Scheir, 2016). To control their environment, those concerned about calories would minimize the availability of high-calorie foods at home, and those concerned with physical fitness would sign up for fitness classes or join a running or bicycling group. Methods of managing stimuli include making lists, tracking performance (weight or miles run or days since last cigarette), setting reminders, scheduling events, and eliminating unwanted cues. Reinterpreting stimuli requires **cognitive restructuring** such that previously powerful stimuli (advertisements for ice cream) become

less so. Self-reinforcement strategies include setting attainable goals, maintaining performance records, self-congratulation and telling others of your accomplishment or progress, and taking time off after completing a task. Making a preferred behavior (e.g., eating ice cream or reading a book) contingent upon completing a less-preferable behavior (e.g., exercising) is a common way to regulate one's behavior (Kazdin, 2020). Because many forms of reinforcement such as recognition, praise, and attention are social, it is useful to spend time with others who appreciate and share similar health behaviors. Indeed, it is rewarding and fun to exercise with your friends, and it is difficult to eat differently than your housemates.

Observational Learning

A lot of human behavior is the product of observation. People can learn by observing the experience of others. The process of learning through the observed experience of others occurs through vicarious reinforcement and modeling. **Vicarious reinforcement** is the process by which a person learns how to interpret stimuli and anticipate reinforcement by observing the reinforcement of others' behavior. For example, skateboarders do not need to personally experience lacerations and broken bones to understand the importance of safety equipment because they can observe the experience of others. Depending on individual goals, personal characteristics, and previous experience, some skateboarders may develop an appreciation for safety equipment, while others may conclude that the risk of injury is acceptable, might not happen to them, or makes the sport attractive.

By observing other people, we learn what behavior is normative and expected. Thus, the behavior of others provides models for our own behavior. The first day at a new school or attending a new group for the first time, we learn what is expected by observing the social effects of others' behavior. For example, when adolescents first experience cigarettes, alcohol, marijuana, and other drugs, the group's reaction to these behaviors indicate social norms and the likelihood of social reinforcement for trying or not trying the drug.

Behavioral modeling by certain others is particularly influential, and the greater perceived similarity of the model to the individual, the greater the influence on behavior. Intentionally or not, some people serve as models for preferred behavior. Parents can but don't always model self-restraint with respect to anger, alcohol, and food. Nurses who model placing a newborn on their back to sleep or require that infants are secured in an appropriate car seat model appropriate behavior for new mothers. Parents who wear safety belts model this behavior for their children.

Cognitions

Learning occurs as a function of cognitive processes that enable people to interpret stimuli to determine likely consequences and determine how to manage their own behavior to maximize the potential for reinforcement. That is, information in the form of feedback from responses to the environment is cognitively stored in memory and retrieved as necessary to evaluate the potential for reinforcement in various contexts.

Behavioral Capability Behavioral capability is the SCT term for essential knowledge and skills. As every health educator knows, knowledge and skills are essential but not necessarily sufficient to promote the adoption and maintenance of health-promoting behaviors. Still, if a complex behavior is to be performed, a person must be knowledgeable about the behavior and have relevant practical skills that would allow correct performance under a variety of relevant conditions. Before trying something, people want to know what it is and how to do it. Behavioral capability enables performance and enhances motivation. Behavioral capability can result from training, observation, and experience. Infant car seats

are notoriously complicated to install and use correctly, and training can reduce errors, while modeling and training increase motivation (Brooks & Wilson, 2018).

It is sometimes the case that people develop skills, but not to the point of mastery, so they are able to perform the behavior under ideal but not actual circumstances. For example, in our research on adolescent problem behavior, where we teach middle school students social skills to enable them to deal with difficult peers and complex social situations, the difficulty many students have is being able to employ their new skills outside the classroom in situations that are dynamic and emotional (Simons-Morton & Farhat, 2010). Behavioral capability implies practical and useful understanding of knowledge that is essential for performing a skill or task under a range of practical situations.

Self-Efficacy Self-efficacy is a unique SCT construct (Bandura, 1997), adopted by other theories, such as the Health Belief Model and Theory of Reasoned Action. Self-efficacy refers to confidence in one's ability to undertake a specific action successfully, even when barriers are present. Confidence increases self-directed behavior, while a lack of confidence discourages self-directed behavior. Self-efficacy is associated with a wide range of health behaviors, higher self-efficacy with more-healthful behavior and low self-efficacy with less-healthful behavior (Bandura, 1997). Behavioral capability improves self-efficacy. Environmental facilitators can support or hinder the development of behavioral capability. In our car seat example, parents may develop different values regarding the possible outcomes depending on their level of confidence. If a mother is confident that she can deal with her husband's impatience, her baby's fussiness, and the complexity of the car seat fittings, she may develop more positive outcome expectations and expectancies and be more likely to employ the car seat. Self-efficacy is thought to be enhanced by successful experience and undermined by failure or frustration. Therefore, a common method for enhancing self-efficacy is to provide instruction and practice to mastery.

Outcome Expectations The cognition, outcome expectation, is the anticipated consequences of behavior. SCT posits that a person develops generalized expectations about the likely outcomes of possible responses to stimuli. Accordingly, people anticipate the consequences of their actions in advance of actually engaging in the behavior and sometimes in advance of encountering situations in which the behavior would be possible and relevant. Outcome expectations are developed primarily through actual and vicarious experience and are stored as memories and emotions. For example, a mother's expectations about the likely outcomes of installing a car seat and putting her young child in the seat are developed from past experience with car seats and from observing others using car seats for their children. Similarly, more favorable outcome expectations are associated with parent management of teenage driving (Simons-Morton, 2019).

Expectations describe both the potential outcomes and the value placed on these anticipated outcomes based on individual goals. Each individual may experience unique **perceived likelihood** or expectations of each possible outcome and also value the outcome differently, requiring that they "calculate" the relative advantages. Outcome expectations are based on past experience, which may not always provide an accurate gauge of the likelihood of reinforcement. Therefore, SCT methods have been developed to alter expectations by providing examples and models. For example, positive expectancies for alcohol use are associated with drunkenness (Osberg & Boyer, 2018; Walther, Pedersen, Cheong, & Molina, 2017). Alcohol use and abuse prevention programs seek to alter expectations by providing accurate information about the outcomes of drinking (Scott-Sheldon, Terry, Carey, Garey, & Carey, 2012). Parental limits on the driving privileges of newly licensed teenagers are mediated by parents' outcome expectations, including the extent to which they believe such limits will protect their children from danger and also the extent to which their teenage children will resist such limitations (Simons-Morton, 2019).

Social Influence

Social influence is a major part of the environment. SCT places special emphasizes on the importance of social learning. By observing and interacting with others, we learn what and under what conditions a response is likely to be reinforced. There are many forms of social reinforcement, attention and praise being two examples. In general, people are highly motivated by the potential for gaining the attention of and praise from those about whom they care, such as family members and close friends, or are otherwise powerful and important, such as teachers and employers. Social influence features prominently in the development of outcome expectations. Adolescents' perceptions of their parents' expectations and their friends' substance use behavior are highly associated with adolescent substance use (Simons-Morton & Farhat, 2010).

Social influence operates at least in part through social norms, which are the accepted beliefs, attitudes, values, and behavior of a group. Norms are powerful influences on behavior. Both actual and perceived norms are influential. Perceived social norms are what the observer believes the norms to be as they apply to particular situations. Actual social norms are reflected by social structures and generally accepted perceptions and values. There will be more emphasis on this in later chapters.

Social norms exist with unique variation at many social levels, nationally, regionally, and locally. Both alcohol and marijuana are generally available in modern society, but norms regarding their use vary according to social context. Notably, norms among adolescents are about equally accepting of marijuana and alcohol (O'Brien et al., 2018). Similarly, breast-feeding is relatively more prevalent among white than African American women, due in part to social norms and self-efficacy (Logan et al., 2016).

Norms are perceptual as well as actual, and perceptions do not need to be accurate to influence behavior. The perception that smoking is a socially desirable behavior, at least among close friends, fosters smoking, while the perception that smoking is unacceptable among close friends discourages smoking (Simons-Morton & Farhat, 2010; Simons-Morton, Haynie, & Noelke, 2009). Although virtually all parents would be upset at the thought that their adolescent child was smoking cigarettes, adolescents who perceive that their parents would be particularly upset with them are less likely to smoke (Simons-Morton, Haynie, & Noelke, 2009).

Additional information about social influences is provided in a subsequent chapter.

Other SCT Constructs

SCT includes a wealth of constructs other than those already described. The interested reader can expect to be well rewarded for reading Bandura's (1986) foundational book, *Social Foundations of Thought and Action: A Social Cognitive Theory*, particularly the descriptions of self-regulation mechanisms, emotional arousal, moral judgment, modes of thought verification, and the like. For example, not only does Bandura describe how cognitive representations of possible future reinforcement mediate intended behavior, but he also elucidates the cognitive mechanisms by which self-evaluation contributes to intent. Moreover, Bandura explains how discrepant information can create informational perturbation (i.e., cognitive dissonance due to the discomfort when new information is discordant with existing cognitions). Bandura also provides a great deal of information of particular relevance to intervention methods. For example,

the chapter on **enactive learning** provides a lucid discussion about how people learn from experience and suggests a number of ways that education and training can be structured to foster learning from doing. With respect to cognitive regulators, Bandura describes how language is representational, suggesting how the words, images, and symbols we use in our programs can motivative behavior. Also, he discusses why goal setting is such a powerful motivator, reminding us that humans are goal seeking and interventions that facilitate goal setting have great potential for success.

Applications of SCT

SCT has been used to guide intervention development across a range of health problems and health behaviors (Logan et al., 2016; Nansel et al., 2009; Sevick et al., 2018; Simons-Morton, 2019). To illustrate the application of SCT to health promotion, we present two case studies. The first application is a weight-loss program for obese women (Annesi, 2019). The second is the prevention of motor vehicle crashes among newly licensed adolescents (Simons-Morton, 2019).

Diet and Physical Activity Self-Regulation Change Among Obese Women

A group-randomized trial was conducted with obese women to evaluate the effect of interventions on self-regulation of eating and physical activity behavior. Community health-promotion centers were randomized to groups, with interventions delivered by wellness instructors. Group 1 received weight-loss information and telephone counseling delivered over 28 weeks. Group 2 participants received six 45-minute sessions over 58 weeks that emphasized goal setting, self-monitoring, performance feedback, identification of barriers and cues, self-talk/cognitive restructuring, and calorie counting. The program included a combination of individual and group sessions designed to increase knowledge and skills (behavioral capability), increase self-efficacy, alter expectations, increase reinforcement, and modify the environment to reduce barriers to physical activity and diet change. Group 3 participants received the same intervention as Group 2, plus five conference calls designed to reinforce self-regulation conducted 8 weeks apart that extended the program to 98 weeks. Significant improvements in emotional eating, negative mood, self-regulation for diet, physical activity, and body composition were found in each group, with significantly larger effect sizes for Groups 2 and 3.

This program is of particular interest not only for its success, which is rare for weight-loss programs, but also because it illustrates the utility of SCT variables, such as goal setting, behavioral capability, self-efficacy, outcome expectations, and reinforcement, and other self-regulatory skills, including self-monitoring, stimulus control, feedback, and self-talk (Berkman, 2016; Carver & Scheir, 2016). The interventions were delivered by skilled health-promotion professionals. The clever intervention methods were based on social cognitive and behavioral theory and sought to facilitate self-regulation. The combination of self-management practices with instruction and feedback over a 1- to 2-year period proved useful in establishing self-regulatory behaviors for physical activity and diet.

Checkpoints Program to Prevent Motor Vehicle Crashes Among Young Drivers

Motor vehicle crashes are the leading cause of death and disability among adolescents (National Center for Statistics and Analysis, 2018). Newly licensed teens are at particular risk due to young age, inexperience, and risk taking. Therefore, novices should drive only under less-risky driving conditions (Simons-Morton, 2019). **Graduated driver licensing** (GDL) is a successful policy innovation designed to reduce exposure by limiting the number of passengers, late night driving, and texting during a provisional licensing stage (Curry, Foss, & Williams, 2017). The effectiveness of GDL policies relies mainly on parents for enforcement, but parents tend not to set and manage limits as strictly as they should (Simons-Morton, 2019).

The Checkpoints Program was developed to increase parental management of teen driving during provisional licensure. The program is based on SCT and consists of a videotape (*Who Wants to Be a Driver?*), persuasive newsletters, and the Checkpoints Parent–Teen Driving Agreement. The video follows the successful experience of several families (models) as they employ the Checkpoints Parent–Teen Driving Agreement with their newly licensed adolescent. The video and newsletters are designed to increase adoption of a parent–teen driving agreement by creating favorable outcome expectations, including threat and coping appraisal, self-efficacy, social norms, and perceived relative advantages. Agreements are a useful type of method for (1) establishing goals that direct behavior in specific ways, and (2) clarifying fair and realistic expectations and the conditions of reinforcement.

The efficacy and effectiveness of the Checkpoints Program have been demonstrated in multiple randomized trials, including two conducted at licensing offices and one conducted in driver education (Simons-Morton, 2019). The Checkpoints Program provided SCT-based methods (see **Table 4.2**), including persuasive communications (video, booklet, mailings, and emails) and a parent–teen driving agreement designed to increase the limits parents set on high-risk driving among newly licensed teenagers. In one study program effects were mediated by changes in risk perception and outcome expectations. The results of these studies show that it is possible to increase risk perceptions and outcome expectations for parental management and that these changes lead to increased limits on novice teen driving (Simons-Morton, 2019).

Table 4.2 The Checkpoints Program to Increase the Limits Parents Set on High-Risk Driving Among Newly Licensed Teenagers

Construct	Context	Intervention
Environment	Parent limits provide safety; how to make parent limit setting a part of the novice driver experience?	Implement intervention in motor vehicle licensing and driver ed settings; create environment where parent limit setting is normative
Situation	How to take advantage of the teachable moment of teen eligibility for licensure when parents are concerned about safety?	Emphasize teen driving risk, benefits of parent limits, and then have parent–teen dyads negotiate agreement
Goal setting	Most parents have no goals for teen driving.	Use the driving agreement to provide context for goal setting
Reinforcement	Parents are reinforced by teen for privileges, not limits; how to reinforce parents for setting limits and minimize negative teen reactions?	Modeling and vicarious reinforcement; provide models for vicarious reinforcement; use the agreement to reinforce parents for setting limits and grant teens additional driving privileges for safe performance
Observational learning	How to provide models of other families dealing with driving limits?	Parents and teens observe others on video and in persuasive communications (PCs) negotiating agreement, reporting satisfaction
Behavioral capability	How to provide negotiation skills for use in negotiating the agreement?	Provide clear and specific instructions; opportunities for practice with feedback
Expectancies	How to increase the expectation of limits and benefits of limit setting?	Use vicarious modeling, information about risk and benefits, testimonials from successful families
Self-efficacy	How to increase confidence in ability to negotiate and maintain restrictions?	Use modeling, instructions, practice in negotiating and maintaining limits
Social norms	How to create social norms that favor parent limit setting?	Provide models and testimonials in video, PC, and information about the prevalence of parent limit setting

Lessons for Public Health Practice

SCT is a grand theory of goal-directed behavior that incorporates cognitive and operant principles in a model of self-regulation called reciprocal determinism. Reciprocal determinism suggests that behavior, environment, and person interact dynamically on goal-directed behavior. The environment shapes behavior, and behavior interprets the reinforcing potential of consequences, while also shaping the environment. The cognitive and affective aspects of the person interpret and store experience uniquely. The person reacts to environmental stimuli and behavioral consequences in somewhat unique ways based on past experience, personality, and personal goals. SCT posits that skill and expectations are central cognitive determinants of behavior. Social influences affect behavior directly through feedback and reinforcement and indirectly through norms and expectations. SCT fits well as a general theory of behavior, with principles that have been adopted by many other behavior theories that have been developed for more narrow purposes. Therefore, it is not uncommon for SCT to be paired with another cognitive theory in multilevel programs, particularly reinforcement- and self-regulation-related theories. Among the many important take-home messages are the following:

1. Reciprocal determinism between the environment, behavior, and the person is the grand concept of SCT. The interaction between the constructs results in a feedback loop that characterizes self-regulation of goal-directed behavior.
2. SCT integrates the concepts of operant condition with those of cognitive psychology and social psychology to explain how self-regulatory processes operate for the self-management of goal-directed behavior.
3. Each person is viewed as having unique goals, personality, and capabilities. The person is influenced by opportunity, situational context, and reinforcement, but responds uniquely to these environmental circumstances.
4. Opportunity provides experience, from which people learn mainly from the experience. People who have not had certain experiences have less information on which to base expectancies.
5. Behavior is largely the product of reinforcement based on past experience. Behavior provides feedback that informs future behavior.
6. Informative feedback from the environment due to behavioral responses is stored in memory and used to determine the conditions and likelihood of future reinforcement.
7. Each person responds uniquely to their environment based on past experience and personal factors such as personality.
8. Behavioral capability, self-efficacy, and outcome expectations are important cognitive determinants of health behavior.
9. Self-regulation methods such as goal setting, feedback, and self-reinforcement facilitate goal-directed behavior by improving self-efficacy, behavioral capability, and outcome expectations.
10. While personal experience is a great teacher, observational (vicarious) learning also occurs. We apply to our own behavior what we learn by observing the behavior of others and their consequences.
11. Social norms influence our behavior through perceived expectations regarding likely social reinforcement.

Discussion Questions

1. Define and describe the elements of reciprocal interaction.
2. How do people learn from experience?
3. How does SCT define the person separate from behavior? Is this a useful concept?
4. What have you ever learned from observation?
5. Define self-efficacy, and apply the concept to a specific health behavior.

References

Annesi, J. J. (2019). Relationship of emotional eating and mood change through self-regulation within three behavioral treatments for obesity. *Psychology Reports*, *122*(5), 1689–1706. DOI: 10.1177/0033294118795883

Bandura, A. (1986). *Social foundations of thought and action: A social cognitive theory*. Upper Saddle River, NJ: Prentice Hall.

Bandura, A. (1997). *Self-efficacy: The exercise of control*, New York: Freeman.

Berkman, E. T. (2016). Self-regulation training. In R. Vohs & K. Baumeister (Eds.), *Handbook of self-regulation: Research, theory, and applications* (3rd ed., pp. 440–457). New York: Guilford Press.

Blair, C. (2016). Bidirectional psychobiological model. In R. Vohs & K. Baumeister (Eds.), *Handbook of self-regulation: Research, theory, and applications* (3rd ed., pp. 417–439). New York: Guilford Press.

Brooks, E. J., & Wilson, D. R. (2018). Car seats. *International Journal of Childbirth Education*, *33*(2), 36–38.

Carver, C. S., & Scheir, M. F. (2016). Self-regulation of action and affect. In R. Vohs & K. Baumeister (Eds.), *Handbook of self-regulation: Research, theory, and applications* (3rd ed., pp. 1–23). New York: Guilford Press.

Curry, A. E., Foss, R. D., & Williams, A. F. (2017). Graduated driver licensing for older novice drivers: Critical analysis of the issues. *American Journal of Preventive Medicine*, *53*(6), 923–927. DOI: 10.1016/j.amepre.2017.06.014

Kahneman, D. (2011). *Thinking fast and slow*, New York: Farrar, Straus and Giroux.

Kazdin, A. E. (2020). *Behavior modification in applied settings* (8th ed.). Long Grove, IL: Waveland Press.

Kersbergen, I., Oldham, M., Jones, A., Field, M., Angus, C., & Robinson, E. (2018). Reducing the standard serving size of alcoholic beverages prompts reductions in alcohol consumption. *Addiction*, *113*, 1598–1608. DOI: 10.1111/add.14228

Logan, C., Zittel, T., Striebel, S., Reister, F., Brenner, H., Rothenbacher, D., & Genuneit, J. (2016). Changing societal and lifestyle factors and breastfeeding patterns over time. *Pediatrics*, *137*(5), e20154473. DOI: 10.1542/peds.2015-4473

Nansel, T. R, Iannotti, R. J., Simons-Morton, B., Plotnick, L. P., Clark, L. M., & Zeitzoff, L. (2009). Long-term maintenance of treatment outcomes: "Diabetes Personal Trainer" intervention for youth with type 1 diabetes. *Diabetes Care*, *32*, 807–809.

National Center for Statistics and Analysis. (2018). Traffic safety facts: Young drivers. DOT HS 812 498 Retrieved from https://crashstats.nhtsa.dot.gov/Api/Public/ViewPublication/812498

O'Brien, F., Simons-Morton, B., Chaurasia, A., Luk, J., Haynie, D., & Liu, D. (2018). Post-high school changes in tobacco and cannabis use in the United States. *Substance Use and Misuse*, *53*(1), 26–35. PMID: 28742412. PMCID: PMC6300995.

Osberg, T. M., & Boyer, A. (2018). College alcohol beliefs and drinking consequences: A multiple mediation analysis of norms, expectancies, and willingness to experience drinking consequences. *Journal of the American College Health Association*, *66*(3), 209–218. DOI: 10.1080/07448481.2018.1431893

Scott-Sheldon, L. A., Terry, D. L., Carey, K. B., Garey, L., & Carey, M. P. (2012). Efficacy of expectancy change interventions to reduce college student drinking: A meta-analytic review. *Psychology of Addictive Behavior*, *26*(3), 393–405. DOI: 10.1037/a0027565

Sevick, M. A., Woolf, K., Mattoo, A., Katz, S. D., Li, H., St-Jules, D. E., . . . Goldfarb, D. S. (2018). Health hearts and kidneys (HHK) study: Design of a 2 x 2 RCT of technology-supported self-monitoring and social cognitive theory-based counseling to engage overweight people with diabetes and chronic kidney disease in multiple lifestyle change. *Contemporary Clinical Trials*, *64*, 265–273. DOI: 10.1016/j.cct.2017.08.020

Simons-Morton, B. (2019). Keeping young drivers safe during early licensure. RAC Foundation. Retrieved from https://www.racfoundation.org/wp-content/uploads/Keeping_Young_Drivers_Safe_During_Early_Licensure_Dr_Bruce_Simons-Morton_September_2019.pdf

Simons-Morton, B. G., Brink, S., & Bates, D. (1987). Effectiveness and cost effectiveness of persuasive communications and incentives in increasing safety belt use. *Health Education Quarterly*, *14*(2), 167–179.

Simons-Morton, B. G., & Farhat, T. (2010). Recent findings on peer group influences on adolescent smoking. *Journal of Primary Prevention, 31*, 191–208. DOI: 10.1007/s10935-010-0220-x

Simons-Morton, B. G., Haynie, D., & Noelke, E. (2009). Social influences: The effects of socialization, selection, and social normative processes on health behavior. In R. DiClemente (Ed.), *Emerging theories in health behavior and health promotion* (pp. 65–96). San Francisco: Jossey-Bass.

Vohs, K. D., & Baumeister, R. F. (Eds.). (2016). *Handbook of self-regulation: Research, theory and applications*. New York: The Guilford Press.

Walther, C. A. P., Pedersen, S. L., Cheong, J. W., & Molina, B. S. G. (2017). Role of alcohol expectancies in the associations between close friend, typical college student, and personal alcohol use. *Substance Use & Misuse, 52*(12), 1656–1666. DOI: 10.1080/10826084 .2017.1306561

CHAPTER 5

Self-Determination Theory and Motivational Interviewing

An appropriate sense of control over life events is a basic human need.

OUTLINE

1. Preview
2. Objectives
3. Introduction
4. Self-Determination Theory Elements
   4.1. Psychological Needs
       4.1.1. Autonomy
       4.1.2. Competence
       4.1.3. Relatedness
       4.1.4. Individual Differences
   4.2. External and Internal Motivation
       4.2.1. External (Controlled) Motivation
       4.2.2. Internal (Autonomous) Motivation
       4.2.3. SDT Examples
5. Motivational Interviewing (MI)
   5.1. MI Assumptions
   5.2. MI Methods
       5.2.1. Open-Ended Questions
       5.2.2. Reflective Listening
       5.2.3. Affirming
       5.2.4. Verbal Summary
       5.2.5. Change Talk
   5.3. MI Spirit
       5.3.1. Conditions for Change
       5.3.2. Overcoming Ambivalence
   5.4. MI Process
       5.4.1. Detachment
       5.4.2. Empathy
       5.4.3. Listening
       5.4.4. Discrepancy
       5.4.5. Rolling with Resistance
       5.4.6. Empowerment and Self-Efficacy
   5.5. MI Example: The Personal Trainer Study
6. The Marriage of SDT and MI
7. Lessons for Public Health Practice
8. Application Exercise
9. Discussion Questions
10. References

PREVIEW

Self-Determination Theory (SDT) and Motivational Interviewing (MI) are concerned with internal motivation—understanding its nature and fostering increases in self-directed behavior. Both perspectives were derived from client-centered psychotherapy, and both are now employed increasingly in the field of public health. SDT is often considered the theoretical basis for MI.

OBJECTIVES

The thoughtful reader of this chapter will be able to:

1. Identify the elements of motivation from the perspective of SDT.
2. Identify and describe the three key psychological needs in SDT.
3. Explain how psychological needs affect motivation.
4. Explain how intrinsic motivation develops.
5. Identify the elements of motivation from the perspective of SDT.
6. Describe how SDT supports MI goals and methods.
7. Distinguish internal (controlled) and external (autonomous) motivation.
8. Explain the purpose of MI.
9. Identify and describe five important MI methods.
10. Define ambivalence and explain its central role in MI
11. Describe empathy.
12. Explain and give examples of rolling with resistance.

Introduction

While there are many theories of behavior, only a few claim to be comprehensive. Most theories are satisfied to deal with certain kinds of behavior or certain types of influences on behavior. Among the grand behavior theories that emphasize the important roles of the environment, personality, and cognition, only Social Cognitive Theory (SCT) provides an explanation of human behavior that is as comprehensive as self-determination theory. While SCT has been part of the training of most psychology and public health students for at least the past three decades, Self-Determination Theory (SDT) has only recently gained substantial recognition outside certain research and psychotherapy communities. Fortunately,

in recent years, SDT has become increasingly popular and influential in psychology and public health.

SDT provides a comprehensive explanation of behavior that has many implications for intervention. SDT is similar to SCT in its emphasis on certain cognitive variables (i.e., self-efficacy), but its primary contribution is its orientation to how interventions should be delivered. Given its emphasis on **intrinsic** motivation, SDT orients the interventionist toward guidance and reflection rather than direct instruction. Many scholars have noted the similarities between SDT and **Motivational Interviewing** (MI). MI is an approach to counseling that seeks to emphasize intrinsic motivation. Therefore, it is now fairly common to consider SDT as a foundational theory for MI.

Both SDT and MI are grounded in the appreciation for intrinsic motivation and client-centered counseling first developed and propounded by Carl Rogers (1951). Rogers was a celebrated educator and psychotherapist in the humanistic psychology tradition who revolutionized counseling methodology by developing the client-centered counseling approach that was widely adopted in education and psychology. Humanistic psychology applies existential and phenomenological philosophy to human development. It adopts a holistic approach to human existence through investigations of meaning, values, freedom, personal responsibility, human potential, and self-actualization. Rogers's client-centered counseling was based on the notion that people are motivated to self-actualize but get stuck in the process. Self-actualization is a term popularized by Abraham Maslow (1954), another post-Freudian theorist. Maslow defined self-actualization as a process of human development in service of self-fulfillment to realize one's capabilities.

Rogers found that he could be most effective not by telling clients how to solve their problems, but by providing genuine warmth, positive regard, and empathy. He found that clients responded to this approach by opening themselves up to their feelings and hopes, which served as an initial and essential first step in personal growth. One of the revolutionary implications for Rogers's work was that the primary training for counselors and educators was in personal development, not in counseling strategies and methods. To be a good counselor and educator, one needed to be genuine, warm, empathetic, and accepting of their clients and students. Becoming a good counselor or educator meant becoming a good person, and by engaging in the process of self-actualization, one learns to be a good counselor. These principles profoundly influence counseling and education, have been incorporated into a variety of training and practice approaches, and are essential in public health practice.

MI is revolutionary in its development of communication methods that can be used to facilitate change within a Rogerian context. In MI the emphasis on the development of the counselor/educator is less implicit, although probably the more "together" the interventionist, the better able to develop **empathy** and positive regard for clients and students. Nonetheless, while MI is not simple or easy to learn, it does provide very specific communication skills based on Rogerian principles that have been demonstrated to facilitate behavior change.

In short, SDT provides a comprehensive theory of behavior in the humanistic tradition of Rogers, and MI provides a comprehensive set of methods based on the Rogerian tradition that have been demonstrated to facilitate change. While both SDT and MI can stand on their own, we believe it makes sense to discuss them in the same chapter, given their common roots and close compatibility. Because SDT and MI share many common characteristics, SDT is commonly thought of as a key theoretical foundation for MI, and MI is increasingly thought of as an important approach for operationalizing the principles of SDT. Increasingly public health professionals are employing SDT

theory and MI methods to better engage with populations of interest.

In this chapter, we provide general descriptions of SDT and MI and brief elaborations of their major constructs. We then describe how SDT provides a theoretical basis of MI, describe how SDT and MI can be used in public health, and provide an example of a successful health-promotion program based on these principles.

Self-Determination Theory Elements

SDT is a macrotheory in that it is an integration of a series of smaller theories. Its development grew out of a frustration with the limits of operant conditioning. Deci and Ryan (2008; Ryan & Deci, 2017), the developers of SDT, recognized that reinforcement and environmental contingencies are powerful influences on behavior, but were frustrated when contingencies were removed and behavior sometimes reverted to the previous state. They concluded that sustained behavior change depends on internal as well as external factors. Thus, for Deci and Ryan began the effort to better understand, explain, and promote self-sustained behavior.

SDT assumes that people are actively directed towards personal growth, as shown in **Figure 5.1**. Similar to Maslow, SDT suggests that people are motivated to grow and change by innate **psychological needs** (Deci & Flaste, 1995). SDT also assumes that gaining mastery over challenges and taking in new experiences are essential for developing a cohesive sense of self. SDT has been compared to SCT because mastery experiences, outcome expectations, and self-efficacy are important in the development of intrinsic motivation. If individuals feel confident in their ability and certain of the outcome, they are more motivated to try something new.

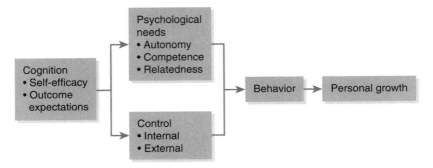

Figure 5.1 Elements of Self-Determination Theory

The growing popularity of SDT may be due in part to its clear and distinct constructs, as well as its success in addressing most of the fundamental issues of human development. For starters it provides cogent descriptions of personality, self-regulation, psychological needs, and life goals and their relationships to motivation, affect, self-regulation, and well-being. It provides explanations for how culture and social factors influence these fundamental developmental issues. It posits that people have basic psychological needs for autonomy, competence, and relatedness, and the extent to which these are satisfied over the life course determines their orientation toward causality and the extent to which their actions matter and their pursuit of life goals. Each of the many constructs in this paragraph refers to complicated themes that have been researched and written about extensively over the past 50 years.

Psychological Needs

SDT provides a comprehensive perspective on core psychological need constructs and integrates them into a broad theoretical orientation with many practical implications for education and psychology. SDT identifies three key psychological needs believed to be both innate and universal: (1) autonomy, (2) competence, and (3) relatedness (Deci & Ryan, 2008). Throughout one's life, from early childhood to the last decade of life, people are motivated by these basic needs. Satisfaction of these needs

is presumed to result in optimal functioning and psychological well-being, while frustration in achieving these needs can lead to dysfunction, poor psychological health, and life dissatisfaction.

Autonomy

Autonomy refers to the perception of control over one's own behavior. People need to feel in control of their own behavior and goals. Autonomy enables action that is consistent with one's values. Autonomy is not exactly the same thing as independence, because a person can behave in an autonomous manner and still be dependent on others for advice and influence. It means having a sense of free will. Autonomy is the sense that ultimately, decisions and behavior are under one's control. This is best viewed from the perspective of human development. Young children cannot be autonomous because they lack sufficient maturity and judgment and must rely on adults to guide and manage their behavior. However, even very young children can begin to develop autonomy over some aspects of their lives by being allowed to choose between prescreened options. Gradually, as children mature and develop better judgment and **self-control**, they can be allowed greater autonomy over their behavior. While this is a process that goes on throughout life, it is perhaps most dramatic during adolescence, when the need for autonomy and experimentation are great, along with the risks for self-damaging behavior. The parents of adolescents struggle to find the correct balance between control and autonomy. During the long developmental process each of us goes through, we develop a certain level of autonomy. Those who fail to develop autonomy are left with the psychological need for it, which is one of the driving forces for their behavior. The lack of autonomy and sense that life is controlled externally are particularly notable among people who engage in addictive and other self-defeating behaviors. Alternatively, developing a great sense of autonomy is an important step in change processes such as quitting smoking or other substance abuse.

Competence

The need for perceived **competence** is seen as basic to human development in SDT. The first of two components of competence is **locus of control**. The basic idea is that people develop a sense of internal or external control over the causes of phenomena. A generalized sense that what happens in their life is a matter of external control, which of course it often is to some extent, reduces motivation. Alternatively, the generalized perception that the causes of phenomena are internal may enhance motivation. Of course, neither extreme would be healthful, because we cannot control everything in our lives, but neither are we helpless. An appropriate sense of control over life events is a basic human need.

One important influence on perceived locus of control is perceived competence. When people perceive that they are capable and self-controlled, they tend to assume a more internal locus of control. Locus of control increases as people master tasks and develop skills. Because they have developed competence in other areas of life, success at school, making friends, getting along, learning new things, they face new challenges with confidence that they can influence the outcome. Ultimately, people want to know how things would turn out and the results of consequences of their actions. Moreover, the development of actual competence increases the sense of capability and motivation. With respect to addictive behaviors intervention, the goal is to develop competencies related to managing behavior, for example, seeking support, avoiding other users, monitoring triggers, and finding alternatives. As skills improve, the sense of control should also increase, providing the basis for change.

Relatedness

One of the basic human drives is to develop satisfactory relationships with others and experience a sense of belonging and attachment to other people. From the Freudian perspective, our relationships with our parents and other family members are extremely important because these are the models from which we learn about how to relate and develop the sense that we are connected with other people. Children's relationships with parents are complicated, of course, by the tension that exists between children's needs for autonomy and parents' responsibility to control their children's lives to protect them and guide them. Children must navigate this difficult path toward autonomy and eventually develop more mature relationships with their parents. Success in developing relationships with family and later with friends and colleagues gives one the sense of belonging and acceptance, which is inherently motivating. In general, our actions and daily activities involve other people, and through this we seek a sense of belonging. Failure in these relationships undermines intrinsic motivation to the extent the person is driven by the need for and insecurity about relatedness. Addictive behavior is facilitated by association with enablers and discouraged by genuine association with those who support freedom from addiction.

Individual Differences

According to SDT theory people vary mainly in the extent to which their needs for autonomy, competence, and relatedness have been satisfied or thwarted. Everyone has these needs, and almost no one experiences complete and constant satisfaction of these needs, but life is a process of seeking to fulfill these very basic needs. Those whose needs have been reasonably satisfied over the course of their life and are better able to achieve and maintain satisfaction of these needs are going to happier and more psychologically healthy than those who have been frustrated at achieving these basic needs and must constantly struggle to obtain needs satisfaction or who give up the effort. Those at the upper extreme of need satisfaction are unusually enlightened, and those at the lower extreme are highly susceptible to mental health and behavior problems and have the most work to do to lead a happy and productive life. In clinical and health-promotion applications of SDT, a primary goal is to facilitate individual achievement of these needs, mainly through a reorientation toward autonomous motivation.

External and Internal Motivation

As discussed in previous chapters, motivation is the tendency to behave in a certain way, and theories of behavior are generally concerned with motivation. When a study concludes that a particular belief, attitude, attribute, environmental factor, or other independent variable influenced behavior, it usually means that changes in the variable had an effect on motivation consistent with a change in behavior. Operant conditioning argues that motivation is the amount of reinforcement required to prompt a response. Social cognitive theory argues that motivation is the product of the reciprocal interactions between the person, environment, and behavior. The Theory of Reasoned Action measures motivation as one's intentions to take a particular action. Personality theories, in general, assume that the amount of motivation for particular actions is more or less genetic, or at least the

potential for certain preferences or tendencies is genetic, and the expression of these tendencies is a product of the environment, in what is known as gene–environment interaction. SDT distinguishes external or extrinsic motivation, called controlled motivation, from internal or intrinsic motivation, called autonomous motivation.

External (Controlled) Motivation

The first of several microtheories within SDT posits that individuals vary in terms of how they respond to environmental influences. Over time, as people are exposed to environmental constraints and external regulations on their behavior from parents and other family members, school, and other sources, they internalize these influences. Initially external environmental factors that regulate behavior, including rules, laws, and social norms, influence behavior through external contingencies—rewards and punishments for following or not following regulations. This is basic operant conditioning.

SDT proposes that the effect of contingencies eventually is internalized, and the person is guided by what they "should" or "should not" do in particular contexts. Eventually, most people come to value these regulations and adopt them as their own. For example, children gradually develop fear of getting caught for doing something against the rules and eventually develop personal values consistent with the rules, which controls their behavior. This is an important form of self-regulation, without which individuals could not function independent of external control, and society would be unmanageable. In a society where people's behavior was controlled only by external rules, we would need police on every corner.

The reason we don't need police on every corner is because the vast majority of people have learned what the rules are, value them, and regulate their behavior to conform to them. This, of course, is a simplification of the pattern of normal development. For example, many adolescents experiment with tobacco, alcohol, and marijuana, which are against the rules. However, as they gain experience and get older, the rules change for them (e.g., smoking and drinking are legal for adults), and they develop mature dispositions about the less-strict rules about these drugs for adults, and they regulate their behavior accordingly. Eventually, the rules become valued, as the individual identifies with them and resolves inherent inconsistencies (e.g., I smoke but I don't favor allowing adolescents to smoke). This is why it is the common case that people who engage in risky behavior as adolescents find themselves as adults on the side of strict regulations that would discourage adolescent experimentation. Here the process has been described in a rather idealized way, when in reality it is a complicated process of gaining experience, obtaining feedback from that experience, and then over a long period of time integrating the results.

Controlled motivation is the product of external regulation, in which one's behavior is a function of the expected and immediate external rewards or punishments associated with an action and the internalization of the lifelong experience of being rewarded and punished for particular behaviors. This internalization of one's lifelong experience with reinforcement is energized by external factors such as the approval of others, the avoidance of shame, maintenance of self-esteem, and ego-involvement. Controlled motivation is experienced as pressure to think, feel, or behave as required. Everyone experiences controlled motivation, and to an extent it is the logical and appropriate outcome of a lifetime of socialization. From the time we are born until we die, other people and human institutions influence how we think, feel, and behave. This is not a bad thing entirely. It is probably useful, maybe even necessary, for people to conform to societal dictates.

The main point here, consistent with almost everything that is known about development and about environmental influences, is that people are influenced by their lifelong experiences with their social and physical environment and the contingencies associated with these experiences, but regulate their behavior only to the extent that they integrate these experiences and adopt values consistent with them. Children, for example, have not yet internalized their experiences with external regulations and rely on parents and other adults to control and guide them. Gradually, most children begin to develop elements of self-control and are able to deal with the environmental restraints of school and family. Over time, self-control develops with experience and maturational processes. Eventually, most young adults have adopted these social regulations as useful and personal, although perhaps with some individual variability in timing and interpretation.

Military training provides an excellent example of this process. Newly recruited soldiers are largely stripped of individual rights as part of basic training. They are almost completely controlled by the environment, from when they get up in the morning (before sunrise), to how much time they have for breakfast, how they get from one activity to another (on the double), how they address their superiors (sir/ma'am), and when they go to bed. Gradually, they gain little bits of freedom, such as the first afternoon weekend leave. By the end of 6 or 8 weeks of training, most recruits have fully adopted the regulations by which they will live as long as they are in the military. Those who are unable to conform or fail to adopt the values of a regimented life do not do well in the military.

Internal (Autonomous) Motivation

While everyone adapts to social contingencies because a certain level of adaptation is required to get along at home, succeed in school, and keep a job, most people are not completely controlled by external contingencies all of the time. Most people also develop some level of autonomous control. While a certain level of controlled motivation is necessary to get along in society, a certain level of autonomous control is necessary for psychological health and self-directed behavior. Autonomous control allows people to pursue their interests and not simply conform to societal demands. Controlled and autonomous motivations exist within each individual in some balance that is unique to each person. Autonomous motivation is thought to be the product of the satisfaction of basic psychological needs for autonomy, competence, and relatedness. Controlled motivation derives from partial satisfaction of basic needs. When basic needs are very poorly satisfied, impersonal motivation occurs, which is highly selfish, guided neither by external regulations nor internal efforts to create, achieve, and connect. Impersonal motivation is associated with antisocial behavior and psychological pathology.

While controlled motivation is **extrinsic**, autonomous motivation is intrinsic, deriving from one's personal needs, interests, and wants (Freud would say drives) and from one's identification with the value of a particular activity and its integration into one's sense of self. Both controlled motivation and autonomous motivation exist within each person, and both are necessary for a balanced life. People may exercise regularly in part because they receive external reinforcement from others and in part because they identify with exercise as something they value and that is meaningful to them (e.g., autonomous or intrinsic motivation). Other people may be unmotivated with respect to exercise, experiencing neither external nor internal motivation in sufficient quantities to do it regularly.

SDT lends itself usefully to counseling and MI (later discussed in this chapter) because there are steps to stimulate intrinsic motivation. When working with individuals, it's important to identify and nurture the individual's wants and needs. Moreover, the individual should engage in active participation in decision making and be given choices, not ideas dictated to them. This is key to the construct of autonomy. Internal states should guide behavior. It is also important to provide optimal challenges to increase competence. Last, to increase relatedness, individuals need emotional support, positive and constructive feedback, and most important, acknowledgment of their challenges and negativity is met with empathy.

SDT Examples

SDT has been widely used in public health research. SDT has established itself as a useful theory to increase motivation in the exercise domain (Bartholomew, Ntoumanis, & Thogersen-Ntoumani, 2009). Hancox, Quested, Ntoumanis, and Thogersen-Ntoumani (2018) found that SDT strategies implemented in group exercise increased participation. Creating a structured program improved competence, and providing meaningful one-on-one instruction and support increased relatedness. The foundation of SDT has also helped dentists lower patients' dental anxiety by supporting the constructs of autonomy, relatedness, and competence through feedback, choices in their care, and empathy and support (Halvari, Halvari, & Deci, 2018). Moreover, SDT has been used to increase motivation, achievement, and well-being using m-learning (Jeno, Adachi, Grytnes, Vandvik, & Deci, 2019) and to even predict binge-watching behaviors (Adachi, Ryan, Frye, McClurg, & Rigby, 2018). For health-promotion specialists, SDT provides a useful way of understanding particular populations, enabling empathy and mutual respect.

SDT has now been employed across a range of behaviors, mostly intractable problems like problematic drinking and other addictions, and increasingly for public health problems such as diet, physical activity, hypertension, and diabetes (Deci & Ryan, 2002;

Sheldon, Joiner, & Williams, 2003). SDT has also been employed successfully to improve learning, persistence, positive mood, cooperative behavior and improved social functioning (Burke, Arkowitz, & Menchola, 2003; Deci & Ryan, 2002).

Motivational Interviewing (MI)

SDT was initially developed as a counseling approach for problem drinking that could be done in a limited number of sessions, rather than extensive psychotherapy. Problem drinking had long been recognized as an intractable problem, with low success rates and frequent recidivism. The idea was to quickly activate patients' motivation for change and adherence, because external methods did seem to work for a large number of problem drinkers. The key was to figure out how to tap into patients' internal motivation for change, and the individual is guided to make their own decisions regarding their health and lifestyle (Miller & Rollnick, 2013). The need to promote internal motivation in a short period of time applies to many public health situations, including, for example, counseling mothers to put their babies to sleep on their backs and in car seats when riding in a vehicle.

A series of studies showed that external reinforcement sometimes undermined task-engagement, initiative, and self-management because people who feel controlled by external factors may not enjoy or value the task for its own sake (Deci and Ryan, 2002; Ryan & Deci, 2017). This is not to suggest that operant conditioning and cognitive behavior management do not work, because there is ample evidence that they are highly effective. However, these approaches are not always effective and even when effective can sometimes have limited long-term success. Hence, at least for some individuals, and possibly for all, a more person-centered approach may be warranted.

MI Assumptions

While SDT was developed as a comprehensive theory of motivation, MI is primarily a set of counseling methods that developed over time by thoughtful psychologists working with difficult clients, many of whom had previously failed to change, despite efforts to do so. MI lacked a comprehensive theory of behavior, but was committed to the Rogerian (Rogers, 1951) approaches that shifted the emphasis from the counselor to the client. It was not the counselor who needed to make the client change, but the clients who were in control over their own behavior. It was up to the client to change, while the counselor's or educator's job was to serve as a guide. Gradually a set of methods developed that reflected the Rogerian spirit of collaboration, evocation, and detachment. The MI approach and methods grew out of a dissatisfaction with operant and cognitive approaches that emphasized contingencies and changing one's mental outlook by managing one's thoughts. MI makes the following assumptions:

- We can enhance but not impose intrinsic motivation.
- MI is collaborative between the client and the counselor.
- Persuasion is not an effective communication style.
- Clients must be willing to discuss their ambivalence for the relationship to be effective.
- Supporting self-efficacy and expressing empathy are useful in eliciting discussion about change.

MI Methods

Motivational Interviewing (MI) is firmly rooted in the client-centered approach developed by the great psychologist, Carl Rogers (1951), who described the counseling process as one of guidance. Rogers emphasized that guidance within an interpersonal context of warmth and regard can facilitate intrinsic motivation to change. Accordingly, the instructor or counselor collaborates with the individual's perspectives and autonomy, develops an understanding of motivations, and provides the conditions for personal growth and autonomous change (Schumacher & Madson, 2015). The purpose is to facilitate positive behavior change to promote health and reduce chronic disease risk. MI helps identify a person's sources of ambivalence, clarify values, and get unstuck.

MI is primarily concerned with **ambivalence**, described as the state in which change is perceived as desirable, but not quite worth the effort. MI describes ambivalence as "being stuck," that condition in which a person wants to change but also wants not to change. Partly, ambivalence is the product of competing motivations that render the individual unable to move on, unsatisfied with the current state, but unable to see a clear path ahead or to take action to change. We have all experienced the state where we consider making a change in our behavior, for example, increasing the amount we exercise, quitting smoking, reducing alcohol or marijuana, losing weight, changing our diets, getting medical care, but we don't do it or we don't stick with it. We want to act, but we also want not to. MI proposes that motivation to change can be increased by information and guidance. Ambivalence is a stage followed by commitment and action. In this phase, MI methods are designed to strengthen commitment to change and develop and implement a change plan. Of course, the client is liable to vacillate between ambivalence and commitment.

MI was initially developed and evaluated as a treatment for addiction, but it has been used in public health increasing over time (Miller & Rollnick, 2013; Schumacher & Madson, 2015). Effective MI-based interventions have been conducted in areas such as addiction, adherence, HIV risk, diet, and physical activity (Martin-Perez et al., 2019).

MI seeks to help people identify the pros and cons of behavior change and overcome ambivalence as they consider their behavior in relation to norms and possible strategies for overcoming ambivalence. MI relies on particular methods of communication to accomplish these goals. These methods include asking open-ended questions, listening reflectively, affirming, and summarizing, and change talk. These methods may seem entirely intuitive and simple, but employing them correctly within the dynamics of interpersonal interactions is actual quite difficult and requires substantial practice. Indeed, professional training is available for the seriously interested, including from the government agency Substance Abuse and Mental Health Services Administration (SAMHSA, 2010).

Open-Ended Questions

Open-ended questions allow the client to do most of the talking. Rather than the counselor instructing the client, the counselor serves as a guide, using open-ended questions (e.g., questions that cannot be answered yes or no) to elicit the client's concerns and ambivalence. Examples include, "Can you tell me more?" "How do you feel about that?" "How has it been going?" "What would you like to do?" "What would help you with that?' "What concerns do you have?" "What are some reasons for that?"

Reflective Listening

Reflective listening restates what the client said. This puts the focus on the client's perspective. Communication is complicated, and people cannot and do not always communicate what they mean accurately. Reflective communication clarifies what the client says without adding the counselor's external frame of reference. Reflection often includes repeating or rephrasing an element of what the client said. Examples of reflective listening questions include, "So, part of you really wants to change (e.g., stop smoking, wear a condom, exercise more often, take your medicine), and another part feels unsure whether you can do it right now." "I hear you say you really like exercising, but it is difficult to get started." Communicating in this manner takes a little practice, but generally can be mastered without extremely intensive and time-consuming training, practice, and feedback.

Affirming

Affirming statements encourage and support. It can be highly rewarding to be understood by another person. Therefore, affirming understanding or appreciating what the client is saying and experiencing is useful. Examples of affirming statements include the following: "You must care a lot about that." "It seems you are working very hard on this." "That sounds complicated." "That must be difficult." "That seems like a good idea."

Verbal Summary

After a time, the counselor provides a verbal summary of their discussion that attempts to link and emphasize the main points. Examples include "So you plan to change a little bit at a time?" "It seems you mainly want more social support for your efforts." "If you were successful, what would be different in your life?" "Am I hearing you correctly that you would like to change that?" Summaries demonstrate attention and provide opportunities to identify and reinforce "change talk."

Change Talk

Change talk is directive and possible only when empathetic communications described have fostered considerable rapport. Open-ended questions are used to elicit from the client thoughts about change, things they might want to change, and ideas for changing. Change talk consists of statements that reflect desire, perceived ability, need, readiness, reasons, or commitment to change. Examples of elicited change talk include, "If I changed my... health would improve; I would feel better about my self; it would make my wife

happier." "I want to change." "I am going to try." "I can make this change." "I intend to change." The counselor then explores these ideas with the client and provides summaries that collect change talk themes.

MI Spirit

The basic spirit of MI is collaborative, evocative, and honoring. It is collaborative in the sense that the counselor or educator seeks to involve the client in a joint decision-making process, recognizing that most change, or at least sustained change, can occur when the client takes responsibility. MI is evocative in that it seeks to evoke from clients their own motivation and resources, rather than imposing these from the outside. The idea is that each person is motivated by their goals, values, aspirations, and dreams, and a goal of MI is to connect the change to what the client values. Naturally, this can only be done if the counselor or teacher understands the client's perspectives and concerns. MI encourages the counselor or teacher to be detached from the outcomes, accepting, even honoring requires prioritizing clients' autonomy over their behavior. The counselor can inform, advise, encourage, but only the client can decide about, commit to, and enact change. Whatever the client decides is honored by the counselor. Implicit in this approach is the recognition that clients and learners have the right not to change.

Conditions for Change

Rather than prescribing change, MI seeks to create the conditions for change. The counselors, health-promotion specialists, health coach, and other interventionists are key to this process, and they are likely to be successful to the extent they are able to develop a relationship with the patient, client, or learner. From the partnership perspective, the counselors avoid argumentation or persuasion with the client. The interaction is different because the traditional role of the professional being the expert and the client being the recipient of the expertise is reversed. MI sees the client as the expert of their own lives, and the process is collaborative with the counselor (Koutsenok, 2012). MI includes specific communication and relationship strategies that must be mastered and employed with great skill and flexibility. However, just learning these skills may not be enough. To foster the spirit of MI, one must be truly collaborative, confident in the client, and accepting of their autonomy. This may seem easy, but it is actually quite difficult, particularly for those trained to promote change through the force of their energy and persuasive abilities. Trained professionals in MI use the client-centered approach to enhance intrinsic motivation and resolve ambivalence (Koutsenok, 2012).

Overcoming Ambivalence

Often, people want to change, but also want not to change. Ambivalence is one of the major reasons people do not change behaviors they wish to change. Many people, perhaps all of us some of the time, suffer from ambivalence, which can be debilitating or at least can impede progress. This is true for many smokers, who would like to quit, overweight people who would like to lose weight, couch potatoes who want to get fit, and patients who would like to better manage their health problems. To a smoker, cigarettes and the process of smoking are rewarding, although mostly they know that it is bad for their health. They may also know that it is not easy to quit, and this impedes their efforts to try. So it is with many behavioral problems and even everyday activities—studying, seeking preventive health care, eating a more balanced diet, and drinking less alcohol. Virtually all cognitive theories of behavior recognize that people experience ambivalence in the form of competing beliefs, attitudes, and values (e.g., smokers may value the freedom and enjoyment they get from smoking and also value their health). Some theories suggest methods for overcoming ambivalence. For example, balance sheet

activities are commonly employed as a way for people to identify and consider their ambivalence. From an operant conditioning perspective, balance sheet activities are useful for identifying competing sources and values of reinforcement. In the transtheoretical model, balance sheet activities are used to bring out aspects of ambivalence at particular **stages of change**. However, perhaps no other approach considers and appreciates ambivalence to the extent that MI does. MI considers ambivalence to be a natural part of the human condition and is fundamentally concerned with fostering resolution of ambivalence to the extent that it impedes the pursuit of personal goals.

MI Process

A number of core principles have come to be associated with MI, although they have been employed in various forms within many counseling approaches. These include **detachment**, empathy, listening, discrepancy, rolling with resistance, and support for self-efficacy. Clearly, these principles are completely consistent with appropriate public health practice.

Detachment

One of the things that draw people to the fields of public health, medicine, and psychology is a sincere desire to help others. When we see our patients, clients, and other populations of interest engaging in self-defeating behavior, damaging their health and feeling badly, our inclination is to help them, telling them how they should do it and trying to persuade them to change. This is the righting reflex—telling people how to behave. This is both natural and often effective with people who are already motivated to change and not overly ambivalent. But with many others persuasion is not always effective and can have the perverse effect of increasing resistance. Traditional persuasive approaches to fostering change may not get at the ambivalence the person is experiencing. Often the person already knows all the good reasons to change. Rather than using persuasion, MI seeks to engage the individual in the process of understanding the nature of their ambivalence and identifying for themselves the relative advantages of change. The idea is to get the individual to voice or document the arguments for change. Curiously, the key is for the health professional to genuinely care about the individual but be detached from specific outcomes. As long as the health professional is invested in obtaining certain outcomes, the individual cannot feel that they have autonomy over their behavior. This is a lot more difficult than it might seem.

Let's say you are working with unmarried teenage mothers to delay another early, unplanned pregnancy. You really want to help these girls because you know that delaying a subsequent pregnancy by even a year can make a huge difference in future economic and health outcomes. You both want to prevent or delay an unplanned pregnancy, but young girls have other needs and wants that can undermine their good intentions. Your effectiveness depends on providing these girls with the tools to change, while recognizing their autonomy and resisting the righting reflex.

Empathy

The reason empathy is so important in MI is that it is the basis for the relationship between the health professional and the individual. Empathy is a major element of trust. Individuals are unlikely to reveal their perceptions and motivations to a health professional unless they develop a sense of being accepted for who there are and confidence that they will not be criticized or looked down upon. Empathy is not simply a matter of health professionals saying they understand what the individual is saying and why they are ambivalent. Empathy, in the MI sense, is personally accepting and valuing the individual, with all the problems and inconsistencies involved. It's the ability to understand the individual's cognitions, motions, and behaviors. This is not as easy as it might sound at first. Most of us are personally offended when our patients

and students fail us by not living up to our expectations. It can even be difficult to accept the failings and shortcomings of our closest friends and family members. Empathy must be genuine to be effective. Empathy is a matter of attitude and affect that can require substantial training and effort. Empathy is natural to most of us in public health, but demonstrating our empathy effectively is a skill that MI emphasizes.

Listening

The purpose of listening is to foster disclosure. Listening, actively listening to what another says, at least as required in MI, is quite difficult and surprisingly rare. Listening involves empathic interest in what the individual says, believes, feels, and wants. Listening requires the health professional to ask questions that get at key issues, that engages the individual in the process of identifying their concerns and perspectives and encourages them to identify acceptable courses of action. The health professional can provide information, support, and alternative perspectives in an effort to help the individual clarify their motivation for change. Okay, maybe listening does not seem like something that needs to be learned and practiced. But in practice, we tend to make a lot of assumptions about people's concerns and plans, but it can be very difficult to really listen to what they say so that you really understand them.

Discrepancy

MI is not a passive activity. Indeed, a major objective is to foster individuals' understanding of the discrepancies between their behavior and their goals. There are many reasons to change negative health behaviors, and any health professional could create a long list of reasons for particular behaviors. However, in MI the important reasons are those of the client or patient and not those of the counselor or health educator. Accordingly, the health professional is interested in individuals' concerns, values, and motivations. To an extent the objective is to help people identify and understand their cognitive dissonance (inconsistencies in knowledge or beliefs, attitudes, and values) with respect to a particular behavior. An early step in the change process is to evoke and explore individuals' current situations and motivations for change. The assumption here is that at some level people know what they want and why. It is the health professional's job to assist individuals to identify and understand their motivations, competing though they might be, so they can move forward. Therefore, a task of the health professional is to explore discrepancies by asking questions, making observations, and exploring their nature and importance.

Rolling with Resistance

The change process is often impeded by conflict and argumentation. MI seeks to avoid these tiresome and self-defeating actions. Many individuals enjoy arguing and are used to conflict with respect to a particular behavior. Many individuals have experienced pressure from family and friends for many years before they seek help from a health professional and are well able to argue their case and to deal with conflict. However, MI seeks to avoid argumentation and conflict and roll with resistance. Argumentation may actually increase resistance. Ambivalence and resistance are viewed as normal and are accepted by the health professional. The most that one does within MI is to encourage the individual to consider alternative perspectives. The goal is to transfer the responsibility for arguing for change to the individual. The primary method for doing this is eliciting change talk and self-motivation statements, similar to strategies employed in Cognitive Behavior Therapy. Change talk recognizes ambivalence and encourages the individual to have a conversation with self about change, **resistance to change**, and reasons for change.

Empowerment and Self-Efficacy

The key to MI is to get the individual to explore how they can make a difference in their own behavior. The individual's own ideas and resources are key to this process. The health professional can provide suggestions, ideas, encouragement, and guidance, but the goal is to empower the individual. Change depends not simply on the desire for it but also on the sense that one possesses the resources and capabilities to overcome barriers and successfully implement change.

MI Example: The Personal Trainer Study

Type 1 diabetes is an autoimmune disease that afflicts some 7.8% of children and youth. The onset of Type 1 diabetes occurs mostly during childhood, but sometimes during adolescence when the body fails to manufacture insulin, a hormone that converts food to energy. Unlike Type 2 diabetes, which is caused by lifelong behavior (lifestyle), Type 1 is a heritable disease and not caused by specific health behaviors. Sadly, those with the disease must adhere to a strict diet and take insulin in the form of shots or an insulin pump buried under the skin designed to maintain glycemic control, measured by blood levels of Hemoglobin A1c. Typically, pediatric patients see a physician, usually a pediatric endocrinologist, every 3 or 4 months. In addition, at most visits they see a diabetes educator and sometimes other healthcare providers. Management of childhood diabetes is a family affair, but during adolescence careful management often falters. Therefore, there is a great need for interventions to improve diabetes management and outcomes. The personal trainer study evaluated the efficacy of an intervention based on MI in improving diabetes control in a sample of children and adolescents (Nansel et al., 2007). Participants were 81 youth, 11- to 16-year-old patients recruited from diabetes, randomized to an information or personal trainer treatment condition.

The personal trainer intervention included six home sessions based on MI. Each participant was assigned a personal trainer who had completed 80 hours of MI training, plus audiotaped practice sessions, to develop competence in MI methods, including particularly authentic listening, resisting the righting reflex, and evocative feedback. The personal trainers arranged visits to the participants' homes. Each participant completed an applied behavioral analysis (ABA) in which they carefully recorded their diabetes management behavior over a period of a week and identified antecedents and consequences of their behaviors. This exercise illustrated discrepancies between the participants' actual management behavior and their desired management behavior and provided focus for the six counseling sessions.

The first three sessions emphasized rapport building and evaluation of the ABA following a semistructured interview. Youth selected their top three potential goals and rated their readiness to change on each goal. The third session focused on a personal plan for at least one target behavior selected by the participant. The final three visits focused on follow-up and continued skill development. With suggestions, encouragement, and feedback from their personal trainers, participants analyzed their behavior, worked on problem solving, and then revised their plan, thereby developing a positive outcome and efficacy expectations.

This is one of the very few studies to show significant effects on both behavior and diabetes control. Program improvements in A1c postintervention and 1-year follow-up was greater among older than younger participants. In postprogram interviews, the participants in the intervention group expressed great enthusiasm for having a personal trainer. The study demonstrated the efficacy of MI for interventions with adolescents in a community setting delivered by trained nonprofessionals. The success of the program was largely due to the personal trainers' development of trusting relationships, empathy rather than persuasion, and the focus on discrepancies between actual and desired management behavior. In the terms of MI, the personal trainers developed the conditions for self-managed change.

From the perspective of SDT, the intervention can be understood largely in terms of its effects on autonomous motivation through fulfillment of needs for autonomy, competence, and relatedness. Accordingly, the personal trainers provided the participants with autonomy by allowing them to set their own goals and through authentic listening rather than persuasion. They facilitated competence by providing the participants with strategies they could use to meet their self-selected goals. Importantly, the personal trainers established trusting relationships with the participants. Viewed from the SDT perspective, the MI-based intervention was effective mainly because it facilitated autonomous rather than controlled motivation.

The Marriage of SDT and MI

SDT and MI stand on their own as important perspectives from which to understand and develop change strategies for a range of health behaviors. However, they share common theoretical origins and assumptions regarding the nature of behavior and how change can best be facilitated (Markland, Ryan, Tobin, & Rollnick, 2005). Therefore, it has been proposed that they be considered as related and complementary theories (Vansteenkiste & Sheldon, 2006). SDT is largely theoretical, while MI is highly applied and methods oriented. Nevertheless, there are many commonalities, and in many ways, they are highly compatible. Not surprisingly, SDT has been proposed as the theoretical basis for MI, while MI can be viewed as a natural application of the principles of SDT. Both SDT and MI share the assumptions about a positive human nature and the potential for change. Both theories assume that people have a natural tendency toward personal development and change with strong inner resources. The goal of intervention is to strengthen inner resources rather than to impose externally controlling strategies.

The SDT concepts of motivation for change may facilitate the understanding of how MI works. The goal of MI is to facilitate the resolution of ambivalence. From the SDT perspective, such facilitation would lead to integrated motivation for change, which is an autonomous (mostly intrinsic) rather than controlled (mostly extrinsic) motivation. SDT suggests that MI serves mainly to enhance a person's identification with change **intention** and its integration into their value system. Hence, a person begins to perform the activity with a sense of self-endorsement rather than with a sense of resistance and pressure.

Although there is ample evidence that MI results in positive outcomes, it is not clear how and why it works. The SDT construct of needs satisfaction may provide a useful explanation for the positive effects of MI. Recall that SDT proposes three universal needs: competence, autonomy, and relatedness. Research has shown that need satisfaction mediates the relationship between supportive context and outcomes such as adherence, persistence, and long-term change (Deci & Ryan, 2008). Accordingly, the goal of intervention would be to facilitate in patients the sense that they have chosen to change their behavior or take action, that they can succeed, and they have developed a relationship with the counselor or other intervening professional.

The core components of MI relate to needs satisfaction. For starters, the empathic and authentic listening style advocated by MI emphasizes the patient's worldview and acknowledges the genuineness and feeling behind the patient's stories. Authentic listening is consistent with people's needs for relatedness and autonomy. Rolling with resistance helps people see for themselves what they are doing, rather than being told, thus helping to satisfy patients' needs for autonomy. MI's emphasis on self-efficacy—enhancing patients' confidence in their capacity to change and cope with setbacks—can enhance patients' need for competence. MI emphasis on providing choice, rationale for options, summarizing, and eliciting the expression of change intention in patients' own words may satisfy needs for autonomy.

Ultimately, it seems that MI can provide SDT researchers with deeper insights into the application of autonomy-support methods, and SDT can provide a better understanding of the theoretical underpinnings of MI. Because they share common theoretical bases, they are increasingly treated as compatible conceptualizations.

Lessons for Public Health Practice

While SDT and MI have mainly been employed in the area of substance abuse treatment, they are increasingly employed in health promotion. The reasons for this growing popularity include the focus on **brief interventions,** the ethical concern for recognizing the person's autonomy, and frustrations with efforts to motivate people to change. SDT provides a useful theoretical orientation for understanding why people are often unable to change self-damaging behavior, despite a recognized need. Developing skill in using MI methods, for which there is excellent online and in-person training, can benefit health-promotion specialists and improve program effectiveness. Here is a brief list of implications of SDT and MI for health promotion.

Viewed from a needs perspective, it is possible to understand the insecurities that keep people from exercising goal-directed behavior.

1. There is a human need for a sense of control over life events, balanced by the understanding that events are not fully controllable. During healthful human development, one learns self-control and orients toward autonomous or internal motivation.

2. According to the MI spirit, the health-promotion specialist should seek to elicit from people their own motivations for change, rather than prescribing change.

3. Many people experience ambivalence, which is the desire to change and also not to change. Only by recognizing one's ambivalence can a person move forward.

4. Resistance to change is common in health promotion, but the MI-informed specialist rolls with resistance, does not try to overcome it, and guides the person around the resistance.

5. The health-promotion specialist should remain detached from the outcomes of their efforts. By remaining detached, the specialist can be objective and unemotional about guiding change, allowing people autonomy.

6. Listening, really listening, is an essential health-promotion skill. By listening and asking open-ended questions, it is possible to elicit self-disclosure about ambivalence and goals.

7. Developing discrepancy fosters motivation.

8. The health-promotion specialist can guide, suggest, and encourage, but the goal of these activities (in the MI spirit) is to empower the individual, not just to facilitate change.

Application Exercise

Using the following scenario, practice your MI skills.

Paul is a 19-year-old male and about 50 pounds overweight. His doctor made a referral to see a health coach as he had two trips to the emergency room within the last 6 months because of elevated blood sugar (above 600 when normal is 80–130 mg/dL). His doctor diagnosed him with Type 1 diabetes when he was 6 years old. Paul's single mother tried to encourage dietary restrictions, but worked two jobs and couldn't always provide healthy meals. Paul struggles eating foods that are low in sugar. Paul is currently enrolled in a welding program at a local vocational school and often eats convenience foods because he is busy. Paul does not like it when his doctor or mother confront him about controlling his blood sugar.

Task: Role-play (in groups of three: health coach, client, and observer scoring use of MI skills) or write a script as both health coach and client. Use open-ended questions, and practice the following:

• Reflective listening
• Eliciting change talk
• Developing discrepancies
• Rolling with resistance
• Providing empathy
• Supporting self-efficacy and affirmations

Discussion Questions

1. Identify and describe the three key psychological needs in self-determination.

2. Explain how psychological needs affect motivation.

3. Identify and describe five important MI methods.

4. Define ambivalence, and explain its central role in MI

References

Adachi, P., Ryan, R. M., Frye, J., McClurg, D., & Rigby, C. S. (2018). "I can't wait for the next episode!" Investigating the motivational pull of television dramas through the lens of Self-Determination Theory. *Motivation Science, 4*, 78–94.

Bartholomew, K. J., Ntoumanis, N., & Thogersen-Ntoumani, C. (2009). A review of controlling motivational strategies from a Self-Determination Theory perspective: Implications for sports coaches. *International Review of Sport and Exercise Psychology, 2*, 215–233.

Burke, B. L., Arkowitz, H., & Menchola, M. (2003). The efficacy of motivational interviewing: A meta-analysis of controlled clinical trials. *Journal of Consulting and Clinical Psychology, 71*, 843–861.

Deci, E. L., & Flaste, R. (1995). *Why we do what we do: Understanding self-motivation.* New York: Penguin Books.

Deci, E. L., & Ryan, R. M. (2002). *Handbook of self-determination research.* Rochester, NY: University of Rochester Press.

Deci, E. L., & Ryan, R. M. (2008). Self-determination theory: A macrotheory of human motivation, development, and health. *Canadian Psychology, 49*, 182–185. DOI: 10.1037/a0012801

Halvari, A. E., Halvari, H., & Deci, E. (2018). Dental anxiety, oral health-related quality of life, and general well-being: A self-determination theory perspective. *Journal of Applied Social Psychology, 49*(5), 295–306. DOI: 10.1111/jasp.12583.

Hancox, J. E., Quested, E., Ntoumanis, N., & Thogersen-Ntoumani, C. (2018). Putting self-determination theory into practice: Application of adaptive motivational principles in the exercise domain. *Qualitative Research in Sport, Exercise and Health, 10*(1), 75–91. DOI: 10.1080/2159676X.2017.1354059

Jeno, L. M., Adachi, P. J., Grytnes, J.-A., Vandvik, V., & Deci, E. L. (2019). The effects of m-learning on motivation, achievement, and well-being: A self-determination theory approach. *British Journal of Educational Technology, 50*(2), 669–683. DOI: 10.1111/bjet.12657

Koutsenok, I., (2012). Motivational interviewing. In H. L. McQuistion, W. E. Sowers, J. M. Ranz, & Feldman, J. M. (Eds.), *Handbook of community psychiatry* (pp. 201–210). DOI: 10.1007/978-1-4614-3149-7.

Markland, D., Ryan, R. M., Tobin, V. J., & Rollnick, S. (2005). Motivational interviewing and self-determination theory. *Journal of Social and Clinical Psychology, 24*, 811–831.

Martin-Perez, C., Navas, J. F., Perales, J. C., Lopez-Martin, A., Cordovilla-Guardia, S., Portillo, M., Maldonado, A., & Villar-Lopex, R. (2019). Brief group-delivered motivational interviewing is equally effective as brief group-delivered cognitive-behavioral therapy at reducing alcohol use in risky college drinkers. *PLoS One 14*(12), e0226271. DOI: 10.1371/journal.pone.0226271

Maslow, A. H. (1954). *Motivation and personality.* New York: Harper and Row.

Miller, W., & Rollnick, S. (2013). *Motivational interviewing: Helping people change* (3rd ed.). New York: Guilford Press.

Nansel, T. R., Iannotti, R. J., Simons-Morton, B. G., Cox, C., Plotnick, L. P., Clark, L. M., & Zeitzoff, L. (2007). Diabetes personal trainer outcomes. *Diabetes Care, 30*, 2471–2477.

Rogers, C. (1951). Client-centered therapy: Its current practice, implications and theory. London: Constable.

Ryan, R. M., & Deci, E. L. (2017). *Self-determination theory: Basic psychological needs in motivation, development, and wellness.* New York: Guilford Publications. Retrieved from ProQuest Ebook Central, https://ebookcentral.proquest.com

Schumacher, J. A., & Madson, M. B. (2015). *Fundamentals of motivational interviewing: Tips and strategies for addressing common clinical challenges.* New York: Oxford University Press.

Sheldon, K. M., Joiner, T., & Williams, G. (2003). *Motivating health: Applying self-determination theory in the clinic.* New Haven, CT: Yale University Press.

Substance Abuse and Mental Health Services Administration (SAMHSA). (2010, July 6). Spotlight on PATH practices and programs: Motivational Interviewing. Retrieved from https://www.samhsa.gov/sites/default/files/programs_campaigns/homelessness_programs_resources/path-spotlight-motivational-interviewing.pdf

Vansteenkiste, M., & Sheldon, K. M. (2006). There's nothing more practical than a good theory: Integrating motivational interviewing and self-determination theory. *British Journal of Clinical Psychology, 45*, 63–82.

CHAPTER 6

Social Influence Theory: The Effects of Social Factors on Health Behavior

Human beings have a remarkable capacity to cooperate, collaborate, conform, and influence each other.

OUTLINE

1. Preview
2. Objectives
3. Introduction
4. Psychosocial Theories That Emphasize Social Influence
5. Elements of Social Influence
   5.1. Social Norms
      5.1.1. Conformity
      5.1.2. Group Membership
      5.1.3. Shared Information
      5.1.4. Actual versus Perceived Norms
   5.2. Social Influence Processes
      5.2.1. Socialization
      5.2.2. Selection
      5.2.3. Selection and Socialization
   5.3. Context, Culture, Capital
      5.3.1. Social Context
      5.3.2. Culture
      5.3.3. Social Networks
         5.3.3.1. Network Connections
         5.3.3.2. Network Benefits
         5.3.3.3. Social Support
         5.3.3.4. Assessing Social Networks
      5.3.4. Social Capital
6. Example: Electronic Cigarette Use
7. Lessons for Public Health Practice
8. Discussion Questions
9. References

PREVIEW

Social influence is the effect of culture and social affiliation on thought and action. This chapter deals with how and to what extent people are socially influenced.

OBJECTIVES

Upon completion of this chapter the reader will be prepared to describe:

1. Social norms and social influence processes.
2. How norms influence conformity.
3. How group membership shapes norms.

4. Theories that emphasize social norms.
5. The role of information in social norms.
6. Perceived versus actual norms.
7. How social selection operates.
8. How socialization operates.
9. How context determines social networks.
10. Why social capital is important to health behavior.

Introduction

Civilization could hardly function if people did not routinely manage their behavior to fit in with others. Fortunately, human beings have a remarkable capacity to cooperate, collaborate, conform, and influence each other. Social influence has a profound effect on attitudes and behavior and is a prominent feature of society, an active field of research, and a goal of politics, commerce, and public health. Because social factors are among the most powerful and pervasive influences on health (Schuz, Papadakis, & Ferguson, 2018), they are of particular interest to health behavior researchers and public health professionals.

Social influence accounts, at least in part, for the remarkable consistency in beliefs, attitudes, values, and behavior among members of social groups (Berkman & Kawauchi, 2000; Forgas & Williams, 2001; Institute of Medicine, 2001). Social connectedness is generally a positive thing. When people feel connected with other people individually or as part of a group (i.e., social integration), they tend to live longer and experience better health and social outcomes (Glass & McAfee, 2006). Patients with good **social support** are more likely to seek necessary health care and follow medical advice than those without good social support (Berkman & Kawauchi, 2000). People who exercise tend to have friends who exercise and make additional friends with those who exercise (McNeill, Kreuter, & Subramanian, 2006). However, social connections also can be bad in some ways. For example, dietary practices are shaped by family eating experiences, suggesting that obesity is at least partly

a social phenomenon (Christakis & Fowler, 2007). Similarly, having friends who smoke or drink increases the likelihood that an adolescent will become a user (Simons-Morton, Haynie, & Noelke, 2009). In this chapter we examine how social influences affect health behavior.

Before starting out, however, consider your own health behavior—diet, physical activity, substance use, drinking alcohol, sexual behavior, hygiene, medical care seeking, driving, etc.—and ask yourself the following questions about how your beliefs, attitudes, and behavior have been influenced. Where did your health beliefs, attitudes, and behavior come from? Has your current behavior been influenced by your family and cultural background? Are the opinions of others persuasive to you? Whose opinions do you most value? Are you more likely to behave in certain ways when you are with particular people than when you are with others? For example, are you more likely to behave one way when in a college classroom with your peers than you would at a party with those same peers; at a sedate party with a few close friends or at a wild party with lots of people? Do you identify with and elect to spend time with others who tend to behave like you do and reinforce your beliefs and behavior? How do your workplace, social organizations, or school affect your beliefs and behavior?

Most of us would admit that our behavior has been influenced for better or worse by our family upbringing and cultural background. Our beliefs about a topic and evaluation of information are influenced by what we learned growing up and how we perceive other members of our social network would think about that information. Our attitudes and behavior at times are influenced by the presence of a particular person and conform to the expectations of the groups to which we belong, and we tend to affiliate with those who support our behavioral preferences. The nature of these influences as they relate to health behavior is the topic of this chapter. In the following pages we discuss in greater detail the complex and important relationships between social norms and behavior and the importance of **social context** and **social networks**, and **socialization** processes among close relations.

Psychosocial Theories That Emphasize Social Influence

Many psychosocial theories include a focus on social influences, particularly the role of norms. The relationship between social norms and behavior is to a great extent a matter of **cognitive consistency**. The principle of consistency is implicit in cognitive theories such as values expectancy and others that view behavior as a cognitive accounting of costs and benefits (Sparks, 2000). The premise is essentially that people tend to be relatively consistent with respect to beliefs, attitudes, and behavior, despite dissonance among these cognitions (Chatzisarantis, Hagger, & Wang, 2008). However, correctly determining the prevailing social norms can be particularly tricky, and misinterpretation is common. Correct or incorrect, perceived norms influence behavior.

As discussed in previous chapters, beliefs, what we perceive to be true, are key elements of behavior. What one believes affects attitudes, which affects behavior. One important type of cognition is perceived social norms about the prevalence and acceptability of specific behaviors. People tend to think and behave in ways that are consistent with and approved of by important others. Notably, the Theory of Reasoned Action (TRA) is primarily concerned with subjective norms (perceptions about others' expectations or pressure with respect to the behavior and the individual) (Ajzen, 1988). **Subjective norms** are the individual's perceptions of what important others (e.g., friends, family) would want the person to do with respect to a particular behavior. (The term *perceptions* here should be considered the same as belief, so perceived norms are what one believes to be the norms.) Accordingly, TRA would suggest that experimentation with smoking would be more or less likely depending on adolescents' perceptions of how important others (e.g., parents, teachers, friends) would perceive them if they were to smoke or what these others would want them to do concerning smoking (Norman, Conner, & Bell, 1999). This contention is well founded in the literature on adolescent and emerging adult substance use (Li, Ochoa, Vaca, & Simons-Morton, 2018; Simons-Morton, 2007; Simons-Morton, Chen, Abroms, & Haynie, 2004; Simons-Morton, Haynie, Liu, Chaurasia, Li, & Hingson, 2016; Simons-Morton et al., 2009; Simons-Morton, Haynie, O'Brien, Lipsky, Bible, & Liu, 2017).

Social norms also figure prominently in other theories. From an operant conditioning and social cognitive perspective, people are reinforced for behaving in ways that meet the approval of important others (Bandura, 1996). With respect to smoking, adolescents learn about potential social reinforcement by observing how smoking is socially reinforced. Based on actual or observed experience, adolescents develop expectations about what behavior is acceptable with respect to smoking. Hence, perceived social norms figure prominently in the literature about operant conditioning and Social Cognitive Theory, as well as persuasion and social marketing (Forgas & Williams, 2001).

Elements of Social Influence

As shown in **Figure 6.1**, the grand social forces of culture and context (time and place) influence social influence processes, which influence social norms, with predictable influences on behavior. Norms provide information about social expectations, but this information can be complicated to decode. Moreover, norms can be subtle and variable across subgroups. The norms that prevail for the larger community

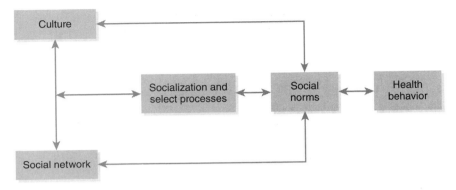

Figure 6.1 Social influences model

may not be the norms favored by each of the many groups of which it is composed. Indeed, it can be difficult to determine exactly what the norms are for a particular group in a particular context. In the following pages we examine the complex relationships between actual and perceived norms, the relationship of social norms and behavior, the social influence process, and finally the role of culture and context, more or less working backward from right to left through Figure 6.1.

Social Norms

Social norms provide direct and powerful influences on behavior, as indicated in Figure 6.1 by the arrow from norms to behavior. We tend to think of social influence in terms of overt pressure, such as when a parent insists you wear a helmet when biking or a friend encourages you to have a beer. But social influence is more about norms than about overt pressure. Social norms are enforced, for better or worse, not only by those we see every day, but also by the groups to which we belong and the culture from which we derive. But what are norms, exactly?

Basically, social norms are the standards for conduct (thought and action) in society. Norms can be very general, referring to cultural understanding (for example, as reflected by stereotypes such as the French are sexy, Americans are aggressive, Swedes

are reserved), or very specific with respect to a behavior and a population group (e.g., smoking among friends at a particular high school; beliefs about binge eating and bulimia among female high school swimmers; attitudes toward condom use among African American males). Norms can vary according to the environment, situation, and culture. There are general rules for public behavior (e.g., dressing appropriately), eating (e.g., not talking with food in your mouth), classroom decorum (e.g., raising your hand before speaking), gender roles (e.g., girls wear pink and boys wear blue), and so on. Social norms contribute greatly to conformity and standards for **group membership**.

Conformity

Social norms encourage **conformity**. Think for a moment about the great extent of conformity of behavior in daily life. People tend to adjust their behavior to fit in with the expectations of others or perceptions about these expectations. For any person and situation, conformity is possible on a continuum ranging from highly compliant to totally defiant. In general, most people tend to prefer the rich social rewards of conformity to the isolation of defiance. Ample research has shown that most individuals tend to go along with the view of the majority, even when they personally view things differently (Forgas & Williams, 2001). **Pluralistic ignorance** describes the common case in which the majority of a group privately reject a norm, but incorrectly assume that most others accept it (Miller, Monin, & Prentice, 2000). Even relatively independent people may not be assertive about their views much of the time because nonconforming behavior is not generally rewarded by the group. When your view is the lone dissenting view, it can be difficult to remain committed to it. Individuals who tend to stray from the group's norms are often rejected, ridiculed, and held back.

Each of us sometimes yields to social pressures to behave in certain ways despite our personal preferences to behave otherwise. Indeed, one of the main requirements for completing and succeeding in school is conforming to rules and expectations. As adults we conform to workplace and community rules and acquiesce to the demands of powerful authorities. Failure to conform in such a situation has substantial consequences. Of course, conformity is not always a good thing. History is replete with examples of people going along with rather horrendous behaviors with which they disagree. Indeed, defiant individuals are often socially persecuted. Thus, nonconforming individuals often seek support and encouragement from other nonconformists. The success of the civil rights movement of the 1960s, for example, was partly the result of Dr. Martin Luther King making nonviolent protest and advocacy normative.

Group Membership

Group membership provides support for shared norms and also enforces normative views and behavior among group members through the administration of rewards and punishments. Group membership may be highly formal, such as belonging to a family, a gang, an organization, a profession, or a clique of friends. Group membership can also be informal, such as identifying with a reputation-based group or crowd (political liberal or conservative, student, worker, athlete, dancer, etc.), each of which has its own set of social norms and limits on nonconformity concerning certain issues. Some groups tolerate substantial dissent and nonconformity, while others tolerate little dissent and demand that dissidents leave the group or be ostracized. Belonging to groups can add additional pressure to conform. When most people think of group behavior, they might conjure up images of peers cheering on someone to drink alcohol or partake in other risky behaviors. However, peer pressure is often indirect, subtle, and noncoercive.

Shared Information

Norms provide information about what is socially expected. Stated differently, social influence is the product of information shared among group members leading to common social norms. Information about norms may be verbalized, written, or implied. No matter how they are described, norms are essentially the rules of how to behave in society. Social influences inform, promote, and enforce social norms. As noted, many behavior theories emphasize the importance of information about social norms. For example, a contention of the theory of planned behavior is that socialization is the product of information sharing (Ajzen, 1988). The information and beliefs that members share form the norms of the group and shape behavior.

People generally prefer that their behavior is consistent with their attitudes and beliefs, including beliefs about accepted social norms. Therefore, people constantly process information about norms and mostly adapt their behavior to conform. However, it can sometimes be difficult to correctly interpret information about social norms. Information about norms is sometimes unclear. Despite constantly gathering information from informal cues, modeled behavior, and formal guidelines, norms are complicated, often unstated, inconsistent, and variable across subgroups and situations. Consequently, despite our best efforts to understand normative expectations, we do not always perceive them accurately. In part this is because social norms are not always obvious. Because social norms are often not written or otherwise specified, misperception is common. In public health, we often see people overestimate the health-damaging behavior of individuals (for example, smoking and drinking), and underestimate healthful behavior (for example, safe and attentive driving). For example, many college students overestimate the alcohol use of their peers, which contributes to overall drinking prevalence (Pape, 2012).

Actual versus Perceived Norms

As noted, it can sometimes be difficult to know precisely what norms prevail among any group for any particular situation. Consequently, perceived social norms are often as important to behavior as actual social norms (Miller et al., 2000). Actual or perceived, norms exert powerful influences on a range of behaviors (Simons-Morton et al., 2009). Because people are social beings, acceptance by others is important, so we try to discern what is socially acceptable. Some information about norms is easy to obtain because it is codified in the form of rules and policies or clearly stated (think about your own parents' expectations for you, or those of your third-grade teacher or high school vice principal). Other information comes indirectly from our interactions with and observations of other people, and we tend to generalize to others our normative perceptions gleaned from a small number of contacts. When we go to a new school or start a new job, we seek out clues about what is acceptable so that we can fit in; we seek out others at that location with views, interests, and behavior similar to our own. We seek information about the norms in particular settings so we can understand the extent to which we fit in.

Adding to the complexity, social norms exist at multiple levels, sometimes with considerable variability among subgroups. It would not be unusual for a wide range of norms to exist within the same school, dorm, or fraternity about marijuana, driving while intoxicated, sexual behavior, and so on. Not knowing the norms of a group makes it difficult to fit in and puts one at a social disadvantage and susceptible to ridicule or embarrassment. In addition to everyday-life examples like these, we also absorb information about the norms for health behavior, including substance use, diet, sex, and medical care seeking. By determining what the norms are, an individual can conform to them and by sharing norms become or remain an accepted member of the group (Kameda, Takezawa, & Hastie, 2005).

The uncertainty of determining actual norms gives rise to well-documented fallacies. As noted earlier, pluralistic ignorance is going along with the perceived norms despite not agreeing with them (Miller et al., 2000). Similarly, "**false consensus**" is the process whereby one incorrectly perceives that one's attitudes and behaviors represent that of the majority when they actually represent the minority (e.g., "because I smoke or my friends smoke, it must be a common and acceptable behavior"). Pluralistic ignorance and false consensus reinforce each other. The majority is silent because they think they are the minority, and the minority is vocal because they think they are the majority (Berkowitz, 2005). Social marketing contributes to both fallacies by feeding to users links to information similar to what they just searched, thereby increasing attention and gaining marketing advantage.

Social Influence Processes

As shown in Figure 6.1, norms are shared directly through **selection** and socialization processes. Socialization processes control and interpret information about social norms, thereby influencing behavior. Friendship

Research on Social Norms and Social Pressure

Simons-Morton and colleagues (Simons-Morton, 2019; Simons-Morton et al., 2019; Simons-Morton et al., 2014) examined the effect of social norms on simulated risky driving. Young male drivers were randomized to drive solo and with a young male confederate passenger portraying either risk-accepting or risk-averse social norms while watching risky driving videos prior to driving. Participants were more likely to run red lights and pass a slowing vehicle in the presence than absence of a passenger, particularly in the presence of a passenger with risk-accepting norms. These findings are consistent with other research indicating that risk-accepting peer passengers sensitize the brain's reward system to risk taking.

In a follow-on experiment, the researchers examined the risky driving when one group of male teenager participants were randomized to drive with a young male passenger (a young male study confederate), who provided pressure to complete the course quickly, and another group drove with a confederate passenger who exercised mild pressure to complete the drive safely by taking few risks. Risky driving (running a red light, time in the intersection, and passing the slowing vehicle) and distraction (failure to stop at an intersection with an occluded stop sign) were greater in the group exposed to mild passenger pressure-to-take-risks. These findings are consistent with theory and research indicating that adolescent risk taking is sensitive to social norms and pressure.

selection occurs largely within particular social networks, the members of which tend to share the same social context. **Social capital** facilitates accurate understanding of social norms and also improves resilience in cases of nonconformity.

Socialization

Socialization is the effect of social relationships on the formation of norms. The term "socialization" is sometimes used to refer to the entire concept of social influence, but it more accurately refers to the process of developing attitudes and behaviors that are consistent with group norms. Social groups include family, school, profession, and other formally constituted groups, as well as less-formal self-identified and reputation-oriented groups such as sport or music fan of some sort, exerciser, or smoker. Being the member of a group, even a self-identified one, is a socializing process to the extent the group is associated with particular norms and holds certain expectations concerning social image and conformity (Evans, Powers, Hersey, & Renaud, 2006). In general, the more individuals are integrated into the group and the more salient the attitudes or behaviors are to the group, the greater the impact on behavior (Friedkin, 2001).

Socialization is often interpreted as peer pressure or **social pressure**. An example of direct and intentional pressure would be when an adolescent who smokes encourages his friends to smoke. There is substantial evidence in the area of adolescent substance use that smokers sometimes pressure their friends to smoke, although it is unclear the extent to which this occurs, and peer pressure is not the only means and probably not the primary means by which adolescents who smoke come to be friends. Basically, behavior among friends is very consistent, so when one adolescent in a group begins to smoke, friends are also likely to start. In one study, friendship groups provided the greatest socializing effects on adolescent smoking uptake, while the behavior of best friends provided the greatest effect on drinking initiation and progression (Urberg, Degirmencioglu, & Pilgrim, 1997). In research on emerging adults, closest friend and five closest friends provided relatively equal predictive association with binge drinking (Simons-Morton et al., 2018). Conversely, parents can successfully pressure their children not to smoke and not to associate with adolescents who do (Simons-Morton et al., 2004).

Indirect social influence is probably more common and possibly more powerful than direct pressure. Indirect social influence occurs through perceived pressure to conform to norms. This can be through modeling or other normative cues. An adolescent who smokes serves as a role model for his friends and acquaintances. Whether he intends to or not, without ever pressuring his friends to smoke, through his behavior the adolescent smoker can influence the social norms of others regarding smoking. Adolescents who associate with smokers are likely to begin to view smoking as an acceptable behavior, maybe even a desirable behavior. Parental smoking may have a similar unintended modeling effect on adolescent smoking (Tilson, McBride, Lipkus, & Catalano, 2004). In this case, social norms were assumed from the behavior of role models.

Being in a friendship group that includes smokers may provide more powerful socializing effects than just knowing people who smoke. Of course, socialization effects also occur within groups that lack smokers and would discourage smoking uptake. The lack of role models and the group's prevailing social norms of believing smoking is not a desirable or acceptable behavior exert social pressure within friendship groups to not smoke.

As previously noted, an adolescent's attitudes about smoking may be influenced by the norms of amorphous groups with which the adolescent affiliates, such as "athlete," "musician," or "student" (Evans et al., 2006; Verkooijen, DeVries, & Nielsen, 2007). Because group norms and perceptions of group norms are powerful influences on behavior, advertising often portrays smoking as normative. Conversely, many intervention programs are at least partly designed to alter social norms of a group indirectly by focusing on group norms rather than the target population directly (Thombs & Hamilton, 2000).

From an operant perspective, socialization is the effect on behavior of reinforcement for sharing the same social norms as the groups and lack of reinforcement for not sharing group norms. Whether a person becomes the member of a group due to social context or volition, membership implies and requires shared social norms. The tendency is to accept the social norms of the group rather than live with the consequences or leave the group. While individuals experiment with views and behavior that are not shared by the group, continued acceptance may depend on the group's tolerance for deviant views and behavior.

According to the Theory of Planned Behavior, subjective (perceived rather than actual) norms are important and influential. Accordingly, perceptions of important others about what thoughts and actions are acceptable and preferred are powerful influences on behavior. In our example of adolescents contemplating experimentation with smoking, perceptions of what proximal and important others want the teen to do with regard to smoking are thought to influence smoking behavior.

Selection

Selection is the process in which an individual associates or identifies with others with similar interests. It is natural to want to spend time with or otherwise identify with others like you and like the same things as you. To the extent possible people associate with others who like the same activities, whether that is sport, music, or drugs. Indeed, the pool of potential social contacts is largely made up of people engaging in similar activities. Such affiliation is powerfully confirming to the extent shared norms provide reinforcement. Research has documented that adolescents interested in smoking are likely to make friends with others who smoke so that the behavior can be shared, is perceived as normative, and is rewarded. (Simons-Morton, 2007).

Selection and Socialization

Selection and socialization processes sometimes work in concert (Simons-Morton et al., 2009). This phenomenon has been well described with respect to the uptake of smoking among adolescents. The extent of agreement in behavior among adolescents and their friends is the most common way to assess peer influence (socialization), and many studies have reported significant associations between peer and adolescent smoking. While there are limits to this research approach (Arnett, 2007), there is substantial evidence that association with substance-using friends leads to increases in adolescent (Simons-Morton et al., 2009) and emerging adult substance use (Simons-Morton et al., 2017).

The more friends an adolescent has who smoke, the more likely the adolescent is to take up smoking (Simons-Morton & Farhat, 2010) and drinking (Simons-Morton et al., 2018). This tendency of adolescents with smoking friends to eventually experiment with smoking may be due to selection or to socialization. Selection effects have been demonstrated in studies showing that adolescents who are experimental smokers tend over time to develop friendships with other adolescents who smoke (Simons-Morton et al., 2004). Selection effects may primarily occur while experimenting adolescents come together to obtain cigarettes, share the experience, and reinforce each other's behavior. Selection could also occur among adolescents who are experimental smokers because smoking represents broader social norms—perceptions of maturity, attractiveness, rebellion, antisocial behavior, or risk taking—that bring adolescents together. The discrete effects of socialization and selection are interactive and difficult to separate. For example, both selection and socialization play a role in the uptake of adolescent smoking (Simons-Morton et al., 2004; Simons-Morton et al., 2009).

Meanwhile, there are other socializing effects on smoking. Notably, while peer influences increase during adolescence, parent influence declines but does not wane entirely. Parents provide important socializing influences on adolescent smoking uptake, partly through pressure on their adolescents not to smoke or drink (Simons-Morton & Chen, 2005; Simons-Morton et al., 2004) and by preventing their adolescent children from making friends with substance-using adolescents or indirectly by restricting activities with certain friends (Simons-Morton et al., 2009). Certain groups of adolescents, particularly those with weak family and school bonds, may be more susceptible to the peer influences of selection and socialization than others (Urberg, Luo, Pilgrim, & Degirmencioglu, 2003). Overall, peer selection and peer and parent socialization processes appear to be important influences on adolescent substance use uptake (Simons-Morton, 2007; Simons-Morton & Farhat, 2010).

Context, Culture, Capital

The bidirectional arrows linking the factors in Figure 6.1 show that social context and social networks shape the processes of socialization and selection, as well as social norms. Social context has both proximal and distal components. At a proximal level, immediate factors such as the setting, location, and who is present can influence behavior. For example, teenagers tend to drive faster in the presence of teenage passengers, particularly male teenage passengers (Simons-Morton & Ouimet, 2017) and take more risks while driving with a male than a female passenger (Simons-Morton, Bingham, et al., 2014; see text box). Similarly, adolescents are more likely to smoke when in the presence of other adolescents who are smoking (Simons-Morton & Farhat, 2010; Simons-Morton et al., 2009). At a distal level, social context is the product of nationality, race, religion, geographic location, socioeconomic status, media exposure, and place of work or school. Over the long term of one's life (and in the immediate sense), social context provides information about what is normative and what is not.

Intentionally or not, individual perspectives tend to conform to generally accepted beliefs and behaviors that are communicated by government, commercial enterprise, media, work, school, and family and represent nested hierarchies with similar values. Culture in the form of prevailing laws, policies, and programs (e.g., public education) transmits, enforces, and inculcates these norms. Norms are established and maintained by the institutions at various social levels. Families ensure that children develop self-control and respect for order. Schools ensure that students develop certain skills and learn order and discipline. Neighborhoods establish norms for public behavior. Indeed, many problems in society stem from family, school, and neighborhood dysfunction (Hirschi, 1969).

Social Context

Social context is about time and place. If you were born a few hundred years ago, your place in society would have been determined by the prevailing norms relating to class. Women were not allowed to work in most trades and professions. A peasant was relegated to being a peasant, a slave a slave, and a nobleman a nobleman. Some would argue that this is largely still true today. However, at least in Western society, there have been dramatic changes in norms regarding the role of women, and the potential for upward mobility is much greater than it once was. The point is that when you were born matters. Also, where you are born and raised matters with respect to future health and success. Growing up in an impoverished environment makes it much more difficult to obtain education and advance socially. Growing up in a wealthy family and neighborhood vastly increases your chances of success and long life (Glass & McAfee, 2006). Prep school provides a different context than public school.

Culture

From a broad cultural perspective, social context is so integral to our experience that we often don't notice it. Cultural norms are thought to be transmitted largely through social-evolutionary processes favoring normative versus deviant behavior (Dawkins, 1989; Shaller, 2001). Basically, conforming members of a group are more likely to mate and reproduce than nonconforming members. Elements of social information in the form of ideas, beliefs, fads, fashions, and biases are transmitted from individual to individual or group to individual and codified as culture.

We don't always appreciate its subtle but profound effects on the way we understand our world or on our values, attitudes, and behavior (Glass & McAfee, 2006). Consider that in some cultures, girls are expected to marry and have their first child soon after puberty, an age that most Americans would consider much too young. Some societies condemn homosexuality, while others accept it as a normal variant in sexual preference. In some societies, cattle are sacred, while in America raising cattle for beef is a big business. In some societies obesity signifies success, but in modern America it is increasingly understood as a health problem. In short, normative perspectives about health behaviors are cultural and contextual.

The profound cultural influences on society are supported and enforced by organizations, including religious groups, Boy Scouts of America, Chamber of Commerce, American Legion, the military, even schools. Immersed in our own culture, it can be difficult to appreciate how at odds it can be with the perspectives of ethnic and sexual minorities, immigrants, and contrarians. For example, environmentalists for decades have urged changes to national policies and practices to counter global warning, which finally today is being recognized by society as an accepted and logical way to think.

Social Networks

Social context largely determines the makeup of our social networks. People in our social network tend to live close by, go to the same schools, belong to the same groups, and have similar racial, ethnic, and religious backgrounds. Glass and McAfee (2006) describe social context as consisting of nested hierarchies, which include one's global, national, work/school/community, family, and social group. Nested hierarchies are interrelated in that they share and reinforce conventional norms and largely determine the perspectives, opportunities, and constraints experienced by its members. Shown in **Figure 6.2** is a conceptualization of concentric circles, or nested hierarchies, of social influences. Accordingly, proximal others, such as family and close others, are likely to have the greatest social influence owing to the closeness of the relationships and the frequency of contact. However, other, more proximal relationships may provide additional influence, either directly on the individual or indirectly through their influence on others within the individual's social circle. Thus, levels are overlapping, and influences are bidirectional, with individuals being exposed to various social influences whether or not they choose to be.

Network Connections Social network is a measure of the extent to which one is connected with others. Social networks are patterns of friendship, advice, communication, or support that exist among members of a social system (Friedkin, 2001). A social network includes everyone with whom one has contact, with whom one interacts, and from whom one obtains information in any form about a particular topic. This includes family members, close friends, fellow group members, acquaintances, colleagues, and people and groups known only by reputation or through media and other vicarious sources. Some individuals have limited social networks, while others have extensive ones. Social networks can be quite widespread and unstructured, existing mainly through vicarious sources such as the Internet, television, or radio. A person can be part of multiple social networks. Social networks can and do evolve over time; they also expand and contract, particularly in response to life transitions like moving to a new city, attending a new high school, leaving for college, or accepting a new job. One's social network is

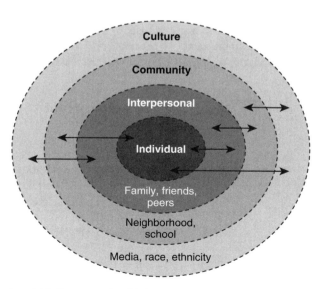

Figure 6.2 Levels of social influence on health behavior

largely determined by social context because the most important venues through which you meet people are residential areas, workplaces, and schools; the organizations and groups to which you belong; and the individuals you already know. The advantage of a relatively larger and more diverse social network is that it affords a wider exchange of information about ideas and behavior. People share information with those they know and obtain new information, interpretations, and values concerning that information.

The primary functions of social networks are providing or gaining support and sharing information about social norms. The more connected or socially integrated into the group, the greater the social influence of the group on the individual (Cohen & Lemay, 2007). Of course, the quality of one's social ties is also important, and the influence of each person in the network may be higher for those who have only a few close relationships than for those who have many trivial social connections. Individuals tend to spend more time with close friends than with distant acquaintances. Moreover, individuals tend to be more influenced by those with whom they have close relationships than those with whom they have weaker ties or connections. People tend to share social resources, such as emotional support, information, and instrumental assistance (help with doing things), with their closest friends.

The social influence of any individual or group is a function of the strength, immediacy, and number of social contacts (Friedkin, 2001). Logically, the greatest social influence is generated by important others with whom we have frequent contact. Strength has to do with status and relationship circumstances. Stronger sources provide greater influence, and respected sources provide relatively greater influence. Close relationships are partly important, because we are most likely to share information with those with whom we most frequently interact. Think about who has influenced the way you think, or the way you

learn about new ways to think and behave. Where do you get your ideas about what is normative and acceptable?

While many overlapping social levels affect norms, the most immediate circle of relationships such as family, friends, and close associates provides important and reasonably well understood effects. Family is the primary social unit for the transmission of values and norms, and family background is substantially associated with a wide range of health behaviors (Harding, 2003). Friends also tend to share many dispositions and behaviors (Kobus, 2003). Group membership is an important influence on social norms, in part because it tends to be based on themes of conformity and identity (Kobus, 2003). For example, when there are four or five groups of students who tend to cluster together, they constitute a friendship "clique." A friendship clique is one in which each individual knows or interacts with everyone else in the group. When most of an individual's relationships are within a single clique, he or she tends to be more influenced by the norms or behaviors of the clique than by individuals who belong to multiple groups. The point is that individuals are influenced not only by the individuals with whom they have direct relationships but also by indirect relationships and the structure of relationships (e.g., belonging to one or more cliques, or friendship groups, instead of just one).

Network Benefits Social networks are important in establishing norms for a number of reasons. Most importantly, the individuals in a social network share information about matters of mutual importance and thereby transmit local norms. New members are generally introduced into a social network through association with another member of the social network. For example, adolescent smoking often begins when the opportunity to do so is provided by a friend or acquaintance (Simons-Morton et al., 2009). Members in a social network often share common values, and they tend to interpret information about ideas and behaviors in ways that reflect those interests and values. Social networks provide the context within which selection occurs and socialization operates (Friedkin, 2001). Not only are individuals influenced by their social ties and connections with others, but also social networks provide social benefits (Luke & Harris, 2007) with important effects on our health and well-being. Social benefits associated with social network affiliations include the following:

1. Social identity: How we define ourselves in terms of social categories, such as married or single, parents, sons and daughters.
2. Access to new social contacts and social roles: We meet many if not most of our friends and colleagues through other friends or family members.
3. Informational support: We receive a wide array of information from our social ties, including what movies to watch, whether a symptom requires a doctor visit, job opportunities, to name just a few.
4. Instrumental support: Help in doing things, such as borrowing money, transportation, help with our studies, and so forth.
5. Affective support: Belief that we are cared for and loved.

Social Support Networks also affect individual behaviors through the provision of social support. People with whom we associate or to whom we are connected through friendship or family ties provide us with social support of various kinds. They help us do things, they provide information, they introduce us to other people, they provide social identity or a sense of who we are, and they provide us with emotional support and feeling cared for and loved. Because social support is obtained through network connections and ties, the amount and kinds of support we receive depend on the networks to which we belong, their structure and size, and the strength of the

ties we have with network members. In the case of smoking, we increasingly find smokers participating in networks in which smoking is prevalent, and members of our network may provide tobacco, or transportation to the supermarket to buy tobacco goods, and may reinforce our smoking through the messages they give us.

Because social networks and close personal ties are an important influence in individuals' health and behaviors, families, social networks, work groups, peers, and neighbors may be important targets of intervention using a variety of network strategies and skills, such as strengthening existing social networks to help them better meet the needs of their members; changing the norms within existing social networks, such as norms around smoking, drinking, or sexual activity; strengthening and enhancing families; developing and implementing social support groups, such as Alcoholics Anonymous, Weight Watchers, or other self-help and supportive organizations; increasing access to more normative groups, such as encouraging adolescent participation in more prosocial groups, such as Boy Scouts or informal after-school organizations; and peer influence approaches, such as using peer leadership models in alcohol and drug prevention.

Assessing Social Networks Social network considerations have recently become more prominent in public health research and practice. An accurate assessment of a population's social network can enable the development of targeted interventions, including two-stage persuasive approaches in which the attitudes and behavior of members of a social network are targeted along with the at-risk population. Understanding the strength of networks is also important. For example, it is well known that younger kids are influenced by teenagers and teenagers are influenced by other risk-prone teenagers. Understanding the effect of peer influence on risk taking might help to improve public health interventions.

More specifically, interventions should focus on social norms and peer expectations rather than the behaviors of the individual (Knoll, Leung, Foulkes, & Blakemore, 2017).

Social Capital

The emerging concept of social capital helps to explain how social networks may be important to health. Social capital is the degree of connectedness, including the breadth and depth of relationships. In the book, *Tipping Point*, Malcolm Gladwell (2008) provided an example of the effects of social capital based on the results of a study of the longevity of a community of people, Rosetans, who resided in Pennsylvania. Despite their love for fatty foods, tobacco, and relatively high levels of obesity, Rosetans rarely developed heart disease before age 65. The study concluded that individual choices about diet and exercise were not as important as cohesiveness of community, families, and friends—social capital.

Indeed, social capital theory is now a prominent concern for public health practice (Kreuter & Lezin, 2002) and is considered an important element of positive psychology (Seligman & Csikszentmihalyi, 2000). This basic concept is, of course, quite easy to grasp for anyone who has ever experienced the benefits of being part of a community. For example, the devastating mental health effects of isolation may be buffered in communities "rich" in social capital simply because the very nature of the community maximizes personal opportunity to spend time with other people. Indeed, the concept of social capital was initially based on the observation that suicide rates were higher in places where social "connectedness" was quite low. This was also exemplified during the COVID-19 global pandemic, when suicide risk increased because of the lack of being able to access and maintain their social capital (Reger, Stanley, & Joiner, 2020)

Social capital has been related to a number of important public health variables such as depression, child welfare, violent behavior,

mortality, and health status (Kawachi, Kennedy, & Glass, 1999). Stated simply, as social capital increases, morbidity rates for given diseases or conditions in a community/society decline. This includes morbidity from chronic diseases such as a diabetes and chronic conditions such as obesity (Holtgrave & Crosby, 2006).

Example: Electronic Cigarette Use

E-cigarettes were created to support smoking cessation by providing the shape and feel of a real cigarette. The use of e-cigarettes (vaping) has grown to over 10.8 million adult users, and 15% of that population were nonsmokers before they started vaping (Amin, Dunn, & Laranjo, 2019). Although the long-term effects of vaping are unknown, e-cigarettes contain toxic chemicals, carcinogens, and metals among other ultrafine particles. E-cigarette use has been shown to make bacterial infections resistant to antibiotics and that lung damage may be similar to conventional smoking (Noland et al., 2016). Moreover, e-cigarette use has been associated with alcohol use and that e-cigarette use can actually increase risk for alcohol abuse (Hefner, Sollazzo, Mullaney, Coker, & Sofuoglu, 2019).

Social connections, social norms, and perceived peer use are associated with vaping behaviors. It was reported that many individuals learned about e-cigarettes, first tried e-cigarettes, and were influenced by family and friends (Amin et al., 2019). Individuals viewed vaping as acceptable by their peer group and that it was a safer alternative and less risky than other tobacco products (Hefner et al., 2019). Among college students, individuals overestimated the use of vaping by roughly 17% (Noland et al., 2016). As we learned, these misperceptions may lead to increases in risky behaviors. There is no question that vaping has become a social phenomenon. The current social acceptability, lack of social stigma, and relaxed public policies will reinforce the acceptance of vaping if interventions and health programming are not quickly adopted to address social influence and social norms.

Lessons for Public Health Practice

In this chapter we have presented a broad conceptualization of social influence processes, taking into account cultural and social contexts and proximal social processes. While there is substantial research on the topic and many theories emphasize aspects of social norms and other aspects of social influence, no grand unifying theory of social influence exists. However, there is theoretical agreement that social influences largely determine the information we obtain and how we interpret it, thereby influencing beliefs, attitudes, values, and behavior.

The strength of the evidence linking social influences and health behavior has important implications for public health. Clearly, the creation of programs designed to alter individual cognitions is insufficient if they are highly dependent on the normative influences of those in their social network, or if interventions do not take social context into account in ways that would increase their effectiveness. Perhaps we could use our knowledge about how ideas are transmitted through social networks to promote health-promoting behaviors in the same manner that industry uses this information to sell tobacco, alcohol, and other consumer goods. One thing for certain is that public health must place greater emphasis on changing social norms and social influence concerning specific health behaviors.

From the perspective of trying to understand behavior:

1. Social influences account for a substantial proportion of the similarity in attitudes and behavior of group members.

2. Social influence is generally considered to be the product of information shared among group members about social norms.
3. Perceived social norms influence behavior. It is not so much what is actually acceptable, but what is perceived to be acceptable and preferred that influences behavior.
4. Group membership provides social capital while requiring adherence to the social norms of the group. Those with wide social networks and substantial social capital appear to do better on many indicators of health and behavior. However, conformity to group norms can also include health-damaging behaviors, such as aggression and crime among gang members, substance use among some adolescents, and condom nonuse among some HIV-infected people.
5. There is no grand unifying theory of social influences, but nearly all behavioral theories emphasize social influences and social norms.
6. Social context and culture provide the broad social backdrop against which proximal norms operate. Interpretations of proximal social norms governed by cultural, national, religious, and racial contexts.
7. Being well connected with many friends and acquaintances, belonging to social groups, and participating in community activities provides social capital, which appears to promote health and behavior.

From an intervention perspective:

1. Social norms are the key to understanding and perhaps to changing socially mediated behavior.
2. Health behaviors are socially mediated through perceived social norms. Therefore, changes in perceived norms may be important intermediate goals of intervention.

3. The interactive nature of socialization and selection processes has several implications for health-promotion intervention:
   a. Peer group, family, and other proximal social influences are important influences on behavior and thus should be targeted by public health programs.
   b. The evidence that social norms, actual and perceived, are powerful influences on health behavior suggests that interventions designed to alter norms may have the best chance of success.
4. Because social influences occur at multiple levels, it is often useful to intervene at more than one social level.
5. Close others are important targets of interventions. Their cognitions can be assessed and then addressed systematically as part of comprehensive, multilevel programs.

Discussion Questions

1. What are social norms?
2. Provide three examples of social norms.
3. How do social norms affect health behavior?
4. What is socialization, and how does it influence a specific personal-health behavior?
5. Why are perceived norms at least as important as actual norms with respect to influence?

References

Ajzen, I. (1988). *Attitudes, personality, and behavior*. Chicago: The Dorsey Press.

Amin, S., Dunn, A. H., & Laranjo, L. (2019). Social influence in the uptake and use of electronic cigarettes: A systematic review. *American Journal of Preventative Medicine, 58*(1), 129–141. DOI: 10.1016/j.amepre.2019.08.023

Arnett, J. J. (2007). The myth of peer influence in adolescent smoking initiation. *Health Education and Behavior, 34*, 594–607. DOI: 10.1177/1090198105285330

Bandura A. J. (1996). *Social foundations of thought and action*. Englewood Cliffs, NJ: Prentice Hall.

Berkman, L. F., & Kawauchi, I. (2000). *Social epidemiology*. New York: Oxford University Press.

Berkowitz, A. D. (2005). An overview of the social norms approach. In L. Lederman, L. Stewart, F. Goodhart, & L. Laitman (Eds.), *Changing the culture of college drinking: A socially situated prevention campaign* (pp. 193–225). Cresskill, NJ: Hampton Press.

Chatzisarantis, N. L. D., Hagger, M. S., & Wang, J. C. K. (2008). An experimental test of cognitive dissonance theory in the domain of physical exercise. *Journal of Applied Sport Psychology, 20*, 97–115. DOI: 10.1080/10413200701601482

Christakis, N. A., & Fowler, J. H. (2007). The spread of obesity in a large social network over 32 years. *New England Journal of Medicine, 357*, 370–379.

Cohen, S., & Lemay E. P. (2007). Why would social networks be linked to affect and health practices? *Health Psychology, 26*, 410–417. DOI: 10.1037/0278-6133.26.4.410

Dawkins, R. (1989). *The selfish gene*. Oxford, UK: Oxford University Press.

Evans, W. D., Powers, A., Hersey, J., & Renaud, J. (2006). The influence of social environment and social image on adolescent smoking. *Health Psychology, 25*, 26–33. DOI: 10.1037/0278-6133.25.1.26

Forgas, J. P., & Williams, K. D. (2001). *Social influence: Direct and indirect processes*. Philadelphia, PA: Psychology Press.

Friedkin, N. E. (2001). Norm formation in social influence networks. *Social Networks, 23*, 167–189.

Gladwell, M. (2008). *Outliers. The Story of Success*. New York: Little Brown and Company.

Glass, T. A., & McAfee, M. J. (2006). Behavioral science at the crossroads in public health: Extending horizons, envisioning the future. *Social Science and Medicine, 62*, 1650–1671. DOI: 10.1016/j.socscimed.2005.08.044

Harding, D.J. (2003). Counterfactual models of neighborhood effects: The effect of neighborhood poverty on dropping out and teenage pregnancy. *American Journal of Sociology, 109*, 305–322.

Hefner, K. R., Sollazzo, A., Mullaney, S., Coker, K. L., & Sofuoglu, M. (2019). E-cigarettes, alcohol use, and mental health: Use and perceptions of e-cigarettes among college students, by alcohol use and mental health status. *Addictive Behaviors 91*, 12–20. DOI: 10.1016/j.addbeh.2018.10.040

Hirschi, T. (1969). *Causes of delinquency*. Los Angeles: University of California Press.

Holtgrave, D. R., & Crosby, R. A. (2006). Is social capital a protective factor against obesity and diabetes? Findings from an exploratory study. *Annals of Epidemiology, 16,* 406–408. DOI: 10.1016/j.annepidem.2005.04.017

Institute of Medicine. (2001). *Health and behavior: The interplay of biological, behavioral, and social influences.* Washington, DC: National Academy Press. DOI: 10.17226/9838

Kameda, T., Takezawa, M., & Hastie, R. (2005). Where do social norms come from? The example of communal sharing. *Current Directions in Psychological Science, 14*(6), 331–334.

Kawachi, I., Kennedy, B., & Glass, R. (1999). Social capital and self-rated health: A contextual analysis. *American Journal of Public Health, 89*(8):1187–1193.

Knoll, L. J., Leung, J. T., Foulkes, L., & Blakemore, S. J. (2017). Age-related differences in social influence on risk perception depend on the direction of influence. *Journal of Adolescence 60,* 53–63. DOI: 10.1016/j.adolescence.2017.07.002

Kobus, K. (2003). Peers and adolescent smoking. *Addiction, 98,* 37–55. DOI: 10.1046/j.1360-0443.98.s1.4.x

Kreuter, M. W., & Lezin, N. A. (2002). Social capital theory: Implications for community-based health promotion. In R. J. DiClemente, R. A. Crosby, & M. C. Kegler (Eds.), *Emerging theories in health promotion practice and research* (pp. 228–254). San Francisco, CA: Jossey-Bass Wiley.

Li, K., Ochoa, E., Vaca, F. E., & Simons-Morton, B. (2018). Emerging adults riding with marijuana-, alcohol-, or illicit drug-impaired peer and older drivers. *Journal of Studies on Alcohol and Drugs, 79*(2), 277–285. DOI: 10.15288/jsad.2018.79.277.

Luke, D. A., & Harris, J. K. (2007). Network analysis in public health: History, methods, and applications. *Annual Review of Public Health, 28,* 69–93. DOI: 10.1146/annurev.publhealth.28.021406.144132

McNeill, L. H., Kreuter, M. W., & Subramanian, S. V. (2006). Social environment and physical activity: A review of concepts and evidence. *Social Science and Medicine, 63,* 1011–1022. DOI: 10.1016/j.socscimed.2006.03.012

Miller, D. T., Monin, B., & Prentice, D. A. (2000). Pluralistic ignorance and inconsistency between private attitudes and public behavior. In D. J. Terry & M. A. Hogg (Eds.), *Attitudes, behavior, and social context: The role of norm and group membership* (pp. 95–113). Philadelphia, PA: Psychology Press.

Noland, M., Ickles, M. J., Rayens, M. K., Butler, K., Wiggins, A. T., & Hahn, E. J. (2016). Social influences on use of cigarettes, e-cigarettes, and hookah by college students. *Journal of American College Health, 64,* 319–328. DOI: 10.1080/07448481.2016.1138478

Norman, P., Conner, M., & Bell, R. (1999). The theory of planned behavior and smoking cessation. *Health Psychology, 18,* 89–94. DOI: 10.1037//0278-6133.18.1.89

Pape, H. (2012). Young people's overestimation of peer substance use: An exaggerated phenomenon? *Addiction 107,* 878–884. DOI: 10.1111/j.1360-0443.2011.03680.x

Reger, M. A., Stanley, I. H., & Joiner, T. E. (2020). Suicide mortality and coronavirus disease—a perfect storm? *JAMA Psychiatry.* DOI:10.1001/jamapsychiatry.2020.1060

Schüz, B., Papadakis, T., & Ferguson, S. G. (2018). Situation-specific social norms as mediators of social influence on snacking. *Health Psychology, 37*(2), 153–159. DOI:10.1037/hea0000568

Seligman, M., & Csikszentmihalyi, M. (2000). Positive psychology: An introduction. *American Psychologist, 55*(1), 5–14. DOI: 10.1037/0003-066X.55.1.5.

Shaller, M. (2001). Unintended influence: Social-evolutionary processes in the construction and change of culturally-shared beliefs. In J. Forgas & K. Williams (Eds.). *Social influence: Direct and indirect processes* (pp. 79–94). Philadelphia, PA: Psychology Press.

Simons-Morton, B. G. (2007). Social influences on adolescent substance use. *American Journal of Health Behavior, 6,* 672–684. DOI: 10.5993/AJHB.31.6.13

Simons-Morton, B. G. (2019). Keeping young drivers safe during early licensure. RAC Foundation. Retrieved from https://www.racfoundation.org/wp-content/uploads/Keeping_Young_Drivers_Safe_During_Early_Licensure_Dr_Bruce_Simons-Morton_September_2019.pdf

Simons-Morton, B. G., Bingham, C. R., Falk, E. B., Li, K., Pradhan, A. K., Ouimet, M. C., Almani, F., & Shope, J. (2014). Experimental effects of injunctive norms on simulated risky driving among teenage males. *Health Psychology, 33*(7), 616–627.

Simons-Morton, B. G., Bingham, C. R., Li, K., Zhu, C., Buckley, L., Falk, E. B., & Shope, J. T. (2019). The effect of teenage passengers on simulated risky driving among teenagers: A randomized trial. *Frontiers in Psychology, 10,* 923. DOI:10.3389/fpsyg.2019.00923

Simons-Morton, B. G., & Chen, R. (2005). Latent growth curve analyses of parent influences on drinking progression among early adolescents. *Journal of Studies on Alcohol, 66,* 5–13. DOI: 10.15288/jsa.2005.66.5

Simons-Morton, B. G., Chen, R., Abroms, L., & Haynie, D. L. (2004). Latent growth curve analyses of peer and parent influences on smoking progression among early adolescents. *Health Psychology, 23,* 612–621. DOI: 10.1037/0278-6133.23.6.612

Simons-Morton, B. G., & Farhat, T. (2010). Recent findings on peer group influences on adolescent smoking. *Journal of Primary Prevention, 31,* 191–208.

Simons-Morton, B. G., Haynie, D., Bible, J., & Liu, D. (2018). Prospective associations of actual and perceived descriptive norms with drinking among emerging adults. *Substance Use and Misuse, 53*(11), 1771–1781. PMID: 29400594. PMCID: PMC6146965

Simons-Morton, B. G., Haynie, D., Liu, D., Chaurasia, A., Li, K., & Hingson, R. (2016). The effect of residence, school status, work status, and social influence on the prevalence of alcohol use among emerging adults. *Journal of Studies of Alcohol and Drugs*, 77(1), 121–132.

Simons-Morton, B. G., Haynie, D., & Noelke, E. (2009). Social influences: The effects of socialization, selection, and social normative processes on health behavior. In R. DiClemente (Ed.). *Emerging theories in health behavior and health promotion* (pp. 65–96). San Francisco: Jossey-Bass.

Simons-Morton, B. G., Haynie, D., O'Brien, F., Lipsky, L., Bible, J., & Liu, D. (2017). Variability in measures of health and health behavior among emerging adults 1 year after high school according to college status. *Journal of American College Health*, 65(1), 58–66.

Simons-Morton, B. G., & Ouimet, M. C. (2017). Teen driving risk in the presence of passengers. In D. L. Fisher, J. K. Caird, W. J. Horrey, & L. M. Trick (Eds.), *Handbook of teen and novice drivers: Research, practice, policy, and directions* (pp. 239–256). Boca Raton, FL: CRC Press.

Sparks, P. (2000). Subjective expected utility-based attitude-behavior models: The utility of self-identity. In D. Terry & M. Hogg (Eds.), *Attitudes, behavior and social context: The role of norms and group membership* (pp. 431–466). Mahwah, NJ: Erlbaum.

Thombs, D. L., & Hamilton M. J. (2000). A test of the perceived norms model to explain drinking patterns among university student athletes. *Journal of American College Health*, 49(2), 75–84. DOI: 10.1080/07448480009596287

Tilson, E. C., McBride, C. M., Lipkus, I. M., & Catalano, R. F. (2004). Testing the interaction between parent–child relationship factors and parent smoking to predict youth smoking. *Journal of Adolescent Health*, 35, 182–189. DOI: 10.1016/j.jadohealth.2003.09.014

Urberg, K. A., Degirmencioglu, S. M., & Pilgrim, C. (1997). Close friend and group influence on adolescent cigarette smoking and alcohol use. *Developmental Psychology*, 33, 834–844.

Urberg, K. A., Luo, Q., Pilgrim, C., & Degirmencioglu, S. M. (2003). A two-stage model of peer influence in adolescent substance use: Individual and relationship-specific differences in susceptibility to influence. *Addictive Behaviors*, 29, 1243–1256. DOI: 10.1016/S0306-4603(02)00256-3

Verkooijen, K. T., DeVries N. K., & Nielsen, G. A. (2007). Youth crowds and substance use: The impact of perceived group norm and multiple group identification. *Psychology of Addictive Behaviors*, 21, 55–61.

CHAPTER 7

Value Expectancy Theories

Your beliefs become your thoughts,
Your thoughts become your words,
Your words become your actions,
Your actions become your habits,
Your habits become your values,
Your values become your destiny.

—Mahatma Gandhi

OUTLINE

1. Preview
2. Objectives
3. Introduction
4. Four Expectancy Value Theories
   4.1. Theory of Reasoned Action
      4.1.1. Key Features and Constructs
         4.1.1.1. Intent
         4.1.1.2. Attitude Toward the Object and Action
         4.1.1.3. Subjective Norms
         4.1.1.4. Motivation to Comply
      4.1.2. Example
      4.1.3. Limitations
   4.2. Theory of Planned Behavior
      4.2.1. Key Features and Constructs
         4.2.1.1. Perceived Behavior Control
         4.2.1.2. Perceived Power
      4.2.2. Examples
   4.3. The Health Belief Model
      4.3.1. Key Features and Constructs
         4.3.1.1. Modifying Variables
         4.3.1.2. Perceived Susceptibility
         4.3.1.3. Perceived Severity
         4.3.1.4. Perceived Threat
         4.3.1.5. Expected Benefits of Action
         4.3.1.6. Cues to Action
         4.3.1.7. Perceived Benefits and Barriers
         4.3.1.8. Self-Efficacy
      4.3.2. Measurement
      4.3.3. Examples
   4.4. The Information–Motivation–Behavioral Skills Model
      4.4.1. Constructs
         4.4.1.1. Information
         4.4.1.2. Behavioral Skill
         4.4.1.3. Motivation
      4.4.2. Measurement
      4.4.3. Example
5. Lessons for Public Health Practice
6. Discussion Questions
7. References

PREVIEW

To some extent, behavior is the product of cognitive self-calculations. Certainly, this is not always the case, but to an important extent, people consider the pros and cons of their actions. The accuracy of these calculations can be questioned because they are based on beliefs that are unique to each individual. Beliefs are the basic element in cognitive calculations, and beliefs about an object or behavior tend to get organized into attitudes. Attitudes are formed by creating a self-understanding of beliefs, and attitudes are evaluations that guide behavior. Cognitive theories are concerned with attitudes, although they go by many different names. Expectancy value theories describe the associations between beliefs and attitudes. Attitude-oriented theories, like those described in this chapter, are important in public health because attitudes change over time and can be changed.

OBJECTIVES

The discerning reader of this chapter will be able to do the following:

1. Describe why attitudes are important to behavior.
2. Define expectancy value.
3. Describe the primary considerations of expectancy value theories.
4. Identify the key constructs of the Theory of Reasoned Action, the Health Belief Model, and the Information–Motivation–Behavior Model.
5. Explain what the Theory of Planned Behavior adds to the Theory of Reasoned Action.
6. Use the key constructs of the expectancy value theories to explain a personal-health behavior.
7. Use the key constructs of the expectancy value theories to explain a health-related behavior.

Introduction

By way of introduction to expectancy value theories, consider your own personal-health behaviors for a moment. Why do you or do you not exercise, eat healthfully, see a counselor when under mental distress, wear a safety belt when riding in a motor vehicle, drink diet or regular soda, water or juice, beer or wine? To what extent does your behavior

depend on your attitudes? Which attitudes are most important? Consider also the possibility of initiating a new behavior, a behavior different from what you have been doing up to now, such as starting a new diet or a new exercise routine. What factors would influence the likelihood of adopting this new behavior, and how important would each factor be?

You might first consider the positives about the behavior, such as how dieting and exercising would help you lose weight, make you look better, make you feel better about yourself, or maybe even impress your friends. Then you consider the negatives, the restraint and hard work involved, the logistics and inconvenience, the time and hassle involved. Of course, you cannot be sure about either the negatives or the positives, but you have some beliefs about them. You know about yourself and about the behaviors from past experience, whether they were positive or negative.

Expectancy value theories were developed to explain how individuals' behaviors are influenced by beliefs and attitudes toward objects and actions. Expectancy value theories provide a theoretical framework for determining the logical and affective calculations that go into decisions and actions. At their core, this group of theories assumes that people behave according to the anticipated or expected personal benefits that an action is anticipated to provide, considering the costs or the relative advantages of the alternatives. In essence, expectancy value theories suggest that behavior is likely when the advantages of a particular action outweigh the costs. This helps explain why you may or may not exercise, get a routine physical, or even attend college.

Thus far it seems that expectancy value is a rather simple concept. However, it is not so easy for any individual to know what the advantages and disadvantages, or benefits and costs of any particular action might be. Two people exposed to similar information about a behavior might decide very differently about adopting that behavior based on their unique subjective evaluation of the relevant considerations. This is because information is not always understood the same way by everyone who receives it, given the variable past histories of each individual. Nevertheless, if you knew a group's dominant beliefs and attitudes about an object or behavior, you could measure them and predict behavior with some level of accuracy. Assessing what beliefs and attitudes predict behavior may provide information that can be used to develop effective interventions, or at least identify the objectives that should be addressed by intervention. After all, attitudes are based on beliefs, and beliefs are based on information, so the introduction of new information relevant to key beliefs and attitudes often leads to changes in beliefs.

The key terms describing the beliefs and attitudes emphasized in expectancy value theories are shown in **Table 7.1**.

Attitudes are formed through a series of beliefs, with some attitudes more strongly held than others (Crano & Prislin, 2008). Some attitudes are highly resistant to change, while others are quite amenable. Attitudes, whether strongly or weakly held, positive and negative, momentary or enduring, influence the likelihood of engaging in the behavior. Ultimately, your attitudes about the behavior and about what it would be like to perform

the behavior lead you to take an action, continue the action, and/or discontinue the action. Of course, once you engage in the behavior, you get new information based on the experience and the consequences of your behavior that affect your beliefs and attitudes about repeating the behavior. Also, attitudes have a tendency to vary by circumstance. For example, your attitudes about a particular TV show might be different than your attitudes toward the legalization of marijuana. Moreover, while attitudes tend to be relatively enduring, they also change over time, as people are introduced to new information and gain experience.

Although beliefs and attitudes are measurable, it can be difficult to know which cognitions might be important and how they might vary from person to person regarding a particular action. Attitudes of concern might be social, emotional, physical, or financial. For example, consider a woman who is concerned that her new male partner may have been exposed to HIV due to his prior sexual history. She cannot know what the chances are that he is infected, and she cannot be sure what the chances are that she could get infected by having sex with him. She could decide not to have sex with him at all, require that he be tested for HIV, require that he use a condom,

Table 7.1 Cognitions

Knowledge	Objectively verifiable truth.
Beliefs	What we believe to be true or factual, even if they are not.
Perceptions	In psychology, perceptions are to become aware of something through our senses. In value expectancy, it is synonymous with beliefs.
Attitudes	Set of emotions, feelings, or beliefs toward a particular object, action, person, or thing. Attitudes can be positive or negative and can change over time as you learn new information and gain new experiences.
Values	Evaluations of the relative importance of various factors, concepts, and actions.

or just hope for the best. Obviously, there are many factors to consider. She could avoid any possibility of being infected by not having sex with him, but she might lose his company entirely. The other options are also complex with uncertain outcomes. Her girlfriend's opinion about what she should do may be important; she knows that her parents would be very upset if she had sex with someone who might infect her with HIV. She realizes that doing nothing might have consequences, just as each of the possible options will have consequences, but she cannot be certain just what they might be. If her concern about the HIV virus is paramount, she might pursue a different course of action than if the most important thing to her was maintaining her relationship with this new man. She does not have all the information she needs to make a decision that has emotional, social, and physical consequences. In this case, doing nothing would have consequences. Nonetheless, in matters such as these, the individual develops beliefs and attitudes that guide behavior, despite not having as much information as would be desirable, or maybe having incorrect information.

The benefits and costs of any action cannot be known in advance and must be estimated. People must rely on uncertain information in developing their expectations about the benefits and costs of any particular action. A young woman contemplating sex with a new man in her life cannot know for sure about his HIV status, about how he would react to her asking him to get tested, or her demand that they use condoms. She can use only the information available to guide her actions. She may assume certain things based on beliefs that later turn out to be unfounded. Indeed, this is the case for many behaviors, where we must develop expectations based on uncertain, often incorrect or incomplete information. If she believes her potential sex partner is not HIV positive, she is likely to behave very differently than if she believes he is or if she is uncertain. Of course, there are uncertain consequences of any action she takes. For

example, she may decide to require her partner to use condoms, thereby reducing her anxiety/fear about possible infection. However, in practice, consistent condom use can be difficult to maintain because the immediate context can sometimes become more important than long-term considerations.

Because existing beliefs and attitudes are based on past information, changes in beliefs and attitudes arise from new information. This is what makes beliefs and attitudes so important in public health. By identifying the beliefs and attitudes associated with behavior, it is possible to provide relevant new information that can alter previously held beliefs and attitudes with hopes to change behaviors and improve health outcomes. Of course, information can come from many sources, including experience, observations of life events, and incidental and purposeful messages.

Collections of beliefs about a particular object or action combine to make up attitudes. This is a very good way of thinking about attitudes, although they are sometimes a good deal more complex than this implies. One cannot just add up all the beliefs a person or group has regarding an object or behavior to come up with attitudes. This is because some beliefs are held more strongly and valued more greatly than others. A more accurate description of attitudes might be that they are an "evaluative integration of cognitions and affects experienced in relation to an object" (Crano & Prislin, 2006, p. 347). Clearly, attitudes are more general than beliefs because they represent an integration of beliefs about an object or action. Moreover, attitudes are distinct from beliefs because they have an affective component that may or may not exist for any particular belief. One can hold particular beliefs more or less strongly, but attitudes convey an emotional quality that beliefs do not.

It is convenient to think that values are made up of a collection of related attitudes. For sure, values are rather more general than attitudes and are sometimes quite grand in scale. I might believe that eating fruit for breakfast is good for health (belief), be upset if I am unable to get fruit for breakfast (attitude), and value opportunities to eat fruit for breakfast. People hold values for small and personal concepts like food, exercise, alcohol, how they spend their time, who they spend it with, and for bigger and less personal concepts things like fairness, competition, patriotism, and religion. Expectancy value theory is so named because it assumes that people tend to behave in ways that they expect will maximize the likelihood of achieving something they value.

Four Expectancy Value Theories

This chapter presents four theories that are predicated on value expectancy assumptions. In this chapter we start with the Theory of Reasoned Action (TRA), developed by Martin Fishbein, who is generally credited with first introducing value expectancy theory. Subsequently, we discuss the Theory of Planned Behavior (TPB), which is an extension of the Theory of Reasoned Action. The Theory of Reasoned Action and the Theory of Planned Behavior have much in common, including measurement and intervention considerations. Next, we present the Health Belief Model, which was developed to explain medication compliance, but has since been used in research and practice addressing a wide range of behaviors. We then present the Information–Motivation–Behavioral Skills, or IMB, Model.

Expectancy value theories propose highly elaborate measurement of beliefs. Indeed, because it cannot be known in advance what beliefs might be important with respect to any particular behavior and any particular population, measurement should involve several steps. The first of these is qualitative assessment of the beliefs of a population of interest, presumably through interviews or general surveys. Based on this initial assessment, more

formal questionnaires would be developed to determine the strength of the identified beliefs. Beliefs and attitudes are generally measured by using scales for each of several variables using bipolar or response options that range on 5- or 7-point scales from strongly agree to strongly disagree. Intentions should be defined very specifically to include the following: (1) time frame for performance of the behavior, (2) an exact description of the action comprising the behavior, (3) the desired outcome (target) of the behavior, and (4) the context of the behavior. For example, intent to use safety belts may be specifically defined as "intent to wear a safety belt every time I ride in a vehicle"; intent to use condoms may be specifically defined as "intent to use condoms for STD prevention (target) in the next 6 months (time) for every act of sexual intercourse." Intention is often measured using scales that include response options that range from very likely to very unlikely, for example, "How likely is it that you will wear your safety belt every time you ride in or drive a motor vehicle in the next month (very likely to very unlikely)?"

Expectancy value theories have been used primarily in **observational research** designed to explain and predict various behaviors and for identifying potential **mediators** that can be addressed by interventions and do not provide specific intervention approaches or methods. However, Ajzen and Manstead (2007) argue that a major strength of the TPB (and by association the TRA) is as a tool for designing interventions, enabling health-promotion professionals to tailor interventions to address those beliefs that have been shown to differ between intenders or performers and nonintenders and nonperformers. Fishbein (2008) and Ajzen and Manstead (2007) have described how these theories can be used to guide intervention development. Notably, these theories emphasize the importance of beliefs and attitudes, suggesting that changing beliefs and attitudes is a good way of changing behavior. Moreover, interventions can focus on increasing **perceived behavioral control** by improving skills or modifying the environment to reduce barriers (Middlestadt, Macy, Dowty, Arrieta, & Jay, 2020).

Theory of Reasoned Action

The Theory of Reasoned Action is one of the most enduring and popular theories in psychology. First introduced by Martin Fishbein and fully described by Ajzen and Fishbein (1980) and Fishbein and Ajzen (2010), the theory provides a rather elaborate description of the relationships between certain beliefs, attitudes, norms, intention, and behavior. At the core of the theory, TRA is made up of three constructs: attitude toward the object or action, subjective norms, and behavioral intent. Behavioral intent is largely influenced by our attitude toward the object or action and subjective norms.

A unique feature of the theory is the proposition that people tend to behave according to their intentions when opportunity allows. Therefore, *intentions predict our behavior*. Certain beliefs and attitudes are associated with intentions. The key beliefs and attitudes are those toward a particular object or behavior and about others' approval or disapproval, known as subjective norms. Basically, human action is influenced by a favorable or unfavorable evaluation of the action (attitude toward the behavior) and perceived social pressure to perform or not perform the behavior (Ajzen & Fishbein, 2005).

TRA has been used in thousands of studies of behavior, including personal-health behavior, health-related behavior, and behavior not related to health at all. Examples include cyberbullying (Doane, Kelley, & Pearson, 2016), physical activity among individuals with disabilities (Kirk & Haegele, 2019), and online shopping using social media (Pookulangara, Parr, Tanoff, & Nix, 2017). The TRA is actually quite elaborate. However, the heart of the theory, shown in **Figure 7.1**, is quite simple.

Key Features and Constructs

The logic of the theory is that behavior is predicted by intentions, intentions are predicted by attitudes, and attitudes are made up of beliefs. People are more likely to do something if they plan or aim to do it than if they don't. Here are the key considerations and features of the theory.

1. Intentions. TRA emphasizes the relationship between attitudes and intention. It posits that intentions are associated with behavior, as shown in Figure 7.1, but intent is the cognitive end point of TRA. Research has long shown that relationships between attitudes and behavior tend to be significant but modest. Fishbein recognized that these relationships were moderated by environmental circumstances and introduced the idea that attitudes are more likely to be associated with intention, a measure of likelihood given certain environmental conditions. That is, a person may intend to use condoms, but actual use would depend greatly on opportunity and circumstance.

    To appreciate the wisdom and utility of this convention, consider how important context and opportunity are to behavior. My attitudes may be consistent with a particular behavior, but I am likely to engage in that behavior only if I have the opportunity. Moreover, I might have the opportunity, but the particular context of that opportunity might not support the behavior. Condom use is a good example. I may intend to use condoms, but if I don't have a partner it may not matter. If I have a partner but no condom is available, my behavior may not be consistent with my attitudes. I may have a partner and a condom, but alcohol undermines good intention. I may intend to use a condom, but only when my partner insists. Something else about the context may not lend itself to condom use. Thus, behavior is often dependent on environmental factors, sometimes regardless of attitudes.

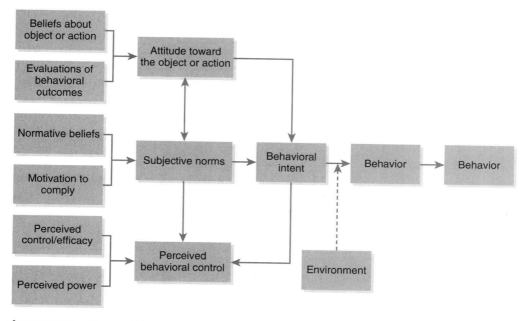

Figure 7.1 The Theory of Reasoned Action with perceived control and perceived power variables from the Theory of Planned Behavior

2. The second key TRA consideration is that intentions are the product of attitudes (Ajzen & Cote, 2008). Shown in Figure 7.1 are arrows linking key attitude to intent rather than to behavior. The most important attitudes are attitudes toward the object or behavior and subjective norms.

3. Both attitudes toward an object and toward a behavior are important. A person may have positive attitudes about the object of physical activity (e.g., it is good for health), but negative attitudes about actually engaging in physical activity (e.g., it takes too much time, it is uncomfortable).

4. Attitudes are based on beliefs. Beliefs are what people think is true or perceive to be true. Beliefs, regardless of their validity, influence attitudes. I may believe that condoms are not reliable, that they hinder sexual enjoyment, that my partner does not favor them, that others like me do not use them, and then these beliefs contribute to my attitudes, intentions, and behavior,

even if they are not true or accurate. If we had to be certain about everything in our lives before we reached a conclusion, we would be paralyzed by the uncertainty and unable to act one way or another.

5. Subjective norms are among the most important beliefs. Perceptions or beliefs about norms include both the prevalence of an action and the preferences of those who are important to us (what others want of us). People feel social pressure to behave in ways that are common and acceptable, particularly with respect to peoples whose opinion are highly valued.

6. TRA argues that intent and behavior are logically based on beliefs, regardless of how factual. This point is important both for understanding intentions and behavior and also for developing interventions to alter them. While it may not be easy to change some beliefs, most beliefs are alterable when new information is provided in a persuasive form.

7. Beliefs can be negative or positive and may be strongly or weakly held. One or two beliefs that are strongly held may provide greater influence on attitudes and intentions than many other beliefs that are not held strongly. This is one reason accurate measurement of beliefs is important.

The key TRA constructs are described in **Table 7.2** and in the following paragraphs.

Table 7.2 Definitions and Examples of Theory of Reasoned Action and Theory of Planned Behavior

Construct	Definition	Example
Intent	Likelihood of taking action	How likely are you to stop smoking in the next 30 days? (VL—VU)*
Attitudes toward object or action	Subjective evaluation of the object or action; positive or negative evaluation about a behavior	Smoking is bad for your health? (SA—SD)*
Beliefs about object or action	Beliefs about object or a particular action	Most smokers quit before age 30 (SA—SD)*
Expected outcomes	Anticipated outcomes of a particular behavior	The earlier one quits, the fewer lasting health effects (SA—SD)*
Subjective Norms	Subjective evaluation of norms and social pressure on behavior	What percent of smokers who try to quit are eventually successful? (0–100%) How important is it to you wife that you quit smoking? (VI—VU)*
Normative beliefs	Beliefs about the prevalence and acceptability of the object or action by the judgement of significant others	Most smokers try to quit? (SA—SD) My wife is very concerned about the effects of smoking on my health (SA—SD)*
Motivation to comply	Importance of the referent's perceived preference	My wife's opinions are important to me (SA—SD)*
Perceived Behavioral Control	Subjective evaluation of one's ability to engage in intended behavior; perception of ease/difficulty of performing a particular behavior	I can quit smoking if I try (SA—SD)*
Perceived control	Subjective evaluation of factors that may facilitate or impede performance of the behavior.	I could quit smoking if my wife (friend, co-workers) quit (SA—SD)* I could quit smoking if I used a nicotine patch (SA—SD)*
Perceived Power	Importance of facilitating and constraining factors	The most important factors in quitting for me are: my wife quits; my friend quits; I use nicotine substitute; the price of cigarettes goes up (1=NI; 10=VU)*

* VL—VU: Very likely to Very unlikely.
SA—SD: Strongly Agree to Strongly Disagree.
NI—VU: Not Important to Very Unimportant.

Intent Intent is a measure of motivation. It is what one plans to do, a decision, based on one's attitudes. However, sometimes life gets in the way of intention, so people do not always follow through. However, given a supportive environment, intention is a good predictor of behavior. Because behavior can sometimes be difficult to measure, for example, measuring a nonbehavior such as not smoking, or not having unprotected intercourse sometime in the future, intentions are a useful proxy. One of the great advantages of intent as the dependent variable in TRA is that it can be easily and accurately measured. People are often asked about their intentions, for example, for whom they will vote and the likelihood they will get a flu shot, exercise, or wear a condom the next time they have sex. For example, you might intend to exercise so you bring gym clothes to work so you can exercise after the workday is done.

Attitude Toward the Object and Action

People develop attitudes toward objects and actions, and these attitudes are associated with intent to act (Ajzen & Cote, 2008). Favorable attitudes toward an object or action are positively associated with intent and action, while unfavorable attitudes toward an object or action are negatively associated with intent and action. Attitudes about a particular behavior are made up of beliefs about the object or behavior and evaluation of the outcomes of the behavior. You can have a positive attitude toward exercising because you know it's good for your health, it can help lower your blood pressure, and you could possibly lose weight. Therefore, because you have a positive attitude toward exercising, the theory implies that you are more likely to exercise.

Remember that attitudes have an affective component that contributes to decision making. The human papillomavirus (HPV) vaccination is recommended for all boys and girls at ages 11–12, but can be given as early as age 9. HPV is a sexually transmitted disease that can cause genital warts and certain types of cancer. Because children are unable to vaccinate themselves, they are reliant on the intentions of their parents, and that intention is largely based on the parents' attitude. Logically thinking, most parents would have the attitude that they will do whatever they can to protect the health of their child, especially from cancer. At the same time, few parents want to imagine that their 9- or 10-year-old could be sexually active. Because parents do not want to imagine this, they might be unlikely to vaccinate their child at that age, even though their attitude is to protect the health of the child.

Attitudes toward an object of behavior are made up of two categories: beliefs about the object or action and beliefs about the **expected outcomes** of an action. A wide range of beliefs about a particular object, action, or behavior might be important, including aspects of desirability, cost, relative advantage over other options, and the like.

Attitudes about the behavior are balanced by the expected outcomes or consequences of actually engaging in the behavior. Outcome expectations are significantly influenced by our past experiences in similar situations, observing others in similar situations, and the emotional or physical response that occurs as a result of the behavior.

Subjective Norms

Subjective Norms Subjective norms provide a set of beliefs that contribute to the formation of intentions. Subjective norms reflect perceptions of social approval. When people feel social pressure to act in a certain way, they tend to do so, and when they feel social pressure not to act in a certain way, they tend not to act in this way. These norms are described as subjective because they are not actual—they are what the individual perceives them to be. I might believe that other people my age behave as I do, even if only some of them do. I might believe that I am the only one who behaves or believes in a certain way, when many others might believe and behave this way. We are not always accurate judges of norms for a variety of reasons. For one thing, we have limited experience. For another, we tend to overestimate the prevalence of behaviors we have observed.

For example, a teenager who knows a few other teenagers who smoke marijuana may wrongly or rightly conclude that a high percentage of adolescents smoke marijuana.

Subjective norms are composed of two sets of beliefs, the first called normative beliefs, the second, motivation to comply. Normative beliefs include beliefs about how normative the behavior is among relevant groups and individuals (called referents) and beliefs about what these referents would want the individual to do or how they would think about the individual engaging in the behavior. Basically, normative beliefs focus on how common and acceptable the behavior is among referents. For example, a parent might want to know if their friends vaccinated their child for HPV or not. Typically, the more common a behavior is perceived, the easier it is to engage in it because one does not need to go against the social norms to engage in the behavior.

In addition to how common the behavior is among particular referents (referents are those whose opinions are of concern), normative beliefs are concerned about the individual's perceptions of how these referents would think about the individual engaging in the behavior. For example, an individual might consider how my friends, my parents, "people like me" or "people I want to be like," or other people whose opinions matter to me would think of me if I engaged in the behavior. If you are a parent and you were to vaccinate your child for HPV, you might think, "Will my friends think I'm allowing my child to be sexually active or do they view me and my decision as being proactive?" Of course, what is important to the individual is what they perceive to be the norms, the subjective norms, and not necessarily what the norms actually are. This is in part because it is not always possible to know what actual norms are, but it is always possible to perceive what they might be.

Motivation to Comply Motivation to comply is how much the individual values the opinions of particular referents with respect

to a particular behavior, what the individual believes the referent would want the individual to do, and how the referent would think about the individual if he or she engaged in the behavior. (Note: This is an important concept but is probably a poor choice of terms, because the entire theory is about motivation, and this particular construct is really about the value of others' opinions, which is generally measured as part of subjective norms.) The importance of each referent with respect to any particular behavior might vary. An adolescent may value the opinions of his or her parents more than the opinions of any others with respect to some behaviors but may value the opinions of friends more than parents with respect to other behaviors. Indeed, for some behaviors I might place the greatest value on my beliefs about the norms of people I know only impersonally, for example, by reputation. The point here is that motivation to comply refers to how valued the opinions of various referents are with respect to a particular behavior.

Example

The behavior of smoking provides a good example. So far we have stated that according to TRA, an individual's intent to smoke or to continue or quit smoking is based on their attitudes toward the behavior and subjective norms, which are the beliefs about how relevant others would regard the individual if he or she were to start smoking, continue smoking, or quit smoking.

Attitudes toward smoking would be made up of beliefs about smoking and about the outcomes of smoking. Beliefs about smoking might include concerns about health. However, because people mostly start smoking as adolescents or young adults, and the health effects of smoking, while substantial and well known, do not manifest for many years and may not be as important as other beliefs about more immediate concerns. People who believe that smoking is attractive, sexy, mature, reflective of independence, and other positive things about the behavior are more likely to smoke than people who believe that smoking is unattractive and gross.

However, as discussed, attitudes toward smoking would be made up of both beliefs about the behavior and evaluation of the likely outcomes of actually smoking. So, my beliefs about smoking, as described earlier, would be important relative to my evaluation of the outcomes, including how likely they are and how important they are. If I believe that smoking causes lung cancer and other health problems, but I don't believe I will get lung cancer if I smoke, then my belief about that health concern might not be a very important influence on my attitudes and intentions regarding smoking. Similarly, I might not be that concerned about the health effects, but I might be concerned about the hassle and cost associated with smoking.

Intentions with respect to smoking may be influenced at least as much by beliefs about the subjective norms as by beliefs about smoking and the outcomes of smoking. People tend to be influenced by the behavior and values of others. It is easier to be a smoker when a lot of other people in your group also smoke because that makes it normative. If I believe my parents would be very upset if I smoke and I value my parent's opinion, I would be less inclined to smoke than if I believed my parents would not be that upset or if I did not highly value my parent's opinions about my smoking. The normative beliefs of my best friend, my spouse, or my colleagues might factor into my smoking intentions. Certainly, perceptions of norms measured as the number of close friends who smoke have shown to influence smoking behavior (Simons-Morton, Chen, Abroms, & Haynie, 2004).

Limitations

There are some limitations to TRA. Intentions do not always lead to the intended behavior. As noted, intention can be affected by the environment or even individual choice. While you had all intention to exercise because you took your gym clothes to work, you might not have exercised because you were too tired, didn't

feel like it, or something more appealing took precedence. Intention is only a strong predictor of behavior in the short term, and the relationship weakens over time. TRA explores the decision-making process as linear and does not consider that it can change over time. The workout clothes you brought to the office might be sitting in your office cabinet, and you have no intention to exercise in the near future. In order to address these concerns and strengthen the theory, Ajzen and Fishbein created the Theory of Planned Behavior (Ajzen, 1985).

Theory of Planned Behavior

The Theory of Planned Behavior is consistent with TRA, distinguished largely by the addition of a fourth key construct, that of **perceived behavioral control** (Ajzen, 2002). Ajzen collaborated with Fishbein on TRA and then elaborated on the theory by adding perceived behavioral control, plus additional explanation and description of TRA. TPB is so closely related to TRA that the two theories are commonly considered together, as they are in this chapter. Nevertheless, there is a rapidly expanding literature on the application of TRA to health-related and other behaviors (Ajzen, 2002; Armitage & Conner, 2001).

Key Features and Constructs

Basically, TPB posits that behavior is the product of attitudes toward the behavior, subjective norms, intention, and perceived behavioral control as shown in Figure 7.1. All of the key features of TRA are retained, including the emphasis on beliefs making up the attitudes related to intention. However, TPB adds to TRA beliefs about perceived control over the factors that may enable, facilitate, or prevent the behavior. Perceived behavioral control can add strength to behavioral intention, but perceived behavioral control is also proximal to behavior and can impact behavior directly. While not noted in Figure 7.1, the key attitudes associated with intention are likely to be moderated by personal factors, such as personality; demographic factors such as age, sex, race, and income; and environmental factors, for example media exposure.

Perceived Behavior Control The key TPB variable is perceived behavioral control, which can be described as an overall assessment of conditional aspects of the behavior that would enable or inhibit engaging in the behavior. Perceived behavioral control is the individual's beliefs about the environment and the extent to which the individual believes he or she has control over the behavior under particular (or conditional) circumstances. If a behavior is perceived to be important and subjective norms seem to favor the behavior, the behavior is more likely if the individual believes that the behavior can be done without too much difficulty or that the individual can control or overcome any obstacles or barriers to action. For example, when you brought your gym clothes to work, you intended to exercise. However, the proximity of the gym might affect your decision. If the gym is close to your work, your perceived behavioral control will be high because it is easy to access. However, if the gym is across town and the weather is poor, your perceived behavioral control is low, and you are less likely to exercise because there are barriers. Beliefs about control are based in part on factors that are external to the person making the decision, but these beliefs should not be confused with the notion that an objective reality exists or that the individual correctly understands either these external factors or the individual's internal resources. Both internal and external aspects of control are based on personal perceptions that may or may not reflect an objective reality. Therefore, the variable, behavioral control, is designed to overcome a limitation of TRA by accounting for the person's perceptions of personal control.

Two sets of beliefs make up perceived behavioral control: perceived control and perceived power. **Control beliefs** are concerned with the likelihood of the occurrence of facilitating and constraining conditions—the subjective evaluation of the likelihood of factors that would facilitate or inhibit action and the importance of each factor. An individual develops beliefs about what and how likely and important these factors are likely to be. Pap testing serves as an excellent example. One factor that may facilitate Pap testing is the perception that it would be convenient to get the test. Other facilitating factors may include beliefs that the clinical environment would be friendly and nonthreatening and the test, itself, not expensive. Beliefs that inhibit or constrain the likelihood of getting the test might include anticipated problems with insurance claims, getting off work, arranging babysitting, and the like. Again, until the individual goes through the bother of getting the test, she will not know for sure about the environmental constraints, but she will base her beliefs about how controllable these environmental factors are on the information available.

Perceived Power A second set of beliefs, labeled perceived power, contribute to the attitude of perceived behavioral control. Perceived power is concerned with the strength of the facilitating and inhibiting factors. This is very much like the concept of motivation to comply that is part of subjective norms. Here, perceived power is the estimation of the importance or strength of the environmental conditions. Perceptions that certain conditions make performing the behavior extremely easy or difficult contribute to overall perceptions of control and intent. For example, time and cost are often important considerations, but when one is poor, cost may be the most powerful factor, overwhelming all others.

Examples

In a recent study, TPB was used to explore texting while driving in college students (Bazargan-Hejazi et al., 2017). The goal was to explore if intent predicted college students' willingness to text while driving. In this cross-sectional study, participants ($n = 243$) were given driving scenarios and asked to respond on a 7-point Likert scale on their willingness to text while driving. Results indicated that intention was mediated by perceived behavioral control. A person's intention to read or send a text was associated with a person's control of the situation (e.g., perceived road conditions, traffic).

Another study reported by Chevance, Caudroit, Romain, and Boiche (2017) explored the constructs of TPB with physical activity and eating behaviors among obese and nonobese individuals. The cross-sectional study ($n = 153$) results revealed a significant association with attitudes toward physical activity and eating behaviors. Attitudes played a significant role in physical activity among the obese, which implies that obese individuals rely more on automatic processes than non-obese individuals.

The Health Belief Model

The premise of the Health Belief Model (HBM) is that beliefs about susceptibility and severity of a health concern and beliefs about the utility of possible preventive action predict the likelihood of action. It is based in value-expectancy because people will behave according to the anticipated or expected benefits they will receive by taking action. For example, you might get a flu shot because you expect that action to prevent you from getting the flu. If you think you're not susceptible to the flu or that the shot is ineffective, you would be less likely to get a flu shot. Similarly, if you think wearing a face mask and

social distancing will prevent you from contracting the coronavirus, you would be more likely to wear a mask and remain socially distant.

Key Features and Constructs

The Health Belief Model has been employed in research and public health practice for more than 50 years and remains popular because of its flexibility in programming. The model takes into consideration events or behaviors that are happening now while also considering future events/behaviors (Champion, 1984). The model posits that people's readiness to take a specific action is based on (1) their desire to avoid illness, get well, or improve their health; and (2) the belief that a specific action will be effective in this regard. The HBM attempts to explain the likelihood of preventive health behavior based on beliefs about the perceived threat and the benefits of the recommended action. According to the HBM, people are ready to act when they regard themselves as susceptible to a condition that has serious consequences, if they believe the course of action would be beneficial. The HBM has widely been used in preventative behaviors such as self-examinations and health management (Janz, Champion, & Strecher, 2002). **Figure 7.2** shows how the HBM constructs are theoretically related. In the following

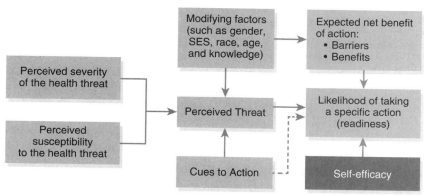

Figure 7.2 The Health Belief Model

paragraphs and in **Table 7.3**, we define and discuss the key HBM constructs.

Modifying Variables As with other expectancy value theories, the HBM suggests that a variety of mainly demographic factors may modify perceived threat. These include age, socioeconomic status, ethnicity, and geographic location.

Perceived Susceptibility This construct is the subjective estimate of individual risk for a particular health problem. This is sometimes conceptualized as a general concern with health, but more often it is concerned with personal susceptibility, being personally at risk or a member of a group that is at high risk. Note that one's actual susceptibility may not matter as much as one's perceived susceptibility. For

Table 7.3 Definitions and Examples of Health Belief Model Constructs

Construct	Definition	Example
Likelihood of action	Readiness to act; made up of perceived threat and cues to action	How likely are you take your medicine for hypertension exactly as prescribed during the next month?
Perceived threat	Overall perception of threat to health	Latent variable made up of susceptibility and severity.
Perceived susceptibility	Belief about the personal likelihood of a health problem	How likely is the occurrence of each of the following health problems in the next 10 years if you take/don't take your HBP medicine?
Perceived severity	Beliefs about the seriousness of the health problem and its consequences	Rate the severity of each of the following health problems that can result from untreated HBP.
Cues to action	Information about perceived threat or benefits and barriers of particular actions	HBP is the silent killer! Remember to take your high blood pressure (HBP) medicine before meals daily.
Expected utility	Subjective evaluation of particular preventive or therapeutic actions; may involve comparison of possible actions; made up of perceived benefits and barriers	Latent variable made up of perceived benefits and barriers.
Perceived benefits	Beliefs about the benefits of action to reduce a health threat	Assuming you take your HBP medicine exactly as prescribed, how effective would it be in preventing the following health problems? (list)
Perceived barriers	Beliefs about the psychological, time, expense, and other costs of action	Rate each of the following barriers to taking your HBP medicine exactly as prescribed: cost, convenience, remembering, etc. (1 = low to 5 = high).
Self-efficacy	Confidence in one's ability to take specific action; linked to readiness to act	How confident are you that you can take your HBP medicine exactly as prescribed under the following conditions?

example, some people are more susceptible to the flu than others because they work with children or in a hospital or other public place where they come into contact with a lot of people during flu season. However, in the HBM, it is the perception of susceptibility that is important, not actual susceptibility.

Perceived Severity Perceived severity is mainly important when there is a perception of susceptibility. Severity may not be an important influence on behavior for one who does not perceive personal susceptibility to the threat, but it may be very important when susceptibility is perceived. Important considerations that make up a person's beliefs about the severity of a health problem include its physical, social, and practical consequences, for example, how long the symptoms last, how painful the condition, and how reversible the condition. In general, the greater the belief that a health problem is severe, the more likely a person is to take preventive action. With respect to the flu, the more severe the illness symptoms are perceived, the more likely you are to take preventive action.

Perceived Threat The basic premise of the HBM is that action is largely a matter of how a particular threat to health is perceived. Perceptions are our interpretation of something we see, hear, or become aware of something. Perceived susceptibility and perceived severity collectively are called perceived threat. For example, perceived threat of getting the flu is made up of beliefs about its severity and one's susceptibility.

Expected Benefits of Action There may be a number of possible actions one can take with respect to a health threat that is perceived to be severe and to which one feels susceptible. Remember, these are perceived options, not all of which may be practical or effective. Nevertheless, in true expectancy value fashion, the HBM posits that people evaluate the available options based on the information at

hand and decide which, if any, to take. One possible benefit of an action is its health-protecting effects. However, these can be uncertain. People must often make decisions about actions that they cannot be certain will have the intended effect. For example, some diagnostic tests have many false positives or false negatives, so it can be difficult to know in advance the benefits of the test. Other benefits may be social or cost. For example, a person may take an action mainly because an important other wants him or her to or because taking the action will result in a reduction in insurance rates. With respect to the flu, one can get vaccinated, attempt to avoid contact with others, wash hands frequently, or ignore the threat.

Cues to Action A variety of cues to action may influence perceived threat. This concept is not well developed in the HBM literature, but basically refers to new information that relates to a perceived threat. A cue to action might be intentional, such as health education in the form of a poster or targeted persuasive communication. However, a cue to action may be incidental, including the comment of a friend or colleague, coming across an article or advertisement, or other chance discovery of new information. Logically, cues to action that are part of a health-promotion program based on the HBM would seek to alter perceptions about severity, susceptibility, and the benefits of the recommended action and how to reduce barriers.

Perceived Benefits and Barriers There are potential benefits and barriers to every possible action. In general, greater perceived benefits and fewer perceived barriers result in higher likelihood of preventive action. Potential benefits include the effectiveness of the action while barriers include the time, cost, effort, and hassle of the action. Barriers can be both physical and psychological. Barriers can include financial responsibility, pain, difficulty, inconvenience, and time consumption (Janz et al., 2002). Some actions have negative consequences having nothing to do with the health problem one is trying to prevent or resolve. The perception that people sometimes get sick from getting a flu shot would be a barrier. Theoretically, cues to action could be directed at perceived benefits and barriers as well as to perceived threat. In general, perceived barriers have been the most predictive construct of behavior change.

Self-Efficacy Although not an original part of the HBM, self-efficacy, generally defined as confidence in one's ability to act in a particular way, has recently been added to the model. The construct can include an estimate of one's ability to overcome barriers. As shown in Figure 7.2, self-efficacy would be expected to influence readiness to act.

Measurement

The measurement of HBM constructs should be done carefully. The main difficulty is that respondents' answers may vary according to their behavior. One cannot simply ask about susceptibility or without controlling for intended or actual behavior. Often an accurate measurement of perceived susceptibility can only be obtained by including in the question a conditional statement about behavior. A conditional statement is one that includes behavior status. For example, consider the question that follows: "In the next year, how likely are you to get the flu?" (very unlikely to very likely). A person who answers by selecting "very unlikely" could do so because he/she truly feels invulnerable to the flu or because that person has been vaccinated against the flu. The solution to this problem is simply to include the behavior in the question stem: "Assuming you obtained appropriate vaccination, how likely would you be in the next year to get the flu?" By asking the question using this structure and then asking the question again rephrased to

include, "assuming you were not vaccinated …" it may be possible to correctly determine perceived susceptibility.

Examples

Recent studies based on the HBM include predicting women's likelihood to screen for breast cancer (Lodyga, 2013; Wang, Chen, Xie, & Zhang, 2019) or men for testicular cancer (Lodyga, 2013), and exploring perceptions about behaviors related to mental illness and mental health services among college students (Nobling & Maykrantz, 2017). According to U.S. survey data, approximately 70% of females participate in breast cancer screenings, and 54% men participate in testicular cancer screenings. Wang et al. (2019) found that 66.8% of the female population were not aware of breast cancer screenings. It was found that women who have more information about breast cancer (perceived threat and cues to action) were more likely to undergo screenings. The most significant barrier associated with screenings were cost and access (Wang et al., 2019). In college students, it was found that only 34% of men and women have performed self-examinations. If they were taught how to perform a self-examination, 76% of women performed at least one breast self-examination and 75.5% of men performed at least one testicular self-examination in the last year. Participants were more likely to perform self-examinations if they felt susceptible to developing cancer and if they had increased self-efficacy in their ability to properly perform one. Participants were also more likely to perform self-examinations if cues to action were provided (e.g., their doctor told them to) (Lodyga, 2013). When exploring mental health and mental health services, Nobling and Maykrantz (2017) discovered that navigating mental health services and perceived sociocultural concerns (e.g., stigma) were the primary barriers to seeking care. Professional treatment was viewed as a perceived benefit, and primary care providers were reported as a critical cue to action.

The Information–Motivation–Behavioral Skills Model

The Information–Motivation–Behavioral Skills (IMB) Model was developed in an effort to better understand HIV risk behaviors (Fisher & Fisher, 1992; Fisher, Fisher, & Shuper, 2009, pp. 25–26). Subsequently, it has been used in other areas, including breast self-examination, motorcycle helmet use, and medication-taking adherence (Fisher, Fisher, Bryan, & Misovich, 2002; Nelson et al., 2018), suggesting that the model may be applicable to other skill-dependent preventive behaviors (Fisher et al., 2002; Fisher, Fisher, Amico, & Harman, 2006; John, Walsh, & Weinhardt, 2017).

The basic idea of IMB is that behavior is often skill dependent, and skills are influenced by information and attitudes (motivation). IMB is an expectancy value theory because it assumes that people act rationally based on the information they have. However, this information is often incorrect and prevents the individual from developing skills and taking preventive actions.

A primary assumption of the IMB Model is that skill is a prerequisite for many behaviors and that skill is largely the product of information and motivation. As indicated in the figure, information and motivation can also influence behavior directly. Motivation includes attitudes and beliefs about the skill and the behavior. Basically, skill and confidence tend to improve as a person obtains useful information

and develops appropriate beliefs and attitudes. Remember, this theory was developed to better understand why many people who would benefit from using condoms failed to do so. Research determined that in many cases condom use failure was due to a lack of skill in managing condom use. Indeed, negotiating successful condom use requires a complex set of skills. It turns out these skills are much higher among those who are knowledgeable and motivated.

The IMB model is shown in **Figure 7.3**, with five important pathways. Accordingly, arrows show that information and motivation are directly related to behavior. However, information and motivation typically influence behavior indirectly, through their effect on behavioral skill. In this context, behavioral skill mediates the influence of information and motivation on behavior. The concept here is that skill develops through the acquisition of relevant and useful information when the individual is motivated to develop the skill. Many health-protective behaviors do require skill, for example, adhering to a low-fat diet, exercising to increase cardiovascular fitness, negotiating condom use, or adhering to complex medical regimen.

Constructs

The key constructs of the IMB model are information, skills, and motivation, and as shown in **Table 7.4**.

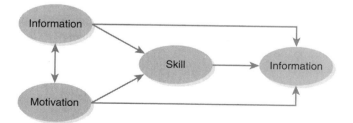

Figure 7.3 The Information–Motivation–Behavioral Skills Model

Fisher, J.D., & Fisher, W.A. (1992). Changing AIDS risk behavior. *Psychological Bulletin*, 111:455-474.

Table 7.4 Definitions of Information–Motivation–Behavioral Skills Model Constructs

Constructs	Definitions
Information	Information that is relevant to the health problem and skills impacts behavior
Motivation	Attitudes toward preventive behavior and social support for the behavior
Skills	Objective and perceived ability to take preventive action

Information IMB suggests that the most important and influential information is relevant to the individual and skill related. Relevant information may remind people about something they are already motivated to do (e.g., exercising or flossing) or facilitate skill acquisition. Information must not only be relevant, it must also be perceived to be relevant, which can be an altogether different thing. People tend to filter information cognitively and linguistically. They can only understand information to the extent it is consistent with their vocabulary and conceptualization of the object or behavior. According to IMB, people tend to be guided by simplified and loosely defined "truths" called heuristics, which are not always accurate. Examples of heuristics relevant to HIV include: "monogamous sex is safe sex" and "known partners are safe partners," which may be generally reliable assumptions, but may also impede protective behavior. Accordingly, it is important to determine what heuristics guide behavior and also to promote heuristics consistent with healthful behavior.

Behavioral Skill Skill is essential in many health behaviors. Returning to our example of negotiating condom use introduced earlier, a range of physical and social skills may be needed. There are certain important skills associated with the correct and effective use of condoms during intercourse, but perhaps more important are the negotiating skills required to get to the point of putting on a condom. Even among experienced adults this can be a tricky

thing even between partners who have known each other for a long time. For example, some heterosexual males use condoms with their secondary partners to avoid contracting an STD, but do not use a condom with their "main partner" out of concern that the main partner might suspect that he had been having sex with other women. IMB emphasizes that correct information and motivation are essential to skill development. People develop skill when they have correct information presented in a way they can understand and when they are motivated to learn.

Motivation As previously emphasized, motivation is the tendency to behave in a certain way and is influenced by a wide range of personal and environmental factors. In expectancy value and other cognitive theories, motivation is measured as beliefs and attitudes, sometimes with a variable like intent. The more consistent an individual's beliefs and attitudes with the behavior, the more likely it is to occur, all other things being equal. Various theories emphasize a range of beliefs and attitudes in terms of their importance in motivation. In the IMB model, motivation refers to personal and social attitudes toward preventive behavior. A wide range of beliefs may be related to motivation, including personal assessments of susceptibility and severity and expectations about the expected outcomes of a particular action or the adoption of a behavior. IMB emphasizes that motivation is often socially inspired and may include perceived norms and social support. Attitudes depend on social context and **perceived social norms** (similar to TRA).

Measurement

The IMB model proposes very specific programmatic activities, described as elicitation, intervention, and evaluation. **Elicitation research** is the IMB term for needs assessment and is very similar to the approach proposed for TRA and TPB of assessing the range of beliefs of the population of interest, recognizing that salient beliefs may vary from group to group (although the categories of beliefs and attitudes would be expected to be consistent). IMB proposes qualitative methods such as in-depth interviews and focus groups, but a wide range of qualitative methods exist and could be useful. The purposes of elicitation research are to gain an understanding about the population, including their vocabulary and popular heuristics and implicit theories. This is one of the features of IMB that makes it an expectancy value theory. IMB assumes that people act rationally based on the information they have. However, that information is often not correct or is misleading or misinterpreted. To develop useful interventions, it is necessary to find out what the at-risk population thinks and believes, what their attitudes are, and what skill they possess. The information gained can be used to develop intervention objectives. Intervention and evaluation follow from the elicitation research.

IMB proposes no specific intervention strategies, but suggests that intervention could be devised based on assessment of the knowledge, attitude, and skill needs evident from the elicitation research. Interventions should be designed to improve knowledge, attitudes, and skills. In one recent clinic-based study with HIV+ individuals, objectives were developed from elicitation research, and motivational interviewing techniques (see Chapter 5) were used to motivate the population to use condoms (Crepaz & Marks, 2002). The evaluation determined that those exposed to the intervention reported fewer unprotected sexual events. Intervention effects on knowledge and attitudes were not reported.

Example

Nelson et al., (2018) explored medication adherence with patients diagnosed with type 2 diabetes. The researchers identified the most common barriers to medication adherence and integrated IMB strategies to improve medication adherence and in turn, hemoglobin A1c (HbA1c). Common barriers identified with medication nonadherence were forgetting doses, not seeing the benefit of taking the medicine, feeling burned out with taking medicine, and low **health literacy**. Those who were young in age and who had lower health literacy were associated with higher barrier scores for information, personal motivation, social motivation, and behavioral skills. Nonwhite participants and participants with less education reported higher barrier scores for information and personal and social motivation. Participants with lower income and participants prescribed insulin reported higher barrier scores for behavioral skills (Nelson et al., 2018). The results provide support for IMB as a behavioral intervention to guide behavior change for medication adherence when working to remove barriers by providing more information and increasing behavioral skills and motivation.

Lessons for Public Health Practice

The expectancy value theories presented in this chapter assume that behavior is basically logical, but sometimes the logic is flawed because it is based on information and beliefs that are not accurate, leading to attitudes that do not support action. Each of the theories presented in this chapter views behavior somewhat uniquely, but each agrees that beliefs and attitudes are important. In the following paragraphs we discuss a few remaining issues about expectancy value theories.

1. Each of the theories were developed primarily to explain behavior, not to change behavior (an argument could be made that IMB has been concerned with behavior change from the start, but the lack of emphasis on intervention approaches and methods limits the validity of this contention). The main implications for intervention are that the key beliefs and attitudes should be assessed and addressed. Methods of intervention are not addressed by any of the theories, but in each case new information and new ways of presenting information are key.

2. Early in the chapter we noted, but do not elaborate on, the point that some beliefs and attitudes are more resistant to change than others. Resistance is an important aspect of research on beliefs and attitudes, and it is well established that some beliefs and attitudes in some people are highly resistant to change. Because public health is mainly concerned with population change, resistance is not a major concern. That is, in most health-promotion programs, we identify and address the beliefs and attitudes found to be most important to the population of interest. If we do a good job of identifying and addressing important cognitions, the group's behavior is likely to change on average, even if some members of the group and even some of the attitudes in the entire group are resistant to change. However, resistance does mitigate the potential for large effects, and additional research is needed to determine if concepts about resistance can be employed usefully to improve the effectiveness of health-promotion interventions.

3. Because each of the expectancy value theories share somewhat common concerns, why are there several such theories and not just one grand theory of expectancy value? This is a common and understandable question that has several answers. In part, there are different expectancy value theories because there are different ways

that behavior can be conceptualized. Also, the theories were developed with different behaviors and populations in mind. For example, the HBM was developed to explain adherence, while IMB was developed to explain HIV-prevention behavior. TRA and TPB have been demonstrated to be useful for explaining both health and nonhealth behaviors. Each theory may be particularly useful for explaining certain behaviors, while it is also the case that more than one theory can be applied to the same behavior. The existence of several theories in this broad category can usefully be thought of as offering a range of theory tools from which to select for particular behaviors.

4. Expectancy value theories have mainly been applied to personal-health behavior and occasionally to the supportive behavior of family members and to the health-related behavior of providers and other health and education professionals. However, these theories have infrequently been applied to other health-related behaviors by planners, administrators, policy makers, and others. However, there does not seem to be any reason that these theories, TRA and TPB in particular, could be employed to explain and possibly change health-related behaviors.

5. Expectancy value theories are concerned mainly with attitudes and beliefs and less with environmental factors. There is no denying that environment widely defined as social and physical is terribly important to behavior. Behavior is more likely when the environment supports it and less likely when it discourages it. Expectancy value theories are concerned with the cognitions that influence action, including perceptions about environmental support. This should suggest to public health professionals the potential of altering perceptions about the environment as well as altering the environment as possible to be supportive.

Discussion Questions

1. Explain the key similarities and differences between each value expectancy theory.
2. How are beliefs related to attitudes? What is a good example?
3. Why is careful measurement of beliefs and attitudes essential for public health program development?
4. Why are cognitions so important in expectancy values?
5. Work through each theory, and explain why or why not a person would take preventative behaviors based on the constructs of the theory. Example preventative measures could be protecting your skin from the sun, routine cancer self-examinations, flu vaccinations, or HPV vaccinations.

References

Ajzen, I. (1985). From intentions to actions: A theory of planned behavior. In J. Kuhl & J. Beckmann (Eds.), *Action control* (pp. 11–39). SSSP Springer Series in Social Psychology. Berlin, Heidelberg: Springer. DOI:10.1007/978-3-642-69746-3_2

Ajzen, I. (2002). Perceived behavioral control, self-efficacy, locus of control, and the theory of planned behavior. *Journal of Applied Social Psychology, 32*, 665–683.

Ajzen, I., & Cote, N. (2008). Attitudes and prediction of behavior. In W. D. Crano & R. Prislin (Eds.), *Attitudes and attitude change*. Frontiers of Social Psychology, *32* (pp. 665–683). New York: Psychology Press.

Ajzen, I., & Fishbein, M. (1980). *Understanding attitudes and predicting social behavior*. Englewood Cliffs, NJ: Prentice-Hall.

Ajzen, I., & Fishbein, M. (2005). The influence of attitudes on behavior. In D. Albarracin, B. T. Johnson, & M. P. Zanna (Eds.), *Handbook of attitudes and attitude change: Basic principles*. Mahwah, NJ: Erlbaum.

Ajzen, I., & Manstead, A. S. R. (2007). Changing health-related behaviors: An approach based on the Theory of Planned Behavior. In M. Hewstone, H. A. W. Schut, J. B. F. De Wit, K. Van Den Bos, & M. S. Stroebe (Eds.), *Scope of social psychology: Theory and applications* (pp. 43–63). New York: Psychology Press.

Armitage, C. J., & Connor, M. (2001). Efficacy of the theory of planned behavior: A meta-analytic review. *British Journal of Social Psychology, 40*, 471–499.

Bazargan-Hejazi, S., Teruya, S., Pan, D., Lin, J., Gordon, D., Krochalk, P. C., & Bazargan, M. (2017). The theory of planned behavior (TPB) and texting while driving behavior in college students. *Traffic Injury Prevention, 18*(1), 56–62.

Champion, V. L. (1984). Instrument development for health belief model constructs. *Advances in Nursing Science, 6*(3), 73–87.

Chevance, G., Caudroit, J., Romain, A. J., & Boiche, J. (2017). The adoption of physical activity and eating behaviors among persons with obesity and in the general population: The role of implicit attitudes within the theory of planned behavior. *Psychology, Health, & Medicine, 22*(3), 319–324.

Crano, W. D., & Prislin, R. (2006). Attitudes and persuasion. *Annual Review of Psychology, 57*, 345–374.

Crano, W. D., & Prislin, R. (Eds.). (2008). *Attitudes and attitude change*. Frontiers of Social Psychology. New York; Psychology Press.

Crepaz, N., & Marks, G. (2002). Towards an understanding of sexual risk behavior in people living with HIV: A review of social, psychological, and medical findings. *AIDS, 16*, 135–149.

Doane, A. N., Kelley, M. L, & Pearson, M. R. (2016). Reducing cyberbullying: A theory of reasoned action-based video prevention program for college students. *Aggressive Behavior, 42*(2), 136–146.

Fishbein, M. (2008). A reasoned action approach to health promotion. *Medical Decision Making, 28*, 834–844.

Fishbein, M., & Ajzen, I. (2010). *Predicting and changing behavior: The reasoned action approach*. New York: Psychology Press. DOI:10.4324/9780203838020

Fisher, J. D., & Fisher, W. A. (1992). Changing AIDS risk behavior. *Psychological Bulletin, 111*, 455–474.

Fisher, J. D., Fisher, W. A., Amico, K. R., & Harman, J. J. (2006). An information–motivation–behavioral skills model of adherence to antiretroviral therapy. *Health Psychology, 25*, 462–473.

Fisher, J. D., Fisher, W. A., Bryan, A. D., & Misovich, S. J. (2002). Information–motivation–behavioral skills model-based HIV risk behavior change intervention for inner-city high school youth. *Health Psychology, 21*,177–186.

Fisher, J. D., Fisher, W. A., & Shuper, P. A. (2009). The information–motivation–skills model of HIV preventive behavior. In R. J. DiClemente, R. C. Crosby, & M. C. Kegler (Eds.), *Emerging theories in health promotion practice and research* (2nd ed., pp. 21–64). San Francisco, CA: Jossey–Bass.

Janz, N. K., Champion, V. L., & Strecher, V. J. (2002). The health belief model. In K. Glanz, B. K. Rimer, & F. M. Lewis (Eds.), *Health behavior and health education: Theory, research, and practice* (3rd ed., pp. 45–66). San Francisco, CA: Jossey-Bass.

John, S. A., Walsh, J. L., & Weinhardt, L. S. (2017). The information–motivation–behavioral skills model revisited: A network-perspective structural equation model within a public sexually transmitted infection clinic sample of hazardous alcohol users. *AIDS and Behavior, 21,* 1208–1218.

Kirk, T. N., & Haegele, J. A. (2019). Theory of planned behavior in research examining physical activity among individuals with disabilities: A review. *Human Kinetics Journal, 36*(1), 164–182.

Lodyga, M. G. (2013). *The relationship between health belief model constructs and factors influencing cancer self-examinations in college students* [Unpublished doctoral dissertation]. Southern Illinois University.

Middlestadt, S. E., Macy, J. T., Dowty, R., Arrieta, A., & Jay, S. J. (2020). Moderating effect of partner smoking on pregnant women's intention to stop smoking: Applying the reasoned action approach. *Addiction Research & Theory, 28*(6), 510–516. DOI: 10.1080/16066359.2019.1708904

Nelson, L. A., Wallston, K. A., Kripalani, S., LeStourgeon, L. M., Williamson, S. E., & Mayberry, L. S. (2018). Assessing barriers to diabetes medication adherence using the information–motivation–behavioral skills model. *Diabetes Research and Clinical Practice, 142,* 374–384. DOI:10.1016/j.diabres.2018.05.046

Nobling, B. D., & Maykrantz, S. A. (2017). Exploring perceptions about and behaviors related to mental illness and mental health utilization among college students using the health belief model. *American Journal of Health Education, 48*(5), 306–319.

Pookulangara, S., Parr, J., Tanoff, L., & Nix. (2017). Insta-shopping: Examining use of Instagram for shopping online using theory of reasoned action. International Textile and Apparel Association Annual Conference Proceedings. St. Petersburg, FL.

Simons-Morton, B. G., Chen, R., Abroms, R., & Haynie, D. L. (2004). Latent growth curve analyses of peer and parent influences on smoking stage progression among early adolescents. *Health Psychology, 23*(6), 612–621.

Wang, X., Chen, D., Xie, T., & Zhang, W. (2019). Predicting women's intentions to screen for breast cancer based on the health belief model and the theory of planned behavior. *The Journal of Obstetrics and Gynecology Research, 45*(12), 2440–2451.

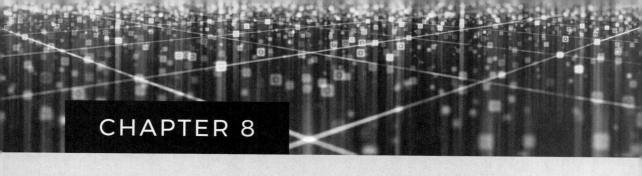

CHAPTER 8

Stages of Change: The Transtheoretical Model

Behavioral change is a process that unfolds over time through a sequence of stages.

OUTLINE

1. Preview
2. Objectives
3. Introduction
    3.1. Assumptions
    3.2. Stages
        3.2.1. Precontemplation
        3.2.2. Contemplation
        3.2.3. Preparation for Action
        3.2.4. Action
        3.2.5. Maintenance
    3.3. Change Dynamics
    3.4. Stage Tailoring
    3.5. Cognitions
    3.6. Change Processes
    3.7. Matching Change Processes and Methods to Stage
    3.8. Examples
4. Lessons for Public Health Practice
5. Discussion Questions
6. References

PREVIEW

Stage theories are based on the premise that intentional behavior change occurs in stages.

Stage models have been popular as a way of thinking about decision-making behavior for many decades, and there are many advantages to thinking about change from a stage perspective. Identifying a person's stage of change may help facilitate appropriate intervention strategies for that individual (or group) at that point in time.

OBJECTIVES

The readers of this chapter will be able to do the following:

1. Describe what the term *transtheoretical* means in the context of stages of change.
2. Explain how people are thought to advance through the stages of change in the Transtheoretical Model (TTM)
3. Describe the processes of change in the TTM.
4. Describe the advantages of stage-related intervention.
5. Identify the type of persuasive messages that might be useful at each stage of change.

Introduction

Stage theories are based on the premise that behavior change is a natural process that typically involves passing through a series of stages of decision making and behavior change.

Stage theories attempt to identify the stages people go through and the processes they use to advance from one stage to another and use this information to promote change. The potential advantage of stage models is that they allow intervention efforts to be tailored to stage, where the objective is to target the objectives relevant to the stage of the population of interest and facilitate movement to the next stage, gradually getting closer to actual behavior change and maintenance. From the perspective of intervention, decision-making stage theories emphasize the following: (1) assess stage or readiness, and (2) tailor messages to stage. Based on these criteria, it may be ineffectual to provide the same intervention to people at very different stages with respect to a particular behavior.

Stage models are **transtheoretical** in that they borrow methods from other theories and orient them to specific stages. This is why they are referred to as stage models versus stage theories; however, either term is appropriate. The stage idea is that there are specific and unique cognitive and informational needs at each of the multiple decision points. Accordingly, decision-making stages include the following: (1) precontemplative, unaware; (2) contemplative, deciding, thinking about it; (3) preparation, planning, actively considering; (4) initiation, action, trying out change; and (5) maintenance, incorporation into lifestyle.

Stage theories have been around a long time going back in time to the early research on the decision-making processes as described by Kahneman and Tversky (2000) and Rogers (2005). Stage theories recognize that people are confronted with myriad decisions regarding everyday life, many of which concern health. Of course, a lot of behavior is automatic, requiring little **volitional decision making**. Habitual smokers do not reflect each time they light up. Thus, the prevention challenge is to stimulate contemplation. Many other behaviors demand thoughtful consideration such as quitting or cutting back on smoking and other substance use, deciding to seek medical attention when symptoms appear, or deciding to wear a helmet for biking or skateboarding. One of the most popular models that exemplifies the decision-making process is the Transtheoretical Model (TTM), developed by Prochaska and colleagues (Prochaska, DiClemente, & Norcross, 1992). TTM is a stages of change model widely used in behavior change research and programs.

The TTM was developed through research on the methods people use as they progress through the decision-making process, termed stages of change (Prochaska et al., 1992). The model is transtheoretical in that it borrows concepts, strategies, and methods from a range of theories of behavior and behavior change. TTM seeks to build on the vast literature indicating that it is possible to facilitate changes in behavior through psychological counseling, education, and persuasion (Krebs, Norcross, Nicholson, & Prochaska, 2018). The TTM seeks to identify the natural progress of change and the processes people employ as they change and harness this information for intervention development.

Today, the TTM is a popularly employed model in public health research and practice. The initial research on the TTM and much of it since has focused on substance use and addictive behavior (Prochaska et al., 1992). From the initial studies of smoking, the TTM has rapidly evolved to include application to myriad other health behaviors. Much of the research on TTM has focused on the processes employed to quit smoking (Erol, Balci, & Sisman, 2018; Prochaska, Hall, & Hall, 2009; Prochaska, Velicer, Prochaska, Delucchi, & Hall, 2006), but it has also been applied to a range of other behaviors, including weight control and obesity (Kim & Kang, 2020), efforts to improve type 2 diabetes (Arafat, Ibrahim, & Awaisu, 2016), and breast cancer survivorship (Scruggs, Mama, Carmack, Douglas, Diamond, & Basen-Engquist, 2018). The diversity of applications has, overall, provided empirical support for the core constructs of the TTM.

TTM seeks to integrate processes and principles of individual-level behavior change across major theories of behavior and psychotherapy, hence the name *transtheoretical.* Prochaska and colleagues have noted that the intellectual impetus for developing the TTM was "the lack of an overall guiding theory, the search for the underlying principles, the growing acknowledgement that no single therapy is more 'correct' than any other, and general dissatisfaction with their often limited approaches" (Prochaska et al., 1992). The model is noted to have emerged from a comparative analysis of leading theories of psychotherapy and behavioral change. The search was for a systematic integration in a field that had fragmented into more than 300 theories of psychotherapy (Prochaska et al., 1992).

The initial research on the TTM, conducted with people attempting to deal with substance abuse and addiction, showed that people go through stages of change rather than changing all of a sudden. At first it was thought that change involved four discrete stages, but later it was determined that five stages characterized change better than four. Further, it was determined that people tend to use a range of **change processes** as they pass from one stage to another. Ten experiential and behavioral processes of change were identified that were consistent with methods employed in behavior change programs and psychotherapy. The modern TTM describes the five stages that people who manage to change their behavior go through on their way and the processes they tend to employ as they adopt, modify, or eliminate a behavior.

Assumptions

The core assumptions or principles of TTM about how people change their behavior include the following:

Assumption 1. No single theory can account for all the complexities of behavioral change. Therefore, a more comprehensive model will most likely emerge from an integration across major theories.

Assumption 2. Behavioral change is a process that unfolds over time through a sequence of stages.

Assumption 3. Change is a process and not an event.

Assumption 4. There is no inherent motivation to progress through the stages of intentional change.

Assumption 5. In attempting to change a behavior, a person typically cycles through these stages of change.

Assumption 6. Specific processes and principles of change need to be applied at specific stages (matched to stage) if progress through the stages is to occur.

Assumption 7. Chronic behavioral patterns are influenced by some combination of biological, social, and self-control factors. Stage-matched interventions have been designed primarily to enhance self-control.

Assumption 8. Each of the stages of change should be navigated for lasting change to occur.

Assumption 9. Insight alone does not change behavior.

Assumption 10. Overt action without insight is likely to lead only to temporary change.

Assumption 11. Relapse, or falling back into old behaviors, can occur.

Assumption 12. If relapse occurs, individuals can reenter an earlier stage.

These assumptions, of course, are subject to empirical verification for each behavior and population group but are useful considerations for program development.

Stages

There are several important advantages to conceptualizing stages of change, including the following: (1) stages facilitate baseline evaluations to determine the educational needs of the target population; (2) interventions can be tailored to stage and delivered according to stage; and (3) it is possible to evaluate the success of the intervention in terms of stage advancement. The explicit goal of health-promotion programs using stage approaches is to facilitate progress from an earlier to a later stage. It makes sense to employ certain intervention approaches with those not considering change (precontemplative) and other approaches with those actively considering change or working on maintenance of change. The stages of TTM have been modified a few times, but currently consist of the following five independent stages.

Precontemplation

People at this stage have no particular interest in changing the behavior in question in the foreseeable future. They may not even be aware that a change would be useful, healthful, or needed. They may be uninformed about the consequences of their behavior, or they may have tried to change a number of times and have become demoralized about their ability to change. They tend not to read, talk, or think about the particular behavior, certainly not about adopting or changing it. They also see the disadvantages as greater than the advantages of behavior change. However, their family and friends are commonly aware that they should change. Substance abusers, including smokers, alcoholics, and problem drinkers who have not recognized that their behavior is not in their best interests, serve as good examples of precontemplation. However, the concept could also be applied usefully to people who are not concerned about their health-risk behavior, including those who eat without concern for their weight or health, those who are seldom or ever physically active, those who have sex with people whose HIV and STD status are not known, even those who are not aware that they should be screened for a particular health problem.

Contemplation

Contemplation is the stage at which people are aware that change might be beneficial and are considering it. They have not made a commitment to change but tend to be open to information about it and may actively seek new information about it. People may remain in this stage for long periods. (This is similar to ambivalence in Motivational Interviewing). Many of us have personal familiarity with this stage as we contemplate changing some health behavior or other. For example, at any particular time a person might be considering losing a little weight, beginning a regular exercise routine, quitting smoking, or cutting back on the amount of alcohol consumed. People in this stage are not resistant to change and may be open to suggestion and persuasion, but may not take action on their own because of low self-efficacy and commitment.

Preparation for Action

People at this stage plan to take action in the near future, usually defined as within the next month. These individuals intend to take action of some sort, such as taking a course, seeking alternatives to substance use, joining a fitness club, consulting a counselor, talking to their physician, or employing a self-help approach. They may have already taken some significant action in the past year but were unsuccessful in establishing the new behavior. They score high on both contemplation and action, but do not qualify for the action stage because their efforts to change are not recent or sustained. Those at the preparation stage often lack the skill and resources needed to establish lasting change, but they are more committed.

Action

At the action stage people have made specific modifications in their behavior within the past 6 months. (As emphasized in Social Cognitive Theory, action is important because it provokes the environment, leading to feedback and reinforcement.) The term *action* here represents substantial behavior change and not just a single action. Action is considered substantial when it is sufficient to reduce risk of disease or promote health. For smoking, for example, only total abstinence would qualify. Cutting back on smoking would be considered preparation and not action. For physical activity, one would need to engage in at least an hour of moderate to vigorous physical activity an average of three times a week or more for at least several months to qualify. Occasionally going for a walk or jog would qualify as preparation, not action. Similarly, changes in diet should reach certain standards, such as 500 fewer calories per week or no more than 30% of calories from fat for a period of 6 months or more, depending on the purpose of the diet. Because behavior change is difficult, this is the least stable stage, and individuals are likely to experience a setback if they experience a challenge. A setback is known as relapse. When relapse occurs, individuals can reenter at any stage. For example, an individual could return to their newly changed behavior and enter back into the action stage, while another individual could see their relapse as a failure and completely quit their newly formed behavior, thus reentering back into the precontemplation stage.

Maintenance

People at the maintenance stage work to prevent relapse and consolidate the gains they have made. The goal here is self-regulation for long-term maintenance. For addictive behaviors maintenance is usually defined as change meeting a certain standard lasting at least 6 months. With addictive behaviors the goal is the prevention of relapse. For other behaviors, diet, physical activity, adherence to medical recommendations, for example, the time frame for maintenance could be one's entire lifetime, and the goal is to better integrate the change into one's lifestyle.

Change Dynamics

The stages of change conceptualization have sometimes been described as a stepladder, with rungs labeled precontemplation,

contemplation, action, and so on. Behavior change is not always linear and tends to cycle through adjacent stages over time. A key underlying assumption of the TTM is that individuals must progress through each stage of the model, but it is anticipated that many people will recycle through one or more stages over time. How long a person or group stays at a particular stage and how stable they are within a particular stage may vary greatly by behavior and population group. Thus, an individual may be in contemplation (thinking about changing a health behavior) for many years without actually progressing to preparation for action. Many people think about changing a particular health behavior for a period of time before they actually make any serious attempts to change. A person may reach the action stage, but after a time revert to the preparation stage, and this may occur over and over for a long time and may even become a more or less permanent cycle. Many people quit smoking many times, often for long periods, only to relapse, before finally quitting altogether. Indeed, most successful quitters have quit in the past and relapsed before establishing lasting change.

Physical activity is a good example of the application of the transtheoretical model. Notably, for any particular sample of people, some may not be considering increasing their activity, others may be considering it, others planning, some trying out a new fitness routine, and others working on incorporating fitness activities into their life. Rather than moving through the stages in an orderly way, it is common for people to cycle through stages, overcoming ambivalence, considering, trying, reconsidering, quitting, starting again. Assessments of stage can be as simple as asking people about their physical activity (e.g., how many times in the past week have you engaged in leisure (not work) activity for at least 30 minutes that increased your heart rate and breathing? Similarly, in interviews, questionnaires, or surveys people can be asked to indicate their readiness to change. It can also be useful to assess perceived barriers to change, which may also be associated with stage. At the ambivalence stage a likely barrier is knowing little about physical activity, while at the preparation stage, the lack of equipment, access to facilities, or exercise buddies may be most important, and at the action and maintenance stages environmental barriers are likely important. Assessing readiness or stage is useful for assessing program effectiveness and suggests what messages might be most motivating.

Stage Tailoring

Each stage has corresponding cognitive needs and informational messages and other interventions that address these cognitions and can move people along the behavior change continuum, from one stage to the next. For example, the cognitive needs for those who are unaware of the need for change include knowledge and beliefs about benefit, and messages would need to capture attention and create dissonance between their existing and new ways of thinking about fitness. This is not so simple because for some ambivalent people, messages that physical activity is fun and easy may be motivating, while for others the health or weight control benefits may motivate further consideration. At the contemplation stage attitudes are particularly important, and messages would need to focus on creating positive attitudes, possibly by presenting examples of others like the contemplator who have started working out and improving efficacy and outcome expectations. Self-evaluation is a useful activity at the contemplation stage. Completing a decision balance sheet that examines and weights the pros and cons of a change in exercise can be helpful at this stage. When a person is preparing to act, they need to know how, and messages would focus on correct performance, practice, and adding activity into lifestyle, possibly by conducting an environmental reevaluation of current

PA resources, barriers, stimuli, and contingencies. At the later other stages of action and maintenance cognitive needs are largely about managing the environment, described as environmental reconstruction, that works on controlling stimuli and creating favorable contingencies, such as a sense of community that supports PA.

A premise of the TTM is that stages are easily identified, and interventions can be developed that are most appropriate for that stage. This process of "**staging**" can provide valuable information about a person's or a group's readiness to change, enabling the tailoring of interventions to stage. This is one of the most important and useful features of the TTM.

Identifying a person's stage of change is only the initial step in developing stage-appropriate behavior change interventions. Staging algorithms, or computable steps to achieve a desired result, have been developed for some behaviors. **Figure 8.1** shows a staging algorithm for decisions stages for increasing exercising.

Once a person's or group's stage is known, it is possible to identify strategies for promoting progress to the next stage of change. Because moving through the stages requires individuals to think about their behavior, their environment, and themselves, processes of change were developed to help individuals progress from one stage to the next.

Cognitions

One of the important considerations that requires more attention in TTM is a formulation of the cognitions that may be associated with each stage. By definition, each stage is linked to a certain level of motivation, but as we have emphasized in previous chapters, motivation is the tendency to behave in certain ways, and cognitions are highly associated with behavior. Therefore, in a transtheoretical model, one would expect more attention to cognitions. The only cognitive variable emphasized in the

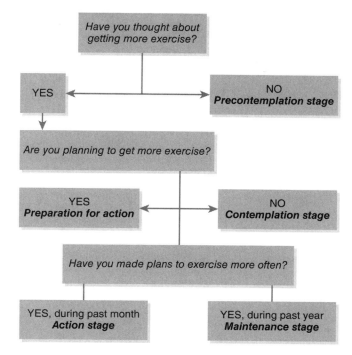

Figure 8.1 Staging algorithm for decisions stages for increasing exercise

transtheoretical model is self-efficacy, derived from groundbreaking research of Albert Bandura (1997) (self-efficacy is discussed in greater detail throughout the book). Self-efficacy refers to one's confidence in one's ability to do something despite obstacles. Given its grounding in psychotherapy and not in education, the role of information, both information seeking and sharing to change cognitions related to decision making, is not well considered.

Change Processes

The TTM suggests a number of change processes, which are observable ways that people go about changing their behavior, even if they are not aware of these processes or what they are called. The TTM emphasizes processes that have been identified from various sources with variable theoretical orientations. It is suggested that these processes are universal and can derive from any theory, not just the TTM. These processes have been widely employed

in behavior change programs and gathered and not developed by TTM. For example, stimulus control, contingency management, and reinforcement are commonly employed in operant conditioning and self-management programs.

Some of these processes derive from community psychology and social change theory, for example, consciousness raising and self-liberation. Some are not really processes so much as counseling methods, so these can be viewed as natural processes that people employ or as counseling strategies to foster appropriate decision making. The 10 popular change processes described in **Table 8.1** are thought to be employed by individuals on their own (although not necessarily known by these names) as they advance on their own from one stage to the next, and these processes can inform or be adapted for use in programs. Experiential processes are emphasized in the earlier stages, while behavioral processes are emphasized in the later stages.

Table 8.1 Ten Common Processes (Methods) of Change

Processes (Methods) of Change	Description/Definition
Consciousness raising	Enhance knowledge and awareness of health risks and protective behaviors.
Dramatic relief	Enhance emotional reaction to health risk behaviors. Experiencing and expressing feelings toward the behavior.
Self-reevaluation	Looking at life with and without the healthy risk behavior.
Environmental reevaluation	Develop appreciation for how personal behaviors affect others and their environment.
Self-liberation	Establish the belief that one can change and make commitments to change (New Year's resolutions; contracts; goal setting).
Helping relationships	Obtain support for the healthful behavior change; utilize supportive others to support behavior change.
Counterconditioning	Substitute healthful behaviors for unhealthy behaviors; e.g., walk instead of eating; chewing gum instead of smoking.
Contingency management	Focuses on the consequences of behavior; reward positive behaviors; keep records for behavior; alter the environment.
Stimulus control	Manage cues that stimulate behavior; remove or avoid cues for unhealthy behaviors, and create cues that support health-promoting behaviors.
Social liberation	Involves actions to promote social causes consistent with the desired and healthful behavior; e.g., lobbying for smoke-free environments, advocating for low-fat and vegetarian restaurant options and fitness facilities at workplaces; transcending socially designated norms and practices to adopt health-protective behaviors.

Matching Change Processes and Methods to Stage

We noted in a previous section of this chapter that the advantage of viewing behavior from the perspective of TTM is that it may be possible to determine the stage of a person or group and promote processes or apply methods most likely to facilitate advancement to the next stage. This is called a "stage-tailored" or "stage-matched" intervention, where the processes of change become strategies that help individuals to progress from one stage to the next. Stage-matching is more an art form than an empirical process, but the TTM suggests which change processes may be most commonly and usefully employed at each stage. In general, the research suggests that in early stages of precontemplation and contemplation, processes such as consciousness-raising, dramatic relief, and environmental reevaluation may be most useful and effective because it helps individuals cognitively assess how their behavior is affecting their own health and the health of those around them. At the action and maintenance stages, helping relationships, counterconditioning, and reinforcement and stimulus management processes may be best because they support the individual's new behavior change by removing triggers, avoiding high-risk cues, providing rewards, and developing a support system. However, the matching of change processes to stage is a subject that needs further research. **Table 8.2** provides cognitions at each stage including which process of change and intervention method to employ.

As noted, TTM describes the process of change from one stage to another and emphasizes 10 processes that can be useful in promoting change. However, a great deal is left to the imagination and creativity of program developers. Notably, each of the change processes can be operationalized in a variety of ways. Developing specific methods out of these processes requires familiarity with the at-risk population, creativity in developing methods, and thorough knowledge of the behavior.

Examples

There is an extensive literature on the effects of stage-matched and processes of change interventions based on the TTM (Hall & Rossi, 2008; Johnson et al., 2006; Johnson et al., 2008). In a recent study, Romain, Horwath, and Bernard (2018) measured self-reported moderate and vigorous physical activity by using the Processes of Change, Stages of Change, and International Physical Activity questionnaires. The cross-sectional study among adults ($M = 35.12$) revealed an association between the experiential and behavioral ($\beta = 0.123$; $P = 0.017$) processes of change for moderate exercise using hierarchical regression models. The behavioral processes of change were a significant predictor for both total exercise ($\beta = 0.261$; $P < 0.001$) and vigorous physical activity ($\beta = 0.297$; $P < 0.001$). In another example, Scruggs and colleagues (2018) explored if breast cancer survivors would adopt a physically active lifestyle to improve survivorship using the TTM and

processes of change. Sixty sedentary cancer survivors were randomized to participate in a 6-month physical activity program or standard care. The processes of change were measured at 3 and 6 months using repeated measures analysis of variance. The intervention group had significant improvement in self-efficacy and identified fewer barriers to exercise. At the 6-month mark, the processes of change self-liberation, counterconditioning, and reinforcement management were significantly associated with progression through the stages. Both studies provide evidence that TTM and the processes of change can improve health behavior and outcomes.

Lessons for Public Health Practice

Stage models of behavior change can be valuable in guiding the development, implementation, and evaluation of health-promotion programs across a diverse range of health behaviors. Additional research is needed to determine the range of possible applications, relative efficacy, impact, and cost-effectiveness of programs based on stage models relative to programs based on nonstage models. Moreover, research investigating whether these models can be applied beyond the individual level is needed. Specifically, could stages apply to health-protective behaviors? Could community leaders be "staged" and stage-related change processes applied? Also, what is the relative efficacy of stage-matched interventions for chronic as opposed to infrequent or episodic health behaviors? These models, as is true for all models of behavior change, are dynamic and continue to evolve as new empirical data are discovered and integrated into the models. As these models continue to gain momentum within the field of public health research and practice, a growing body of empirical evidence will be available to evaluate the models' applicability for new health behaviors.

Table 8.2 Cognitions, Processes (Methods), and Intervention Methods at Each Stage of Change

Stage of Change	Precontemplation	Contemplation	Preparation	Action	Maintenance
Cognitions	Not considering or does not want to change behavior	Acknowledges the problem and sees the need for change but not ready to commit	Intends to take action and performs tasks to prepare for behavior change	Has changed behavior; continues behavior change with increased confidence and less tempted to relapse	Continues behavior change with increased confidence and less tempted to relapse
Process (methods) of change	• Consciousness raising • Dramatic relief • Environmental reevaluation	• Self-reevaluation	• Self-liberation	• Helping relationships • Counterconditioning • Contingency management	• Stimulus control • Social liberation
Intervention methods	• Public education • Media campaigns • Role play • Discussions with family	• Clarifying values • Guided imagery	• Policy interventions • Empowerment	• Social support • Reinforcing behavior with rewards • Substituting healthy behavior for problem behavior	• Avoiding high-risk cues • Removal of triggers • Restructuring environment • Accountability

Stage theories are useful and popular in public health research and practice. They should not be mistaken, however, for the theory answer to every behavior problem and population. Identifying the stage of a person with respect to a particular behavior is just a starting place, maybe a very good starting place, but not the whole solution. Here we discuss important issues with respect to stage theories in relation to public health research and practice.

1. Applications: Stages of change approaches can logically be employed to a range of decision-making behaviors. It has mostly been employed in situations where people are dealing with addiction-related decisions. Increasingly, it is being employed with other personal-health behaviors such as physical activity.

2. Thinking in terms of stages: The primary value of thinking about behavior in terms of stages of change is that it facilitates identification of barriers and related cognitive and psychological factors associated with each stage. This allows and facilitates the development of interventions that are stage related, which can be effective and efficient relative to approaches without stages.

3. Early stage change: The goal of health-promotion programs is always to achieve action and maintenance of healthful behavior, but changes in earlier stages can reflect cognitive progress and serve as evaluation criteria.

4. Other theories compatible with stages: Many studies now use stage theory and another theory to guide assessment of cognitive factors at each stage. In this sense, stage theories are transtheoretical.

5. Processes and methods: Stage theories are primarily interested in the processes employed to advance from one stage to the next. These processes, as described in the TTM, are very useful and have even been linked to particular stages. However, to make programmatic use of these processes, the health-promotion professional must develop methods that address specific objectives within the context of the program parameters.

Discussion Questions

1. Identify the cognitions and behaviors at each stage of change using a poor health behavior (smoking, poor diet, etc.).
2. Explain why the action stage of change is most vulnerable for relapse.
3. Explain the usefulness of stage identification when working with behavior change.
4. Provide strategies for each process of change.

References

Arafat, Y., Ibrahim, M. I., & Awaisu, A. (2016). Using the transtheoretical model to enhance self-management activities in patients with type 2 diabetes: A systematic review. *Journal of Pharmaceutical Health Services Research, 7*(3), 149–156. DOI: 10.1111/jphs.12138

Bandura, A. (1997). *Self-efficacy: The exercise of control.* New York: Freeman Press.

Erol, S., Balci, A. S., & Sisman, F. N. (2018). Effect of transtheoretical model based smoking cessation program on high school students. *Journal of Nutritional and Health Sciences, 5*(3), 1–6.

Hall, K., & Rossi, J. S. (2008). Meta-analytic examination of the strong and weak principles across 48 health behaviors. *Preventative Medicine, 46,* 266–274.

Johnson, S. S., Driskell, M.-M., Johnson, J. L., Prochaska, J. M., Zwick, W., & Prochaska, J. O. (2006). Efficacy of a transtheoretical model-based expert system for antihypertensive adherence. *Disease Management*, 9(5), 291–301.

Johnson, S. S., Paiva, A. L., Cummins, C. O., Johnson, J. L., Dyment, S. J., Wright, J. A., Prochaska, J. O., Prochaska, J. M., & Sherman, K. (2008). Transtheoretical model-based multiple behavior intervention for weight management: Effectiveness on a population basis. *Preventive Medicine*, 46(3), 238–246. DOI: 10.1016/j.ypmed.2007.09.010

Kahneman, D., & Tversky, A. (Eds.). (2000). *Choices, values, and frames*. New York: Russell Sage Foundation; Cambridge, UK: Cambridge University Press.

Kim, Y., & Kang, S. (2020). Effects of a weight control intervention based on the transtheoretical model on physical activity and psychological variables in middle-aged obese men. *Journal of Women & Aging*, 1–13. DOI: 10.1080/08952841.2020.1728183

Krebs, P., Norcross, J. C., Nicholson, J. M., & Prochaska, J. O. (2018). Stages of change and psychotherapy outcomes: A review and meta-analysis. *Journal of Clinical Psychology*, 74, 1964–1979.

Prochaska, J. J., Hall, S. E., & Hall, S. M. (2009). Stage-tailored tobacco cessation treatment in inpatient psychiatry. *Psychiatric Services*, 60, 848–856.

Prochaska, J. J., Velicer, W. F., Prochaska, J. O., Delucchi, K., & Hall, S. M. (2006). Comparing intervention outcomes in smokers treated for single versus multiple behavioral risks. *Health Psychology*, 25, 380–388.

Prochaska, J. O., DiClemente, C. C., & Norcross, J. C. (1992). In search of how people change: Applications to the addictive behaviors. *American Psychologist*, 47, 1102–1114.

Rogers, E. M. (2005). *Diffusion of innovations* (5th ed.). New York: Free Press.

Romain, A. J., Horwath, C., & Bernard, P. (2018). Prediction of physical activity using processes of change from the transtheoretical model: Experiential, behavioral, or interaction effect? *American Journal of Health Promotion*, 32, 16–23. DOI: 10.1177/0890117116686900

Scruggs, S., Mama, S. K., Carmack, C. L., Douglas, T., Diamond, P., & Basen-Engquist, K. (2018). Randomized trial of a lifestyle physical activity intervention for breast cancer survivors: Effects on transtheoretical model variables. *Health Promotion Practice*, 1, 134–144.

Communication and Messaging

Essentially, behavior change is the product of effective communication. Section 3 includes one chapter on contemporary health communication theory and social marketing and one chapter on the Diffusion of Innovations Theory.

CHAPTER 9   Health Communication and Social Marketing 163

CHAPTER 10   Diffusion of Innovations Theory 189

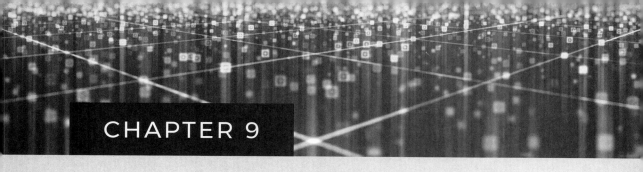

CHAPTER 9

Health Communication and Social Marketing

Information is essential for intentional behavior change. In whatever form it is delivered, information can contribute to knowledge, challenge beliefs, shape attitudes, and facilitate behavior change.

OUTLINE

1. Preview
2. Objectives
3. Introduction
4. Information Revisited
    4.1. Cognitive Dissonance
    4.2. Cognitive Resistance
5. Models of Communication Processes
    5.1. Action Model
    5.2. Interactive/Transactional Model
    5.3. Intermediary Model
    5.4. Ecological Model
6. Persuasion
    6.1. Elaboration Likelihood Model
        6.1.1. Peripheral Route Processing
        6.1.2. Central Route Processing
    6.2. Inoculation Theory
        6.2.1. Threat
        6.2.2. Refutational Preemption
7. Social Marketing
    7.1. Processes
    7.2. Ethics
8. Theory-Based Message Framing
    8.1. Theory of Reasoned Action and Theory of Planned Behavior
    8.2. Health Belief Model
    8.3. Social Cognitive Theory
    8.4. Social Influence Theory
    8.5. Diffusion Theory
9. Theory-Based Social Marketing Applications
    9.1. Smoking Prevention
    9.2. Preventing Excessive Drinking
    9.3. Reducing Consumption of Sugared Beverages
    9.4. Increasing Face Mask Wearing to Prevent COVID-19
10. Lessons for Public Health Practice
11. Discussion Questions
12. References

PREVIEW

Health communication processes and methods are essential to public health practice and central to health promotion. This chapter describes the theoretical underpinning and practical applications of communication methods and processes.

OBJECTIVES

After reading this chapter, readers should be able to:

1. Define communication and health communication.
2. Identify models of the communication process.

3. Describe the central role of information in health communication.
4. Describe how cognitive dissonance is an important aspect of persuasion.
5. Describe the elements of persuasive communication.
6. Distinguish social marketing from other commercial marketing.
7. Explain how behavior theories can improve social marketing
8. Explain the special ethical responsibilities of social marketing.

Introduction

Information is an essential element of public health programs. Information is rarely the only ingredient and should not be, but it is an essential part of nearly all prevention activities and behavior change theories. Regardless of the topic or the mode of intervention, we seek to impart information about health and behavior that is clear, honest, accessible, and persuasive. People cannot know how to behave healthfully if they do not know what healthful means and how to achieve it. Communication is the process by which information is shared. **Health communication** is the process of sharing information about health and health

behavior. Developing and delivering effective messages is both interesting and complicated.

The growing diversity of the U.S. population, sophistication of new technology, and sheer amount of information and variety of sources pose extreme health communication challenges as well as opportunities. The limited capacity of vulnerable populations to obtain, process and comprehend basic health information (termed *health literacy*) needed to make appropriate health decisions is a growing public health concern. Those for whom health literacy may be particularly challenging include the elderly, immigrants, minorities, low-income groups, and those with chronic health conditions. Notably, many medical conditions require relative sophisticated understanding of the prescribed regimen, the effects and contraindications of medicines, and how to schedule appointments and complete required paperwork. Accordingly, improving health literacy is one of several national health objectives for health communication, shown in **Table 9.1** (Office of Disease Prevention, n.d.).

Health communication methods are frequently employed in public health programs, as reflected by the objectives in Table 9.1. Theoretically, communication that considers the needs of the intended audience by thoughtfully

Table 9.1 Examples of Health Communication Objectives, *Healthy People 2030*

Description
• Increase social marketing by health departments
• Increase health literacy
• Increase health communication by health providers
• Increase access to medical records
• Increase electronic health information
• Improve information about emergencies
• Increase preventive cancer interventions
• Increase preventive health services among adolescents

employing sound communication principles can enable the useful transfer, receipt, and utility of information about health. As a key health-promotion practice, health communication is a core subject for public health professionals and a growing subspecialization (Parvanta, Nelson, & Harner, 2018). Meanwhile, communication is an independent field of study outside public health that emphasizes commercial and social marketing, politics, and publicity. Communication Theory provides essential foundations for conceptualizing the development of informative and persuasive messages about health and directing them in ways that **receivers** attend, comprehend, and act on them.

Communication can be thought of as a process of transmitting and receiving information that creates shared meaning. Good communication can make sense of otherwise disconnected and overwhelming amounts of information and facilitate meaningful attributions about it. Modern communication theory and practice emerged in recent decades mainly as the product of social-psychology studies of communication processes among members of social groups. Early communication studies focused largely on the processes by which messages were sent and received. Subsequent theory and research focused on how people processed and interpreted information and the effect of communication on knowledge, beliefs, attitudes, and behavior.

In this chapter, we discuss how communication is related to the transfer and acquisition of information, the role of information in persuasion, the special responsibilities of social marketing, the role of behavior theory in social marketing, and the effects of health communication on cognitions. First, let's revisit the importance and nature of information in communication.

Information Revisited

Information is the substance of all communication processes. Previously, we noted that information processing is a predominant interest of cognitive psychology, concerned with how people obtain, perceive, interpret, remember, and react to information. People are constantly processing information from many sources, including their own behavior, observation of others, routine conversations, newspapers, advertising, TV, social networking apps, and the Internet. New information is filtered through our memories and evaluated in relation to existing cognitions. In general information processing is simple, but the specifics are complex. How and to what extent does information get to the intended audience; what contributes to attention, comprehension, and recall? What information is heard but never processed? How does information create knowledge, alter beliefs, affect attitudes, contribute to values, and change behavior?

Cognitive Dissonance

To understand the importance of information to behavior it is useful to review Cognitive Dissonance Theory (Festinger, 1957), an elemental theory that provides the basis for most other communication theories and health communication efforts. The theory concerns itself with the common question, what do individuals do when confronted with information that is dissonant (does not agree) with their current knowledge, beliefs, attitudes, values, or behavior? New information can be evaluated by a person as consonant (aligning with their current attitudes), dissonant, or irrelevant (and thus not worth attending to). The significant implication of cognitive dissonance for health communication is that strategies can be (often are) designed to create dissonance in the target audience while providing explicit suggestions for how to resolve the resulting tension.

When information aligns with current attitudes or beliefs, it reinforces existing cognitions. However, as illustrated in **Figure 9.1**, when presented with information that is substantially dissonant (i.e., "I smoke cigarettes," and "Cigarettes cause cancer."), we experience cognitive distress and instinctively seek

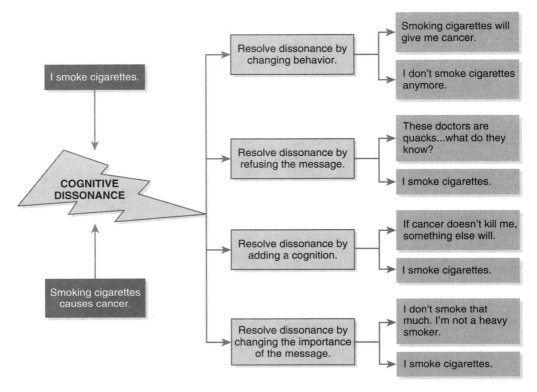

Figure 9.1 Example of cognitive dissonance

to resolve it because we much prefer to be consistent, and dissonance is experienced as stress. The greater the personal interest in the topic and the stronger and more salient the new information, the greater the urgency to resolve the dissonance. While people can tolerate unresolved dissonance for some time, mostly they seek to resolve it quickly.

Cognitive Resistance

There are three basic ways a person may act to resolve cognitive dissonance. Consider how a smoker may respond when confronted with information about the health risks associated with smoking. First, a person may ignore, discount, or reinvent the information. The smoker may think "… because I am not a really heavy smoker, I am not really at that much risk." Second, the smoker may

embrace counterinformation or prioritize alternate information that is more consistent with existing cognitions, for example, by thinking not all smokers get lung cancer. Third, the smoker might change existing cognitions to be consistent with the new information. By attending to the message, the smoker is challenged to consider its potential validity and importance, thereby experiencing dissonance to the extent existing cognitions and behavior are inconsistent with the new information. Therefore, the smoker must tolerate the dissonance or change cognitions to be consistent with the new information. These considerations for smoking also apply to other behaviors, such as diet and physical activity (Stellefson, Wang, & Klein, 2006).

For better or worse, people are resourceful in their efforts to reduce their exposure to dissonant information or reduce dissonance when it occurs. In particular, people reduce their likelihood of experiencing cognitive dissonance by actively avoiding dissonant information, termed **selective exposure**. We are selective about what we read, watch, listen, and otherwise attend. Given the dramatic amount of information available in modern society, people must be selective about the information to which they attend. However, selective attention is also a strategy for avoiding information that conflicts what we already believe, thereby preventing the tension that comes with dissonance. Instead, we commonly seek and attend to information that is consonant with existing cognitions to the exclusion of dissonant information. Accordingly, it is not difficult to find information that supports existing cognitions, and often people suffer from confirmation bias, where they selectively attend to information consistent with their beliefs and ignore other information. Indeed, commercial marketing is designed to generate advertising income by selectively feeding us links related to the information previously obtained to increase the likelihood we will click and attend. Sadly, a lot of such information is unregulated and its veracity questionable, which poses a growing challenge for those who seek to promote healthful behavior based on sound knowledge and attitudes.

To be clear, information that generates knowledge can alter beliefs and attitudes, but does not always for a number of reasons. For one thing, it can be difficult to reach people with new information. Given the vast amount of information constantly transmitted, people must be selective with their attention. Even the information that gets through to a receiver can be ignored, disbelieved, countered, or reinterpreted. People are highly selective, often deflective (antagonistic to other beliefs), harbor biased heuristics (reactive beliefs without reflection or further consideration), are prone to false consensus (believing your beliefs and behavior are normative, even when they are not), suffer from confirmation

bias (seeking information that conforms to existing beliefs), and resort to pluralistic ignorance (going along with what you think others believe, even when you do not). Under the best of conditions, people must evaluate the preponderance of consonant and disconsonant information, while considering the consequences of changing current cognitions and behavior. Consequences can be social, such as explaining change to others, or emotional, such as giving up a long-held belief or an activity like smoking that has been an important habit for many years. Therefore, to be effective new information must not only inform but also persuade. However, before we take up the topic of persuasion, an examination of basic communication processes is warranted.

Models of Communication Processes

While communication may seem like a simple process, think about how difficult it can be sometimes to get what you think and feel across to other people, even people you know very well. Consider common examples of difficult communications such as telling a friend that you don't approve of her behavior, maybe drinking too much, eating too little, or riding with her boyfriend when he has been drinking. What words to use? What logic would make sense to her? When to have this talk? How often? Should you get someone else to deliver or reinforce the message? The complexities magnify when you take this to the population level. For example, impaired driving is unsafe and illegal. Should the public health messages be about the dangers of impaired driving, the relationship between blood alcohol level and impairment, the likelihood of a serious crash or of getting arrested? A person who has been drinking becomes less inhibited and more likely to DWI, so maybe the message should be delivered to the friends of drinkers and maybe the message should be about the role of friendship (e.g., friends don't let friends DWI)? Should the message be delivered at bars or via the Internet, so people get it before they go drinking? Just announcing to the public that roadside sobriety tests will be performed on certain dates may reduce DWI if messages are widely shared and the target audience appropriately exposed (Centers for Disease Control and Prevention [CDC], 2015).

The following models have been developed to capture the complexity of communication processes: (1) action model, (2) transaction model, (3) interactive/intermediary model, and (4) ecological model. These models account for a great deal of complexity that is inherent in the communication process.

Action Model

The Shannon–Weaver model (1963), shown in **Figure 9.2**, is an early and formative description of communication processes that has been hugely influential in practice and the subject of extensive research (Verdú, 2000). The model provides a useful and essential set of definitions that have informed other models and provides the working vernacular for the following discussion of seven components of the communication process:

1. *Sender*: The person or source of the information. The sender would be the individual, organization, or agency that originated the message.
2. *Encoding*: The way the information is packaged for transmission. When a message is encoded, it uses particular wording, language, symbols, and style that are designed to make the message relevant to the intended receiver.
3. *Message*: The selection of content. It can be simple or complex, long or short, humorous or serious; it can appeal to logic or emotion, which also relates to the length of the message and how easily it can be decoded and interpreted.
4. *Channel*: The medium used to transmit the message. Typical channels include face-to-face, telephone, social networking apps, e-mail, newspaper, radio, television, and website. Any or all of these channels can be used to communicate a specific message. In health communication, channels are selected strategically based on what media the target audience is thought to use most.
5. *Decoding*: Is what the receiver actually takes away from the message. There is often variability in how the receivers decode the message based on their existing cognitions and dispositions. A well-designed message will be decoded by most of the receivers as planned.
6. *Receiver*: The person or target audience of the communication.
7. *Noise*: Interference of the communication that prevents the message from being received or attended. Interference may occur while sending, such as a technology glitch and factors that inhibit the receipt or comprehension of the message such as distractions and competing messages.

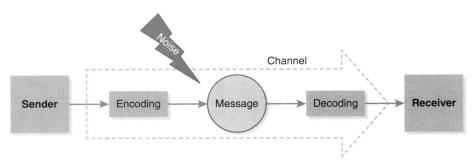

Figure 9.2 Shannon–Weaver model of communication

The model captures the essential elements of communication. The first four elements focus on information transmission, while the last three concern information receiving. Theoretically, all of the elements interact, enabling a mathematical calculation of communication effect. However, this is largely a static, one-way model of communication, like a healthcare provider prescribing a certain drug for a patient (e.g., "... take one tablet 3 times a day"). Applied to the COVID-19 pandemic, the action model might be employed to produce communication from authoritative sources that encourage people to wear face masks in public, which would be a good start, but maybe not enough to achieve the desired effect on the behavior.

Interactive/Transactional Model

Communication is often interactive and sometimes transactional in the sense that it involves dynamic interactions. The transaction model, shown in **Figure 9.3**, recognizes that information sharing is often iterative and cyclical, more like conversations over time. All of the elements of the action model are relevant, but messages are understood to be stated and restated, interpreted and reinterpreted as participants build understanding. In this model, both parties are simultaneously senders and receivers of messages, which flow back and forth across the channel. Consider communications you have with your family and friends where you discuss the same topic many times and many ways. Sometimes this leads to new understanding, sometimes not. Returning to our example of a drug prescription, the

interactive model would encourage a discussion between the physician and the patient about how the drug works, why it should be taken according to a particular routine, possible side effects, and what the patient should do if concerns arise.

Now think about this process in a health-promotion program, for example, seeking to convince people to wear face masks to prevent spreading COVID-19. The message is simple, sort of. Actually, at the start of the pandemic in 2020 there was a lot of confusion about mask wearing, with national health leaders, including the director of the CDC and the U.S. Surgeon General, in addition to antiscience political leaders, publicly discouraging mask wearing. In the absence of clear, unambiguous messaging, people sought information from various sources (not all of it credible). Were masks personally protective (they are modestly) or only useful for preventing contagion (much more important)? How and when should you wear them? Can they be reused? **Transactional communication** played out over months with the public demanding information, and massive amounts of information, a lot of it incorrect and misleading, were disseminated via every possible channel, including radio, television, and the Internet. Fortunately, public health academics spread the science-based message that mask wearing could prevent the spread of the virus, which helped reduce uncertainty and increased use, if belatedly. The pandemic was a humbling example of public health leadership, and a wonderful example of the importance of research, science-based information, and the importance of public health academics in getting the correct information to the public. It was also a good example of transactional communication. Essentially, the pandemic created a sense of urgency for useful information, but inconsistent information was rampant early on, which created extreme cognitive dissonance that people were motivated to resolve, either by seeking new information or by ignoring new sources of information and relying on existing beliefs, regardless of the facts.

Figure 9.3 Interactive/transactional model of communication

Intermediary Model

The intermediary model of communication, shown in **Figure 9.4**, acknowledges that often there are gatekeepers who mediate the content and flow of information from the transmitter to targeted receivers (Katz & Lazarsfeld, 1955). Rogers (2003) noted the role of **opinion leaders** in his research on the **diffusion** of innovations (see Chapter 10). Opinion leaders, sometimes called gatekeepers, can include anyone whose opinions about a topic are influential, including parents, teachers, community leaders, and print and electronic media professionals.

During the COVID-19 pandemic, opinion leaders from academia, government, and the private sector were recruited by media sources to provide information about the virus, the epidemic, and its prevention, and these opinion leaders provided messages that changed behavior. Unfortunately, there was a lot of **noise** in the messaging at first because there was a lack of scientific evidence and later because many opinion leaders were ill-informed or politically motivated, which made it more difficult for credible opinion leaders to get the right messages across. Sadly, many religious and local leaders, concerned about the economy, insisted on in-person contact at events, restaurants, and stores, resulting in dramatic viral spread and local hotspots. Of course, the **intermediary communication** process played out among individuals and families across the world, asking each other about masks and social distancing, and the most highly informed and socially connected individuals became opinion leaders. It was a dynamic process where people were desperate for information and sought the opinions of others, who got their information from still others and the media. Of course, as research

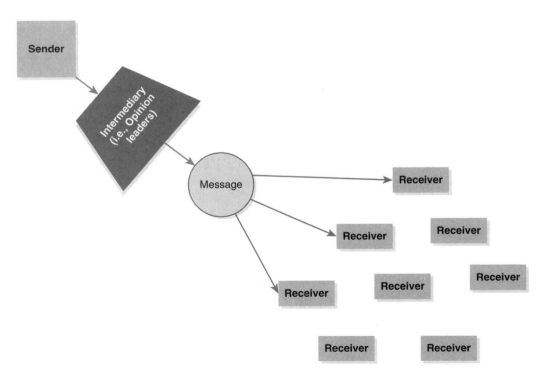

Figure 9.4 Intermediary model of communication

advanced, the benefits of mask wearing became overwhelmingly clear. Planned or not, the process consisted of lots of information being provided, much of it conflicting, and opinion leaders interpreted and remessaged the information to those in their social network.

Ecological Model

Given that health communication campaigns are directed almost exclusively at individual behavior, they cannot expect to be successful when the infrastructure is not conducive. Therefore, it is recommended that health communication campaigns be conducted in concert with other programmatic activities directed at community, policy, and other structural and environmental changes (Institute of Medicine [IOM], 2015). Foulger (2004) described a comprehensive ecological model of the communication process. The model includes the usual considerations of message transmission and receipt, but also emphasizes that information is embedded in a system that consists of social structures, history, and politics. This model emphasizes message symbols and language specific to the media channel such as text messages and social networking websites. Essentially, the ecological communication model accounts for contextual factors that influence how messages are created, translated (both **encoding** and **decoding**), and interpreted, as well as the outcome of the communication. With respect to the example of the pandemic, in an ideal world, an information campaign would inform about individual behavior, including face mask wearing, social distancing, hand washing, monitoring symptoms, and seeking care immediately upon infection. Community resources would be available to make these individual behaviors most effective and give people confidence that their efforts are part of a larger solution. This would include routine testing, personal protective equipment, and clear containment policies regarding social gatherings and the like.

Persuasion

Beliefs are what we think to be true, attitudes are affective evaluations, and values represent collected attitudes. These cognitions are established over time based on inculcated information from many sources that guide our behavior (along with environmental context). Despite some resistance, cognitions are malleable and subject to persuasion, making them the obvious target for intervention. Persuasive communications describe how information can be communicated in ways that are persuasive.

The early research on persuasion indicated that the persuasiveness of communications depended on three general factors: (1) the credibility and attractiveness of the source, (2) the salience and utility of the content, and (3) the characteristics and receptiveness of the receiver (Hovland, 1953). McGuire's (1989) "communication/persuasion matrix" elaborated on these factors, providing fundamental perspectives on the inputs and outputs of persuasion that are routinely employed by modern advertising and social marketing. The inputs (or transmission variables) of the communication/persuasion matrix include familiar elements from the action model of communication, including the following: source, content, intended recipient, channel, and context. These variables serve as column headings in the matrix shown in **Table 9.2**. In analyzing the effectiveness of particular persuasive efforts, termed outputs or outcomes, the characteristics of each message element can be identified and evaluated. For example, evaluation of message source characteristics may reveal the degree of credibility, expertise, and effectiveness as perceived by the intended audience. Indeed, thousands of scientific papers and countless marketing dollars have been spent on research on these input variables to determine the best message content, how receivers respond to different sources, how best to reach the target audience, the variability in receiver response to messages under differing contexts

Table 9.2 **Persuasion Matrix of Message Inputs and Outcomes**

Message Inputs	Definitions
Receiver	Who are the intended targets?
Source	What is the source of the information; is source authoritative or common? (Who sponsors the message? Who delivers the message?)
Content	What is the substance and intended meaning of the message?
Channel	By what medium are messages delivered (e.g., paper, radio, TV, Internet/digital)?
Context	In what location/situation does the message reach the receiver (e.g., health care, worksite, community)?
Outputs	
Exposure	How many of the intended targets received the messages?
Attention	To what extent did the receivers view or listen?
Interest	How much interest did the receivers show?
Comprehension	Did the exposed receivers understand the message as intended? How did they understand it?
Acquisition	To what extent could the receivers apply the message to the intended behavior?
Yielding	To what extent did exposure affect attitudes?
Memory	How long could the exposed receivers remember the message?
Retrieval	Could receivers recall the message in relevant contexts or situations?
Decision	Did exposure affect intent to behave as intended?

(at the doctor's office, at school, at work, in a magazine, etc.). In practice, message transmission characteristics related to recipient, channel, and context are often determined by program logistics, while source credibility and aspects of content can be guided by theory (as discussed later in the chapter) and pilot tested.

The outputs (targeted outcomes) of the communication/persuasion matrix are the impact or effect of the communication on the receiver. They include exposure, attention, interest, comprehension, acquisition, yielding, memory, retrieval, decision, action, reinforcement, and consolidation, as shown in the row headings in **Table 9.3**. These represent possible outcomes, most of

which are measurable, although evaluations are generally selective regarding which variables are actually evaluated. Evaluations of delivered messages or campaigns with multiple measures often examine the extent of exposure, including how many and what percent of the target population were exposed to the message; paid attention to it; and found it of interest, relevant, and understandable. Important, but more difficult to evaluate output measures deal with receiver cognitions, including remembering the message; ability to retrieve the message such that it is useful; changes in knowledge, beliefs, and attitudes; deciding to act, acting, and reinforcement of action; and consolidating the information with

Table 9.3 Communication-Persuasion Matrix: *Let's Move* Example

	Message Source	Message Content	Message Recipient	Communication Channel	Context
Evaluation	*Michelle Obama*	*Encourage children to be active and model physically active lifestyle*	*Parents, caregivers, teachers, community leaders*	*Website; television; YouTube*	*Childhood obesity epidemic; President Obama's administration*
Exposure				X	
Attention		X	X		
Interest		X	X		
Comprehension		X	X		
Acquisition		X	X		
Yielding		X	X		
Memory		X	X		
Retrieval		X	X		
Decision		X	X		
Action		X	X		
Reinforcement		X	X		
Consolidation		X	X		

existing attitudes and behaviors in ways that are consistent (not dissonant) and resistant to competing arguments. While some outputs may be independent, generally they are assumed to be related and interactive. For example, the extent of immediate knowledge acquisition is related to eventual consolidation.

The Let's Move Campaign, championed by former First Lady Michelle Obama, shown in Table 9.3, serves as a useful illustration of the persuasion matrix. This highly publicized campaign targeted childhood obesity prevention, with messages aimed mainly at parents of young children, with additional messages aimed at schoolteachers and administrators and community program leaders. The central message was for parents to encourage their children to be physically active by serving as an example of an active lifestyle. In the matrix, the output rows include the message source, content, recipient, channel, and context. Presumably, the former First Lady is a highly credible source for most parents. The content was varied to reflect the many ways families could establish an active family lifestyle. Other message input characteristics described in the table were piloted prior to program rollout. Output exposure was well evaluated, primarily exposure to Internet messages. Some evaluation was conducted of message attention, comprehension, and immediate effects on cognitions. Parents may be more inclined to attend to the message, which can foster interest. Theoretically, changes in family activity would occur consistent with message exposure, attention, comprehension, and so on.

The utility of the communication/persuasion matrix, then, is that it identifies multiple factors that interact to affect the persuasiveness of messages on cognitions and behavior. In addition, it illustrates the possible relationships between transmission (input) and receiver (output) variables. Decades of research has focused on the relationships among these inputs and outputs, processes for developing effective inputs, and the relationships among output variables. Cialdini (2009) has synthesized the vast literature on persuasion with the following principles of persuasion, which are now a staple of commercial marketing: (1) reciprocity: receivers feel obligated to return favors; (2) consistency: new information that creates dissonance challenges existing cognitions; (3) social proof: receivers conform to social norms; (4) authority: receivers evaluate the credibility of the source; (5) liking: receivers are susceptible to messages and messengers they like; (6) **scarcity**: receivers value less available things; and (7) unity: receivers are attracted to a sense of shared identify. These research-based principles provide a decided advance over the outdated commercial marketing practices known as the four "P's": product, place, price, promotion.

It should be abundantly clear that there are clear guiding principles for effective persuasive communications. Next, it is useful to review some of the theories (or models) that have extended the logic of the persuasion matrix and elaborated on mechanisms of information processing.

Elaboration Likelihood Model

The key concept of the elaboration likelihood model (ELM) is that persuasive information is processed and affects attitudes through central and peripheral information processing routes (Petty & Cacioppo, 1986). The model is so named because it highlights factors that influence a person's likelihood to elaborate (make practical use of) the message content as a result of information processing. Peripheral processing involves attention, while central processing entails active involvement that can yield high elaboration. ELM emphasizes factors related to message attention and the processes by which that information results in persuasion.

Peripheral Route Processing

Peripheral route processing occurs when information generates attention but generally passive consideration. People process most information passively, particularly when the topic is not of high and immediate importance. Because the amount of information is vast, people are selective and attend only to certain messages. Messages that are frequent, unique, visual, and emotional are thought to attract attention (see **Table 9.4**). Because attention is a necessary step prior to action, fear arousal and other emotional messages are commonly employed.

Table 9.4 Elaboration Likelihood Model Peripheral Route Processing Messaging Priorities

Message Category	Description
Consistency	Establish consistency of new information with existing cognitions
Source characteristics that increase message salience	Expertise Trustworthiness Attractiveness
Social proof	Focus messages on social norms
Reciprocity	Elicit a sense of obligation
Scarcity	Establish sense of urgency

Central Route Processing

Central route processing requires the receiver to be an active participant, thoughtfully evaluating the information with respect to possible action. This sort of information processing is highly desired because it facilitates message retention and fosters resilience to counter-arguments, leading to changes in attitudes. Central route processing occurs mainly when the receiver judges the topic to be personally important and immediate. When acceptable options are available, action is likely. While other message characteristics are important, the strength of the argument made by the message is an important factor in central route processing.

Peripheral and central processing are not independent and typically occur simultaneously. ELM provides an "elaboration" on the persuasion/communication matrix and has generated substantial research on message input and output. Receiver elaboration of messages is highly desirable as it represents active engagement leading to changes in cognitions or at least cognitive dissonance. Messages can actively involve the receiver by personalizing messages and providing acceptable actions. Note how closely ELM aligns with cognitive dissonance with its emphases on resolving tension created by information inconsistent with existing cognitions and behavior.

Inoculation Theory

In the modern age there is a lot of competing information on any particular topic, much of it sponsored by marketers encouraging unhealthful behavior, for example, smoking, drinking, and eating high-calorie foods. **Inoculation** theory focuses on strengthening resistance to persuasion by repeated exposure to counterarguments (Niederdeppe, Gollust, & Barry, 2014). The primary focus is on the persuasion (output) variables of yielding (relevant attitudes) and consolidation (integrating the information into existing cognitions). The key components of the theory are threat and **refutational preemption**.

Threat

People respond to threats and are motivated by warnings about impending threatening events. Therefore, messages that arouse emotions can increase readiness to take action. Fear-arousing threats that are too extreme tend to be rejected by the receiver, but threats that increase emotional arousal, particularly when linked to an acceptable remedy or course of action, can be highly effective.

Refutational Preemption

People are sometimes bombarded with threats, often from sources that are not credible or concerned with the receivers' best interests. Preparation for people to resist such messages can be directed at logical defenses or counterarguments. Just being warned that a message is biased can be protective. People are even better defended when armed with preemptive arguments against the biased message. Effective preemptive arguments are thought to stimulate cognitive defenses against biased arguments (e.g., why I don't smoke or drink to excess). For example, a refutational preemption arguments against smoking uptake might focus on the avarice of tobacco companies, social norms against smoking, disadvantages such as cost, and negative health effects. Equipping people with refutational arguments for specific counterarguments stiffens resistance to persuasion.

Inoculation theory is most applicable to health behaviors that pull people to them, but are not good for them, for example, drugs and risk taking, but also being sedentary, overeating, and other obesogenic behaviors. However, in the age of the Internet, with so much misinformation, there is a need for messages that provide arguments that preempt dangerous and misleading information about health, for example, drinking bleach or taking other unproven and potentially or actually dangerous treatments to prevent illness.

Social Marketing

So far, we have been discussing communication processes that could relate to commercial or social topics. **Social marketing** combines communication and marketing principles with traditional program planning strategies to affect behavior (Lee & Kotler, 2019). Social marketing was originally employed by public and private nonprofit groups to foster healthful or socially beneficial behavior. Today social marketing is a lucrative business model that seeks to sell information about user preferences and interests to advertisers. The communication and persuasion theories just discussed are entirely relevant to both nonprofit and profit-oriented social marketing, although the focus of the following discussion is on nonprofit uses of social marketing. For example, social marketing has been applied to the topics related to public health, safety, the environment, and community development, including a wide range of specific health behaviors such as diet, physical activity, smoking, and medication taking (Lee & Kotler, 2019). Distinctions between commercial and social marketing are noted in **Table 9.5**.

Processes

Basically, social marketing combines principles of persuasion with the principles of program planning within a socially responsible context. The steps involved are recognizable to any public health professional and second nature to those trained in health promotion as key to the planning processes. Social marketing processes include the following: (1) formative evaluation of inputs, (2) message and materials development, (3) pretesting and adjusting inputs, (4) implementing and disseminating messages, and (5) evaluating outputs (outcomes).

1. **Formative evaluation**. Surveys, interviews, or other qualitative or quantitative formative methods can determine the following:

   a. Source: Credibility and attractiveness (likeability) of possible sources.

   b. Receivers: Possible subgroups of intended receivers for special attention and the possible utility of focusing on social referents rather than or in addition to the primary target.

Table 9.5 Key Differences Between Social and Commercial Marketing

Characteristic	Social Marketing	Commercial Marketing
Desired outcome	Societal benefit	Financial gain
"Product" sold	Social or health behavior	Goods and/or services
Competition	Alternative cognitions and behaviors	Organizations offering similar products or services
Behavior targeted	Behavior that provides benefit to society or to personal health, often requiring sacrifice or restraint	Money for product or service
Context	Socially responsible: unbiased, not manipulative; planning includes representatives of target population	Sometimes misleads and manipulates

c. Channel and context: Logistics of message delivery — where, when, how often should which messages be placed?

2. **Message content and format**. For any target output there are many possible messages and many possible ways to express a theme. What cognitions should the message address? Message development can be tricky, considering how complex language is, how it must be adapted to each channel, and how it is subject to variable interpretation by various receivers. Only through pilot testing can the acceptability and correct interpretation of the message be determined. In addition, the message often consists not only of words, but also of symbols, other visuals, and sounds, which can interact with source and context factors.

3. **Pretest and adjust**. Prototypes should be formatively evaluated before finalization. This work is to determine the extent to which the message reaches the target audience; their attention, comprehension, and reaction to the message; the utility of message delivery; and so on.

4. **Implementation and dissemination**. Experience teaches us that even the most carefully planned program activity can fail to realize its potential. Implementation requires advance planning, problem resolution, staff energy and enthusiasm, and resources. Great messages can be widely disseminated, more so through careful planning and substantial effort.

5. **Evaluation of outputs** (outcomes). Evaluating the many possible outcomes requires careful planning and resource allocation to determine the extent to which the following questions were answered.

a. Exposure: Did the messages get to the intended audience?
b. Attention: Did the receivers pay attention?
c. Comprehension: Did the receivers understand the information?

d. Cognitions: Did the message affect the targeted beliefs and attitudes (yielding, remembering, retrieval)?
e. Behavior: Did behavior change (decision, action, reinforcement, consolidation) as a result of the social marketing campaign?

Take the example of a social marketing program to prevent drinking and driving. Extensive media campaigns launched over the past several decades have been credited with contributing to the decline in prevalence. Ubiquitous public service announcements (PSAs) developed by The Ad Council emphasized the messages, "Friends don't let friends drive drunk" and "Drinking and driving will kill a friendship." These messages addressed social norms regarding DWI and the responsibility of friends to prevent DWI. This was a well-funded campaign by a sophisticated marketing firm with resources to pilot test messages, develop multiple messages for particular population subgroups and context, with ongoing evaluation of outputs. The success of the campaign has been credited to the broad exposure to the messages over a long period of time, which has long been recognized as an essential element of success (IOM, 2015). At the same time critical issues other than personal responsibility were being addressed, including changes in the legally allowed blood alcohol concentration (BAC), the development of technology for immediate results of BAC testing, and increased priority of DWI by law enforcement.

Ethics

While social marketing applies principles and practices common to commercial marketing, it has special responsibilities and challenges (IOM, 2015). Commercial advertising is regulated to an extent by federal legislation that requires "truth in advertising," although mostly it is up to marketers to self-regulate. Social marketing is held to a higher standard by its practitioners (IOM, 2015; Lee & Kotler, 2019). Here we mention a few of the most important.

1. Receivers. Although targeting receivers most "ready to adopt" may yield the greatest results, **high-risk** and vulnerable populations should also be addressed. However, the special needs and characteristics of these population groups should be considered.

2. Channel. A great deal of social marketing, indeed of all marketing, is digital these days. Digital marketing has the potential for good and for not so good with respect to responsible marketing. The language, visuals, and symbols employed should be fully vetted to ensure they do not represent bias or misrepresentation.

3. Messaging. While social marketing employs persuasion methods, it must adhere to a higher standard than commercial marketing with respect to receiver integrity. The goal of most social marketing programs is behavior change, but messaging must be honest, factual, and not manipulative. Message development should involve representatives of the target receivers, and pilot testing should evaluate emotional and related receiver responses to draft messages. Great caution should be exercised in using emotional appeals that are known to capture attention, but could manipulate particularly vulnerable populations

4. Exposure. Many social marketing campaigns achieve inadequate exposure. Sometimes this is because the campaign is not sufficiently funded and must rely on public service announcements placed in passive channels such as public radio or TV. Sometimes it is simply not sufficient message distribution or improper channel selection. At other times it is a matter of insufficient duration or failure to repeat the messages sufficient to gain attention and other desirable receiver input characteristics. Social marketing cannot be successful unless the messages are frequent and persistent.

5. Environmental context. Social marketing programs, like all health communications, address individual behavior. Because environmental factors are so important with respect to both behavior and health, social marketing in the absence of efforts to overcome factors that pose barriers to change and efforts to advance factors that facilitate healthful change is unlikely to be successful and could contribute to **blaming the victim** (Niederdeppe, Shapiro, Kim, Bartolo, & Porticella, 2014). Moreover, effective social marketing programs are usually part of a multilevel and multistrategy program. At the very least, a responsible social marketing program development carefully considers the limits of individual-level change in the presence of environmental adversity and in the absence of environmental change.

6. Government-based and supported social marketing, while completely legitimate, must exercise particular caution to avoid manipulation given that government messaging and persuasion sources may be particularly powerful for some populations.

Theory-Based Message Framing

Communication strategies are designed to deliver relevant, accurate, useful information to those who need it in a way that affects their behavior. Successful information campaigns are guided by the principles generated from Communication Theory dealing with the message and the receiver. However, even the most highly technical and well-funded program will not be successful if it does not understand the receiver (target population) and the key cognitive determinants of their behavior. Some messaging considerations can be intuited, for example, context may be a given—if the intended receivers are medical patients, they may best be reached in healthcare settings; if the receivers are adolescents, then schools might be the context of choice. The source of the communication and the channel or channels by which it might be delivered might require a little more than a bit of piloting to determine feasibility. Message content, however, is best guided by behavior theory. Toward the end of determining the content of messages behavior theory is useful if not essential as follows: conceptualizes behavior, provides constructs and variables that can be measured, and facilitates the interpretation of output variables. Behavior theory can guide the development of specific messages.

Behavioral theories are generally concerned with cognitions, some more interested in beliefs, others in attitudes; some mostly concerned with beliefs about self, others with beliefs and attitudes about social norms. Cognitions are building blocks of behavior, so changing cognitions increases the likelihood of behavior change. A communication campaign, commercial or social marketing, would benefit from selecting a theoretical perspective; crafting and conducting surveys, interviews, or other needs assessments; and interpreting the outcomes (outputs) of the campaign (e.g., did it affect the targeted cognitions). Earlier in this chapter we discussed cognitive dissonance as a foundational Communication Theory and Elaboration Likelihood Theory as an extension of Persuasion Theory. In **Table 9.6** we present the key cognitions for each of several other behavior theories, each of which is described in detail in previous chapters. The list of

Table 9.6 Selected Behavior Theory Constructs for Health Communication Messaging

Theory	Construct for Possible Messaging
Theory of Reasoned Action (TRA); Planned Behavior (TPB)	Information influences beliefs, attitudes, intentions: • Beliefs about the object, action, behavior • Subjective norms/perceived prevalence • Social pressure/injunctive norms • Personal behavioral control
Health Belief Model (HBM)	Information influences beliefs related to behavior • Perceived risk • Perceived benefit • Perceived susceptibility • Self-efficacy
Social Cognitive Theory (SCT)	• Outcome expectations • Behavioral capability • Self-efficacy • Self-control • Social norms
Social Influence Theory (SIT)	• Social identity • Perceived and actual social norms • Perceived and actual social pressure • Sources of information, support
Diffusion Theory	Innovation characteristics • Compatibility • Complexity • Trialability • Observability • Relative advantages

theories is meant to be representative and not comprehensive. Other behavior theories may have logical and useful social marking applications. The included theories are meant to provide examples of how behavior theory can augment and, indeed, are essential to the development of effective social marketing. The discussion is brief and meant to be read in the context of the more detailed descriptions in previous chapters. Here we provide a brief discussion about how the key constructs from each theory might facilitate social marketing. The goal is to create appreciation for how valuable these theories are for developing health communications, leading the reader back to the relevant chapters.

Theory of Reasoned Action and Theory of Planned Behavior

Each of the overlapping theories of reasoned action and planned action are commonly employed in health communication programs because the constructs generalize to many health problems. Beliefs about the action or the behavior, including subjective and **injunctive social norms** and personal behavioral control, can be applied to many personal-health behaviors, including diet, physical activity, and adherence to a medical regimen. The theories also emphasize a measure of motivation, intention, that is useful for measuring outputs.

Health Belief Model

The premise of the health belief model is that beliefs about susceptibility and severity of a health concern and beliefs about the utility of possible preventive action predict the likelihood of action. These constructs are easily understood, although not so easily measured accurately, and applicable to a range of health problems. HBM was developed to understand compliance/adherence to medical regimen, and that remains its most useful

application, although it has been applied to many health behaviors. Assuming compliance is the behavior of interest, an information campaign would determine the target populations' specific beliefs (perceptions) about the severity of the health problem, their personal susceptibility to its effects, and the benefits of compliance. The model also provides a useful summary measure of motivation or readiness to take action for use in output evaluations.

Social Cognitive Theory

Social Cognitive Theory (SCT) provides a wealth of cognitions for consideration in information campaigns. The best known of these are outcome expectations, behavioral capability, and self-efficacy. In addition, a wide range of self-regulatory variables are prominent, including self-evaluation, monitoring, and self-control. Outcome expectations is a particularly noteworthy variable for information campaigns. Beliefs about the outcomes of a particular action is a key cognition that translates readily to messaging. For example, with respect to physical activity, expectations about the benefits of increased activity, including fitness, weight control, self-perceptions, and social advantages, are logical variables to assess and message. In addition, SCT provides guidance about how to create cognitive dissonance and representational language that can increase persuasion.

Social Influence Theory

Social Influence Theory elaborates the powerful role that group membership, social relations, and social norms have on behavior. Here we focus on selected variables that can logically be addressed by social marketing. The premise of social norms theory is that people share cognitions with others, particularly with the groups with which they are directly associated, such as family, friends, and coworkers. These are people from whom we develop personal identify and from whom we seek information and support. Additionally, we share cognitions with groups with which we identify indirectly or remotely, such as peers or colleagues outside our close circle of friends and reputation-based groups such as athletes, influencers, gamers, or musicians. Examples include social networking sites such as Facebook, Twitter, Instagram, Snapchat, and Pinterest. Other sources of influence can be a result of YouTube, TikTok, and blogs. Influence is the product of social norms and pressure, which can be actual, but is largely perceived and often not entirely correct. Perceptions about norms lend themselves to informational messaging. Notably, adolescents and young adults perceive that a greater proportion of their friends drink alcohol routinely than is actually the case (Moreira, Smith, & Foxcraft, 2010). This overestimation of peer behavior applies particularly to youthful perceptions of their general peers, young people their age or grade. Similarly, there may be misperception about how acceptable drinking or other risk behavior is among those in our social network. Adolescents and young adults may feel social pressure to drink or engage in other risky behaviors than is actual. These perceptions lend themselves to informative messages. It is now common for university-based social marketing programs to "advertise" the actual drinking prevalence of students, which tends to be lower than perceived by individual students, particularly incoming students. The theory also suggests possible messages related to sources of correct information or assistance.

Diffusion Theory

Diffusion Theory is based on the study of adoption patterns—how an innovation diffuses over time in a population. This is just what social marketing attempts to promote healthful behavior. The theory provides a wealth of useful communication concepts relating to the receiver, discussed in terms of specific types of receiver knowledge (about the innovation, its practical application and use, and the principles upon which it is based), **adopter categories** (early to late adopters), and stages of adoption (which predates other stages of change theories), which provide exceptional guidance for social marketing program development. Notably, the theory emphasizes two-step communication processes based on the influence of personal recommendations from close others. The theory also elaborates on persuasion strategies not described elsewhere. Notably, Diffusion Theory emphasizes the characteristics of the innovation that could be targeted. These include compatibility with current practice, complexity, **trialability**, **observability**, and relative advantage. (The next time you have a chance to view a few commercials, think about which of these innovation characteristics it uses.) Just for fun, review the ad in **Figure 9.5** from the perspective of persuasive communications inputs. What are the message source(s), intended audience, and message contents? What would be the logical channels and contexts for this message?

Theory-Based Social Marketing Applications

Examples of how health communication strategies have been employed for science, policy, health care, emergencies, and other topics are reported in Parvanta et al. (2018). Here we focus on examples of theory-based communication efforts. Kurt Lewin noted that there is nothing so practical as a good theory. Accordingly, behavior theory is a prominent component of many social marketing campaigns. In this section we provide examples of social marketing programs based on behavior theory and sound health communication principles.

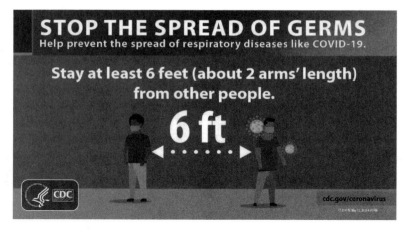

Figure 9.5 Example of a persuasive communication

Centers for Disease Control and Prevention (2020). Stop the spread of germs. Retrieved from https://www.cdc.gov/coronavirus/2019-ncov/downloads/stop-the-spread-of-germs-11x17-en.pdf

Smoking Prevention

During the past decade the Florida Department of Health enacted the Tobacco Free Florida media campaign to encourage smoking cessation (Duke et al., 2020). This was a well-funded campaign in the community context with frequent media messages using a wide range of paid advertising **channels**, including television, radio, and Internet. The intended **receivers** were adult smokers. The **source** of the message was Tobacco Free Florida and the Florida Department of Health, which would seem credible and authoritative sources. Messages were based on the Elaboration Likelihood Model of parallel processing. The contents of most messages were highly emotional designed to capture attention and arouse a sense of fear, consistent with peripheral information processing. Other messages focused on specific actions smokers could take to quit, consistent with **central route processing** that requires receiver involvement, possible only when the receiver was exposed and was emotionally aroused to reconsider current cognitions and behavior. The effects of the campaign were evaluated in statewide surveys of smokers. The research found that 17% of smokers quit during the period of

study, and quitting was greater among those who reported being exposed to at least one message. The research findings were consistent with an effect of messages based on parallel cognitive processing, where high-arousal messages combined with active messages that encourage specific actions increased smoking quit attempts.

Preventing Excessive Drinking

Social influence is highly associated with behavior and a key construct in numerous cognitive theories. Cognitions and behavior are socially mediated by through social relationships, both immediate and distant. Of the many ways social influence works, perceived social norms appear to play a particularly powerful role with respect to college drinking behavior (Perkins, 2002). In particular, the overestimation of drinking prevalence is related to drinking and media campaigns that have been conducted to correct misperceptions of prevalence. Dejong et al. (2006) randomized 18 colleges to a social norms–oriented media campaign, half administering the intervention and half serving as controls. In addition to media, the intervention schools were expected to provide other appropriate prevention measures, including standard drinking misuse policies and alcohol-free events. The media campaign in the college context consisted of messages that sought to correct misperceptions by advertising the actual drinking prevalence from routine surveys conducted at each school. The intended audience of **receivers** included the entire population of students, with emphasis on younger students and those on campus. The **message** content was labeled as "just the facts" and reported statistics on actual drinking prevalence and the reported extent of overestimation of prevalence. Communication **channels** included dormitory and other group housing, student cafeterias and other campus gathering places, and local businesses. The **source** was identified as the university and "Just the Facts." Output measure of exposure was the average weekly activity score of the number of media messages delivered. Measures of drinking in the SNM (intervention group) colleges relative to the control colleges included lower perceptions of drinking prevalence among students, lower recent amount of maximum consumption, and fewer drinks at parties and per week. Message intensity was greater in some schools than others, and this was related to drinking outcomes, suggesting a dose response.

Reducing Consumption of Sugared Beverages

Routine consumption of sugar-sweetened beverages (SSB) is a potential cause of obesity and diabetes due to the intake of "empty" calories and the metabolic effects of sugar. In the context of a single city (Philadelphia), a social norms media campaign targeted the parents/caregivers (receivers) of children 3–16 (Bleakley, Jordan, Malya, Hennessy, & Piotrowski, 2018). Messages were delivered as public service announcements on cable TV channels popular with the intended receivers. Message content was based on the **Theory of Reasoned Action**. The content of the messages included information about the health harm of excessive SSB consumption, **social norms** regarding the expectations of other parents (normative pressure or injunctive norms), and personal control of their children's SSB consumption. The message sources portrayed in the PSAs were low-income African American women similar to the target population. Survey findings indicated that over 60% of the sample reported being exposed to at least one PSA over the study period. Greater exposure was associated with several outputs, including stronger beliefs that reducing SSB would be good for health (diabetes and overweight in particular) and would not make mealtimes less enjoyable. Greater exposure was also associated with stronger **intention** to reduce SSB among their children. The findings were consistent with an effect on beliefs and intentions of media messages based on theory of reasoned action.

Increasing Face Mask Wearing to Prevent COVID-19

The national response to the 2020 COVID-19 pandemic in the United States is recognized as among the worst in the world. The administration of the federal government failed to establish centralized planning, leaving states to fend for themselves in their efforts to obtain appropriate protective equipment and testing kits and come up with their own policies to prevent further contagion, leading to millions of cases, overburdened hospitals and healthcare workers, and repeated outbreaks of the disease. Infected people spread the disease while traveling, despite state and local travel restrictions (but no national policy). Of all the well-earned criticism of the federal response, none was greater than the lack of consistent messaging about how people should behave to prevent contagion. President Trump convened a national advisory group, but sidelined the scientist and public health representatives, while undermining the importance of social distancing and mask wearing. The government failed to provide personal protective gear, ventilators, and other badly needed medical equipment. It could not settle on reasonable advice, while resident and other national figures undermined public health guidance with off-message noise. The belated shutdown of the economy was inconsistent across the country and lifted before the infection was under sufficient control. Blame was earned by national and state leaders who failed to take appropriate action, the CDC for its failed testing procedures and inconsistent prevention messages, and even members of the advisory committee, who were late to recognize the importance of social distancing and mask wearing. While many governors, mayors, and other local leaders took concerted action, the lack of leadership and fumbling national reaction to the threat resulted in confusion and distrust such that the public actions necessary to contain the virus, social distancing and mask wearing, quickly and widely adopted in other countries, were not widely or uniformly adopted, which allowed the contagion to continue to spread unabated for months. Had the administration taken decisive action and encouraged reasonable public health measures many of the more than half a million deaths and millions of COVID cases could have been prevented. Imagine how things might have been different if there had been thoughtful leadership and a well-planned media campaign. Here we present ideas for such a media campaign designed to encourage consistent mask wearing in public settings, which, combined with social distancing, is one of the most effective ways of preventing the spread of the virus. This is an exercise in the application of the persuasion matrix of message inputs and outputs.

The goal of the hypothesized program, for simplicity's sake, is to increase the prevalence of mask wearing in public, particularly indoors, where the concentration of the virus and people make contagion most likely. Possible input and output variables are described in **Table 9.7**. Diffusion Theory provides constructs that could help conceptualize and measure inputs and outcomes.

The prevalence and characteristics of receivers in each adopter category would be assessed in needs assessments from surveys and interviews with people in a range of public contexts, particularly high-risk settings such as restaurants, bars, and public gatherings where the concentration of the virus and people make for likely contagion. Quickly, profiles of early adopters and innovators, late adopters, laggards, and never wearers would be developed. Academics and public researchers would be enlisted and supported in a concerted effort to examine mask-wearing behavior and its cognitive and other predictors in various jurisdictions and contexts. Some of the information generated would provide baseline information for later program evaluation and enable message targeting for different populations. Some surveillance activities would be conducted repeatedly to monitor changes in prevalence and perceptions.

The channels, contexts, sources, and content would be assessed, including demographics, media use, mask-wearing behavior, and innovation characteristics identified in Diffusion Theory. Channels and programs popular with mask nonusers would be targeted. While the authoritative sources of the messages would be the CDC, they would be delivered by respected national leaders, as well as people with whom the receivers would identify. Message content themes would likely include receiver knowledge about the hows, whys, whens, and relative advantage of mask wearing (it is amazing how ill-informed people are about these seemingly simple issues), along with beliefs and attitudes about the relative advantages and social norms regarding mask wearing. To establish refutational preemption, messages might focus on defenses against counterarguments (e.g., "don't let people tell you it is not masculine or politically incorrect to wear a mask"). Messages could also focus on the complexity of mask wearing, some on compatibility

Table 9.7 Persuasive Communication Matrix Applied to Mask Wearing to Prevent the Spread of COVID-19 Based on Diffusion Theory

Input	Description
Receivers	Based on needs assessments, the market would be segmented to include adopter categories (e.g., innovators to laggards).
Channels	Multiple channels would be employed, including PSAs and paid advertisements for radio, TV, and Internet.
Contexts	Worksites, businesses, bars/restaurants, etc.
Sources	Authoritative source: CDC. Social referent sources: members of the public similar to the targeted receivers.
Content	Content would be modified for various receivers, but would generally include social norms, civic responsibility and patriotism, correct and appropriate mask-wearing behavior and its compatibility, simplicity, trialability, observability, and relative advantages, plus other themes identified in needs assessments.
Output	
Exposure	What percentage of the target receivers recall messages?
Attention, interest	Attitudes about the messages.
Comprehension	Understanding the messages.
Yielding	Believing the truth, accuracy, and value of the messages.
Memory, retrieval, acquisition	Remembering the message content and applying it to relevant contexts.
Decision	Strength of commitment to wear a mask in specified contexts and conditions.
Action, consolidation	Population prevalence and individual consistency in wearing masks in high-risk public contexts.
Reinforcement	Perception that mask-wearing behavior is supported.

(e.g., have your mask with you always, like your wallet or phone). Masks have high trialability because they are inexpensive (use a rag or cutoff T-shirt sleeve if you don't have an actual mask), not permanent, and reversable. Because masks mainly protect other people from infection, the relative advantages of mask wearing are social. Messages would probably need to emphasize and convince the receiver that appropriate mask

wearing is a socially advantageous, responsible behavior that is mature, patriotic, law-abiding, and expected, and failure to do so poses the risk of social sanctions and exclusion.

Various outputs would be routinely monitored to determine message exposure, attention, interest, and comprehension. Repeated surveys would assess receiver cognitions and behavior. Would such a social marketing program be effective if it included all the ingredients required for success? It certainly would have helped, but as with all social marketing efforts, success would depend not just on the quality of the program, but also on social conditions and events outside it. Aspects of the pandemic were in dynamic flux, as research rapidly discovered how the virus spread and could be contained, changes in rates of infection were reported (this or that area is a hot spot or has declining infections), and the progress on vaccines was the subject of daily news. The maximum potential of such a program would require national leaders emphasizing the national importance of mask wearing, with as little off-message noise as possible. If only....

Lessons for Public Health Practice

Communication is the process of sharing information, the essential ingredient of health communications and an important element of nearly all public health programs. Social marketing is a meld of health communication and program planning. Public health professionals should develop familiarity with social marketing concepts, methods, and principles. Here we provide a brief list of essential points regarding health communication and social marketing.

1. Information is essential for intentional behavior change. In whatever form it is delivered, information can contribute to knowledge, challenge beliefs, shape attitudes, and facilitate behavior change.
2. Given the profusion of information, much of it factually suspect, and a diverse and vulnerable population, the communication of unbiased, accurate, easily accessible, and useful information about health is greatly needed. Such information should deal with issues of low health literacy and variable cultural considerations.
3. Information processes include the top-down action model, the interaction model, the intermediary model, and the community/ecological model. Each model provides useful perspectives on communication processes.
4. Cognitive dissonance is the basis for most Communication Theory. Information that is inconsistent with current cognitions and behavior creates tension that the receiver seeks to reduce by disregarding the information, living with the tension, or changing cognitions.
5. Because people have well-developed mechanisms for avoiding dissonance, messages must gain receivers' attention, arouse interest, and provide acceptable solutions.
6. Persuasion applies communication in ways designed to alter cognitions and behavior. The persuasion matrix includes inputs and outputs that are routinely used in commercial and social marketing to overcome resistance and alter cognitions and behavior.
7. Social marketing employs persuasion variables to develop social- and health-related campaigns. Social marketing combines the principles of persuasion and program planning. Social marketing has special ethical and practice requirements, including honest, factual, and snonmanipulative messages.
8. Behavior theories contribute to social marketing, including providing conceptualization, variables for needs assessments, methods for message development and delivery, evaluation criteria, and contexts for interpreting results.
9. There are many examples of social Marketing programs that employ behavior theory to guide the development and evaluation of messages.

Discussion Questions

1. What are the key features of the intermediary model of communication?
2. What distinguishes social marketing from other communication processes?
3. What are the input features of the persuasive communication model?
4. What are the advantages of behavior theory in social marketing?
5. Identify two distinct ethical requirements of social marketing.

References

Bleakley, A., Jordan, A., Malya, G., Hennessy, M., & Piotrowski, T. (2018). Do you know what your kids are drinking? Evaluation of a media campaign to reduce consumption of sugar-sweetened beverages. *American Journal of Health Promotion*, 32(6), 1409–1416. DOI: 10.1177/0890117117721320

Centers for Disease Control and Prevention. (2015). Sobriety checkpoints. Retrieved from https://www.cdc.gov/motorvehiclesafety/calculator/factsheet/checkpoints.html

Cialdini, R. B. (2009). *Influence: The psychology of persuasion*. New York: Harper Collins.

DeJong, W., Schneider, S. K., Towvim, L. G., Murphy, M. J., Doerr, E. E., Simonssen, N. R., Mason, K. E., & Scribner, R. A. (2006). A multisite randomized trial of social norms marketing campaigns to reduce college student drinking. *Journal of Studies on Alcohol and Other Drugs*, 67, 868–879.

Duke, J. C., Woodlea, R., Arnold, K. Y., MacMonegle, A. J., Nonnemaker, J. M., & Porter, L. (2020). Effect of a statewide media campaign on smoking cessation among Florida adults. *Preventing Chronic Disease*, 17, 190271. DOI: 10.5888/pcd17.190271

Festinger, L. (1957). *A theory of cognitive dissonance*. Stanford, CA: Stanford University Press.

Foulger, D. (2004). *An ecological model of the communication process*. Unpublished manuscript. Retrieved from http://davis.foulger.info/papers/ecologicalModelOfCommunication.htm

Hovland, C. I. (1953). *Communication and persuasion: Psychological studies of opinion change*. New Haven, CT: Yale University Press.

Institute of Medicine. (2015). *Communicating to advance the public's health: Workshop summary*. Washington, DC: The National Academies Press. DOI:10.17226/21694

Katz, E., & Lazarsfeld, P. F. (1955). *Personal influence*. New York: Free Press.

Lee, N. R., & Kotler, P. (2019). *Social marketing: Influencing behaviors for good*. Thousand Oaks, CA: Sage. https://us.sagepub.com/en-us/nam/social-marketing/book260584

McGuire, W. J. (1989). A meditational theory of susceptibility to social influence. In V. Gheorghiu, P. Netter, H. J. Eysenck, & R. Rosenthal (Eds.), *Suggestion and suggestibility: Theory and research* (pp. 305–322). Heidelberg: Springer.

Moreira, J. J., Smith, L. A., & Foxcraft, D. (2010). Social norms interventions to reduce alcohol misuse among university or college students. *Cochrane Collaboration*. London: John Wiley and Sons, Ltd. DOI: 10.1002/14651858.CD006748.pub2

Niederdeppe, J., Gollust, S. E., & Barry, C. L. (2014). Inoculation in competitive framing: Examining message effects on policy preferences. *Public Opinion Quarterly*, 78(3), 634–655. DOI: 10.1093/poq/nfu026

Niederdeppe, J., Shapiro, M. A., Kim, H. K., Bartolo, D., & Porticella, N. (2014). Narrative persuasion, causality, complex integration, and support for obesity policy. *Health Communication*, 29(5), 431–444. DOI: 10.1080/10410236.2012.761805

Office of Disease Prevention and Health Promotion. Health Communication. (n.d.) *Healthy People 2030*. U.S. Department of Health and Human Services. Retrieved from https://health.gov/healthypeople/objectives-and-data/browse-objectives/health-communication

Parvanta, C. F., Nelson, D. E., & Harner, R. N. (2018). *Public health communication: Critical tools and strategies*. Burlington, MA: Jones & Bartlett Learning.

Perkins, H. W. (2002). Social norms and the prevention of alcohol misuse in college students. *Journal of Studies on Alcohol and other Drugs*, Supplement #14, 164–172.

Petty, R. E., & Cacioppo, J. T. (1986). *Communication and persuasion: Central and peripheral routes to attitude change*. Heidelberg: Springer.

Rogers, C. E. (2003). *Diffusion of innovations* (5th ed.). New York: Simon & Schuster.

Shannon, C. E., & Weaver, W. (1963). *The mathematical theory of communication*. Champaign: University of Illinois Press.

Stellefson, M., Wang, Z., & Klein, W. (2006). Effects of cognitive dissonance on intention to change diet and physical activity among college students. *American Journal of Health Studies*, 21(4), 219–227. Retrieved from https://link.gale.com/apps/doc/A164105497/PPSM?u=viva_vpi&sid=PPSM&xid=071e55a3

Verdú, S. (2000). Fifty years of Shannon theory. In S. Verdú and S. W. McLaughlin (Eds.). *Information theory: 50 Years of discovery* (pp. 13–34). Piscataway, NJ: IEEE Press.

CHAPTER 10

Diffusion of Innovations Theory

Make a better mousetrap, and the world will beat a path to our door.

—Ralph Waldo Emerson

OUTLINE

1. Preview
2. Objectives
3. Introduction
4. Key Concepts
   - **4.1.** Communication Channels
   - **4.2.** Social Systems
   - **4.3.** Time and the S-Shaped Diffusion Curve
   - **4.4.** Innovation-Decision Process
     - **4.4.1.** Stage 1: Knowledge
       - **4.4.1.1.** Awareness Knowledge
       - **4.4.1.2.** Practical Knowledge
       - **4.4.1.3.** Principles Knowledge
     - **4.4.2.** Stage 2: Persuasion
     - **4.4.3.** Stage 3: Decision
     - **4.4.4.** Stage 4: Implementation/Trial
     - **4.4.5.** Stage 5: Confirmation
   - **4.5.** Adopter Categories
   - **4.5.1.** Innovators
   - **4.5.2.** Early Adopters
   - **4.5.3.** Early Majority
   - **4.5.4.** Late Majority
   - **4.5.5.** Laggards
   - **4.5.6.** Adopter Categories in Context
   - **4.6.** Characteristics of the Innovation
     - **4.6.1.** Relative Advantage
     - **4.6.2.** Communicability
     - **4.6.3.** Compatibility
     - **4.6.4.** Impact on Social Relations
     - **4.6.5.** Reversibility
     - **4.6.6.** Risk and Uncertainty Level
     - **4.6.7.** Trialability
     - **4.6.8.** Complexity
     - **4.6.9.** Time and Effort
     - **4.6.10.** Commitment
     - **4.6.11.** Modifiability
     - **4.6.12.** Observability
     - **4.6.13.** Implications of Innovation Characteristics
5. Example: Diffusion of an Innovation at the System Level
   - **5.1.** Innovation Characteristics of Graduated Driver Licensing (GDL)
   - **5.2.** Communication and Relative Advantage
6. Lessons for Public Health Practice
7. Discussion Questions
8. References

PREVIEW

An innovation is a new idea or practice. Diffusion Theory considers the characteristics of innovations, adopters, and processes of adoption over time.

OBJECTIVES

The discerning reader will be able to do the following:

1. Describe three public health innovations that diffused rapidly in the past decade, including one personal-health behavior, one health-related behavior, and one health-protective behavior.
2. Describe and apply the four main elements of Diffusion Theory to a public health innovation.
3. Identify five important characteristics of a public health innovation.
4. Analyze a public health innovation in terms of adoption characteristics.
5. Explain the implications of the "S-shaped" diffusion curve.
6. Describe one typical characteristic of each of the categories of adopters.
7. Explain the importance of opinion leaders in two-stage communication approaches.
8. Describe the role of the change agent, and give examples of change agent activities.

Introduction

An innovation is "... an idea, practice, or object that is perceived as new ..." (Rogers, 2003, p. 12). Diffusion Theory is concerned with how ideas and practices are adopted over time, specifically how innovations spread through a social system through formal and informal **communication channels** and processes. The theory developed out of research looking backward in time at the rate innovations were adopted. Additional research then examined the characteristics of adopters at each stage. Other research examined how the characteristics of innovations affected the

rated of adoptions. It turns out some innovations spread very rapidly, others more slowly. According to the theory, the rate and extent of adoption depends largely on innovation characteristics, communication elements, social system dynamics, and individual decision-making processes. Ultimately, the rate of adoption of most innovations resembles an S-shaped curve, slowly at first, increasing for a period of time, flattening, and then declining. Innovations that have certain and obvious advantages and are easy to understand and try out tend to diffuse rapidly and broadly. Innovators and early adopters are among the first to adopt an innovation, and late adopters and laggards are among the last. Diffusion Theory provides a framework for understanding how innovations diffuse. The principles of Diffusion Theory can be used to promote the adoption of healthful innovations and to understand the adoption of health-damaging innovations, for example, new designer drugs.

Key Concepts

Diffusion Theory has been well described by Rogers (2003). Malcolm Gladwell (2000, 2007, 2008) popularized the concepts of Diffusion Theory in a series of best-selling books describing the dramatic successes and failures of business and social innovations, decision-making processes in the adoption of innovations, and the unique characteristics of innovators. For nearly a century diffusion has been a popular topic of research in sociology and anthropology. A wide range of innovations has been studied, including many health and health-related practices, but much of the early research focused on innovations in agriculture. Early research examined the adoption by Iowa farmers of a new variety of hybrid corn that was more resistant to disease and pests than previous grain, which occurred over a period of 15 years. Nearly all farmers eventually adopted the new variety, but some farmers adopted the new variety soon after it became available, others much later. Ultimately, the cumulative rate of adoption created an S-shaped curve, with about 10% of farmers planting the hybrid corn in the first 5 years, 40% more within another 3 years, and the rest over the next 10 years or so. Earlier adopters were more open to new ideas in general, often willing to take chances, and were well connected with other farmers, while the later adopters tended to be more cautious about risk in general, more committed to conventional ways, and less connected with other farmers.

The phenomenon where some people adopt a new practice early on, others somewhat later, and still others much later, has been observed with respect to numerous innovations. Health innovations that have been adopted according to this pattern at the individual and system level include evidence-based programs (Pashaeypoor, Ashktorab, Rassouli, & Alavi Majd, 2017), health services (Greenhalgh, Robert, Bate, Macfarlane, & Kyriakidou, 2005), bicycle sharing (Therrien et al., 2014), physical activity (Glowacki, Centeio, Van Dongen, Carson, & Castelli, 2016), and safe sex practices (Eke et al., 2019), to mention only a few.

Ultimately, the decision to adopt a new idea, behavior, or program related to health is not much different than a farmer's decision to plant a new variety of corn seed. In each case there is inherent uncertainty involved in adopting something new. People seek to resolve uncertainty by gathering information from multiple sources to determine the relative advantages of the innovation. A particularly important source of information comes from trusted and well-informed others who have already adopted the innovation and have firsthand experience.

The spread of the SARS-CoV-2 virus that caused the COVID-19 pandemic of 2020 and infected millions of U.S. citizens and led to hundreds of thousands of deaths provides examples of the rapid diffusion of health-related innovations, including social distancing and face-mask wearing. Because the

virus is spread through expired air from an infected person (coughing, sneezing, breathing) face masks and social distancing can effectively deter contagion. In countries such as Japan and South Korea, where wearing face masks has long been a common form of hygiene, most people immediately adopted the practice of routinely wearing face masks. In contrast, wearing a face mask for any purpose was uncommon in the United States, and adoption of the practice to prevent the spread of the virus occurred gradually over a period of months following the outbreak of the pandemic. Because there was a shortage of suitable protective face masks, some innovators and early adopters began crafting homemade face masks for themselves and to share with others. Some businesses converted their workshops into factories for face-mask development.

Still, face-mask wearing languished, in part because initial guidelines from the CDC and the federal White House Coronavirus Task Force discouraged face masks as a preventive measure, except in special circumstances, such as when dealing with an infected family member. Eventually, when it became known that people could be infectious for days without obvious symptoms, the CDC guidelines were revised to encourage everyone to wear face masks in public places. Initially, masks were encouraged only to protect healthcare workers and others in direct contact with those infected, but gradually it was understood that the primary purpose of wearing a mask in public was not to protect oneself but to prevent the spread of the virus from those infected, even if not symptomatic, to others. Basically, if the majority, maybe 60% or more, of the population wore a face mask routinely and honored social distancing guidelines of remaining six feet from non–family members in social contexts, the spread of the virus could be dramatically reduced. However, with a lack of national leadership, each state was responsible for establishing protective measures. Sadly,

President Trump and others made face-mask wearing a political issue, arguing that it was a personal decision, rather than a public health responsibility. These logic-contradicting messages from the White House, government agencies, and the media, and strong resistance to face masks by reactionary news sources and groups, resulted in some states and municipalities encouraging social distancing and mask wearing much later and less aggressively than others. Consequently, while face-mask wearing increased substantially nationwide, the rate and period to maximum adoption varied dramatically from one state to the next. Moreover, while many municipalities and states eventually required face masks in public, the proportion of those who adopted the recommended behaviors varied. Some individuals started wearing masks before it was required, others wore them once it was required and they saw most people wearing them, and some refused to wear masks or only would wear a mask when requirements were actually enforced.

Social distancing, a much more complex set of measures than face-mask wearing, reflected similar adoption patterns and characteristics. Thus, the COVID-19 pandemic of 2020 provides a dramatic example of how public health innovations diffuse in populations over time and how adoption was influenced by the characteristics of the innovations, adopter characteristics, and both formal and informal patterns of communication.

Diffusion Theory is concerned with the following key elements of innovation **adoption**: (1) communication channels, (2) the social system, (3) time, (4) the innovation decision process, and (5) characteristics of the innovation.

Communication Channels

Innovations diffuse through a social system via two distinct communication channels. The first channel is formal media—television, radio, Internet, and print media—which serve primarily to convey information or knowledge that the innovation exists and something about its characteristics. Advertising and other media frequently mimic informal communication channels. For example, many advertisements show a knowledgeable adopter extolling the virtues of their new car or other product being marketed. Governments are responsible for formally communicating guidelines, rules, and policies to promote public welfare. Sadly, formal communication about the COVID-19 pandemic was erratic, poorly coordinated, and not always correct, which contributed to the spread of the virus.

Informal, interpersonal communication is the second channel. People tend to talk to each other about things of interest, particularly things that are new to them and things they want to know more about. Those who have tried something new, or in diffusion terms "adopted an innovation," may convey to others their **subjective evaluation**—their opinions about the uses and relative advantages of the innovation. Having experience with the innovation makes an adopter a particularly credible source of information. The attitudes of known adopters regarding the innovation shape the attitudes and intentions of others with respect to the innovation. Those who have not yet adopted the innovation develop their initial impressions about it largely from talking with experienced others. If a friend or family member shares their experience with an innovation that is of interest to you—a new technology, fitness activity, diet, or safety behavior—you will likely pay attention and learn all you can. When something interests you greatly, you will ask those you know about it.

Social influences stem from communication within social networks. This form of social influence was described in somewhat different terms in previous chapters, where it was noted that behavior depends greatly on the perceived descriptive (e.g., prevalence) and subjective norms (e.g., expectations for others regarding the behavior), the observed behavior of close others (modeling), and the expectations of those in our social networks. It has been widely demonstrated that simply knowing someone who has adopted a certain practice increases adoption, including losing weight (Christakis & Fowler, 2007), starting to smoke (Simons-Morton, 2007), and quitting smoking (Christakis & Fowler, 2008). Early in the COVID-19 pandemic there was substantial Internet chatter as people sought to find out who in their social network was practicing social distancing and wearing face masks and the particulars of these behaviors.

Interpersonal communication occurs mainly among acquaintances with similar backgrounds, interests, and norms, a phenomenon described as **homophily**. The opinions of people who are like us in important ways tend to be trusted and valued. However, if everyone talked only with people just like them, few new ideas would emerge. The broader our sources of information, the more informed we are and the earlier we gain information. Those with a broad social network and access to information from many sources tend to be particularly influential information sources because they help spread new ideas.

For public health, the important implication of informal social influences on adoption is the **two-stage communication** approach. One-stage communication involves messages directed at the target population, those who could benefit by adopting the innovation. The second step addresses opinion leaders in the hope they will spread the word about the innovation. While these are somewhat natural processes, they can be adopted programmatically by directing communication both to the target population and to influential people who are likely to share information about the innovation with others, thereby influencing adoption.

Social Systems

We all live within social systems made up of extended families, workplaces, neighborhoods, religious and social groups, and virtual connections. Social systems are characterized by shared beliefs and norms that define the social structures within the community and establish patterns of communication. Social systems provide boundaries for communication structures, influencing which innovations are discussed and what information about them is discussed. Within social systems, both formal and informal communication structures operate. Colleges and universities have well-established policies regarding formal interactions with faculty, for example, required office hours and assigned academic advisors. Some institutions of higher learning assign students and faculty to a "college," often without regard to their academic specialties or lodging. Sometimes meals and other social activities are organized within these cross-discipline structures in the effort to create informal structures for communication. Even without formal structures like this, new students learn from upperclass students how best to navigate the system, take the best courses, and graduate on time. Informal communication structures are especially important in diffusion because they promote exchanges of information about ideas and practices.

The distinction between formal and informal structures is not always distinct. Business, industry, and academia promote both formal and informal structures to support the exchange of information. For example, many academic units encourage formal presentations by faculty and students, as well as outside speakers. As part of these formal structures, informal information is exchanged during the Q&A, at lunch, or during informal discussion. Outside experts tend to be innovators and opinion leaders who travel frequently, are in contact with other experts, and have access to the latest information. Similarly, academic conferences and meetings have many formal presentations and opportunities for informal communication over coffee, drinks, and meals. Sometimes, the informal exchange of information and ideas can be as important as the formal presentation.

Time and the S-Shaped Diffusion Curve

Diffusion occurs over time. Some innovations diffuse rapidly and extensively, while others diffuse more slowly and less extensively. Essentially, adoption is quite slow at first, gains speed over time, and then slows. This general pattern occurs regardless of the extent of adoption, although the entire adoption process can play out in a matter of months or decades. In all cases, cumulative adoption forms an **S-shaped curve**, as shown in **Figure 10.1**.

In the modern age of expansive communication structures, innovations can become widely adopted rather quickly. The Internet, itself, has been adopted quite rapidly, and while it may still be in ascendance, a plot of cumulative adoption would form an S-shaped curve in terms of the number of users and frequency of use. This is the same for face-mask wearing, bike sharing, and all other innovations.

Ultimately, adoption involves decisions on the part of the individuals in the social system as they learn about a particular innovation. In diffusion parlance, this process of deciding about adopting an innovation is called the **innovation-decision process**.

Innovation-Decision Process

Diffusion is a process that reflects individual decisions. As noted, communication channels and social systems largely determine how information is disseminated and understood. However, in the final analysis, individuals make personal decisions about adopting an innovation. The complexity of this decision-making process influences the rate and extent of adoption. Decision making is not necessarily rational or linear, where the more people learn about an innovation, the greater the adoption. Sometimes people remain committed to their current ideas or practices and are reluctant to change. Nevertheless, when people find out about something of interest to them, a new smart phone app, for example, they may quickly decide to adopt it or think about it for a long while as they gather information. Regardless of how long it takes, adopters typically experience certain innovation-decision stages. The length of time it takes eventual adopters to proceed through the stages of adoption determines the rate of diffusion. The innovation-decision process includes specific stages that involve the active or passive collection and evaluation of information about the innovation. As people learn more about the innovation,

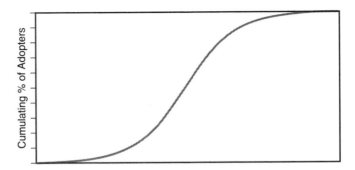

Figure 10.1 S-shaped diffusion curve. Adoption of innovations tends to begin slowly and gradually increases in rate until most have been adopted

Rogers, E. M. (2003). *Diffusion of innovations* (5th ed.). New York, NY: Free Press.

they gain confidence in their decision making. Rogers described the process as one of collecting information about the innovation to reduce uncertainty before making a commitment.

The innovation-decision process described in Diffusion Theory is similar to stages of change models that were initially developed by the Transtheoretical Model to describe addiction recovery (Prochaska, DiClemente, & Norcross, 1992) or HIV prevention (Weinstein, 1988). The five stages of the innovation-decision process are included in **Table 10.1** and described in the following paragraphs.

Stage 1: Knowledge

One must know about the existence and characteristics of an innovation before it can be adopted. Three types of **knowledge** are particularly important in adoption: **awareness knowledge**, practical knowledge, and principles knowledge.

Awareness Knowledge Awareness of the existence of the innovation is a requirement for an affirmative adoption decision. Awareness occurs mainly when we come into contact with others who know about the innovation. Therefore, those with a broader social network are more likely to find out about certain innovations. Awareness knowledge can also come about through media and education. Providing information to people in public health programs is seen as necessary and fundamental to fostering the broad adoption of healthful innovations. However, people may be unlikely to pay much attention to messages promoting an innovation unless they first perceive a need for the innovation. Knowledge awareness would include finding out that wearing a face mask can protect against infection from coronavirus.

Practical Knowledge After becoming aware of an innovation, practical knowledge about the personal utility of the innovation and how it can be employed becomes important in the decision process. Practical knowledge is similar to Bandura's concepts of essential knowledge and behavioral capability. Theoretically, the more people know about how the innovation works, how they would apply the innovation, and the skills required, the more prepared they are to decide about adopting it. Practical knowledge, including the required skills, increases self-efficacy and the likelihood of adoption. For example, practical knowledge about safe sex practices, leading to increased self-efficacy and adoption, would include the ability to negotiate safe

Table 10.1 Five Stages of the Innovation-Decision Process

Stage	Description
Knowledge	• Awareness of the existence of the innovation • Practical knowledge about how the innovation works or how to use it • Knowledge of the underlying principles of the innovation
Persuasion	Strong and positive attitudes toward the innovation
Decision	Accepting or rejecting the innovation
Implementation	Initial adoption or trial of an innovation
Confirmation	Commitment to use innovation or discontinue the use of the innovation

Rogers, E. M. (2003). *Diffusion of Innovations* (5th ed.). New York, NY: Free Press.

sex practices with partners (Winter, 2013). Awareness about face masks was followed by great interest in how to create or obtain a face mask and how and when to wear one.

Principles Knowledge Knowledge about the principles that underlie the innovation, **principles knowledge**, can influence the adoption process and may be particularly important at the confirmation or maintenance stage. For example, safe sex practices are more likely to be adopted by those who understand the underlying principles and not just how to employ them (Eke et al., 2019). Use of face masks was supported by research about how the coronavirus behaved when expelled and the extent to which even simple cloth masks could prevent the spread of infection.

Stage 2: Persuasion

Attitudes and related cognitions are important at the persuasion stage, when the potential adopter is evaluating the innovation. The term *persuasion* refers here to becoming persuaded through personal evaluation of the innovation. As people learn about the innovation, they develop subjective feelings about its relevance, importance, usefulness, and acceptability. The formation of positive beliefs about the relative advantages, attitudes toward the innovation, social norms, and expected outcomes can increase the likelihood of adoption (Eke et al., 2019). With respect to face masks, over a matter of weeks and months attitudes became more favorable as the behavior became more widely adopted.

Stage 3: Decision

This is the stage where people decide to accept or reject the innovation. Deciding is similar to what in other theories is called contemplating or intending, preliminary to actually adopting the innovation. Deciding increases the likelihood of adoption, but environmental factors can discourage or delay actual adoption. Theoretically, adoption is more likely if the innovation can be sampled or tried without

requiring a major commitment. As information about how to obtain, make, and use face masks increased, more people wore them.

Stage 4: Implementation/Trial

This stage refers to the initial adoption or trial of an innovation. Implementation does not always result in continuation or maintenance, but it is a level of commitment consistent with action. Implementation provides practical experience, from which adopters learn firsthand about the relative advantages of the innovation and its personal applications. Not surprisingly, at this stage adopters frequently **reinvent** and adapt the innovation for their own unique purposes. The primary purpose of an innovation may not be the one some adopters find appealing. During the COVID-19 pandemic, innovators came up with many designs and materials for face masks, and this information rapidly spread via social media, leading to rapid marketing. T-shirts, socks, rubber bands, coffee filters, and other household products were quickly repurposed to make protective face masks.

Stage 5: Confirmation

The experience gained from adopting a behavior provides feedback about the innovation, its uses, and consequences. Actual trial provides information about the innovation that informs the decision to confirm and commit to it. People who have a good experience with the innovation are likely to confirm their decision or commit to it. The routine use of face masks increased when state and local governments required their use in public locations, people were obligated to wear them, and they become normative.

Adopter Categories

Looking backward in time after an innovation has been widely adopted, it is possible to classify adopters according to when they adopted (Bhattacharya & Singh, 2019). Shown in **Figure 10.2** is a normal curve with adopter categories and expected percentages of adopters

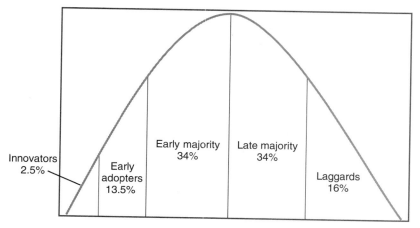

Figure 10.2 Adopter categories

Data from: Rogers, E. M. (2003). *Diffusion of innovations* (5th ed.). New York, NY: Free Press.

included. Based on research on the pattern of adoption of many different innovations, it turns out that of all eventual adopters, whether many or few, they are characterized by the categories and proportions shown Figure 10.2.

The characteristics of adoption groups are fairly consistent across innovations. Some people adopt early, some to adopt late, and some not at all. Those who adopt early are of particular interest because they influence adoption by others (Gladwell, 2008). In public health we are often most concerned about those who delay or fail to adopt healthful innovations. We can only know for sure who fits into each adopter category sometime after the introduction of an innovation when there is enough data to plot an adoption curve. An understanding of typical characteristics of each adopter category can inform program development, although detailed assessment of actual characteristics is even more useful. The five adopter categories are described in **Table 10.2** and in the following paragraphs.

Innovators

Innovators have a proclivity for experimentation and can be daring and bold when it comes to trying something new. Typically, innovators make up a relatively small proportion

(approximately 2.5%) of those who ultimately adopt any particular innovation. Innovators actively seek new ideas, practices, and technologies, which they consider, try out, and adopt or discard. This is an important group because they actively seek new information, are open to innovation, and experiment, thereby providing an initial baseline about the characteristics, uses, and advantages of the innovation. However, innovators tend not to hold central positions within communication structures, and they generally are not role models and not particularly interested in sharing what they have learned. Innovators do the early testing of the innovation, providing information about its characteristics that others can pick up on.

Early Adopters

Early adopters tend to have access to a variety of media and have a broad social network, presumably including many innovators, which allows them to find out before most others about innovations and their relative advantages. Many early adopters hold central positions within their communication structures. They tend to be generally well respected and even admired by others in the social system and are seen by others in the

Table 10.2 Descriptions of Adopter Categories

Adopter Category	Description
Innovators	Tend to have a proclivity for experimentation
Early adopters	Tend to have access to a variety of media and a wide and varied social network
Early majority	A normative population that is not that innovative but adopts after more innovative others have already adopted
Late majority	People who ultimately appreciate the advantages of the innovation and are finally able to gather the resources needed to adopt it
Laggards	Extremely traditional with a limited social network, narrow access to information, and limited resources of time and money

Rogers, E. M. (2003). *Diffusion of innovations* (5th ed.). New York, NY: Free Press.

social system as ahead of the crowd but not radical. Therefore, many early adopters are opinion leaders whose opinions and behavior can "ignite" a diffusion effect that can rapidly spread through the social system with a high degree of efficiency. Early adopters typically represent about 13.5% of a social system.

Early adopters are particularly important to the diffusion process because they tend to be opinion leaders whose opinions and behavior influence the opinions and behavior of others. Typically, opinion leaders are "located" within the center of their respective social networks, tend to be have elevated social status, and have frequent contact with others and a broad social network (Gladwell, 2008). Their generally high education level enables them to develop informed opinions about the innovation, and their relatively high economic status allows them to be among the first to try an innovation. Although not the first to adopt, opinion leaders tend to be among the first to comprehend the advantages of an innovation, explore their uses, and promote those they like.

Early Majority

Members of the early majority (about 34% of ultimate adopters) are not the first to learn about an innovation, but they are ahead of most eventual adopters because they are quick to recognize innovations with obvious advantages and appreciate those that are trending. Early adopters largely determine the extent of diffusion by their communication of their experience with the innovation to others. Early adopters may not be particularly innovative, but they are not resistant to change, able to appreciate new ideas, and sensitive to the influence of early adopters. The experience that the early majority has with the innovation influences what others will learn about the innovation. Given the sheer number of people this represents, we consider the idea to be mainstream once the innovation is adopted by the early majority.

Late Majority

The late majority (typically composing about 34% of eventual adopters) includes people who finally develop an appreciation for the possible advantages of the innovation and are finally able to gather and commit the resources needed to adopt it. The late majority tends to have relatively modest access to information sources and is typically reluctant to accept change. Their initial uncertainty may be overcome only at the point that the innovation is established well enough that it is relatively common, they have heard about it frequently, and they know others who have successfully and satisfactorily adopted the innovation. To overcome uncertainly, they need time to process information and vicariously experience the positive benefits of the innovation by observing those who have adopted.

Laggards

Finally, about 16% of eventual adopters are labeled laggards. Laggards tend to be extremely traditional, have a limited social network and narrow access to information, and have limited resources of time and money. Laggards may have few ties to the key opinion leaders of a social system and tend to resist change.

Adopter Categories in Context

These categories are not meant to be labels, simply general descriptions. There may be many reasons that one person adopts an innovation early and another later, including personal resources and opportunities. Some innovations are expensive and time consuming. Some innovations require substantial expertise. Some innovations are culturally neutral, while others meet substantial cultural resistance. For example, with the advent of electronic health records, patient portals have become a common part of medical practice. Patient portals are repositories for patient records and also provide a medium for appointment scheduling and communication between patients and providers. A recent study found that use of patient portals was greater among younger, higher-income patients (Emani et al., 2018). This finding is consistent with other literature on the digital divide in adoption that indicates those who are more confident with electronic and computer services and have ready access to them use them more often than others (Yamin et al., 2011).

Characteristics of the Innovation

Innovations diffuse through populations at variable rates largely as a consequence of the characteristics of the innovation. Innovations perceived to have favorable characteristics will be more quickly and broadly adopted, while innovations with less favorable characteristics, for example, more complex or expensive and notable downsides, will be adopted more slowly and by fewer people. Innovations that can be quickly understood, with characteristics that are easy to explain, have diffusion advantages. However, there are many examples of innovations with favorable characteristics that languished for many decades before finally being adopted. For example, the safety benefits of seat belts were known for decades before they became routinely available as standard equipment in vehicles. Similarly, logical policies are often ignored while counterproductive ones are retained, for example, current drug interdiction and penalties mainly increase the cost of drugs and bolster criminal activity, but appear not to reduce use, while harm reduction approaches that decriminalize and regulate drug use have not been widely adopted, despite their relative advantages.

Remember that an innovation can be an idea, practice/behavior, program, product/object, technology, or policy, and it must only be new to a particular population of potential adopters. Only a few decades ago, seat belts and bicycle helmets, now common safety devices, were novel innovations. Today, bike share programs have increasingly been promoted and adopted in the United States and Europe (Therrien et al., 2014). Suntan lotion was introduced as a product to assist tanning but is now used to protect skin from damaging ultraviolet rays.

Uncertainty is a barrier to adoption. Some people can accept a greater amount of uncertainty than others, but uncertainty undermines confidence and commitment. The innovation-decision process is largely devoted to collecting information about the characteristics of the innovation to reduce uncertainty and inform decision making. This is why a gym will offer a 30-day free membership and mattress outlets allow shoppers to try out a new bed for 60 days. **Table 10.3** provides a listing of 12 characteristics of innovations. The table is divided into three sections. Seven characteristics best apply to the decisions that people make before they adopt the product or practice, three apply to the actual process of adoption, and two apply mainly to the continuation or maintenance of adoption. Generally, most of the variance in rate and extent of diffusion rates can be explained by five main characteristics of innovations.

Relative Advantage

Successful innovations are those that have **relative advantages** over the alternatives. In addition to possible advantages, some innovations have disadvantages such as cost, time, and effort. Some innovations require giving up a current practice that competes with the innovation. The relative advantages of safety belts and air bags are now well established due to extensive research, but their initial adoption was delayed because their safety benefits had not been demonstrated. At some point a tipping point occurred when these safety devices were fully embraced by the safety community, policy makers, manufacturers, and the public. During the COVID-19 pandemic, the advantages of face masks became so well recognized that not wearing a mask in certain contexts (such as grocery stores) became unacceptable in many communities.

The concept of relative advantage is related to the social cognitive theory concept of outcome expectations and the Health Belief

Table 10.3   Twelve Key Characteristics of a Successful Innovation

Characteristic	Description
Relative advantage	Innovations with advantages over current practice are more likely to be considered.
Communicability	Easily understood innovations are more likely to be considered.
Compatibility	Innovations that are compatible with current practice are more likely to be adopted.
Impact on social relations	The less the impact on social relations, the greater the likelihood of adoption.
Reversibility	Reversible innovations are more likely to be adopted.
Risk and uncertainty level	The lower the risk and uncertainty, the greater the likelihood of adoption.
Trialability	Being able to try the innovation increases adoption.
Complexity	Less complex innovations are more readily adopted.
Time and effort	The less time and effort, the greater likelihood of adoption.
Commitment	Minimal commitment increases continued use.
Modifiability	Modifiable innovations are more likely to be maintained.
Observability	Seeing the effect of the innovation increases continuation.

Rogers, E. M. (2003). *Diffusion of innovations* (5th ed.). New York, NY: Free Press.

Model concept of net expected utility. While the perception that the innovation has relative advantages over the alternative may be sufficient for trial or implementation, it is often necessary for confirmation. Wearing a face mask became common during the COVID-19 pandemic because there was little competition, and the advantages were obvious. Other than social distancing, about the only way to prevent unwitting spread of the virus was to wear a mask.

Communicability

Innovations than can be simply, clearly, and easily described are more likely to be considered for adoption. The "6-foot" rule of social distancing was an effective way of describing how far apart people should be to avoid contracting the coronavirus.

Compatibility

This characteristic applies to sociocultural beliefs and values, current practices, and needs of potential adopters. In short, innovations that are consistent with a person's current attitudes and behavior and do not depart too radically from past ideas or innovations of a similar nature are more likely to be adopted. Perhaps most important, the innovation must be perceived by the potential adopter as meeting a critical need and being consistent with values and current practice. It is much easier to add a new program or application to a PC than to change to a Mac, or vice versa. The popularity of sunscreening lotion can be attributed in part to its **compatibility** with the practice of using suntanning lotion. Safety belts were viewed for many years by auto industry executives as inconsistent with the image of carefree transportation. During the COVID-19 pandemic, face-mask wearing was adopted widely and immediately in countries where they had commonly been used, but adopted only gradually and not by everyone in the United States, where they were not compatible with common practices.

Impact on Social Relations

Innovations that do not affect others upon adoption are more likely to be considered. Innovations that involve others, particularly that affect others' behavior and their perceptions of the adopter, are less likely to be considered. Social distancing greatly impacted social relations, and during the COVID-19 pandemic it was a persistent issue for families and friends negotiating relationships.

Reversibility

Reversible innovations are more readily adopted. Face masks, for example, could be obtained easily and worn when logical, making their use "reversible" or at least not irreversible.

Risk and Uncertainty Level

Greater risk and uncertainty discourage adoption. During the COVID-19 pandemic as restaurants reopened, people needed to consider the increased risk of infection from indoor association with other patrons.

Trialability

Innovations that can be tried without expensive and time-consuming commitment may diffuse more rapidly than those that involve an "all or nothing" decision. Innovations that can be tried at low cost and are reversible, for example, are more likely to be adopted than innovations that require expense and long-term commitment. People do not want to make a substantial commitment to an innovation only to find out that it does not work well for them. It is a lot easier to take up running, which only requires a pair of sneakers, then skiing, which generally requires a lot of equipment and travel. Being able to try an innovation without making a substantial commitment can resolve this uncertainty. Some protective behaviors, however, cannot be tried and then discontinued—they require either a "yes" or "no" decision, for example, getting a vaccine or purchasing an exercise bike or treadmill.

Complexity

Complex innovations, those that require extensive knowledge and skill, tend to be adopted at slower rates and by fewer people than innovations that are less complex. Complexity thwarts adoption because it increases uncertainty, which can only be resolved through substantial intellectual commitment. For example, adopting a new exercise routine is a surprisingly complicated thing, given the time, equipment, facilities, range of possible exercises, and skill required. Infant car seats and toddler booster seats are examples of innovations that diffused slowly because they were perceived to be expensive, complicated to install, and a bother all around. The relative widespread adoption of face masks could be attributed to how simple they are to acquire and try.

Time and Effort

Time and effort matter with respect to adoption. Those innovations that require a lot of either are less likely to be adopted than those that require little. The time and effort required to get vaccinated against COVID-19 may have discouraged some potential adopters.

Commitment

The greater the commitment, the lower the likelihood of adoption and continued use. Social distancing during the COVID-19 pandemic was a huge commitment that was negatively associated with compliance.

Modifiability

Innovations that can be modified to be consistent with current practice or otherwise consistent with adopters' lifestyles and cognitions, or otherwise personalized, are more likely to be maintained.

Observability

Innovations that are observable are more likely to be adopted than those that cannot be observed. Observing the experience of others can greatly reduce uncertainty. Direct observation provides vicarious experience. The experience of others in words, pictures, or graphics can also be useful. The observability of face-mask wearing facilitated its rapid adoption during the COVID-19 pandemic.

Implications of Innovation Characteristics

Innovations are easily promoted when they have obvious relative advantage, are readily observable, can be tried without commitment, are not exceedingly complex, and are compatible with current practices. Emani et al. (2018) found that relative advantage, complexity/ease of use, and trialability were the best predictors of the use of a patient portal. Of course, the relative advantages of an innovation are not always obvious and may require education or persuasion, while more complex innovations require training. Therefore, it is sometimes the task of the public health professional to figure out how to clearly communicate to potential adopters the characteristics of the innovation.

Example: Diffusion of an Innovation at the System Level

Diffusion Theory provides insight into how useful innovations are adopted and how to facilitate their adoption programmatically. Here we discuss in diffusion terms the rapid adoption of a highly effective safety policy innovation, graduated driver licensing (GDL). GDL developed out of a concern about the high crash rates among teenaged drivers (Williams, 2017). Crash risk among novice teenagers is uniquely high when first licensed and remains elevated until the mid-20s owing to the combination of young age, inexperience, and risk taking (Simons-Morton, 2019).

Most novices learn to manage a vehicle with only a few hours of practice, but developing the judgment required to drive safely in traffic requires years of experience (remember how long it took to learn algebra, play a musical instrument, ride a bike, yoyo, or play golf?). Therefore, experts have long recommended minimizing driving under higher-risk driving conditions for a time to allow novices to gain experience and develop safe driving skills. The policy innovation of GDL was the solution to this dilemma (Simons-Morton, 2019).

Over the past two decades GDL policies have been adopted by all U.S. states and by many other countries (Williams, 2017). Of course, some states adopted early, while others much later, reflective of how systems are similar to individuals in adopter characteristics. GDL policies manage exposure to risk, reducing driving by novices under the highest-risk driving conditions. GDL includes the following three stages: (1) a prolonged supervised practice driving period; (2) provisional licensing with restrictions on high-risk driving conditions such as late night and teen passengers; and (3) unrestricted licensing usually at age 18. The prolonged practice period during the first stage delays licensure, reduces the amount of driving, increases practice, and allows months of maturation before licensure (Williams, 2017). Provisional licensure, stage 2, allows teens to drive without supervision, except under certain high-risk conditions such as late at night and with multiple teen passengers. Allowing novices to drive, but not under the highest-risk conditions, GDL policies represent a compromise between safety and mobility.

Innovation Characteristics of Graduated Driver Licensing (GDL)

GDL is a policy innovation adopted over time by complex systems. How did this policy become so widely adopted in such a short period of time? Licensing policy is established by state legislatures. Typically, the state motor vehicle administration, with input from transportation professionals and interest groups, provides recommendations about licensing policies to elected representatives. There is uncertainty and political differences that must be resolved for any policy to be adopted. GDL is a marvelous example of an innovation with nearly ideal characteristics of relative advantage, compatibility, adaptability, and observability that reduced uncertainty in the decision-to-adopt process that played out in each state. The relative advantages of GDL compared with the traditional two-stage licensing policy are now well established, but initially it was just a simple idea for transforming existing policy to help resolve an important safety concern (Williams, 2017). Fortunately, GDL is highly compatible with existing licensing policy, and its simplicity and flexibility have allowed each state to adapt it to meet local requirements and for incremental changes over time, resulting in improvements over time as the policy has been amended and revised. Each state has tended to adopt a slightly unique version, while retaining the key elements.

Communication and Relative Advantage

Presenting the innovation as "graduated licensing" made it consistent with existing licensing policies, and its flexibility allowed states to adopt specific and unique versions of the policy, reducing uncertainty in decision making by policy makers. GDL was modifiable to be consistent with each state's unique considerations. The positive experience of the early adopting states provided observable experience, and as more states adopted the policy and it became normative, a great deal of practical knowledge emerged. Critical and highly publicized research demonstrated effectiveness in reducing statewide crash and fatality rates, with the strictest policies resulting in the best outcomes, and high parent satisfaction with GDL (Williams, 2017). Government, academic groups, and private safety organizations actively promoted GDL, increasing its acceptability to policy makers, who could point to the evidence of effectiveness, while also adapting the policy to the needs of their state, for example, by allow specific exceptions, such as driving to work and carrying teen siblings.

In summary, GDL is an example of a policy with characteristics that enabled its rapid diffusion. The flexibility of the policy allowed each state to reinvent the policy and adopt a state-specific form. Adopter uncertainty was reduced by research demonstrating its effectiveness and substantial parental acceptance. Thus, the safety community and advocacy groups had evidence they could present about the relative advantages of GDL. Gradually a consensus emerged about the benefits of GDL as a policy solution to the problem of young driver motor vehicle crashes.

Lessons for Public Health Practice

Above all, Diffusion Theory is about the role of information and how it is communicated and received. It is a theory about the role of information in the adoption of innovations. Diffusion Theory is based mainly on retrospective research on the adoption of innovations. Less research has examined the application of elements of Diffusion Theory to promoting or discouraging adoption. Some public health goals are to increase the rate and extent of adoption of healthful innovations such as physical activity, safe sex, social distancing, and face masks and discourage health-damaging innovations such as opioids and other harmful drugs. Public health programs can employ principles of Diffusion Theory in a variety of ways.

1. **Innovations.** Almost any change in a behavior, program, or policy can be considered an innovation. Thinking in diffusion terms suggests interesting considerations about how to craft messages that describe the characteristics of health innovations, adopters, and the adoption process in ways that would increase adoption. Indeed, a good way to think about

developing program goals and measuring outcomes is the extent to which adoption of a health innovation increases due to programmatic effort. For example, a goal relating to the face masks might be "increase to 80% of adults making appropriate use of face masks in public spaces." In addition, Diffusion Theory suggests the importance of describing innovations in terms that best describe their relative advantages.

2. **Adoption Process.** Adoption occurs in stages, basically progressing from acquiring knowledge about the innovation, to considering its relative advantages, deciding to try/implement it, and then confirming, maintaining, or discontinuing adoption. Of course, people can get hung up at any stage and not progress at all or not progress very rapidly or uniformly through the stages. Public health programs can tailor messages to different decision stages, awareness information for those who don't know about the innovation, affective appeals to those at the persuasion stage, how-to information for those considering, and information about underlying principles for those at the confirming stage. The more that is known about the stage of adoption, the better able planners are to provide information appropriate to the innovation-decision process. Thus, needs assessments are essential to determine stages and what information would be most appropriate for those at each stage.

3. **Adopter Categories.** Some adopters learn about an innovation earlier than others, evaluate the potential advantages, try it, and incorporate it into their lives. Innovators and early adopters are good at seeking useful information and adopting healthful innovations, late adopters often are of concern because the longer they delay, the greater harm to their health. To attract people to healthful innovations, we need to learn as much about them as possible so that we can design appropriate interventions for specific population

groups, target groups. Early adopters are easy to work with because they have wide communication channels, actively seek out information, are receptive to change, and are good at creating personal environments that support their behavior. The strategy here is to provide useful information, including detailed "how-to" and "how the innovation works" information. Late adopters tend to need more intensive sorts of intervention, just to introduce them to the idea and provoke consideration. Laggards tend to be so busy with the stresses in their lives that it makes change difficult, and sometimes their culture and social network are not supportive of change. Generally, most change occurs in the early and late majorities, and the goal with these groups is to reduce the amount of time before the innovation is adopted or in some cases to improve adoption **fidelity**. Surveys and other needs assessment tools can be useful for categorizing or segmenting target populations and the program components can be specifically designed for adopter categories. Information about adopter characteristics allows programs to target particular populations with particular messages.

4. **Innovation Characteristics.** Some innovations are adopted more quickly and more extensively than others. In public health we are concerned about increasing the rate and extent of adoption of healthful innovations. A major task is to present or frame the characteristics of these innovations in ways that reduce the uncertainty of potential adopters because uncertainty prevents the formation of positive attitudes toward the innovation. For example, during the COVID-19 pandemic, messages that indicated the expired virus could generally travel no more than 6 feet framed and clarified this aspect of social distancing, while messages that simple masks could prevent the spread of infection, even if they did not prevent getting infected, increased use. Thus, in addition to framing healthful innovation in

terms of tangible personal characteristics, programs can emphasize social norms and social benefits of the innovation.

5. **Two-Stage Communication and Opinion Leaders.** Consistent with two-stage communication approaches, Diffusion Theory emphasizes the importance of the position of potential adopters within a social system and their access to information through various communication channels. Accordingly, people learn about innovations directly via media and also from other people. Therefore, determining the information sources for a population group of interest can facilitate communication development and delivery. This is where Diffusion Theory and network analyses intersect. It may be important to determine where the target population gets their information and which information sources are most credible to them. In this manner, health-promotion programs can be crafted to provide information that is accessible and useful.

   Of particular importance are opinion leaders, who tend to have somewhat more extensive social contacts than others in the social system and are well respected within their social system. The attitudes and behavior of opinion leaders greatly influence the attitudes and behavior of others in the social system. Opinion leaders are sometimes targeted by intervention because they may be particularly open to innovation or as a way of getting to later adopters. During the COVID-19 pandemic opinion leaders were instrumental in promoting face masks and social distancing.

6. **Change Agents.** Unlike most theories with origins in psychology, the origins of Diffusion Theory are sociology and anthropology. Hence, some of the terms and concepts it employs are somewhat unique. Notably, Diffusion Theory uses the term **change agent** to describe a person who seeks to promote change within a population. A change agent could be a government official; a social worker;

a neighborhood activist; a healthcare professional, health educator, or other public health professional; or an influential nonprofessional. For example, church leaders have been recruited as change agents for cardiovascular disease prevention (Glick et al., 2016). The concept of change agent is a very good one for health promotion because it nicely captures the sense of promoting change, using Diffusion Theory concepts and methods. Change agents, regardless of their training, provide information to alter how an innovation is portrayed by media, demonstrate the advantages of an innovation, make the innovation available and provide opportunities for people to try it out, recruit opinion leaders, and alter environmental conditions so that they are more supportive of the innovation.

Discussion Questions

1. What is an innovation? What are some examples of health-related innovations?
2. What factors influence the rate and extent of adoption of an innovation? Take the example of wearing a mask to prevent the spread of the SARS coronavirus or taking aspirin to prevent heart disease.
3. How do adopter characteristics vary, for example, early versus late adopters?

References

Bhattacharya, S., & Singh, A. (2019). Using the concepts of positive deviance, diffusion of innovation and normal curve for planning family and community level health interventions. *Journal of Family Medicine and Primary Care*, 8, 336–341, DOI: 10.4103/jfmpc.jfmpc_392_18

Christakis, N. A., & Fowler, J. H. (2007). The spread of obesity in a large social network over 32 years. *New England Journal of Medicine*, 357, 370–379.

Christakis, N. A., & Fowler, J. H. (2008). The collective dynamics of smoking in a large social network. *New England Journal of Medicine*, 358, 2249–2258.

Eke, A. N., Johnson, W. D., O'Leary, A., Rebchook, G. M., Huebner, D. M., Peterson, J. L., & Kegeles, S. M. (2019). Effect of a community-level HIV prevention intervention on psychosocial determinants of HIV risk behaviors among young Black men who have sex with men (YBMSM). *AIDS and Behavior*, 23, 2361–2374. DOI:10.1007/s10461-019-02499-4

Emani, S., Peters, E., Desai, S., Karson, A. S., Lipsitz, S. R., LaRocca, R., Stone, J., Suric, V., Wald, J. S., Wheeler, A., Williams, D. H., & Bates, D. W. (2018). Perceptions of adopters versus non-adopters of a patient portal: An application of diffusion of innovation theory. *Journal of Innovation in Health Informatics*, 25(3), 149–157. DOI: 10.14236/jhi.v25i3.991

Gladwell, M. (2000). *The tipping point: How little things can make a big difference*. New York: Little, Brown.

Gladwell, M. (2007). *Blink: The power of thinking without thinking*. New York: Little, Brown.

Gladwell, M. (2008). *Outliers: The story of success*. New York: Little, Brown.

Glick, D. C., Sharif, M. Z., Tucker, K. L., Prelip, M. L., Ammerman, A. S., Keyserling, T. C., Torres, S. E., & Pitts, S. J. (2016). Community-engagement to support cardiovascular disease prevention in disparities populations: Three case studies. *Journal of Health Disparities Research & Practice*, 9(1), 92–108. http://digitalscholarship.unlv.edu/jhdrp/

Glowacki, E. M., Centeio, E. E., Van Dongen, D. J., Carson, R. L., & Castelli, D. M. (2016). Health promotion efforts as predictors of physical activity in schools: An application of the diffusion of innovations model. *Journal of School Health*, 86, 399–406.

Greenhalgh, T., Robert, G., Bate, P., Macfarlane, F., & Kyriakidou, O. (2005). *Diffusion of innovations in health service organizations: A systematic literature review*. Malden, MA: Blackwell.

Pashaeypoor, S., Ashktorab, T., Rassouli, M., & Alavi Majd, H. (2017). Experiences of nursing students of evidence-based practice education according to Rogers' diffusion of innovation model: A directed content analysis. *Journal of Advances in Medical Education & Professionalism*, 5(4), 203–208. PMCID: PMC5611430

Prochaska, J. O., DiClemente, C. C., & Norcross, J. C. (1992). In search of how people change: Applications to the addictive behaviors. *American Psychologist*, *47*, 1102–1114.

Rogers, E. M. (2003). *Diffusion of innovations* (5th ed.). New York: Free Press.

Simons-Morton, B. G. (2007). Social influences on adolescent substance use. *American Journal of Health Behavior*, *31*(6), 672–684. DOI: 10.5993/AJHB.31.6.13

Simons-Morton, B. G. (2019). *Keeping young drivers safe during early licensure*. RAC Foundation. Retrieved from https://www.racfoundation.org/wp-content/uploads/Keeping_Young_Drivers_Safe_During_Early_Licensure_Dr_Bruce_Simons-Morton_September_2019.pdf

Therrien, S., Brauer, M., Fuller, D., Gauvin, L., Teschke, K., & Winters, M. (2014). Identifying the leaders: Applying diffusion of innovation theory to use of a public bikeshare system in Vancouver, Canada. *Transportation Research Record*, *2468*, 74–83. DOI: 10.3141/2468-09

Weinstein, N. D. (1988). The precaution adoption process. *Health Psychology*, *7*, 355–386.

Williams, A. F. (2017). Graduated driver licensing (GDL) in the United States in 2016: A literature review and commentary. *Journal of Safety Research*, *63*, 29–41. DOI: 10.1016/j.jsr.2017.08.010

Winter, V. R. (2013). Diffusion of innovations theory: A unifying framework for HIV peer education. *American Journal of Sexuality Education*, *8*, 228–245. DOI: 10.1080/15546128.2013.838512

Yamin, C. K., Emani, S., Williams, D. H., Lipsitz, S. R., Karson, A. S., Wald, J. S., & Bates, D. W. (2011). The digital divide in the adoption and use of a personal health record. *Archives of Internal Medicine*, *171*(6), 568–574. DOI: 10.1001/archinternmed.2011.34

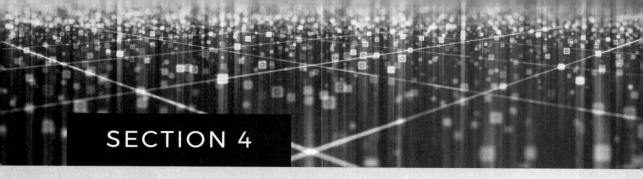

Nothing So Practical as Theory

Section 4 includes a chapter on applying theory to practice. In case you were wondering how to select among the many theories for intervention and programming, we provide a section on selecting theory. The last chapter in the book explains why there are so many theories.

| **CHAPTER 11** | Applications of Theory to Public Health Practice....211 |
| **CHAPTER 12** | Why So Many Theories?.............................225 |

Applications of Theory to Public Health Practice

OUTLINE

1. Preview
2. Objectives
3. Introduction
4. Theory in Practice
   4.1. Program Planning Phases and Steps
   4.2. Example: Theory-Based Planning to Reduce College Drinking Problems
      4.2.1. Multilevel Planning
         4.2.1.1. Intrapersonal Level
         4.2.1.2. Interpersonal Level
         4.2.1.3. Institutional, Community, Policy Levels
      4.2.2. Program Development
         4.2.2.1. Needs Assessment
         4.2.2.2. Components
         4.2.2.3. Evaluation
      4.2.3. Theory Utility
5. Choosing a Theory
   5.1. Theory Selection Principles
   5.2. Common Errors in Selecting Theory
6. Lessons for Public Health Practice
7. Discussion Questions
8. References

PREVIEW

Now that you have a good understanding of behavior theory, having read previous chapters, how can you use this knowledge to plan health-promotion programs? In this chapter we explain how theory can be integrated in the program-planning process and illustrate this process using the example of college drinking problem prevention.

OBJECTIVES

The discerning reader of this chapter will be able to:

1. Explain the relationship between theory and research.
2. Describe the phases and steps of program planning.
3. Identify the role of theory at each planning phase.
4. Identify the planning steps where theory is most useful.
5. Identify the Social Cognitive Theory (SCT) variables of interest for needs assessment.
6. Identify the SCT intervention methods of possible use in program development.
7. Identify at least one theory other than SCT, and apply it to the three planning phases.
8. Identify ways to select theory for use in planning a health-promotion program.

Introduction

Theory can help public health professionals understand behavior, identify potential determinants, select intervention strategies and methods, and evaluate program effectiveness.

Theory contributes to systematic health-promotion program planning. In this chapter we deal with two questions. First, how can theory be integrated into program planning? Second, what is the process for selecting theory for particular problems and programs?

Theory in Practice

Planning is essential for effective program development. Several useful and commonly employed health-promotion planning frameworks are available. Of these, PRECEDE-PROCEED (Green & Kreuter, 2016) is perhaps the most influential. It encourages education and epidemiological problem assessment at multiple levels, leading to potential intervention approaches at behavioral and environmental levels. MATCH (Simons-Morton, McLeroy, & Wendel, 2011) is a planning framework that details the steps involved in multilevel intervention development. A key distinction is the identification of targets of intervention (TOI) at each level of analysis. The TOI is usually the same as the target population at the intrapersonal level, but at the interpersonal and institutional/community/policy levels the TOIs are those with influence over environmental objectives. Intervention mapping (Bartholomew Eldredge et al., 2016) provides brief descriptions of theory and potential intervention approaches within the framework of three general program planning phases. In each of these planning frameworks, the role of theory is discussed in relation to societal level and planning phase. In this chapter we adopt a simple, three-phase planning framework to elaborate the process for integrating theory into program planning.

Program Planning Phases and Steps

The three major program planning phases, each with several steps, are shown in **Table 11.1**. The steps of Phase 1, needs assessment, include (1) conceptualize the problem, (2) define the

outcomes (goals) at multiple levels, (3) identify potential determinants (behavioral and environmental), and (4) determine delivery options, including possible intervention settings, contexts, sources, and channels. Phase 2, program development, includes steps to (1) create goals, (2) create objectives at multiple levels, and (3) develop program components. In multilevel programs, this would be done separately for each level-specific component (think of the social ecological perspective from Chapter 2). Phase 3, evaluation, includes steps for (1) assessing exposure, (2) measuring changes in goals and determinants, (3) interpreting results, and (4) providing feedback for program revision and theory validity.

Each planning phase can be informed by both theory and research. To illustrate the role of theory and research in planning, we apply the planning phases and steps to the example of program development to prevent college drinking problems. College drinking is a useful example because it is an important and timely public health concern that has been well researched and to which theory has been applied to programs addressing various aspects of the problem.

Example: Theory-Based Planning to Reduce College Drinking Problems

Theory informs the conceptualization and definition of the problem. Theory guides research, and research findings provide information about the utility and applicability of theory. Well-researched topics provide a wealth of information about the topic that contributes to a conceptual understanding of causes and solutions. Most theory-based research has been conducted at the intrapersonal and interpersonal levels, which lend themselves to experimental evaluation. However, there is also literature and conceptualization of the problem at the institutional, community,

Table 11.1 Program Planning Phases and Steps

Phase	Steps
1: Needs assessment	Step 1. Conceptualize the problem from multiple levels. Step 2. Define goals/outcomes at each societal level. Step 3. Identify potential determinants, target of intervention at each level, and cognitions. Step 4. Determine program delivery options: settings, contexts, sources, levels, and channels.
2: Program development	Step 1. Create goals. Step 2. Create objectives at multiple levels. Step 3. Identify intervention methods. Step 4. Develop program components.
3: Evaluate program	Step 1. Measure program exposure. Step 2. Measure changes in outcomes and determinants. Step 3. Interpret the results. Step 4. Feed results into program revisions and theory utility.

and policy levels, where theory tends to give way to more general **conceptual models** and frameworks for understanding the relationships among and between variables. For simple illustrative purposes, in the following example of the role of theory in program planning to prevent college drinking problems, we emphasize a single theory, Social Cognitive Theory, because it is highly relevant, it operates at multiple levels, and key variables have been well studied. Of course, other cognitive and social theories have similar relevance and could be employed in such an exercise.

Multilevel Planning

There is vast literature on drinking prevalence, problems, and determinants concerning college drinking. This literature, both theoretic and empirical, makes it clear that alcohol is best understood from a multilevel perspective. While the following summary of findings is much too brief to do justice to this complicated problem, some very strong conclusions can be drawn even from this selective review.

Alcohol is a central nervous system depressant that reduces inhibition almost immediately upon ingestion, leading to altered mood and increased confidence, but at the cost of impaired judgment and self-control. The mild mood-altering effects of social drinking, as when having a few drinks with friends, has made alcohol a popular and prevalent drug in most of the world. However, the effects of alcohol are dose dependent, with predictable impairment in cognitive and motor function with increasing blood alcohol concentrations. Episodic drinking to excess is associated with many negative outcomes, including impaired driving, violence, and social problems. The more common and societally acceptable behavior of moderate social drinking facilitates social interaction and reduces the likelihood of excessive use. Of course, the potential for moderation or abuse depends on a combination of cultural and social restraints and individual cognitions related to drinking.

Typical of nearly all behaviors, culture establishes the acceptability of particular drinking practices, while individuals must learn from experience how to manage their personal drinking behavior. Given the dangers associated with impairment, alcohol is a regulated drug, illegal to possess in most states before age 21. Restrictions on sales, public use, and legal consequences are designed to limit underage and dangerous drinking behaviors. However, most young people are exposed to drinking during adolescence when it is an illegal and risky behavior. College students encounter an environment where alcohol is readily available with limited restrictions and tolerance for underage and excessive drinking. At whatever age one starts to drink there is a steep learning curve. Drinking is a surprisingly complicated drug with both pharmacologic and social effects on behavior. Young drinkers who fail to develop the skills required for safe social drinking are likely to experience alcohol-related problems.

Drinking prevalence, generally measured as one or more drinks in the past 30 days, increases dramatically with age, from less than 20% in the 10th grade to nearly 40% in the 12th grade and over 53% the year after high school (Schulenberg et al., 2020; Simons-Morton et al., 2016). Curiously, drinking prevalence is higher among adolescents who go to college than those who do not (Schulenberg et al., 2020; Simons-Morton et al., 2016). In college, the majority of students report monthly drinking, and over 40% report recent binge drinking (Simons-Morton et al., 2016). College students experience many drinking-related problems. In one national survey, over 20% of college student drinkers reported a recent blackout, which is associated with greatly increased risk of DWI, injury, blackouts, and school, work, legal, and social relation problems (Hingson, Zha, Simons-Morton, & White, 2016). The contributions of theory and theory-informed research contribute to the conclusion that the prevalence and nature of college drinking problems are best understood from a multilevel perspective (Hingson, 2010).

Intrapersonal Level From an Operant Conditioning and Social Cognitive Theory perspective (SCT) (Bandura, 1986), the immediate effects of drinking are reinforcing for many imbibers, leading to repeated events, even when they do not always result in positive outcomes.

A wide range of cognitions, examined within the context of a range of values expectancy and social cognitive theories, are associated with drinking problems among college students (Wrye & Pruitt, 2017). From the SCT perspective, drinking is viewed as the product of personal characteristics (some emerging adults are more susceptible, expectant, and less behaviorally capable than others), the behavior (some emerging adults learn from the positive and negative consequences of their drinking experiences and adjust their expectations, while others maintain extreme drinking expectations and behavior), and the environment (environmental cues and conditions are associated with drinking). SCT emphasizes the self-regulatory processes of behavioral capability, reinforcement, modeling, expectations, and self-efficacy. Of the many cognitive variables that have been studied, the relationship between exaggerated and unrealistic drinking expectancies and drinking problems is very strong (Lac & Luk, 2019). Curiously, as important as alcohol and drinking are to the college experience, at least for many students, behavioral capabilities (knowledge and skills) with respect to alcohol and drinking appear to be quite deficient among many college students (Miller, Merrill, Singh, DiBello, & Carey, 2018). Many youthful drinkers do not know how many drinks would make them legally drunk, how to moderate their drinking, how to resist social pressures to drink, how to evaluate social norms regarding drinking, and how to deal with their friends who drink to excess. Erroneous social norms and expectancies are common. Theoretically, increased behavioral capability regarding alcohol and drinking would increase self-efficacy and other self-regulation capabilities needed to manage drinking and prevent alcohol-related problems.

Interpersonal Level Social cognitive and other theories suggest that social influences are powerful predictors of behaviors. While the influence of parents wanes once emerging adults head off to college, the influence of peers and close friends increases. Not surprisingly, there is a very strong literature on peer influences and drinking (Simons-Morton, Haynie, Bible, & Liu, 2018). Indeed, friends' drinking is probably the single best predictor of emerging adult drinking. Those who report no close friends who drink are several times less likely to drink or to drink to excess than emerging adults with at least one friend who drinks (Simons-Morton et al., 2018).

The general peer culture, or at least perceptions of it, also seems to be important. For example, college students who belong to a fraternity or sorority, which tend to have strong drinking cultures, report more drinking than other students (DeSimone, 2009; Tyler, Schmitz, Ray, Adams, & Simons, 2018). Social influences of this sort, of course, could be the result of selection, where emerging adults join fraternities (or other social groups) in part because the members favor drinking, or socialization, where members tend to drink because it is normative in that group, or both selection and socialization (Simons-Morton et al., 2018).

There is considerably less empirical literature on the protective behaviors of peers, which are known to occur (Buckley, Sheehan, & Chapman, 2009), but in unknown quantity and quality. It is clear that adolescents and emerging adults with few friends who drink or get drunk, relative to those with many such friends, are much less likely to drink or get drunk (Simons-Morton et al., 2016). Protective peer behaviors might include encouraging friends and acquaintances to engage in alternative, socially acceptable activities and persuading them not to drink to excess, drive after drinking, spend time with heavy-drinking mates, attend alcohol-centric events, drink rather than study, or engage in dangerous or obnoxious alcohol-related behavior.

Clearly, peers have great potential to contribute to the prevention of alcohol-related problems and would seem to be important targets for intervention at the intrapersonal level. SCT indicates that increasing peer prevention actions would indicate that they develop important knowledge and skills that would increase confidence and self-efficacy for successfully engaging in protective social behaviors.

Institutional, Community, Policy Levels

The culture, policies, and practices at the institutional and community level are important influences on drinking behavior among adolescents and emerging adults (Fairman, Haynie, Goldstein, Simons-Morton, & Gilman, 2019; Fairman, Simons-Morton, et al., 2019). The drinking cultures of some colleges and college communities are more alcoholcentric with less thoughtful alcohol policies and practices than others. However, increasingly colleges and universities seek to limit the emphasis on alcohol at school events and in the college community (Keller, 2014). The high prevalence of college drinking and drinking problems may, to some extent, be the inevitable product of bringing many emerging adults together with upper-grade students 21 and older who provide ready access to alcohol. However, it suggests that many colleges and universities have not done a good job of creating healthful environments that allow social drinking as appropriate and legal, but strongly discourage excessive drinking and attendant problems. By establishing clear policies and programs, with substantial education and training for students and administrators, colleges and universities could moderate student drinking and reduce the prevalence of drinking problems.

While research has identified many individual-level determinants of college student drinking problems, there is little or no research on the key cognitive variables related to college administrator actions with respect to college drinking problems. As noted, some colleges are more proactive than others, with relatively sophisticated harm reduction programs to prevent such problems. Hypothetically, from an SCT perspective, we might seek to measure among relevant college administrators' behavioral capability (knowledge and skills regarding the problem, its causes, and potential solutions), expectations with respect to the potential for adopting and implementing prevention programs, attitudes regarding preventive actions, likelihood of positive reinforcement for taking action, and confidence (self-efficacy) in effectively altering the campus drinking culture. Examples of successful programs could serve as vicarious efficacy models.

From the point of view of reciprocal determinism (i.e., triadic influences of environment, person, and behavior), it is understood that colleges reside within local communities and have many stakeholders, including alumni, parents, students, community businesspersons, and law enforcement, not to mention students, all of whom can be part of the problem or part of the solution. Theoretical and empirical community policies and practices matter with respect to problem drinking (Fairman, Haynie, et al., 2019; Fairman, Simons-Morton, et al., 2019). Therefore, successful prevention might require a number of actions in addition to college/university programs. Because alcohol is a regulated drug, specific policies and practices contribute to the overall culture related to drinking. Policies and practices related to alcohol availability, consumption, and management include sales restrictions, bartender and "bouncer" training, ID for purchase requirements, intervention with unruly patrons, limits on tailgating and similar events, enforcement, alcohol-free events, and so on. Possibly, successful prevention would require the serious activation of local task forces consisting of representatives of the many stakeholders that would seek to create a safe drinking culture that would reduce alcohol-related problems. By changing the environment, including enforcing policies and creating a culture shift that alters the social norms surrounding alcohol, it is likely that individuals' cognitions will change and the problem drinking behavior reduced. SCT would suggest the utility of promoting model programs that could be adapted to local needs. Model programs increase expectations for success and provide examples of program activities and methods.

A comprehensive approach to the problem would suggest many possible settings and contexts for intervention, including on-campus and off-campus housing, Greek life, and the local community. A variety of communication channels might be employed, and the source of messages might include local officials, trusted administrators, campus personalities, and opinion leaders, all under the same programmatic umbrella.

Program Development

Based on the preceding limited review, some tentative considerations about program development to prevent college drinking problems are listed in **Table 11.2** and discussed in the following pages.

Needs Assessment As shown in Table 11.2 for Phase 1, the SCT-based needs assessment would provide information leading to a conceptualization of college drinking as a multilevel concern. Because college drinking is largely normative and for the most part not problematic, the goals/outcomes of the program would be to reduce alcohol-related problems, including drunkenness; academic, social, and legal problems blackouts and DWI. At the intrapersonal level the goal would be to transform the social culture related to drinking to one that prioritizes and ensures safety and security. At the institutional and community levels, the goal would be to create a culture on campus and in the community that proactively discourages alcohol-related problems.

SCT-related determinants assessed at the intrapersonal level would include college student drinking-related behavioral capabilities, normative reeducation (drinking to excess is not socially acceptable behavior), expectations for drinking and for peer behavior, and self-efficacy for managing pressures to drink irresponsibly. At the interpersonal level the focus would be on college students' normative reeducation, behavioral capabilities, and self-efficacy for enacting protective behaviors

Table 11.2 Program Planning to Reduce College Drinking Problems Informed by Social Cognitive Theory

Phase	Steps
Phase 1. Assess prevalence and determinants.	Step 1. Conceptualize as a multilevel problem involving the environment, person, and behavior at the intrapersonal, interpersonal, and institutional/community levels.
	Step 2. Define multilevel outcomes. Intrapersonal: Alcohol-related problems of students (drunk, social, academic, legal problems). Social: Friend and peer attitudes and behaviors. Institutional: College and community drinking culture, policies, programs, resources, and commitment.
	Step 3. Identify targets of the intervention and potential determinants. Intrapersonal: TOI = college students; Cognitions = knowledge and skills, perceptions, and expectations. Social: TOI = college students; Cognitions = knowledge, skills, and behaviors regarding dealing proactively with friends' drinking and bystander training. Institutional: TOI = decision makers and leaders of college, students, and community; Cognitions = attitudes toward and commitment to prevention, priorities, plans, and policies to prevent alcohol-related problems.
	Step 4. Program delivery. Settings, contexts, channels: Multiple campus and community settings, events, and locations. Saturate communication channels with messages about responsible drinking. Sources: Deliver messages under a single program umbrella, with recognizable symbols, slogans, and messages coming from local officials, trusted administrators, campus personalities, and opinion leaders.
Phase 2. Develop program.	Step 1. Program goals. Reduce prevalence of alcohol-related problems, dangerous drinking.
	Step 2. Objectives. Interpersonal/individual level. Drinking-related behavioral capability outcome expectations, self-efficacy, and social norms. Intrapersonal level. Alter perceived social norms, and develop behavioral capability and expectations for preventing peer drinking problem behavior. Institutional/community/policy level. Create safe drinking culture by adopting comprehensive programs, education, providing alternatives, enforcement, etc.

(continues)

Table 11.2 Program Planning to Reduce College Drinking Problems Informed by Social Cognitive Theory   *(continued)*

Phase	Steps
	Step 3. Create program components. Intrapersonal/interpersonal levels: • Training at orientation for new students. • Educational messages at student housing, etc. • Required training for students who engage in alcohol-related problem behavior. • Training for student leaders of clubs, teams, residences, etc. Institutional/community/policy level: • Adopt a wide range recommended prevention activities. • Form and participate in community-wide prevention task force.
Phase 3. Evaluate outcomes.	Step 1. Measure program exposure. Maintain and evaluate records of the number of program activities, participants, and evaluations of these activities.
	Step 2. Measure changes in outcomes and determinants. • Survey students periodically during the year. • Assess administrator attitudes. • Measure campus and community prevention activities annually.
	Step 3. Interpret the results in terms of how well the program achieved the outcomes, including changes in cognitions, behavior, and environmental change.
	Step 4. Feed results into program revisions and theory utility; identify needed changes in program resource needs and allocation at each level: targeted outcomes, cognitions, and environmental changes.

to discourage peers from problem drinking behavior. At the institutional/community/policy level, the focus would be on university and community stakeholders dedicated to creating a local culture and environment that would reduce the emphasis on drinking and prevent alcohol-related problems with comprehensive education, policies, and programs.

Components Assuming the overall program goal of reducing alcohol-related problems among students, the objectives at the individual level would be to improve behavioral capability, improve self-efficacy, and alter drinking expectancies among students.

At the intrapersonal level the objective would be to foster behavioral capability for preventing peer drinking–related problems. At the institutional level the objective would be to establish a comprehensive prevention program.

Potential program components would include methods and strategies for each component. Social Cognitive Theory would guide the selection of methods and strategies, including modeling, reinforcement, persuasion, and reflection, where appropriate, with the goal of increasing the individuals' behavioral capability and self-efficacy and changing the expectations about drinking. These methods would be incorporated into the various program components. At the intrapersonal level the components might include training for new students regarding responsible drinking, messages on responsible drinking delivered at student housing and various campus locations, and remedial skills training for students who engage in alcohol-related problem behavior. At the interpersonal level, program components might include orientation for new and continuing students, peer-mentoring, training for student leaders, and normative education. At the institutional/community/policy level a task force would bring in experts to engage them in the process for adopting and implementing recommended activities and coordinating across task force members.

Evaluation Evaluation follows naturally from the measures collected during the earlier needs assessment phases and steps. Program exposure would be measured by evaluating the records of program activities, including the number of events, number of participants, and evaluations of their utility. The overall outcome, alcohol-related problem prevalence, would be assessed through student surveys and campus and community records of alcohol-related problems. Measuring the effects of program activities on the objectives at each level would be accomplished by surveys of students, administrations, and community representatives. The results would be summarized in a report and interpreted in terms of changes in drinking prevalence, particularly the number of drinking-related problems. The interpretation would seek to determine the extent to which activities worked, why or why not, and how they could be improved. This information would be used as feedback for program refinement and further development and theory validity. The findings should provide useful information about program effects for use in revising and improving the program. Similarly, the results would be evaluated to determine the utility of SCT in general and in particular the methods and activities for

the problem and for each component. Was the SCT conceptualization useful? Were the SCT variables related to the problem? Were the SCT methods effective and manageable within the program structure? The interpretation of theory utility would provide useful information for programs to be developed elsewhere.

Theory Utility

As noted, a range of theories could be and have been applied to college drinking program development. For this chapter we selected Social Cognitive Theory as an exercise to illustrate how theory could guide program development. Of course, other theories could have provided similarly useful examples. Also, different theories could have been employed for different program components or social levels. For example, at the interpersonal level we emphasize SCT variables, but social influence and social norms theories could have been employed, as is common for social norming programs. However, SCT variables have been well studied and effective when applied to alcohol-prevention programs.

Program development is much more complicated and elaborate than described here. We identified possible program components but did not dig into the details of how to create such programs, including operationalizing the key variables and crafting theory-based learning and skill development activities. We did not discuss how to implement programs, which is more practical than theoretical, but quite arduous and difficult.

Hopefully, the example makes clear that theory is useful at each phase of program development, guiding conceptualization, identifying measures, crafting components, and interpreting results. We used SCT as an example of how theory could be employed in program development because the theory is familiar to us, well studied, and logically relevant at multiple societal levels. However, many factors could be considered when evaluating which theory to employ for a particular program. The remainder of the chapter deals with that question.

Choosing a Theory

One of the goals for this book is to introduce public health professionals to a range of theories for use in program planning. As we have discussed each specific theory, we have sought to provide useful examples of how the theory has been and could be applied. Any of a number of theories could be applied to a specific health behavior or health problem. Indeed, most theories have many possible applications; however, no one theory can be employed for all problems. Learning how to choose a theory requires working knowledge and familiarity with behavioral theories.

The status of research on behavioral theory that would make it more useful for program planning has been criticized. In particular, the seeming proliferation of theories, overlapping variables, inconsistent terminology, and lack of studies comparing theories have been emphasized (Noar & Zimmerman, 2005). Clearly, there is a need for research on these aspects of behavior. It can be bewildering to come across the same variable, for example, self-efficacy, in multiple theories (Social Cognitive Theory, Self-Determination Theory, Health Belief Model). It is also disconcerting that basically identical constructs are labeled and measured differently by different theories. In part this is because many constructs are complicated. Social norms, for example, include actual prevalence and perceived prevalence and expectations. Perhaps, there is a need to convene an expert consensus panel to standardize terminology.

There have been efforts to address the theory proliferation issue. Several expert panels have been convened in an effort to meld the best of most prominent intra- and interpersonal theories into a single, all-encompassing theory, or at least a short list of important variables (Fishbein, 2000; Institute of Medicine [IOM], 2002). Basically, the disappointing result of this exercise was a list of key variables, intent, self-efficacy, and norms. These, of course, are among the most well-studied variables, so they are good candidates for a short list. The report, however, limited the exercise to already motivated populations with prerequisite knowledge and skills. Sadly, these conditions are rare and largely ignore the environmental conditions (beyond social norms) that substantially influence behavior. Rather than already motivated and skilled target populations, we mostly find reticent target populations with incorrect knowledge and lack of skills, as well as low self-efficacy and inaccurate perceptions of social norms. We agree that social norms and self-efficacy are important, but also quite complex. Intent is a reasonable measure of motivation, but intent reflects a lot of other important beliefs and attitudes that need to be measured and intervened upon to increase intent and change behavior (Fishbein et al., 2001). Moreover, intent goes largely unacted upon when environmental conditions are unsupportive. Outside the context of fully elaborated theory, it is difficult to determine what to measure, how to intervene, and how to interpret results. Simplifying theory by integrating key variables seems logical but may not fully hold together. Not surprisingly, this integrated theory approach has seldom been employed in practice, and there are no empirical validations.

While there is a need for additional research comparing theories and evaluating constructs, it seems most important that public health professionals understand and appreciate that theory, like practice, is dynamic, naturally resulting in elaborations and specifications. While this makes selecting a theory more difficult, it also provides more options. While more research on the salience of specific theories is needed, the best place for public health professionals to start is by studying the theories presented in this book.

Clearly, selecting a theory involves the consideration of numerous factors, and the more experience you have with the health and behavior of concern, the theories that have been used to explain the concern, and the evaluation of the effectiveness of theory-based programs, the better prepared you will be to select and employ theory. At this point it may be helpful to review some of the key principles involved in selecting and applying theory to particular problems.

Theory Selection Principles

1. **Understanding the problem.** Before considering theory, consider the problem. Learn all you can about it from as many different sources as possible (e.g., literature, experts, experienced practitioners, key informants, members of the at-risk populations). The better you understand the nature, variability, complexities, and practices related to the problem, the better equipped you will be to create an effective prevention program. Seek to understand the problem in terms of how it is conceptualized and defined. Determine what kind of problem it is (chronic or contagious; personal or environmental, etc.). Who is at risk (age, sex, location, characteristics, etc.)? Are there different stages or characteristics of the problem (preventive, healthcare seeking, treatment, rehabilitation; immediately dangerous or risk factor, etc.)? What societal levels are involved, and who are the appropriate targets of intervention at each level? What are the individual and environmental determinants (these will become the target of the intervention)? What individual and environmental determinants need to change to improve the health condition? Which of these are most important? Which is most changeable? When looking at those determinants, you can match the constructs from theory to the theoretical problem. The theory that matches well with the determinants is a good place to start.

2. **Identify theories previously employed.** While reading the literature, identify theories that have been used to define the problem and develop prevention programs in the past. Theories that may have been used for the same problem with effective intervention results can help validate theory selection. It's important to note that different theories may have been used for different aspects or stages of the problem. Taking the example of college drinking, certain theories, for example, Social Cognitive Theory, may be best for multilevel conceptualization of the problem, Communication Theory may be useful for developing primary prevention messages, Social Norms Theory may be most useful for creating prevention activities to prevent problem drinking, and counseling theories, like Motivational Interviewing or operant conditioning, might best be employed to develop programs for repeat offenders and addicted drinkers. Often, elements of different theories are combined to create a program, as in the Transtheoretical Model.

3. **Theories employed for similar problems.** In cases where a problem has not been well studied, theories applied to similar problems may be relevant. Notably, many theories started out to address particular problems (i.e., Diffusion Theory was developed to explain the adoption of social innovations, the Transtheoretical Model for smoking cessation, the Health Belief Model to explain compliance with a medical regimen). For example, the Transtheoretical Model, originally developed to explain and study smoking cessation, has proven applicable to a range of behaviors and might be useful for a problem like college drinking to the extent smoking cessation and problem drinking are similar addictive behaviors.

4. **Consider societal level.** Some theories are best applied at a particular level or a few levels. For example, social influence theories operate at an individual level in relation to perceived social norms, while actual norms operate at the interpersonal

level. Different theories are best suited to different levels of intervention (individual, group, community).

5. **Consider logical other theories.** Certainly, "try out" theories with which you are most familiar. Does the theory logically explain the problem? Consider the theories described in this book. Possibly, think "outside the box" by considering theories applied to remotely different problems, for example, economic theory scarcity to heroin addiction.

6. **Pilot-test theory.** There are a number of simple and practical ways to pilot-test ideas about theory.

   a. Beyond logic, explore how the constructs of a theory explain the problem or its prevention. For example, expectations and self-efficacy are cognitive constructs emphasized by social cognitive theory. For a particular problem, perhaps college drinking problems, how do these constructs apply? If they do not apply, the chosen theory might not be the right theory moving forward because they do not explain the problem. When measured, are the responses logical and informative?

   b. Expert testimony. Ask experts in theory and/or in problem to suggest appropriate theory and to discuss theory relevance for proposed program development.

   c. Logic testing. Form a group of interested and knowledgeable professionals to discuss how selected theory or theories could be applied to the problem.

   d. Develop theory-relevant questions and interview individuals or hold group discussions with members of the at-risk population and potential influences such as peers, family, administrators, practitioners, and policy makers.

7. **Test theory validity.** When all is said and done and the program has been developed, implemented, and evaluated, enlist health-promotion academics to help you evaluate the data and examine the validity of theory, as applied, for this problem and for specific components.

Common Errors in Selecting Theory

1. **One theory.** The same theory does not apply to every problem. Like a kid with a stick or a man with a hammer, a public health professional who knows only one theory is likely to apply it to every problem regardless of fit.

2. **Problem definition.** Theory can best be considered when the problem is well defined. Is the problem largely personal-health behavior, health-protective behavior, or health-related behavior? What specific behaviors are most important? What is most changeable? What is the social context? What other environmental considerations are important? Are different theories relevant for different parts of the problem?

3. **Early adoption.** Theories are best chosen when important and changeable determinants have been identified. As Sherlock Holmes said, "Never theorize before you have data. Invariably, you end up twisting facts to suit theories instead of theories to suit fact."

4. **Societal level.** Health and health behavior generally have influences at multiple societal levels. Considering only one level may not be adequate for effective multi-level planning. One or several theories may be relevant at each level.

5. **Inappropriate target of the intervention.** There are different potential intervention targets at each level, with variable determinants of behavior. While many theories are relevant to the behavior of every intervention target, unique theoretical considerations are necessary depending on determinants and societal level.

6. **Lack of imagination.** Applying theory can be a creative process. A certain amount of imagination is required to figure out how to apply theory to a problem. In general, does the theory make sense of the problem? Are there particular constructs that may be applicable? Has the theory been applied usefully to a similar problem? How could the theory contribute to an understanding of behavior? For example, the core of every behavior theory is reinforcement (operant conditioning), drive, and/or cognitive dissonance. Specific theories elaborate on these core influences on behavior. Sometimes it can be useful to focus first on the big picture (what drives, cognitions, and environmental factors are related to the behavior) before seeking a more specific theory.
7. **Lure of novel theories.** It is tempting to select a novel theory for a particular problem. This can suggest creative solutions but should not be considered seriously before a thorough review of existing literature on the problem and the theory.
8. **Failure of application versus failure of theory.** While evaluating the literature, seek to determine the extent to which null findings are due to a lack of sufficient exposure or poor application of methods and to what extent the research represents a failure of theory.

Lessons for Public Health Practice

1. Theory is a practical tool for health-promotion program planning.
2. Theory and research are interactive. Good research is stimulated by theory that is based on theoretical tenets and provides results that inform the utility and validity of theory for that problem and context.
3. Theory informs problem conceptualization and definition (goals).
4. Theory suggests multilevel considerations.
5. Theory provides variables for needs assessments.
6. Theory suggests potential intervention activities and methods.
7. Theory guides evaluation of results for feedback for program revision and theory considerations.
8. Not every theory is useful for every problem, but most problems can be understood from a variety of theoretical perspectives.
9. The better one understands theory, the more able one is to apply it usefully to program development.
10. While theory gives way to conceptual modeling at higher social levels, changing behavior at every level is informed by behavioral theory.

Discussion Questions

1. How does theory inform research?
2. How does theory inform needs assessments?
3. How does theory inform program component development?
4. What are some ways to go about selecting theory?

References

Bandura, A. J. (1986). *Social foundations of thought and action*. Englewood Cliffs, NJ: Prentice Hall.
Bartholomew Eldredge, L. K., Markham, C. M., Ruiter, R. A. C., Kok, G., Parcel, G. S., & Fernandez, M. E. (2016). *Planning health promotion programs: An intervention mapping approach* (4th ed.). San Francisco, CA: Jossey-Bass.
Buckley, L., Sheehan, M., & Chapman, R. (2009). Adolescent protective behavior to reduce drug and alcohol use, alcohol-related harm and interpersonal violence. *Journal of Drug Education*, 39(3), 289–301.
DeSimone, J. (2009). Fraternity membership and drinking behavior. *Economic Inquiry*, 47(2), 337–350.

Fairman, B., Haynie D., Goldstein, R., Simons-Morton, B. G., & Gilman, S. (2019). Neighborhood context and binge drinking from adolescence into early adulthood in a US national cohort. *International Journal of Epidemiology, 49*(1), 103–112. PMID: 31263877

Fairman, B. J., Simons-Morton, B., Haynie, D. L., Liu, D., Goldstein, R. B., & Gilman, S. E. (2019). State alcohol policies, taxes, and availability as predictors of adolescent binge drinking trajectories into early adulthood. *Addiction, 114*(7), 1173–1182. PMID: 30830991. DOI: 10.1111/add.14600

Fishbein, M. (2000). The role of theory in HIV prevention. *AIDS Care, 12*, 273–278.

Fishbein, M., Triandis, H. C., Kanfer, F. H., Becker, M., Middlestadt, S. E., & Eichler, A. (2001). Factors influencing behavior and behavior change. In A. Baum, T. A. Revenson, & J. E. Singer (Eds.), *Handbook of health psychology* (pp. 3–17). Mahwah, NJ: Erlbaum.

Green, L.W., & Kreuter, M. (2016). *Health program planning: An educational and ecological approach* (4th ed.). New York: McGraw-Hill.

Hingson, R.W. (2010). Magnitude and prevention of college drinking and related problems. *Alcohol Research and Health, 33*(1–2), 45–54.

Hingson, R., Zha, W., Simons-Morton, B. G., & White, A. (2016). Alcohol-induced blackouts as predictors of other drinking related harms among emerging young adults. *Alcoholism, Clinical and Experimental Research, 40*(4), 776–784. PMID: 27012148. PMCID: PMC4820355

Institute of Medicine. (2002). *Speaking of health: Assessing health communication strategies for diverse populations.* Washington, DC: National Academies Press.

Keller, A. (2014). New college students and risky alcohol behaviors. National Social Norms Center. Retrieved from https://socialnorms.org/new-college-students-and-risky-alcohol-behaviors/

Lac, A., & Luk, J. W. (2019). Pathways from positive, negative, and specific alcohol expectancies to weekday and weekend drinking to alcohol problems. *Prevention Science, 20*, 800–809. DOI: 10.1007/s11121-019-0986-x

Miller, M. B., Merrill, J. E., Singh, S., DiBello, A. M., & Carey, K. B. (2018). College student knowledge of blackouts and implications for alcohol intervention: A qualitative analysis. *Psychology of Addictive Behaviors, 32*(8), 933–943.

Noar, S. M., & Zimmerman, R. S., (2005). Health Behavior Theory and cumulative knowledge regarding health behaviors: are we moving in the right direction? *Health Education & Research. 20*(3), 275–290. DOI: 10.1093/her/cyg113. PMID: 15632099.

Schulenberg, J. E., Johnston, L. D., O'Malley, P. M., Bachman, J. G., Miech, R. A., & Patrick, M. E. (2020). *Monitoring the future national survey results on drug use, 1975–2019: Volume II, College students and adults ages 19–60.* Ann Arbor: Institute for Social Research, The University of Michigan. Retrieved from http://monitoringthefuture.org/pubs.html#monographs

Simons-Morton, B., Haynie, D., Bible, J., & Liu, D. (2018). Prospective associations of actual and perceived descriptive norms with drinking among emerging adults. *Substance Use & Misuse, 53*(11) :1771–71781. PMID: 29400594. PMCID: PMC6146965

Simons-Morton, B. G., Haynie, D., Liu, D., Chaurasia, A., Li, K., & Hingson, R. (2016). The effect of residence, school status, work status, and social influence on the prevalence of alcohol use among emerging adults. *Journal of Studies of Alcohol and Drugs, 77*(1), 121–132. PMID: 26751362. PMCID: PMC4711312

Simons-Morton, B. G., McLeroy, K. R., & Wendel, M. L. (2011). *Behavior Theory in Health Promotion Practice and Research.* Burlington, MA: Jones & Bartlett.

Tyler, K. A., Schmitz, R. M., Ray, C. M,. Adams, S. A., & Simons, L. G. (2018). The role of protective behavioral strategies, social environment, and housing type on heavy drinking among college students. *Substance Use & Misuse, 53*(5), 724–733. DOI: 10.1080/10826084.2017.1363235. PMID: 28952844.

Wrye, B. A. E., & Pruitt, C. L. (2017). Perceptions of binge drinking as problematic among college students. *Journal of Alcohol and Drug Education, 61*(1), 7–90.

CHAPTER 12

Why So Many Theories?

OUTLINE

1. Preview
2. Objectives
3. Introduction
4. Behavior Theory and Public Health
    4.1. Personal-Health Behavior
    4.2. Health-Protective Behavior
    4.3. Health-Related Behavior
    4.4. Program Planning
        4.4.1. Conceptualization
        4.4.2. Needs Assessment
        4.4.3. Program Development
        4.4.4. Evaluation
    4.5. Multilevel Thinking
5. Many Useful Theories
    5.1. External Influences on Motivation and Behavior
    5.2. Internal Influences on Motivation and Behavior
        5.2.1. Personality
        5.2.2. Cognitions
        5.2.3. Behavior
6. The Value of Each Theory
    6.1. Grand Theories of Behavior
    6.2. Somewhat Grand Theories of Behavior
    6.3. Possible Integration of Cognitions Across Theories
7. Theory as a Way of Thinking
8. Lessons for Public Health Practice
9. Discussion Questions
10. References

PREVIEW

While there are many theories, each has particular features and applications. Therefore, theory-proficiency is essential to public health practice.

OBJECTIVES

The discerning reader will be able to discuss with confidence the major themes discussed in the book, including:

1. How behavior theory relates to public health practice.
2. What multilevel means.
3. Why there are so many theories.
4. Theory as a way of thinking.

Introduction

Having read the book chapters, viewed the PowerPoint presentations, completed the assignments, and taken the tests, it may be timely to review some of the book's core concepts. Now that the central ideas are familiar to the reader, this chapter emphasizes the essential role of behavioral science theory to public health practice and to the everyday life of public health professionals.

Behavior Theory and Public Health

Public health is about preventing health problems from occurring or getting worse on a population level. Because prevention is complicated, there are numerous public health subspecialties, including environmental health, population dynamics, infectious or chronic disease, health services, epidemiology, biostatistics, and health behavior/health promotion/health education. Behavior theory may seem mostly relevant only to this last group, but once in the field, many public health professionals assume important practice responsibilities relating to health behavior. In part this is because behavior is important in most, if not all, public health problems. In part this is because public health is generally underfunded, requiring the too few public health professionals to manage a wide range of responsibilities. Despite its well-recognized importance, public health must compete with other priorities for public funding. Policy makers within institutions, communities, and government agencies must determine how much of limited tax dollars to spend on water pollution, vaccinations, and substance abuse prevention, relative to roadways, schools, police, and infrastructure. Therefore, even where public health is a well-recognized and appreciated public responsibility, state and local entities tend to hire too few public health professionals for the necessary work. You might have trained as an epidemiologist, a health services specialist, or a substance abuse counselor, but when there is a public health crisis you will need to focus on disaster relief or preventing the spread of a contagious disease like COVID-19. Also, on a daily basis, even within the niche of your selected subspecialty, you will constantly compete for resources and are likely to have responsibility for developing, managing, or conducting programs in which health behavior is a critical element. These are some of the reasons public health training requires basic competence in behavioral science, of which behavior theory is a major element.

Many health behaviors are so closely related to health outcomes that they become the primary focus of the program, for example, safe sex to prevent HIV, responsible drinking to prevent impaired driving, and mask wearing and social distancing to prevent COVID-19. Because many health behaviors occur well in advance of the health outcomes with which they are related, they serve as proximal prevention targets. For example, lifelong physical activity and healthful diet behaviors can increase or decrease the likelihood of obesity, diabetes, and heart disease. Because behaviors are both observable and measurable, they provide objective program outcomes. Hence, health behavior is not only the primary focus of health-promotion and health education specialists, but also an essential focus of other public health professionals.

In short, prevention involves behavior. Examples of personal health behaviors include getting a flu shot, complying with medical recommendations, wearing a face mask in public, not smoking in restricted areas, and driving responsibly. Of course, public health is also about the environment, air and water pollution/purity, safe transportation, restaurant sanitation, safe harbors for abused family members, and so on. But even considering primarily environmental issues, public health success requires appropriate personal behavior such as not polluting, driving safely, seeking health care, complying with health regimens, moderating substance use, using contraception responsibly, discouraging health-damaging behavior, and supporting public health. In addition, public health professionals must be concerned with the behavior of institutional and government decision makers with respect to policy decisions regarding the support of prevention programs. We argue that the success of public health practice often depends on the extent to which public health professionals can get people other than the at-risk population to behave in ways that support healthful behavior and environments. Here we review the three basic types of health behavior of concern to public health professionals.

Personal-Health Behavior

Successful prevention requires that people behave in ways that are consistent with health. Personal-health behaviors include those taken with health as a concern (if not the sole or overriding concern), such as being physically active, eating a healthful diet, getting vaccinated, moderating drug use, driving safely, and not spreading infection. The theories described in this book provide cogent explanations for why people do or do not practice these health behaviors and how to facilitate behavior change.

Health-Protective Behavior

Some behaviors are intentionally taken for the benefit of others' health. Parents, friends, neighbors, and public health professionals do this routinely. People in a position to reach large audiences, including teachers, city planners, policy makers, and politicians, sometimes engage in behaviors that can positively affect others' health by creating a healthful social and physical environment. Examples include legislators passing legislation to improve water quality, business leaders advocating for road safety, civic leaders encouraging parks and bike routes, and school administrators opting for healthful school meals. Behavior theory relating to information processing, social influence, communication, diffusion of innovations, and social change is relevant to health-protective behavior.

Health-Related Behavior

Actions that affect the health of others, intentional or not, are health related. A parent who smokes indoors exposes household members to sidestream smoke. Inebriated drivers put other road users at risk. A litterer disposes toxic substances into the water supply. A reluctant citizen fails to wear a mask in public, increasing others' risk of infection. These behaviors are not taken to affect others' health, but they can and do. Successful prevention (consider the COVID-19 pandemic) requires efforts to alter these unintended but risky behaviors. These behaviors should be included in multilevel program planning. Theories and models can help explain these behaviors and identify what information or skill development is needed for effective intervention.

Program Planning

Behavior theory is integral to multilevel program planning and intervention processes.

Conceptualization

In combination with the empirical literature on a particular topic, behavior theory facilitates conceptual perspectives on the topic's nature, the role of behavior, theoretic constructs and empirical factors that may be associated with behavior and health.

Needs Assessment

Successful planning includes epidemiologic and behavioral assessment. Epidemiologic assessment focuses on the prevalence of the problem and the populations at risk. Behavioral assessments reveal the cognitive and social factors associated with the problem. Together they guide the development of program goals and objectives.

Program Development

The results of theory-based need assessments guide the development of goals and objectives. Theory also provides a range of possible intervention methods and strategies.

Evaluation

Just as theory can guide need assessments, it can guide evaluation of the extent to which the program altered cognitions and behavior and if these changes resulted in changes to health status. It is difficult to interpret evaluation data without a theoretical perspective.

Multilevel Thinking

Throughout the book and in detail in an earlier chapter, we emphasized multilevel thinking. Understanding behavior is complex because there are multiple factors and multiple levels that contribute to behavior. Bronfenbrenner (1979) theorized concentric circles of social levels extending outward from the individual, shaping development and behavior. Behavior does not occur in a vacuum; it occurs as a product of the lifelong interaction of the individual with the environment. Here we emphasize a few key issues that were discussed in detail in an earlier chapter.

1. **Environment**. Behavior is substantially determined by the environment. Social and physical environments provide context, opportunity, and informative feedback about the potential for future reinforcement under similar conditions. Environmental influences on health and behavior, for example, community, culture, policy, and economics, are sources for program goals and outcomes, not interventions. Public health professionals cannot create policies, improve the economy, or change culture, but they can facilitate changes in cognitions and behavior of individuals with influence over these conditions. Because behavior is behavior, the same theories that operate for cognitions related to personal-health behavior also operate for health-protective and health-related behavior.
2. **Norms**. Social norms are among the most powerful environmental influences on behavior. Behaving counter to the norms of one's social contacts, institutional affiliations, culture, and politics is generally unrewarding. Therefore, most people most of the time conform to perceived social pressure and normative

expectations. Many theories address the role of social influence in behavior and suggest possible intervention approaches.

3. **Societal Levels**. Because behavior is greatly influenced by the many levels that make up the environment, we must assess the influences on the individual at each level, take these influences into account when intervening at the individual level, and establish program goals for changes in policies and practices at other societal levels. Achieving improvements in population health often requires changes not only in personal health behavior of the target population, but also changes in the health-protective and health-related behaviors of influential others. Thus, policies and practices that affect personal-health behavior are program goals.
4. **Targets of Intervention**. Each societal level has key influencers. At the intrapersonal level, this is the target population that includes those at risk and whose behavior and health are the focus of program goals. The knowledge, attitudes, beliefs, and skills of the target population form the objectives of most programs. However, it can be useful and sometimes essential for programs to focus on those with influence at other societal levels. At the interpersonal level, family, friends, and peers may be important targets of interventions designed to alter health-related and health-protective behaviors. At more distal levels, the targets of intervention may be institutional or government managers, policy developers, and leaders if they control or influence environmental factors that, in turn, influence the behavior and health of the target population. Therefore, the cognitions and behavior of these key individuals warrant programmatic attention.
5. **Theory**. Behavior theory is best at explaining how people cognitively process information, make decisions, and respond to the environment. These theories

are commonly employed in public health programs to affect personal-health behavior. However, behavior is behavior, and the same theories relating to cognitive and social processes are involved in health-protective and health-related behavior. Models of how broader social levels affect health and behavior provide insight into the environmental influences on health behavior. The specific cognitive factors that influence personal-health behavior may not be the same as those that affect health-related or health-protective behavior, but the same behavior theories apply. Understanding the mask-wearing and social distancing behavior of those at risk of being infected, those who might infect others, and those responsible for relevant policies and practices are all influenced by cognitions, social influences, and broader environmental factors.

Many Useful Theories

Actually, most theories derive from only a few elemental conceptualizations about internal or external factors, or their interactions. Most theories are elaborations on how these primary influences operate. The seeming proliferation of theories, with overlapping variables and terminology, is a natural and useful development, but has been a concern of some researchers (Noar & Zimmerman, 2005). While there is a need for additional research comparing theories, as argued by Noar and Zimmerman, it seems most important that public health professionals understand and appreciate that theory, like practice, is dynamic, so elaborations on basic theories is natural, warranted, and welcome. Elaborations and specifications of theory can make selecting theory more difficult, but also provide more options by indicating how the theory can be applied in specific situations or to specific behaviors.

Despite the seeming proliferation, behavior theory is essentially concerned with external (extrinsic) and internal (intrinsic) processes and the dynamic interactions of these processes. At the risk of oversimplifying theory, the following is meant to provide a review of theory and framework within which practitioners can broadly appreciate the application of theory to specific behaviors.

External Influences on Motivation and Behavior

Behavior is largely the product of reinforcement in the manner described by operant conditioning and Social Cognitive Theory. When the consequences of particular responses increase the frequency of response, it has been reinforced. Stimuli provide information about how likely reinforcement would be for a particular response. Reinforcement is complicated because stimuli and consequences are subject to interpretation, and certain behaviors become habits that need little additional external reinforcement. The principles of operant conditioning can be applied to personal behavior in the form of self-management practices, the application of operant principles to personal behavior.

Reinforcement also explains how the larger environment influences behavior. To the great extent that behavior is social, it is influenced by the norms of family, friends, colleagues, group members, and culture. Whether by overt social pressure or standards of acceptability, people conform to normative expectations. Not always, but most of the time. Indeed, most behavior is so embedded within social and cultural context that we may not even realize we are conforming. Many policies and practices at institutional, community, and government levels serve the function of establishing normative behavior. Codes of conduct, speed limits, no smoking ordinances, age limits for alcohol possession and use, mask requirements, seat belts, bike helmets, HIV and COVID-19 tracing, and on and on. Many of these normative standards include enforcement for violation in the form of fines, imprisonment, employment censorship, or other severe consequences. Of course, some people sometimes drive too fast, drink too much, and ignore bicycle helmet laws and other safety measures, but with or without enforcement, when policies directed at these behaviors are effective. The establishment of policies provides sanctions, but more important, they reflect and alter social norms. Smoking is an excellent example. Not so long ago, people could smoke on airlines, at work in office buildings, and in bars and restaurants. Today, these behaviors are rare, although violators are seldom actually penalized. This is because the policies both reflect and threaten to enforce norms. Policies regarding social distancing and mask wearing to prevent the spread of the coronavirus and other contagious germs reflect social norms. They work mainly because they reflect a social consensus about the behavior. Ultimately, because behavior is greatly influenced by the larger environment, public health intervention must include key environmental factors as objectives.

Internal Influences on Motivation and Behavior

Each person is unique due to genetic, social, behavioral, and environmental factors. People have distinct personalities owing to their genetic heritage and lifelong experiences. No two people have identical personalities, in part because only identical twins have the same genes, and no two people have the same life experiences. Indeed, people learn from their behavior, to the extent the environment provides feedback and reinforcement. Individual differences are generally measured as personality traits and cognitions.

Personality

Personality is thought to be substantially heritable, but genetic propensities are shaped by the environment. Developmental psychologists emphasize challenges that define each age, shaping personality along the way. Parenting is particularly important in this

regard, but schools and neighborhoods, among the many sources of life experiences, challenge individuals as they develop and shape personality. Personality is probably not the only heritable characteristic that distinguishes individuals, but personality traits are measurable, relatively stable over time, generally associated with behaviors, and specifically associated with many health behaviors. For example, using the Big Five Personality Traits, it is likely that a high extraversion scorer is going to be sociable, optimistic, and friendly. Someone with a high neuroticism score will be insecure and worry about the little things. Others, such as with the trait of openness, will be imaginative and curious, while conscientious people will be self-disciplined and hard workers. Individuals with agreeableness traits are likely to be gullible, be helpful, and agree with most opinions. Those with an internal versus external locus of control are more likely to embrace healthful behaviors. It may be possible for public health professionals to tailor intervention strategies to personality types.

Cognitions

Specific knowledge, skills, beliefs, attitudes, and past behavior are predictive of future behavior. One cannot manage one's behavior without knowing how or without the skills to do so. Attitudes are made up of beliefs, and both can be influenced by new information, particularly information delivered in ways that obtain attention and create dissonance. Impressions from experience are stored in memory as cognitions. While cognitions reflect past experience, they are mutable by information. Cognitions, therefore, are the product of information gained from the experiences provided by the environment, which includes family life, schooling, work, TV viewing, religious training, cultural background, and so on. New information struggles to compete with existing cognitions and the generalized heuristics (generalized cognitions) upon which they are based. Generally, people are resistant to new information, particularly if it does not conform to their existing cognitions. Only through repeated exposure to new information, variously expressed by credible sources, does new information get through to reluctant people. Of course, people sometimes seek new information about topics of interest, and during these heightened periods of interest they may be particularly susceptible to new information (truthful or not).

Behavior

In addition to personality, cognitions develop from experience over time. Behavior is a powerful teacher. By acting or observing others act, we can determine how the environment responds, allowing us to determine the likelihood, nature, and amount of reinforcement. Thus, our behavior is another important aspect of individual differences.

The Value of Each Theory

Therefore, we need to determine the specific cognitions of the target population so that our programs can address them systematically. Behavior theories provide cognitive constructs associated with behavior that can be assessed and addressed by intervention. Here we describe macro- and microcategories of behavior theory. While this is a somewhat arbitrary categorization, it serves to illustrate important points about theory.

Grand Theories of Behavior

Social Cognitive Theory (SCT) and Self-Determination Theory (SDT) are macrotheories that seek to integrate **external** and **internal influences** on deliberative behavior. These theories seek to explain comprehensively how the interaction between internal and external factors influence behaviors of all kinds.

As described in an earlier chapter, SCT (Bandura, 1986) includes three interactive elements: environment, person, behavior. As described for operant conditioning, the environment provides opportunity and reinforcement. "Person" represents the unique characteristics of each individual, including personality and cognitions stored in memory. The most important SCT cognitions include self-efficacy, outcome expectations, personal goals, and behavioral capability (knowledge and skills). SCT emphasizes that behavior, in addition to providing experience by eliciting environmental responses (reinforcement) from which people learn, alters the environment. For example, the behavior of that first cigarette or alcoholic drink can set off a cascade of environmental responses that occur in response to that behavior.

SDT (Deci & Ryan, 2008) is a grand theory that seeks to explain the development of intrinsic or internal motivation. Deci and Ryan, like Bandura, were trained in operant conditioning, interested in self-regulatory processes, and disappointed that changes in behavior from external reinforcement were often not maintained when external reinforcement was removed. While SDT and SCT have much in common, with outcome and efficacy expectations as key cognitive variables, SDT uniquely emphasizes psychological needs. As you recall from our discussion in an earlier chapter of Freud and psychoanalytic theory, the satisfaction and resolution of innate drives shape personality. SDT emphasizes the psychological needs of autonomy, competence, and relatedness. Resolution of these needs facilitates autonomous or intrinsic motivation, a key element of self-regulation.

Somewhat Grand Theories of Behavior

With no criticism intended, we classify theories other than SCT and SDT as somewhat grand or micro because they are less comprehensive in breadth and focus. They are great for conceptualizing the internal cognitive factors that influence behavior with some emphasis on the environment, particularly the proximal social environment. Here we provide only a few prominent examples of intrapersonal- and interpersonal-level theories, without consideration for important institutional, community, policy, and economic influences.

The values expectancy and Transtheoretical theories identify key cognitive variables related to behavior. These theories assume that people are rational, at least to some extent, calculating the relative advantages of particular responses by adding up perceived pluses and minuses. These theories also share the underlying assumption that information that does not conform to existing cognitions creates cognitive dissonance. To a greater or lesser extent, dissonance motivates individuals to reconsider existing cognitions or otherwise resolve the resulting tension. Of course, this is not always the case, as people develop powerful mechanisms to avoid dissonance and change.

Information and skill development are powerful tools of persuasion for creating change. Some theories focus largely on how information can be communicated effectively. Communication theories explain how information in the form of planned messages is best able to penetrate cognitive defenses. The Transtheoretical Model and Diffusion Theory examine the susceptibility to new information at various stages in the change process. Diffusion theory elaborates on communication and stage theories as they relate to the process of adopting innovations (new ideas, practices, things, behaviors).

Of the values expectancy theories, the Theory of Reasoned Action and the Theory of Planned Behavior envision that behavioral intention is the product of beliefs about likely outcomes. There are many possible beliefs, some in opposition to others. Individuals, therefore, must somehow calculate the relative advantages by weighing these many disparate beliefs. New information addressed to salient beliefs could alter this calculation, leading to behavior change.

Possible Integration of Cognitions Across Theories

Efforts to meld the best of the most prominent intra- and interpersonal theories into an integrated theory have identified efficacy and outcome expectations and norms perceptions as key cognitions. Social influences and self-efficacy are prominent in many theories because of their explanatory and predictive power. Social influences, for example, are central to Social Cognitive Theory and Theory of Reasoned Action and have been elaborated as independent theory. Self-efficacy is proximal and can facilitate change through a personal sense of confidence. Self-efficacy, of course, develops from experience and is largely dependent on knowledge and skills, in addition to other beliefs about self and the extent to which the environment is supportive. Therefore, it is important for intervention to include proper training and skill development, attainable goals, and positive social role modeling, in addition to persuasion.

Rather than adopting a set of variables as theory, a more conceptual orientation to theory and practice may be more useful. Accordingly, **Figure 12.1** illustrates the integration of key concepts presented in this book. The arrow across the top of the figure indicates the persistent interaction of the person and the environment over the life course. The circle to the left includes the internal personal factors of personality, cognition, and past behavior. The circle to the right includes the environmental factors of social, institutional, community, policy, and economics areas. The arrow joining these two circles represents the interaction of these internal and external factors.

Within each circle is a list of the possible targets of intervention. The target of intervention in the person circle is the target population, whose personality, cognitions, and behavior can be assessed to determine intervention objectives. The targets of intervention listed in the environment circle are those with influence over policies and practices,

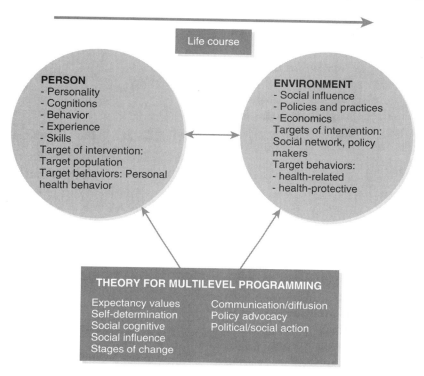

Figure 12.1 Illustration of the interaction of the person and environment in ecological context

including social network members, policy and practice decision makers, and the public.

The box at the bottom includes theories that can be employed to identify possible goals/outcomes, cognitive determinants, and intervention strategies and methods. Each behavior theory and model can provide insight into behavioral determinants, possible target outcomes, and useful intervention strategies and methods. Theory can guide assessment and suggest appropriate intervention approaches. Assessment at the environment level provides program goals and objectives (e.g., improve health-related behavior, change policies and practices, increase public support for healthful policies and practices) and possible change strategies. In a multilevel program, for example, to prevent college drinking problems, a wide range of goals would be identified as part of assessment and intervention components created to alter personal-health

behavior related to drinking and health-related and health-protective behaviors of the college community and policy makers.

Theory as a Way of Thinking

We have presented behavior theory as a tool for use by public health professionals to create more systematic and comprehensive programs. It is also a way of thinking using the scientific method that depends on **inductive** and **deductive reasoning**. Theories are based on *inductive* reasoning where observed patterns lead to hypotheses and then to theory for testing. Each of the theories described in this book is based on inductive reasoning, and for each there is substantial evidence of their validity, some generally and others for specific behaviors and contexts. Meanwhile, in developing programs, we employ *deductive* reasoning by assuming that theory will usefully explain the behavior of concern. Accordingly, we adopt an appropriate theory, apply its hypotheses to the specific health concerns, create measures of the constructs, implement intervention programs, and as a part of evaluating program effects, we confirm the utility of the theory at least for the problem and context at hand.

Theory can also be relevant at a personal level. Health behavior is deeply personal, and our behavior is a reflection of our character. Therefore, studying health behavior is not abstract; it applies to our own behavior as well as to the behavior of others. Most public health professionals tend to behave in reasonably healthful ways. This may be because those particularly interested in health and health behavior gravitate to the profession. It may also be that public health training exposes new professionals to new information that is of personal interest and to which they are cognitively open. This may lead to cautious reexamination of personal heuristics and related cognitive perspectives developed over time that students bring with them to public health training. As we know, new information can create cognitive dissonance by challenging existing heuristics. While public health is a population science, public health training is a personal experience that can lead to changes in cognitions and behavior.

At both the personal and professional levels, we encourage you to employ scientific reasoning to your life endeavors. Based on the knowledge gained from reading this book, think like a behavioral scientist by applying the scientific method to your own behavior as well as to the behavior of others. Extrapolate the theories into real-world experiences by making hypotheses about the possible cognitive and environmental factors associated with behavior. Use theoretical constructs to explore how and why behavior varies. This manner of thinking has the potential to make you a better person, as well as a more successful professional.

Lessons For Public Health Practice

1. Each behavior theory has particular features and applications.
2. Health behavior is the primary focus of many public health programs that require adherence to medical regimens (taking prescribed medications or going to rehab) or compliance with preventive recommendations (get a flu shot, wear a mask in public, use protection during sex).
3. Hence, competence in the application of behavior theory is essential to public health professionals regardless of subspecialty.
4. Behavior theory facilitates multilevel conceptualization of health problems.
5. At an elemental level behavior theory is about the relationship between external and internal influences.
6. The grand behavior theories of Social Cognitive Theory and Self-Determination Theory integrate internal and external factors, thereby providing comprehensive explanations of behavior.
7. Other theories provide specific applications and methods.
8. Theory provides a scientific way of thinking that involves inductive reasoning that involves the development of hypotheses from verifiable observations, and deductive reasoning involving generalizing understanding about the nature of things to specific concerns, including health behaviors.

Discussion Questions

1. Why is behavior theory important to public health?
2. How can theory contribute to health program development?
3. Why should public health professionals be concerned about multiple societal levels of influence?
4. What does it mean to intervene at social levels beyond the interpersonal and intrapersonal?
5. What is the role of information in policy advocacy?

References

Bandura, A. J. (1986). *Social foundations of thought and action.* Englewood Cliffs, NJ: Prentice Hall.

Bronfenbrenner, U. (1979). *The ecology of human development: Experiments by nature and design.* Cambridge, MA: Harvard University Press.

Deci, E. L., & Ryan, R. M. (2008). Self-determination theory: A macrotheory of human motivation, development, and health. *Canadian Psychology, 49*(3), 182–185. DOI: 10.1037/a0012801

Noar, S. M., & Zimmerman, R. S. (2005). Health behavior theory and cumulative knowledge regarding health behaviors: Are we moving in the right direction? *Health Education Research, 20*(3), 275–290. DOI: 10.1093/her/cyg113

Glossary

[Note: The following are the definitions of terms as employed in the book. However, some of these terms have broader or other definitions as well.]

Adopter categories. Descriptions of when adoption occurs, from early to late.

Adoption. A decision to make use of an innovation as the best course of action; decision to implement a program or program component.

Affirming statements. In Motivational Interviewing, affirming statements are positive messages that encourage and support the client.

Agency. The ability to engage in self-directed behavior.

Ambivalence. In Motivational Interviewing, ambivalence reflects the simultaneous desire to change and the desire not to change.

Antecedent. An event that precedes a behavioral response.

Applied behavioral analysis (ABA). A method for assessing responses and their antecedents and consequences.

Association. Factors correlated with an outcome, for example, a cognitive or environmental variable with a behavior.

At-risk population. The population whose behavior and health is of concern in a program.

Attitude. A collection of beliefs and feelings with regard to a person or thing.

Attribution. What the person believes to be the cause of an action or outcome.

Autonomy. The ability to act in one's self-interest consistent with one's values.

Awareness knowledge. Knowledge of the existence of an innovation.

Behavior modification. The use of operant methods to guide training programs.

Behavior. Observable actions.

Behavioral capability. The Social Cognitive Theory term for knowledge and skills essential for self-directed behavior.

Beliefs. What we think is true, whether it is or not. (Belief is sometimes termed *perception*, which more correctly describes what the mind interprets as what is seen.)

Blame the victim. Assigning responsibility for health behavior or outcomes that are not fully under personal control, for example, when people are simply responding to the environment.

Brief intervention. Limited to a single intervention activity, contact, event, or session, often of brief duration.

Central route processing. Information that requires active participation in the process of determining the quality of the information and what action should be taken.

Change agent. A person who promotes an innovation.

Change processes. Actions taken to produce behavior change.

Change talk. In Motivational Interviewing, open-ended questions elicit from the client thoughts about change, things they might want to change, and ideas they have for changing.

Channel. The medium through which information is delivered.

Cognitions. Mental processes that involve perception, knowledge, beliefs, attitudes, values; cognitive representations of thoughts and feelings.

Cognitive consistency. The tendency to maintain alignment of cognitions and behavior.

Cognitive dissonance. Inconsistency between current knowledge, attitudes, and behavior that can create tension and motivate change.

Cognitive restructuring. Cognitive Behavior Therapy processes for restructuring thoughts in a manner consistent with personal goals and healthful behavior.

Communication channels. Formal and informal sources of information.

Communication. Process by which information is shared; processes of transmitting and receiving information.

Compatibility. The extent to which an innovation is consistent with current practice and values.

Competence. Sense of capability and self-control.

Concept. Cognitive representation of meaning; abstract or mental symbol of knowledge.

Conceptual model. Representation of the hypothesized relationships of constructs and outcomes; forerunner to theory.

Conditioning. Automatic or learned responses to stimuli.

Confirmation bias. Attending mainly to information consistent with existing cognitions to the exclusion of conflicting or dissonant information.

Conformity. The tendency to adapt cognitions and behavior to fit the expectations of others.

Consequence. An outcome that follows a response.

Construct. An essential element or core idea of a theory; such as a particular cognition or environmental factor in relation to a behavior.

Contingent. Dependent on particular conditions.

Control beliefs. The subjective evaluation of the likelihood of factors that would facilitate or inhibit action and the importance of each factor.

Counseling. The process of instruction and facilitation that focuses on individuals or small groups rather than classrooms with a focus on the dynamic interaction between the counselor and the client.

Culture. Broad social structures and norms owing to nationality, religion, socioeconomic status, and geography.

Decoding. The way or ways a message is understood by the receiver.

Deductive reasoning. Theory-based explanations of phenomena that starts with a general statement or hypothesis and examines possibilities to confirm the conclusion.

Deliberative behavior. Behavior involving conscious thought.

Detachment. Allowing others to decide for themselves.

Determinant. A variable that is prospectively associated with an outcome; factor associated with an outcome.

Diffusion. The adoption of an innovation over time; the process in which an innovation is communicated through certain channels over time among the members of a social system.

Discrimination. Unfair policies, practices, and behaviors that unfairly apply to people based on race, ethnicity, gender, sexual orientation, or other characteristics.

Dissonance (cognitive). The tendency for new information, that is inconsistent with existing cognitions and/or behavior, to create tension that is uncomfortable and often leads to change.

Drive. Innate desire for pleasure and avoidance of pain.

Ecological. The interaction of multiple factors and social levels.

Effectiveness. The degree to which a program is capable of producing specific, desired outcomes, particularly in more than one context.

Efficacy. Indicates evidence of programmatic effects on target objectives in a given intervention in a given context; a measure of programmatic effects on cognitions.

Elicitation research. In IMB theory, qualitative assessment of what the at-risk population thinks and believes, what their attitudes are, and what skills they possess.

Empathy. Personally accepting, understanding, and valuing others.

Enabling factors. Conditions that facilitate action.

Enactive learning. Learning by doing; practice to mastery.

Encoding. The way information is packaged for transmission.

Environment. Physical and social conditions, including policies, practices, and programs.

Epidemiological transition. A change in population growth in a country or region due to a decrease in mortality.

Expectancies. The value placed on anticipated outcomes.

Expectancy value/value expectancy. The idea that behavior occurs according to the individual's expectations about the benefits of engaging in the behavior, accounting for the costs and alternatives.

Expectations. Anticipated or expected outcomes.

Expected outcomes. Anticipated consequences of engaging in a behavior.

External influences on behavior. Influential social (including interpersonal and institutional/policy) and physical environmental factors with reinforcement potential.

Extrinsic. External factor.

Facilitating behavior. Person, place, or thing that helps with behavior change.

False consensus. Incorrect perception that one's attitudes and behavior represent those of the majority.

Feedback. Information about the likelihood of future reinforcement.

Fidelity. Accuracy, exactness, and faithfulness of program implementation.

Generalized expectations. General thoughts based on experience about the potential for reinforcement in particular situations.

Germs. Microorganisms invisible to the eye.

Goal-directed behavior. Behavior under individuals' control oriented toward attaining personal goals.

Graduated driver licensing. A system that includes three stages—supervised, provisional, and independent.

Group membership. Affiliation that can be highly formal, such as belonging to a family, a gang, an organization, a profession, or informal, clique, group, or crowd.

Health communication. Processes by which health information is shared.

Health education. A profession concerned with educating people about health; planned learning experiences based on sound theories that provide individuals, groups, and communities the opportunity to acquire information and skills needed to make quality health decisions.

Health-promotion specialist. A health or education professional whose work is devoted to health promotion.

Health literacy. The degree to which individuals have the capacity to obtain, process, and understand basic health information and services needed to make appropriate health decisions.

Health promotion. Processes for enabling healthful living by changing personal behavior and environmental influences on behavior.

Health-protective behavior. Behaviors that are undertaken specifically, if not exclusively, out of concern for the health of others.

Health-related behavior. Behavior that affects others' health and health behavior, even if not purposefully undertaken for health reasons.

Heuristics. Generalized memories or intuition that guides behavior in the absence of concerted thought.

High-risk groups. Those who are more likely to develop a risk factor or health outcome.

Homophily. Populations that are alike with shared interests, values, and behaviors.

Hypothesis. An explanation for the occurrence or cause of phenomenon.

Impact evaluation. Evaluation of the effect of the program on proximal objectives.

Incentive. An inducement, often material, to encourage a particular response.

Individual differences. Psychological characteristics that distinguish one person from another, including intelligence, personality traits, and cognitions.

Inductive reasoning. Hypotheses based on observed phenomena.

Injunctive norms. Perceptions about how close others would think about one behaving in a particular manner (similar to subjective norms in TRA).

Innovation. An idea, practice, or object that is perceived as new by a potential adopter.

Innovation-Decision Process. The stages of adoption include knowledge, persuasion, decision, implementation, and confirmation.

Inoculation. Exposure to counterarguments.

Intention. A cognitive determination to behave in a certain manner.

Intermediary communication. Information interpreted by a third party who is neither the transmitter nor the receiver.

Internal influences on behavior. Individual differences in response to stimuli due to unique personality, experience, and cognitions.

Internal validity. Ability to draw accurate conclusions about the achievement of objectives in a particular program based on implementation and exposure.

Intervention. A specific set of actions designed to accomplish specific objectives and outcomes.

Intrinsic. Internal factor such as a cognition.

Knowledge. Objectively verifiable truth; what we know to be true that is actually true.

Learning theory. Refers to how people develop cognitions and patterns of behavior.

Locus of control. The extent to which individuals attribute events to internal (such as effort) or external factors (such as luck, fate, or chance).

Logic model. A systematic visualization, figure, or conceptualization that illustrates possible relationship among variables.

Mediator. A variable that alters the relationship between an independent variable and a dependent variable varies, for example, the relationship between peer influence and substance use may vary by sex or age.

Medicine. Profession and practices concerned with health at an individual level.

Message. Information about a specific topic that is intentionally communicated.

Modeling. The process by which the observation of one's behavior influences the behavior of others; or the process by which observation of others behavior influences one's behavior.

Moderator. A variable that changes the extent of a relationship between an independent variable and a dependent variable; for example, the magnitude of the relationship between peer influence and substance use may vary according to parenting behavior.

Morbidity. The extent of a health problem measured as a rate.

Motivation. The tendency of an individual or group to think and behave in certain ways.

Motivational interviewing spirit. A counselor–client relationship that is collaborative, evocative, and honoring.

Multilevel thinking. Recognition that multiple factors and societal levels may contribute to health outcomes.

Noise. Interference in an intervention due to unplanned causes.

Norm (social). Understood rules of behavior that are considered acceptable by a group or society.

Observability. The degree to which the operation and results of an innovation are visible to others.

Observational learning. Learning that occurs through observing the behavior of others; a form of social learning.

Observational research. Nonexperimental research that studies natural phenomenon.

Operant. A response that is controlled by its consequences.

Opinion leaders. Individuals who are well informed, with extensive social contacts; influential members of a social network.

Outcome evaluation. Evaluation of the program outcomes, which can be health, health behaviors, or environmental factors.

Outcome expectations. Cognitions about anticipated consequences of behavior.

Pathogen. Agent such as a germ or physical factor that contributes to the cause of injury or disease.

Perceived behavioral control. One's beliefs about the environment and the extent to which one believes s/he has control over the behavior under particular circumstances.

Perceived likelihood. Belief about taking action or changing behavior.

Perceived severity. The believed seriousness of a health problem.

Perceived social norms. What people think are the prevailing and accepted beliefs, attitudes, values, behaviors, and standards by a group or society.

Perception. Commonly defined as beliefs, but better understood as how the mind interprets the observed environment.

Peripheral route processing. The passive consideration of information.

Person. The unique characteristics and goals of the individual.

Personal-health behavior. Behavior that affects one's own health, intentional or not.

Personality traits. Characteristics of personality that are relatively stable over time, differ among individuals, and contribute to behavior.

Personality. A dynamic and organized set of characteristics, inherited and shaped by experience, that contribute to individual differences interpreting experience and develop cognitions, motivation, and behaviors.

Persuasion/persuasive communications. Information designed to affect cognitions and behavior.

Pluralistic ignorance. The sharing of incorrect information among members of a group.

Predisposing factors. Cognitions linked to health behavior.

Prevention. Actions designed to reduce the prevalence, severity, recurrence, and consequences of illness, disease, and/or injury.

Principles knowledge. Knowledge about the how an innovation works; underlying mechanisms.

Process evaluation. Examines the extent to which the planned activities were delivered and their fidelity and quality; assessment of the extent to which a program is implemented as designed.

Psychological needs. Basic needs for autonomy, competence, and relatedness.

Psychosocial. The psychological development and behavior of the individual in relation to social context.

Public health. Health at a population level that is generally measured by statistics, such as mortality and morbidity rates. Also, a discipline with many subspecialties, all of which function to prevent health problems and improve wellness.

Qualitative research. The collection and analyses of non-numerical data such as text, audio, video, and/or interviews, to generate new research ideas or gather in-depth insights into a problem.

Receiver. The person or target audience of the specific information.

Reciprocal determinism. The dynamic interaction of environment, person, and behavior; also called triadic reciprocity.

Refutation preemption. A key component of Inoculation Theory that refers to the arguments developed against anticipated counterarguments before they are articulated.

Reinforcement. A consequence that increases the likelihood or frequency of a response.

Reinforcing factors. Factors that support health behavior.

Reinvention. The degree to which an innovation is changed or modified by a user in the process of its adoption and implementation.

Relative advantage. The degree to which an innovation is perceived as better than the existing or competing alternatives; advantages and disadvantages of adopting an innovation.

Resistance to change. Unwillingness to alter cognitions, actions, or behaviors.

Response. An incident of a particular behavior, for example, smoking one cigarette or taking a walk (versus the general behavioral categories of smoking and exercising).

Reward. A prize for performing a behavior; may be reinforcing.

Risk factor. A variable associated with an increased risk of injury or disease; also called a determinant.

Risk reduction. Reducing the prevalence or severity of risk factors.

Scarcity. A feeling of urgency created by information that the opportunity is limited by time or circumstance.

Selection. Affiliating with others with similar beliefs and behavior; the process whereby social relationships are established, maintained, or strengthened on the basis of shared characteristics.

Selective exposure. Avoiding information that may be dissonant with existing cognitions.

Self-actualization. High-level desire or drive for self-fulfillment.

Self-control. Processes for managing impulse control.

Self-directed behavior. Actions based on individualized goals.

Self-efficacy. The perception of one's ability to perform a behavior or otherwise exercise control in various situations and overcome obstacles.

Self-management. The self-application of operant methods to facilitate self-regulation of behavior and environment.

Self-regulation. Cognitive processes for controlling one's behavior, emotions, and thoughts in the pursuit of goal-directed behavior.

Social approval. Positive appraisal or acceptance by a social group.

Social capital. The degree of social connectedness.

Social context. Social norms and conditions specific to place and time.

Social ecology. The effect of multiple societal levels on health and health behavior.

Social influence. The effect of others on cognitions and behavior; the product of information shared among group members leading to common social norms.

Social marketing. The combination of communication and marketing principles for social programs.

Social network. Connections between individuals; patterns of friendship, advice, communication, or support that exist among members of a social system.

Social norms. The accepted knowledge, attitudes, values, behaviors, and standards of members of a population group; may be actual or perceived.

Social pressure. Actual or perceived pressure from others to adopt particular norms.

Social support. The physical and emotional comfort given to us by our family, friends, coworkers, and others.

Social systems. Specific sets of social connections such as extended families, workplaces, neighborhoods, religious and recreational groups, and friends.

Socialization. The effect of others on behavior; the cumulative effect of social influences from all sources on attitudes and behavior.

Source. The person or agency transmitting a message.

S-shaped cumulative diffusion curve. The tendency of innovations to be adopted slowly at first, then more rapidly, before tapering off; the distribution of cumulative adoption over time makes an S-shape.

Stages of change. Categories of change from awareness to action.

Staging, tailoring, stage tailoring, and stage matching. Interventions that are appropriate for a person's stage of change.

Stimulus. An antecedent event or condition that is linked to potential consequences.

Subjective evaluation. Opinions of adopters of the relative advantages of an innovation.

Subjective norms. Perceptions about the prevalence and acceptability of an objective, cognition, or behavior.

Susceptibility. Subjective estimate of individual risk for a particular health problem.

Targets of intervention. Those with influence at a particular social level identified for programmatic attention.

Teaching. A means of transmitting information, generally through formal (more or less) instructional units (curricula), strategies and methods, and environmental contexts.

Theory. A description of hypothesized relationships; a hypothesis supported by data.

Training. Teaching designed to develop specific skills or prepare others to teach specific skills.

Trait (personality). Enduring patterns of perceiving and responding to the environment.

Transactional communication. Interactive communication leading to shared understanding.

Transtheoretical. Integrating concepts and methods across theories.

Trialability. The degree to which an innovation may be experimented with on a limited basis.

Two-stage communication. Directing messages to opinion leaders, as well as to the target population.

Value. Evaluation of the relative importance of various factors, concepts, and actions.

Values expectancy/expectancy value. The idea that behavior occurs according to the individual's expectations about the benefits of engaging in the behavior, accounting for the costs and alternatives.

Variable. The specific definition and measurement of a construct.

Vicarious reinforcement. The process by which a person learns how to interpret stimuli and anticipate reinforcement by watching others.

Volitional decision making. Deciding or committing to an action independently and without influence. Decisions can be made consciously, or they can be automatized as habits over time.

Index

A

ABA. *See* applied behavioral analysis (ABA)
action, 152–153. *See also* Theory of Reasoned Action
    attitude toward object and, 135
    belief about, 135
    cues to, 141
    expected benefits of, 141
    model of communication, 168–169
    preparation for action stage, 152
actual *versus* perceived norms, 114
adopter categories, 181, 196–199, 204–205
    in context, 199
    descriptions of, 198
adopters, 192
adoption, 190, 192
affirming statements, 101
agency, 48
agreeableness, 62
AIDS, 129–130
Ajzen, I., 131, 137
alcohol, 213–214
algorithms, 154, 155
ambivalence, 100
    overcoming, 102
American Public Health Association, 9
antecedent, 58
applied behavioral analysis (ABA), 60, 78, 105, 119
assessment. *See also* needs assessment
    research, 22
association, 39
at-risk population, 21
attention, 177

attitudes, 20, 128–130
    about the behavior, 135
    toward an object of behavior, 135
    toward object or action, 135
    toward smoking, 136–137
attribution, 27
autonomy, 94–95
awareness knowledge, 195

B

Bandura, Albert, 155
barriers, 141–142
behavior, 177, 231
    attitude towards an object of, 135
    environment and, 50
    external influences on, 229–230
    goal-directed, 77
    grand theories of, 231–232
    health and, 14–17
    internal influences on, 230–231
    motivation and, 53–71
    reciprocal determinism, 81
    self-directed, 77
    stimulus–response model of, 59, 76
    theories, 26–27, 58
behavioral capability, 83
behavioral skill, 144
behavior theory, public health and, 226–227
beliefs, 34, 128–130. *See also* expectancy value theories
    about object or action, 135
    about smoking, 136–137
    control, 138
    normative, 136
benefits, 130
Big Five Personality Traits, 230
Black Lives Matter, 44
blaming the victim, 178
blogs, 181

blood alcohol concentration (BAC) testing, 177
breast cancer, 142
brief interventions, 106
Bronfenbrenner, U., 34, 228

C

cable TV channels, 183
Cacioppo, J. T., 174
cause-specific mortality, 6
central route processing, 175, 182
certification as a health education specialist (CHES), 19
change agent, 205–206
    opinion leaders and, 198
change dynamics, 153–154
change processes, 151
    health promotion, 20–22
    TTM and, 155–156
change talk, 101
channel, 168, 178, 183
    advertising, 182
    and context, 177
Checkpoints Program
    to prevent motor vehicle crashes among young drivers, 86, 87
CHES. *See* certification as a health education specialist (CHES)
choosing a theory, 220–222
    common errors in, 222–223
    principles, 221–222
Chua, A., 45
classical conditioning, 58, 59
cognition, 34, 177, 230–231
    with expectancy value theories, 129–130
    self-regulatory processes, 83–84
    of targets of intervention, altering, 50
cognition–theory–change continuum, imperfection in, 28

Cognitive Consistency Theory, 64–65
cognitive dissonance, 64
    example of, 166
    for health communication,
        165–166
Cognitive Dissonance Theory, 165
cognitive psychology, 64–66
cognitive resistance, 166–167
cognitive restructuring, 82
college context, 183
commercial marketing
    social marketing *vs.*, 176
commitment, 202
common errors in selecting theory
    early adoption, 222
    failure of application *versus*
        failure of theory, 223
    inappropriate target of the
        intervention, 222
    lack of imagination, 223
    lure of novel theories, 223
    one theory, 222
    problem definition, 222
    societal level, 222
communicability, 201
communication. *See also* health
        communication
    action model of, 168–169
    ecological models in, 171
    interactive model of, 169
    intermediary model of, 170–171
    persuasive, 171–174
    and relative advantage, 203–204
    transactional model of, 169
communication channels, 190,
        192–193
    formal media, 192
    informal, interpersonal,
        192, 193
    two-stage communication, 193
communication/persuasion
        matrix, 173
    utility of, 174
community context, 182
community level, 41–42
compatibility, 201
competence, 95
complexity, 202
comprehension, 177
concept, 4
conceptualization, 227
conceptual models, 213
conditioning
    classical, 58, 59
    operant, 25, 59–60
conditions for change, 101–102

confirmation, 196
confirmation bias, 65
conformity, 112–113
conscientiousness, 62
consequences, 12
constructs, 25
consumption of sugared beverages,
        183
contemplation stage, 152
context, 183
context of a single city
        (Philadelphia), 183
contingent, 80
control beliefs, 138
coronavirus, 139
cost, 130
counseling, 20
COVID-19, 169, 170. *See also* face
        mask wearing
    social distancing and, 192
    spread of, 191
    wearing face mask to prevent,
        183–186
crude mortality, 6
cues to action, 141
cultural level, 44–45
culture, 34, 118

D

death, causes of, 7
decision, 196
decision-making processes
    Rogers, E., on, 150
decoding, 168, 171
deductive reasoning, 233
deliberation, 78
descriptive norms, 192
detachment, 102–103
determinants, 20
    of health behavior, 22–23
    of health outcomes, 22–23
developmental theory, 63–64
DiClemente, C. C., 195
diet and food choices
    physical activity self-regulation
        change among obese women,
        85–86
diffusion, 170
diffusion of innovation theory,
        189–207
    communication channels in,
        190, 192–193
    examples of, 202–204
    innovation-decision process
        and, 194–196

    introduction to, 190
    key concepts of, 190–192
    lessons for public health
        practice, 204–206
    social systems and, 193
    at system level, 202–203
    time and S-shaped diffusion
        curve in, 194
Diffusion Theory, 181, 184
discrepancy, 103–104
discrimination, 44
diseases, 4
    causation, 5–6
    incidence rate, 6
    prevalence rate, 6
dissemination, 177
Drinking and driving will kill a
        friendship campaign, 177
drinking problems among college
        students, 212–219
drive, 61

E

early adopters, 197–198
early adoption, 222
early majority, 198
ecological models in
        communication, 171
ecological perspectives
    multilevel programs and, 23–25
economic health and well-being, 8–9
economic level, 45–46
effectiveness, 22
efficacy, 22
    and effectiveness research, 23
elaboration likelihood model
        (ELM), 174–175, 182
elaboration likelihood theory,
        174–175, 179
    central route processing and,
        175
    overview of, 174
    peripheral route processing
        and, 174
electronic cigarette use, 122–123
elicitation research, 145
Emerson, Ralph Waldo, 189
empathy, 103
empowerment, 104
encoding, 168, 171
environment, 48, 228
    and behavior, 50
    reciprocal determinism, 80–81
environmental context, 178
epidemiological transition, 7

Erickson, E. H., 63
ethics, 177–178
evaluation, 219. *See also* program
    evaluation
    program planning, 227–228
    subjective evaluation of
        innovations, 192
evaluation of outputs, 177
expectancies, 79
expectancy value theories, 127–148
    cognitions with, 129–130
    definition of, 131
    Health Belief Model (HBM), 131,
        139–142, 180
    Information–Motivation–
        Behavioral Skills (IMB)
        model, 131, 143–145
    introduction to, 128–131
    lessons for public health
        practices, 145–146
    TPB, 131, 137–139, 180
    TRA, 131, 132–137, 180
expectations, 39
expected benefits of action, 141
expected outcomes, 135
exposed, 183
exposure, 177, 178, 183
external (controlled) motivation,
    96–97
extraversion, 62
extrinsic, 98

F

Facebook, 181
face mask wearing, 169, 193, 200
    benefits of, 171
    messages about, 184–185
    persuasive communication
        matrix applied to, 185
    to prevent COVID-19, 183–186
    as political issue, 192
    in public places, 191
failure of application *versus* failure of
    theory, 223
false consensus, 114
fear-arousing threats, 175
feedback, 70
Festinger, L., 165
fidelity, 205
Fishbein, Martin, 131
    TPB and, 137
    TRA and, 131, 132
flu, 139, 141
formal media communication, 192
formative evaluation, 176–177

Foulger, D., 171
Friends Don't Let Friends Drive
    Drunk campaign, 177

G

Gandhi, Mahatma, 127
gatekeepers, 170
GDL. *See* graduated driver licensing
    (GDL)
generalized expectations, 81
germs, 5
Gestalt Theory, 63
Gladwell, M., 122, 190
Glass, T. A., 119
goal-directed behavior, 77
graduated driver licensing (GDL),
    86, 203
grand theories of behavior, 231–232
Grossman, M., 45
group membership, 112, 113

H

Haddon matrix, 5
Hancox, J. E., 98
Harari, Y. N., 45
health, 4
    behavior and, 14
    public, 9–11
    status, measures of, 4
health behaviors, 3–30
    category of, 17
    caveats, 28–29
    determinants of, 22–23
    health-protective behavior,
        15–16, 227
    personal-health behavior, 15
Health Belief Model (HBM), 131,
    139–142
    definitions and examples of, 140
    examples of, 142
    health communication and, 180
    key features and constructs of,
        139–142
    measurement of, 142
health communication, 163–187
    cognitive dissonance for,
        165–166
    cognitive resistance and,
        166–167
    defined, 164
    information processing and, 165
    introduction to, 164–165
    lessons for public health
        practice, 186

messaging, 179
objectives, 164
selected behavior theory
    constructs for, 179
theory-based message framing,
    179
health, dimensions of
    economic health and well-being
        as, 8–9
    health and well-being as, 6–9
    interactive, 9
    mental health as, 7–8
    social health as, 8
health literacy, 145, 164
health objectives for the nation,
    13–14
health promotion, 14, 18–19
    assessment research, 22
    caveats, 28
    change processes, 20–22
    definition of, 18
    determinants of health behavior,
        22–23
    determinants of health out-
        comes, 22
    efficacy and effectiveness
        research, 23
    evaluation, 19–20
    goals of, 24
    implementation/management,
        19–20
    processes, 19–23
    program planning, 19–20
    theories and, 26
health-protective behavior, 14–16,
    227
health-related behavior, 15, 16–17,
    227
Healthy People 2020, 13–15, 68
Healthy People 2030, 164
heuristics, 78, 144
high-risk population, 178
HIV, 129–130, 144, 226, 229
homophily, 193
human papillomavirus (HPV)
    vaccination, 135
hypothesis, 25

I

impact, 23
implementation, 177
    in innovation-decision process,
        196
inappropriate target of the
    intervention, 222

incentives, 40
individual differences, 95–96
individual variability, 58
inductive reasoning, 233
infant mortality, 6
influential information, 144
informal or interpersonal
        communication, 192, 193
Information–Motivation–Behavioral
        Skills (IMB) model, 131,
        143–145
    basic idea of, 143
    definitions of, 144
    example of, 145
    information and, 144
    key constructs for, 143–145
    measurement of, 145
    primary assumption of, 143
Inhelder, B., 63
innovation characteristics,
        199–202, 205
    commitment as, 202
    communicability as, 201
    compatibility as, 201
    complexity as, 202
    of graduated driver licensing
        (GDL), 203
    implications of, 202
    modifiability as, 202
    observability as, 202
    relative advantage as, 200–201
    reversibility as, 201
    risk and uncertainty level
        as, 201
    time and effort as, 202
    trialability as, 201
innovation-decision process,
        194–196
    five stages of, 195–196
innovations, 41, 204
    subjective evaluation of, 192
innovators, 197
inoculation theory, 175
    refutational preemption in, 175
    threat in, 175
inputs, 171
Instagram, 181
Institute of Medicine (IOM), 9
intent, 135
intention, 106, 183
    to smoking, 137
interaction of the person and
        environment in ecological
        context, 233
interactions between societal
        levels, 46

interactive model of
        communication, 169
intermediary communication,
        170–171
internal (autonomous) motivation,
        97–98
interpersonal level, 214–215
interpersonal (social) level, 39–40
intervention, 20
    approaches, 49
    multilevel considerations,
        49–50
    targets of, 48–49
intrapersonal (individual) level,
        38–39, 214
IOM. *See* Institute of Medicine
        (IOM)

K

Kahneman, D., 150
King, M. L., 113
knowledge, 195–196
    awareness, 195
    practical, 195
    principles, 196

L

lack of imagination, 223
laggards, 199
late majority, 198–199
learning theory, 39
Let's Move Campaign, 173
Lewin, K., 63, 181
life expectancy, 6
listening, 103
locus of control, 95
logic model, 39
longevity, 6
lure of novel theories, 223

M

macroeconomics, 45
maintenance stage, 153, 196
Manstead, A. S. R., 131
Maslow, A., 64, 67, 93
MATCH. *See* Multilevel Approach to
        Community Health
McAfee, M. J., 119
measurement
    in HBM, 142
    in IMB, 145
media campaign, 182

mediators, 131
medication compliance, 131
medicine, 9
mental health, 7–8
message, 63, 168
message content, 183
    and format, 177
message framing, theory-based,
        178–180
messaging, 178
MI. *See* motivational interviewing
        (MI)
modeling, 67
modifiability, 202
modification, 70
morbidity, 6
mortality, 6
    cause-specific, 6
    crude, 6
    infant, 6
Motivational Interviewing (MI), 92–93
    assumptions, 99
    examples, 104–105
    methods, 99–101
    process, 102–104
    Self-Determination Theory and,
        105–106
    spirit, 101–102
motivation and behavior, 144–145
    behavior theories, 58
    cognitive psychology, 64–66
    to comply, 136
    external influences on, 229–230
    individual variability, 58
    influences on, 57
    internal influences on,
        230–231
    Psychoanalytic Theory, 60–64
    Reinforcement Theory, 58–60
    social psychology, 66–67
    sociology, 67–68
    theories of, 53–71
    theory commonalities,
        68–70
Multilevel Approach to Community
        Health (MATCH), 212
multilevel program planning,
        213–216
    ecological perspectives and,
        23–25, 29
    interpersonal level, 214–215
    intrapersonal level, 214
multilevel thinking, 17, 228–229
multiple societal levels, intervening
        at, 47
Myers-Briggs Type Indicator, 62

N

needs assessment, 219–219, 227
NEO Personality Inventory, 61–62
neuroticism, 62
noise, 168, 170
Norcross, J. C., 195
normative beliefs, 136
norms, 228
    descriptive, 192
    perceived social, 145
    subjective, 135–136, 192
Ntoumanis, N., 98

O

Obama, Michelle, 173
obesity, Let's Move campaign
    for, 173
object, belief about, 135
observability, 181, 202
observational learning, 82–83
observational research, 131
open-ended questions, 100
openness to experience, 62
operant conditioning, 25, 59–60
opinion leaders, 170, 198, 205
organizational/institutional
    level, 40–41
outcomes
    evaluation, 23
    expectations, 79, 84
    expected, 135
    of smoking, 136–137
outputs, 171, 183
    evaluation of, 177

P

parents/caregivers, 183
pathogen, 5
patient portals, 199
peer culture, 215
perceived behavioral control, 131,
    137, 138
perceived benefits and barriers,
    141–142
perceived control, 133, 138
perceived likelihood, 84
perceived power, 133, 138
perceived severity, 141
perceived social norms, 145
perceived susceptibility, 140–141
perceived threat, 141
perceptions, 39, 111

peripheral information
    processing, 182
peripheral route processing, 174
person, reciprocal determinism, 82
personal-health behavior, 11, 14,
    15, 227
personality, 55, 230
    definition of, 61
    development, 62
    traits, 56, 61–63
personal trainer study, 104–105
persuasion
    communication/persuasion
        matrix, 173
    in innovation-decision process,
        196
    matrix of message inputs and
        outcomes, 172
persuasive communication, 50,
    171–174
    matrix applied to mask wearing,
        185
Petty, R. E., 174
physical environment level, 43–44
physical well-being, 7
Piaget, J., 63
pilot-test theory, 222
    beyond logic, 222
    develop theory-relevant
        questions, 222
    expert testimony, 222
    logic testing, 222
Pinterest, 181
pluralistic ignorance, 113
policy analysis, 42
policy intervention, 42–43
policy level, 42–43
population, vulnerable, 178
practical knowledge, 195
PRECEDE-PROCEED model
    (PPM), 212
precontemplation stage, 152
predisposing factors, 56
preparation for action stage, 152
pretest and adjust, 177
preventing excessive drinking, 182
prevention, 9, 28
    COVID-19 pandemic, 17–18
    primary, 11–12
    secondary, 12–13
    tertiary, 13
primary prevention, 11–12
principles knowledge, 196
problem definition, 222
process, 23
Prochaska, J. O., 150, 195

program evaluation, alcohol-related
    problem and, 219
program objectives, 47–48
program planning, 227–228
    conceptualization, 227
    evaluation, 227–228
    needs assessment, 227
program planning phases and steps,
    212, 213
Psychoanalytic Theory, 60–64
psychological needs, 93–96
psychology
    cognitive, 64–66
    social, 66–67
psychosocial factors, 55
psychosocial theories, 111
public health, 9–11
    behavior theory and, 226–227
    essential services, 10
    goals of, 24
    practice, 29
    social ecology and, 35–36
public health practice, lessons for,
    223, 234
    in diffusion of innovation the-
        ory, 204–206
    in expectancy value theories,
        145–146
    in health behavior, 29
    in health communication, 186
    in motivation and behavior,
        70–71
    in SCT, 88
    in SDT and MI, 106–107
    in social ecological perspective,
        50–51
    in Social Influence Theory,
        123–124
    in stages models, 157–159

Q

qualitative methods, 45
Quested, E., 98

R

readiness to act, 142
receivers, 165, 168, 176, 178,
    182, 183
reciprocal determinism, 79–82
    behavior, 81
    environment, 80–81
    person, 82
reciprocity, 174

referents, defined, 136
reflective listening, 100–101
refutational preemption, 175
reinforcement, 69, 76, 229
    theory, 58–60
    vicarious, 82
reinvent, 196
relatedness, 95
relative advantage, 200–201
    communications and, 203–204
relevant information, 144
research, elicitation, 145
resistance to change, 104
response, 58
reversibility, 201
rewards, 80
risk and uncertainty level, 201
risk factors for chronic diseases, 5–6
risk reduction, 11
Rogers, C. E., 99–100, 170
Rogers, Everett
    on decision making
        processes, 150
    on diffusion of innovation
        theory, 195
rolling with resistance, 104

S

Safety Belt Connection Program, 80
safety belts, 131
SAMHSA. *See* Substance Abuse
    and Mental Health Services
    Administration (SAMHSA)
SARS-CoV-2 virus, 191
scarcity, 174
SCT. *See* Social Cognitive Theory
    (SCT)
SDT. *See* Self-Determination Theory
    (SDT)
secondary prevention, 12–13
selection, 114, 116
    and socialization, 116–117
selective exposure, 167
self-actualization, 64
self-control, 94
Self-Determination Theory (SDT),
    57–58, 69, 92, 231
    elements, 93–94
    examples, 98–99
    and Motivational Interviewing,
        105–106
self-directed behavior, 77
self-efficacy, 83–84, 104, 155
    in HBM, 142
self-management, 59, 60

self-regulation, 60, 77–78
self-regulatory processes, 82–84
sender, 168
severity, perceived, 141
Shannon-Weaver model of
    communication, 168–169
shared information, 113–114
Simons-Morton, B., 115
smoking, 136–137
    prevention of, 182
Snapchat, 181
social approval, 76
social capital, 115, 122
Social Cognitive Theory (SCT), 57,
    69, 79, 83, 85, 92, 180, 231
    applications of, 85–87
    program planning to reduce
        college drinking problems
        informed by, 212–219
social context, 111, 118
social distancing, 192, 193
social ecology, 33–51
    conceptualizations, 34–35
    environment, 48
    intervention approaches, 49
    multilevel intervention consid-
        erations, 49–50
    program objectives, 47–48
    and public health, 35–36
    target of interventions, 48–49
    theory and social levels of,
        36–47
social health, 8
social influences, 84–85
Social Influence Theory, 109–124,
    180–181
    elements of, 111–112
    processes, 114–117
    psychosocial theories, 111
    social norms, 112–114
socialization, 66, 111, 115–117
    selection and, 116–117
social marketing
    applications, theory-based, 181
    vs. commercial marketing, 176
    ethics, 177–178
    government-based and sup-
        ported, 178
    processes, 176–177
social network analysis, 40
social networks, 111, 118–122
    assessing, 121–122
    benefits, 120–121
    connections, 119–120
social norms, 39, 112–114, 183,
    228

social pressure, 115
social psychology, 66–67
social support, 110, 121
social systems, 34, 193
sociology, 67–68
source, 176, 183
source, of message, 182
S-shaped diffusion curve, 194
stage-matched intervention, 156
stage models, 149–160
    introduction to, 149–151
    lessons for public health
        practice, 157–159
    TTM, 150–159
stages of change, 102, 195
    action stage, 152–153
    cognitions, processes (methods),
        and intervention methods
        at, 158
    contemplation stage, 152
    maintenance stage, 153, 196
    precontemplation stage, 152
    preparation for action stage, 152
    TTM and, 150
stage tailoring, 154
stage theories, issues with, 159
staging, 154
    algorithm, 154, 155
stimulus, 76
stimulus–response model of
    behavior, 59, 76
stronger beliefs, 183
subjective evaluation of innovations,
    192
subjective norms, 135–136, 192
Substance Abuse and Mental Health
    Services Administration
    (SAMHSA), 100
susceptibility, 5
    perceived, 140–141
systems, social, 193

T

tailoring, stage, 154
targets of intervention (TOI), 40,
    212, 228
teaching, 20
tertiary prevention, 13
texting while driving, 138–139
theories, 228–229
    -based message framing,
        178–180
    behavior, 26–27, 231
    cognitions and, 230–231
    cognitive consistency, 64–65

commonalities, 68–70
constructs as element of, 25
definition of, 25–26
developmental, 63–64
in ecological context, 27
gestalt, 63
grand theories of behavior, 231–232
and health promotion, 26
hypotheses and, 25
lessons for public health practice, 234
personality and, 230
possible integration of cognitions across, 232–233
psychoanalytic, 60–64
psychosocial, 111
public health and, 226–227
social cognitive, 57, 69, 79
social influence, 109–124
and social levels, 36–47
useful, 229
values expectancy, 65–66
values of, 29, 231
as a way of thinking, 233–234
theory-based planning to reduce college drinking problems, 212–219
institutional, community, policy levels in, 215–216
multilevel planning in, 213–216
needs assessment in, 216–219
program development, 216–219
theory-based social marketing applications
increasing face mask wearing to prevent COVID-19, 183–186
preventing excessive drinking, 182–183
reducing consumption of sugared beverages, 183
smoking prevention, 182
theory in practice, 212
Theory of Planned Behavior (TPB), 116, 131, 137–139, 180
examples of, 138–139
Fishbein and, 137
Theory of Reasoned Action (TRA), 111, 131, 132–137, 180, 183

definitions and examples of, 134
example of, 136–137
Fishbein and, 131, 132
health communication and, 180
key considerations and features of, 132–134
limitations of, 137
"theory of the week" approach, 26
theory selection principles, 221–222
considering logical other theories, 221–222
considering societal level, 221–222
identifying theories previously employed, 221
pilot-test theory, 222
test theory validity, 227
theories employed for similar problems, 221
understanding the problem, 221
theory to public health practice, 212
applications of, 211–224
choosing a theory, 220–222
example, 212–219
introduction to, 211–224
lessons for, 223
program planning phases and steps, 212, 213
theory selection principles, 221–222
Thogersen-Ntoumani, C., 98
threat, 175
TikTok, 181
time, 194
time and effort, 202
Tobacco Free Florida media campaign, 182
TOI. *See* targets of intervention (TOI)
TPB. *See* Theory of Planned Behavior (TPB)
training, 50
transactional model of communication, 169
Transtheoretical Model (TTM), 150–159
change dynamics in, 153–154
change processes and, 155–156
cognitions and, 154–155
core assumptions of, 151
examples of, 157

matching stages and, 156–157
overview of, 150–151
stages of change and, 150, 151–153
stage tailoring and, 154
TRA. *See* Theory of Reasoned Action (TRA)
trialability, 181
Trump, Donald, 192
TTM. *See* Transtheoretical Model (TTM)
Tversky, A., 150
Twitter, 181
two-stage communication, 193, 205
type 2 diabetes, 145

U

unconscious drives, 61

V

values, 130–131
values expectancy theories, 65–66
variable, 54
variables
modifying, in HBM, 140
variables, modifying, 140
verbal summary, 101
vicarious reinforcement, 82
volitional decision making, 150
vulnerable population, 178

W

Weinstein, N. D., 195
well-being
economic health and, 8–9
physical, 7
Wertheimer, M., 63
WHO. *See* World Health Organization (WHO)
World Health Organization (WHO)
on health, 4
on health promotion, 18

Y

YouTube, 181